DEPARTMENT OF ECONOMIC AND SOCIAL AFFAIRS

# National Development Strategies

## Policy Notes

United Nations
New York, 2008

# DESA

The Department of Economic and Social Affairs of the United Nations Secretariat is a vital interface between global policies in the economic, social and environmental spheres and national action. The Department works in three main interlinked areas: (i) it compiles, generates and analyses a wide range of economic, social and environmental data and information on which States Members of the United Nations draw to review common problems and take stock of policy options; (ii) it facilitates the negotiations of Member States in many intergovernmental bodies on joint courses of action to address ongoing or emerging global challenges; and (iii) it advises interested Governments on the ways and means of translating policy frameworks developed in United Nations conferences and summits into programmes at the country level and, through technical assistance, helps build national capacities.

## Note

The designations employed and the presentation of the material in this publication do not imply the expression of any opinion whatsoever on the part of the Secretariat of the United Nations concerning the legal status of any country, territory, city or area or of its authorities, or concerning the delimitation of its frontiers or boundaries.

The term "country" as used in the text of this publication also refers, as appropriate, to territories or areas.

The designations "developed" and "developing" countries or areas and "more developed", "less developed" and "least developed" regions are intended for statistical convenience and do not necessarily express a judgement about the stage reached by a particular country or area in the development process.

The views expressed in the signed articles are those of the individual authors and do not imply the expression of any opinion on the part of the United Nations Secretariat.

Mention of the names of firms and commercial products does not imply the endorsement of the United Nations.

UN2
ST/ESA
2008N12

United Nations publication

ISBN 978-92-1-104579-6

Sales No. E.08.II.A.4

# Contents

## Macroeconomic and growth policies

## State-owned enterprise reform

## Investment and technology policies

# Social policy

# Foreword

The economic record since the early 1980s shows that markets can indeed suffer serious failures. The same record also shows how proactive policy measures can make a difference. Yet, there are no easy solutions or quick fixes for developing countries seeking to sustain growth and integrate with the global economy on terms that can contribute to sustained development. Considerable differences exist among countries, and when it comes to development policy, no one size fits all.

What countries need most is the "space" to adopt policies that will work for them, due to their own particular historical, economic, social and political conditions. This essentially means securing and preserving greater policy space than is currently permitted when countries seek assistance from international financial institutions or donor countries, or join the World Trade Organization.

At the 2005 World Summit (A/RES/60/1), world leaders called on all countries to develop and implement more ambitious national development strategies, taking into account the internationally agreed development goals and the United Nations development agenda. For this purpose, the United Nations Department of Economic and Social Affairs (DESA) has prepared this series of Policy Notes, which offer practical guidance on how to operationalize policies aimed at promoting growth with equity, besides enhancing and diversifying national productive capacities, while emphasizing human development and decent work for all.

These *National Development Strategies—Policy Notes* concentrate on critical areas where other sourcebooks and guidelines do not adequately reflect alternative policy options, international agreements and development goals, and the latest research evidence, including on the likely costs and trade-offs that such options entail. They focus on employment-generating macroeconomic policies, inclusive finance for development, reform of state-owned enterprises, trade policy, investment and technology (industrial) policies, and social policy. They have been developed by DESA in cooperation with the United Nations Development Programme (UNDP), and reviewed by Nobel Laureate Joseph Stiglitz and other distinguished development specialists.

This first set of Policy Notes does not pretend to exhaust the complex set of development challenges facing the poorer countries in particular, and more guidance notes are in the pipeline. Nevertheless, it is hoped that these Policy Notes will provide the basis for better informed and nuanced policymaking, both among the various stakeholders in the policy community in developing countries as well as the international development community.

SHA Zukang
Under-Secretary-General for Economic and Social Affairs
United Nations
New York, 1 May 2008

# Preface

The outcome document of the 2005 United Nations World Summit called on countries to prepare national development strategies, taking into account the international development goals agreed in the various United Nations Summits and Conferences of the past two decades. In order to assist countries in this task, the United Nations Department of Economic and Social Affairs (DESA) commissioned a series of notes for policymakers and policy-shapers both in the Government and civil society, in major and interconnected areas relevant to the formulation of national development strategies: macroeconomic and growth policies, trade policy, investment and technology policies, financial policies, social policy and state-owned enterprise reform. The preparation of the notes received generous funding in part from the United Nations Development Programme (UNDP). Colleagues from UNDP also provided helpful suggestions for and comments on the notes.

The Policy Notes, authored by experts in these fields, draw on the experience and dialogues of the United Nations in the economic and social areas, complemented by outside knowledge. The Notes provide concrete suggestions on the means to achieve at the national level, the internationally agreed development goals synthesized in the United Nations development agenda. The Policy Notes are intended to provide those at the country level who shape and set policies, with a range of possible alternatives to the standard policy solutions that have prevailed over the past two decades, rather than to prescribe any single course of action. The Notes serve to help countries take advantage of and expand their policy space—their effective room for manoeuver in formulating and integrating national economic, social and environmental policies.

I encourage readers to see these notes as complementary inputs into the debate at the country level on development challenges faced and the policies needed to meet them. The issues chosen are vital pieces of the policy mosaic that underlies national development strategies, which are ultimately geared to achieving sustained economic growth with social inclusion and environmental protection.

José Antonio OCAMPO
Former Under-Secretary-General for Economic and Social Affairs
United Nations
New York, June 2007

# Acknowledgements

This book, *National Development Strategies—Policy Notes*, has been prepared by the Department of Economic and Social Affairs of the United Nations (UNDESA), with the assistance of the UNDP (United Nations Development Programme) and distinguished academics and other experts. These policy guidance notes have been requested by UN Member States who unanimously committed themselves to designing and implementing nationally owned development strategies to achieve the internationally agreed development goals, including the Millennium Development Goals (MDGs). These internationally agreed development goals refer principally to the commitments associated with the international summits and conferences, especially since the 1990s, and are increasingly referred to as constituting the United Nations development agenda.

Member States have been especially concerned with ensuring genuine "national ownership" of their development strategies making full use of "policy space". With some financial support and colleagues from UNDP, UNDESA commissioned six policy guidance notes on subjects of greatest interest to Member States contained in this volume. C. P. Chandrasekhar, Ha-Joon Chang, Jayati Ghosh, Murray Gibbs, Mushtaq Khan, Isabel Ortiz and Shari Spiegel authored and revised the Policy Notes. The authors worked very hard and quickly, revising drafts through an intense consultative process involving at least three rounds of external review. This collective effort sought to develop this state of the art compendium of innovative development policy guidelines in line with the 2005 World Summit Outcome's commitment to developing national development strategies to achieve the internationally agreed development goals, including the Millennium Development Goals (MDGs). Hence, the project was mindful to ensure meaningful national ownership of development strategy with policy space.

Joseph Stiglitz provided guidance and carefully reviewed all the Policy Notes providing detailed suggestions for substantial revisions. Jose Antonio Ocampo, Alex Izurieta, Richard Kozul-Wright, Jan Kregel, David O'Connor and Isabel Ortiz from UNDESA, Kamal Malhotra, Terry McKinley and Rathin Roy of UNDP, Jenik Radon (Columbia University), Khoo Khay Jin and others all contributed crucially to the speedy completion and publication of the Policy Notes.

Nikhil Chandavarkar and Isabel Ortiz have led and overseen the editing of the Policy Notes for web and print publication, besides translation and customization of the Notes in the different United Nations languages, as well as follow-up work with

Member States. Important support has also come from Marie Oveissi, Nuria Zayas (UNDESA), Diego Aragon and Queenee Chowdhury (UNDP).

Valuable comments and suggestions were also received from UN and other experts. Listed alphabetically, these include: Yilmaz Akyuz (ex-UNCTAD), Yusuf Bangura (UNRISD), Barbara Barungi (UNDP), Sylvie Illana Cohen (UNDESA), Carlos Correa (University of Buenos Aires), Bob Deacon (University of Sheffield), Enrique Delamonica (UNICEF), Randall Dodd (Financial Policy Forum), William Easterly (New York University), Luba Fakhrutdinova (University of Cambridge), Anna Falth (UNDESA), Ben Fine (University of London), Terence Gomez (UNRISD), Siddhartha Gupta (Columbia University), Bob Huber (UNDESA), Katja Hujo (UNRISD), Adil Khan (UNDESA), Gabriele Koehler (UNICEF), Bernardo Kosacoff (ECLAC), Ray Koytcheff (Columbia University), Paul Ladd (UNDP), Lamin Manneh (UNDP), Sebastian Matthew (International Collective in Support of Fishworkers), Darryl McLeod (UNDP), Thandika Mkandawire (UNRISD), Manuel Montes (UNDESA), Shahra Razavi (UNRISD), Dorothy Rosenberg (UNDP), the late Thomas Schindlmayr (UNDESA), Sibel Selcuk (UNDESA), Harry Shutt, Peter Utting (UNRISD), Rudi von Arnim (G24), Wenyan Yang (UNDESA) and Sergei Zelenev (UNDESA).

Jomo Kwame Sundaram
Assistant Secretary-General for Economic Development
Department of Economic and Social Affairs
United Nations
New York, 1 May 2008

# Contributors

**C. P. Chandrasekhar**
Professor
Centre for Economic Studies and Planning
School of Social Sciences
Jawaharlal Nehru University
New Delhi, India

**Ha-Joon Chang**
Reader in Political Economy of Development
Faculty of Economics
University of Cambridge
United Kingdom

**Murray Gibbs**
Former Coordinator of UNDP Asia-Pacific Trade
and Investment Programme
and Senior Adviser to the UNCTAD Secretary General

**Mushtaq H. Khan**
Professor of Economics,
School of Oriental and African Studies (SOAS)
University of London
United Kingdom

**Isabel Ortiz**
Senior Interregional Advisor
Department of Economic and Social Affairs
United Nations

**Shari Spiegel**
Former Executive Director
Initiative for Policy Dialogue (IPD)
Columbia University, New York

# Acronyms

| | |
|---|---|
| ACP | African, Caribbean and Pacific countries (members of Cotonou Convention) |
| ARAMCO | National Oil Company of Saudi Arabia |
| ATC | Agreement on Textiles and Clothing |
| BNDES | Banco Nacional de Desenvolvimento Econômico e Sosial (Brazilian Development Bank) |
| BONOSOL | Bono Solidario (Bolivia's social pension) |
| CalPERS | California Pension Fund |
| DACOM | Data Communications Corp., Republic of Korea |
| DAF | Development Assistance Fund (Viet Nam) |
| DFID | Department for International Development UK |
| EC | European Commission |
| ECD | Early child development |
| EEZ | Exclusive economic zone |
| EMBRAER | Brazilian Aeronautic Enterprise |
| EPC | Engineering, procurement and construction |
| ESCs | Economic and Social Councils |
| EU | European Union |
| FAO | Food and Agricultural Organization |
| FCW | Finnish Cable Works |
| FDI | Foreign direct investment |
| FRW | Finish Rubber Works Ltd. |
| FTAs | Free trade agreements |
| GATS | General Agreement on Trade in Services |
| GATT | General Agreement on Tariffs and Trade |
| GBS | General budget support |
| GDP | Gross domestic product |
| GLC | Government linked companies |
| GPL | General public licence |
| GSP | Generalized System of Preferences |
| HACCP | Hazard analysis and critical control point |
| HDI | Human Development Index |
| HIV/AIDS | Acquired immune deficiency syndrome |
| IDPs | Internally displaced persons |
| ILO | International Labour Organization |
| IMF | International Monetary Fund |
| LDCs | Least developed countries |
| MDGs | Millennium Development Goals |

| | |
|---|---|
| MEAs | Multilateral environment agreements |
| MFA | Multifibre Agreement |
| MFI | Micro-finance institutions |
| MFN | Most favoured nation |
| MNP | Movement of natural persons |
| MOU | Memorandum of understanding |
| MTAs | Multilateral trade agreements |
| MTEF | Medium Term Expenditure Framework |
| MTEF | Medium-term expenditure framework |
| MTNs | Multilateral trade negotiations |
| NAMA | Non-agricultural market access group |
| NGO | Non-governmental organization |
| ODA | Official development assistance |
| OECD | Organization for Economic Cooperation and Development |
| OLJEFONDET | Norway Petroleum Fund |
| PAYGO | Pay-as-you-go pensions |
| PDUSA | Venezuelan State Oil Company |
| PETROBRAS | Brazilian Petroleum Company |
| POSCO | Pohang Iron and Steel Company Ltd, Republic of Korea |
| PPPs | Public-private partnerships |
| PRSP | Poverty reduction strategy paper |
| QRs | Quantitative restrictions |
| R&D | Research and Development |
| RTA | Regional Trade Agreement |
| SARS | Severe acute respiratory syndrome |
| SIDS | Small island developing States |
| SINGTEL | Singapore Telecom Group |
| SMRT | Singapore Mass Rapid Transit Ltd. |
| SOE | State owned enterprise |
| SP | Special Products (agriculture) |
| SPS | Sanitary and phytosanitary measures or regulations |
| SSG, SSM | Special Safeguard Mechanisms (agriculture) |
| SWAps | Sector-wide approaches |
| TNCs | Trans-national corporations |
| TRIMs | Trade related investment measures |
| TRIPS | Trade related intellectual property rights |
| TRQ | Tariff rate quotas |
| TVES | Township and village enterprises |
| UNCTAD | United Nations Conference on Trade and Development |
| UNDESA | United Nations Department for Economic and Social Affairs |

| | |
|---|---|
| UNDP | United Nations Development Programme |
| UNESCO | United Nations Education, Scientific and Cultural Organization |
| UNFPA | United Nations Population Fund |
| UNRISD | United Nations Research Institute for Social Development |
| VPSC | Viet Nam Postal Service Savings Company |
| VTET | Vocational and technical education and training |
| WTO | World Trade Organization |

# Macroeconomic and growth policies

Shari Spiegel*

## Introduction

Since the 1990s, many developing countries have had remarkable success in reducing inflation, as well as improving fiscal and current account deficits. Yet, countries have not been as successful at achieving stability of macroeconomic output and sustainable growth. This is in large part because stabilization policies have focused on price stability—even though *real* stability, not price stability, is what is ultimately important for attracting investment and achieving sustainable development.

This Policy Note lays out a framework for designing macroeconomic policy geared toward real macroeconomic stability *with* growth. This framework is based on the view that there need to be broader goals, additional instruments beyond fiscal and monetary policies (including capital account management, regulations and other microeconomic tools), and a balanced role for government and the private sector. In addition, policymakers need to coordinate fiscal, monetary, exchange rate policies and design programmes based on flexibility and the individual needs of each country.

This note is divided into three sections. The first discusses macroeconomic objectives, and the need for a broader set of policy goals. The second examines the conventional tools of macroeconomic policymaking: fiscal, monetary and exchange rate policies. The third and final section of this note looks at alternative tools for macroeconomic management, with an emphasis on interventions in capital markets. Some of the issues discussed, such as public sector revenue mobilization, are relevant to current policy choices in both low-income and middle-income countries. Some sections—such as aid modalities, aid and the "Dutch disease", and to some extent, direct mechanisms of monetary policy—are geared toward low-income countries. Many issues, such as some of the discussion on prudential regulatory structures and

---

\*   Much of this note is based on Joseph Stiglitz, José Antonio Ocampo, Shari Spiegel, Ricardo Ffrench Davis and Deepak Nayyar, *Stability with Growth*, Oxford University Press, 2006. For a more detailed analysis of many of the issues covered in this note please refer to *Stability with Growth*. The section on aid delivery and absorption is taken from Benu Schneider, "Aid delivery, management and absorption", UNDESA, mimeograph, 2006.

Thanks also to Jomo K. Sundaram, Assistant Secretary-General on Economic Development, UN; José Antonio Ocampo, former Under-Secretary-General for Economic and Social Affairs, UN; Isabel Ortiz and Alejandro Izurieta, UNDESA; Rudi von Arnim, and Sid Gupta and Ray Koytcheff at the Initiative for Policy Dialogue at Columbia University.

accounting for structural deficits, are more appropriate for middle-income countries with greater administrative capacity. But we hope the discussion will give all policy-makers ideas for creative measures that can be used to overcome market failures.

## Macroeconomic objectives

We begin our discussion by focusing on the objectives of macroeconomic policy-making. At the most general level, the goal of economic policy is to maximize long-run societal well-being in an equitable and sustainable manner. Much of the recent discussion of economic policy has focused on intermediate variables, such as price stability or the balance of payments. Intermediate variables, however, are not important in their own right. Their importance derives largely from their role as possible indicators of economic performance in terms of truly significant variables, such as growth, development and equity. For example, price stability should be seen as a tool for achieving important long-run objectives, such as greater efficiency and long-term growth. The centre of attention of macroeconomic policymaking should be on "real macroeconomics" and the use of productive capacity—the employment of capital and labour at their highest potential level—and improvements in that productivity.

### Stabilization and growth

What people truly care about is the stability and growth of their real incomes. It should be obvious why growth is important: even small changes in the rate of growth, say, from 2.5 per cent to 3 per cent, add up significantly over time because of the effect of compounding. With a growth rate of 2.5 per cent, incomes double every 28 years; with a growth rate of 3 per cent, they double every 23 years.

It is the overall stability of output and the real economy, and not just price stability, that concerns firms when they make investment decisions. High instability generates an "unfriendly" domestic macro-environment that appears to be a crucial factor in explaining low rates of capital formation: firms have less incentive to invest, and growth will be lower. Similarly, economic policies that lead to fuller utilization of resources today may also lead to higher incomes in the future. This implies that there may be less of a trade-off between growth and stability than orthodox economics suggests.

Issues of stabilization and growth cannot be separated. In general, the conduct of short-run stabilization policy has long-term effects. If the economy's output is low-ered 10 per cent today, the best estimate is that the output path will be 10 per cent lower than it otherwise would have been 10 years from now. That means that most downturns have long-lasting effects, regardless of causes.

There are several links between stabilization (and how it is pursued) and growth. Relying on alternative measures to stabilize the economy (such as the Government expenditures used by the Republic of Korea and Malaysia during the Asian crisis, or the regulations on capital inflows used by Chile and Malaysia during boom pe-riods in the 1990s) may have less adverse effects on long-term growth than relying exclusively on modifying interest rates. An exclusive or even excessive focus on price stability can have a negative impact on growth.

## Inflation

Although mainstream economics has focused on price stability as one of its primary policy objectives, there is considerable confusion as to its role. High inflation is said to signal that the government (fiscal and monetary authorities) is not doing its job well. Inflation is thus a variable that is of concern not in its own right, but as an *indicator* of economic malperformance. There are, however, two problems with this analysis. First, many people have started to view the indicator as the policy objective itself. Second, the links between inflation and real variables may be weaker than usually assumed.

All economic policies involve trade-offs, the question here is whether the benefits of further reducing inflation outweigh its costs. Since 1991 most developed and developing countries have experienced low or moderate inflation, with many countries experiencing relatively low inflation. When inflation is low or moderate, efforts to reduce it further may have smaller benefits and increasing costs, especially when traditional contractionary monetary policy is the only instrument used to fight it. As we will discuss below, this may dampen employment in the short term and growth in the longer term.

Much of the importance placed on fighting inflation in developing countries today stems from the history of *hyperinflation* in several Latin American countries in the 1980s. There were also episodes of very high inflation in some transition economies of Central and Eastern Europe in the early 1990s. But countries in Asia have rarely experienced hyperinflation, and the African experiences have been quite different from the Latin American experiences.

There is general agreement that hyperinflation has large economic costs, and that defeating it should be a top priority. Hyperinflation, and even high and uncertain inflation, creates huge uncertainty about changes in relative prices, which can be devastating for the information quality of prices and for the efficiency with which resources are used. Behaviour gets distorted as firms and individuals work to spend money quickly, before it diminishes in value. In some countries, huge amounts have been spent on institutional arrangements to protect individuals from the effects of inflation. Under more moderate inflation levels (let us say 15 to 20 per cent), these costs will be much lower.

### The impact of inflation on growth

There is little evidence that moderate inflation has a significantly adverse impact on growth. Real growth rates in periods of fairly high inflation have sometimes been impressive—and far better than growth rates in seemingly similar countries that have brought inflation down. Table 1 examines growth in several countries that have experienced episodes of high inflation and hyperinflation, as well as low and moderate inflation. Very high inflation and hyperinflation have been generally associated with low growth or open economic recession, although there are exceptions to the rule, as in Israel in 1979-1985.

*Moderate* rates of inflation have been accompanied by rapid economic growth quite often, as in Argentina in 1965-1974, Brazil in 1965-1980, Chile in 1986-1996, and Poland in 1992-1998. There is agreement across schools of thought that inflation beyond a certain—and possible varying—threshold can accelerate into high, potentially *hyper*, inflation, which is likely to be very detrimental to growth. What constitutes price *stability*, however, is disputed. There is often a range of inflation rates where prices are still perceived as stable, reliable, and thus allow sound business and consumer decisions, providing the basis for strong revenue growth, reduce real debt burdens, and signal demand growth. The view that *very* low inflation facilitates economic growth is *not* valid as a general proposition. For several of these countries, the periods of low inflation have been among those with the slowest rates of economic growth, such as Argentina in 1994-2001, Brazil in 1996-2003, and Israel in recent years.[1]

The hard question, of course, is why the experiences of these countries differ so markedly. Standard statistical techniques are, in theory, able to show whether inflation has been associated with lower growth or more inequality while controlling for all other variables. These cross-country regressions,[2] although imperfect,[3] suggest that inflation is not closely related to growth, as long as inflation is not too high—below a threshold of about 20 per cent.[4]

Unexpected or volatile inflation has been more problematic, and interest rate policy responses can pose a serious problem in economies where firms have borrowed extensively, as was apparent during the Asian crisis. The rise in interest rates led to widespread bankruptcies because firms were carrying large levels of short-term debt that had to be refinanced at extremely high rates. Of course, had there been a history of high volatility of interest rates prior to the crisis, firms probably would not have held so much short-term leverage in the first place, and the volatility in inflation

---

1   Country studies on inflation crises and stabilization programmes can be found in Bruno, et al., eds., 1988 and 1991. For a more general discussion see Bruno, 1995.

2   Levine and Renelt, 1992; Levine and Zervos, 1993; Bruno and Easterly, 1996 and 1998; and Stanley Fischer, 1996.

3   One of the problems with the simple regression models discussed above is that they seldom account fully for important differences in economic structures across countries, as discussed in this section.

4   Many of the studies show no statistically significant relationship when inflation is below a certain threshold. This implies that one cannot reject the hypothesis that there is no relationship below a certain level of inflation. Barro, 1997, shows that there is no (or only a weak) statistically significant relation between economic growth and inflation when inflation is below 20 per cent. Ocampo, 2004*b*, finds that threshold to be 40 per cent for Latin America since the mid-1970s. Others show a small but significant relationship, i.e., an increase of inflation from 3 to 5 per cent might have a statistical relationship—statistically different from zero—but so small that, as long as inflation does not change much, the impact on growth is barely perceptible.

**Table 1. Inflation and growth rates in selected countries**

| | Years | Low inflation | | Moderate inflation | | High inflation/ hyperinflation | |
|---|---|---|---|---|---|---|---|
| | | Inflation | Growth | Inflation | Growth | Inflation | Growth |
| **Argentina** | 1965-1974 | | | 30.5 | 5.1 | | |
| | 1975-1987 | | | | | 259.4 | 0.9 |
| | 1988-1990 | | | | | 1 912.2 | −4.2 |
| | 1991-1993 | | | 69.1 | 10.1 | | |
| | 1994-2001 | 0.7 | 1.4 | | | | |
| | 2002-2004 | | | 12.2 | 1.6 | | |
| **Brazil** | 1965-1980 | | | 36.2 | 7.9 | | |
| | 1981-1986 | | | | | 150.4 | 2.2 |
| | 1987-1995 | | | | | 1 187.8 | 2.0 |
| | 1996-2003 | 8.5 | 1.7 | | | | |
| **Chile** | 1965-1971 | | | 25.7 | 4.6 | | |
| | 1972-1977 | | | | | 269.9 | −0.6 |
| | 1978-1985 | | | 26.9 | 3.5 | | |
| | 1986-1994 | | | 18.9 | 7.4 | | |
| | 1995-2003 | 4.8 | 4.5 | | | | |
| **Israel** | 1965-1970 | 4.7 | 8.0 | | | | |
| | 1971-1978 | | | 30.3 | 5.5 | | |
| | 1979-1985 | | | | | 181.5 | 4.0 |
| | 1986-1996 | | | 17.9 | 5.4 | | |
| | 1997-2003 | 3.8 | 2.2 | | | | |
| **Poland** | 1981-1987 | | | 31.2 | 1.0 | | |
| | 1988-1991 | | | | | 233.8 | −3.7 |
| | 1992-1998 | | | 27.2 | 5.4 | | |
| | 1999-2003 | 5.1 | 3.5 | | | | |
| **Turkey** | 1968-1970 | 5.4 | 4.7 | | | | |
| | 1971-1977 | | | 17.5 | 6.1 | | |
| | 1978-1980 | | | | | 71.4 | −0.5 |
| | 1981-1987 | | | 37.9 | 5.8 | | |
| | 1988-2001 | | | | | 72.8 | 2.8 |
| | 2002-2003 | | | 35.1 | 6.9 | | |

*Sources*: World Bank WDI/EBRD. Dataset from Michael Bruno and William Easterly, 1998, "Inflation crises and long-run growth", *Journal of Monetary Economics*, vol. 41, No. 1, February, pp. 3-26.

would have had far less impact. If firms come to believe that there will be periodic episodes of high interest rates, they will limit their borrowing. But, as explained below, this too can have a significant adverse effect on growth.

Another problem in interpreting data is that shocks to the economic system often lead to inflation, but inflation is not necessarily the cause of the problem—it is merely a symptom of the external shock. Inflation itself is an endogenous variable that should be explained *within* the model. For example, the oil price rise in the 1970s led to inflation in much of the world; growth slowed and poverty increased. The underlying cause of the problem was not the inflation rate, but the higher price of oil. Because greater resources were being spent on oil, fewer resources were available for growth. The effect that the oil price shock had on countries in Latin America is particularly telling. Latin American countries had borrowed heavily to maintain growth during the 1970s, but the long-run costs of this strategy turned out to be enormous. When the United States raised interest rates to extremely high levels many countries defaulted on their loans, ushering in the lost decade of the 1980s.[5]

Policymakers should, of course, undertake policies that mitigate the effects and facilitate a broad adjustment to "shocks". When governments respond to inflation by tightening macroeconomic policy, while doing little to facilitate the broader adjustment, the country is likely to be worse off, especially when the "shock" has already led to an economic slowdown.

Overall, it seems clear that the inflation threshold differs from country to country; but, in general, we can say that the threshold is significantly higher than the extremely low levels advocated in most inflation targeting regimes of the late 1990s and early 2000s. Moderate inflation does not seem particularly bad for growth, and too low inflation (aiming at price stability) may actually be bad for growth.

## The costs of fighting inflation

The benefits of maintaining low inflation have to be offset against the costs. The costs of inflation depend, of course, on how inflation is fought. But whatever the specific tools employed, the fight against inflation usually leads to higher unemployment, at least in the short run,[6] and the risk of lower growth in the medium term.

One of the arguments against excessive inflation is that it impairs the efficiency of the economy, but using tight monetary policy to fight inflation can be equally damaging. In the Russian Federation, excessively tight money from 1993 to 1998—defended on the grounds that it was needed to combat inflation—had ex-

---

5   There is an extensive debate about the cause of the lost decade. See Ocampo, forthcoming; Stiglitz, 2003*a*, argues that it was not that the import-competing strategy eventually came to a dead end. Rather, the problem lay with the totally unexpected and unprecedented high levels of international interest rates that followed from the Federal Reserve's policies of the early 1980s.

6   Some argue that in the long run, there is no trade-off. (The Phillips curve is asserted to be vertical.) While there is little convincing empirical support for this hypothesis, even if it were true, it does not preclude there being a trade-off in the short run.

## Box 1. The impact of inflation on inequality

The litany against inflation also asserts that "inflation is the cruellest tax of all"—that it especially hurts the poor. There are some cases where the distributive effects of inflation are clearly adverse. For example, hyperinflation in Argentina in the late 1980s severely hurt the poor, and price stabilization had a positive effect. However, in broader terms, the evidence is actually ambiguous as to whom—poor or rich—inflation hurts more. The impact of inflation on inequality depends on social and market institutions, as well as on the level of indexation in the economy.

Creditors and holders of nominal financial instruments, such as bonds and loans, are clearly hurt by unexpected increases in the rate of inflation. The wealthy tend to hold financial assets (these assets are less equally distributed than income), so inflation has a negative impact on the rich. In most advanced industrial countries, social security is indexed, so that poor retirees, who depend on social security, are fully protected. In contrast to industrial societies, social security is limited or non-existent in many developing countries. In these countries, inflation can have a greater effect on the elderly poor; though stronger family ties and informal networks in developing countries can somewhat mitigate the impact.

The effect of inflation on workers depends on whether their wages adjust. In places where inflation has been a problem, longer-term contracts often have cost-of-living adjustment clauses. However, in developing countries, many workers are not organized. For these countries, as well as for those without an inflationary history, indexation is not the norm for a significant portion of the workforce. Here, the extent to which inflation impacts workers depends on whether firms are forced to raise wages due to competition in the labour market, or to maintain worker productivity as "efficiency wage" theory indicates they should.[a]

How inflation affects different groups of society is also determined by which sectors of the economy it hits. If inflation is strongest in basic food or necessities, it may have a larger impact on the urban poor, assuming their incomes do not adjust. On the other hand, higher food prices can help agricultural workers and the rural poor. In addition, if inflation mostly affects imported luxury items, the impact on the poor will be low.

Overall, though, depending on market institutions, it seems that inflation—so long as it does not have serious adverse effects on the economy—is worse for bondholders than for most other parts of society. This conclusion conforms to the observed "political economy": financial markets seem most concerned about fighting inflation, far more concerned than most other industries, corporations or workers.

a If they do not, they will lose workers to firms who have adjusted wages in response to inflation. In addition, many firms pay higher wages than is absolutely necessary to attract and retain workers. Furthermore, wages have to be high to ensure that workers have enough nutrition to be productive. See Shapiro and Stiglitz, 1984.

tremely adverse effects on efficiency to the point that between 60 and 80 per cent of all transactions were conducted by barter. High interest rates used to fight inflation can also cause widespread bankruptcies, especially when an economy is characterized by a significant amount of leverage, as was the case in East Asia.

A heavy reliance on monetary policy to stabilize the economy may also lead to interest rates being highly variable. Both high and excessively variable interest rates make funds more expensive. In developing countries, equity markets work poorly, and most outside financing is in the form of debt. If firms are reluctant to take on debt, they will have to rely on self-financing, and will find it difficult to meet their working capital needs. Thus high and variable interest rates impair the efficiency of capital markets, further lowering growth rates.

Sometimes governments address one problem, such as inflation, while exacerbating others. One way to check inflation is to allow the currency to appreciate. This reduces aggregate demand and domestic price pressures at the same time that imported prices in local currencies fall. Even when governments do not deliberately focus on the currency, the exchange rate typically strengthens when the government fights inflation by raising interest rates. While this may reduce inflation, it can have other costs. The strong currency can hurt exports, the sectors that compete with imports and employment generation. The resulting trade deficit may lead to an external balance problem for the future even worse than the problems that might otherwise have resulted from inflation.

## External balance

Like inflation, external balance is an intermediate variable, less important in its own right, and more important for its impact on variables that are of greater concern, such as stability and growth. It is not always easy to evaluate the links between external balance and the more fundamental objectives (just as it is difficult to evaluate the links between inflation and the fundamental objectives). Countries generally try to maintain rough external balance—but what this means is not always clear. Some countries, like the United States, have maintained large trade deficits over extended periods, and for long stretches without apparent problems. The current crisis in US financial markets and the possibility of a recession point to the costs of extreme imbalances. Others, particularly smaller countries, that have to borrow in foreign currencies, seem to face a problem after only a short period of a relatively moderate trade deficit.

In the world of fixed exchange rates that prevailed before the early 1970s, a country that was buying more from abroad than it was selling had to pay for the gap, either by borrowing abroad or selling international reserves. Eventually, a country's reserves would run out, and its creditors would no longer be willing to lend, leading to a crisis.

With flexible exchange rates, the sequence is slightly different, but the outcome is not dissimilar. If the country seems to be borrowing excessively, lenders and other investors may suddenly lose confidence in the country and want their money back. The exchange rate plunges as investors try to take money out of the country, making it even more difficult for those in the country to repay dollar-denominated short-term debt.

Borrowing from abroad has both short-term and long-term consequences, but the nature of those consequences depends on what gives rise to the borrowing. If countries borrow to finance productive investments that will generate returns in excess of the interest rate charged, then growth will be enhanced. Investors will recognize the economy's increased strength and should have more confidence in it. But, by borrowing abroad, the country is taking on foreign currency risk, so that a devaluation of the local currency will raise the amount of external debt relative to domestic GDP. Moreover, short-term investors often look at only a part of the country's balance sheet—the size of fiscal and trade deficits. They often do not look at what gives rise to these deficits. So, even when capital inflows are used to finance productive investments, they might still cause instability as short-term investors worry about the increased deficits.

Frequently, however, capital inflows (especially short-term inflows) go to finance increased consumption. Then foreign investors might be justifiably worried about the country's ability to repay its debts. A lack of external balance might then be heralding a crisis that will have enormous costs to society. Argentina, for example, experienced zero inflation and a strong consumption-led recovery in 1996-1997 fuelled by capital inflows. GDP growth averaged over 6.7 per cent per year. But the current account deficit as a percentage of GDP nearly doubled, and unemployment remained high. The recovery was then followed by a four-year recession (1999-2002), during which GDP fell 18 per cent and unemployment rose.

To summarize, the short-term benefits of a payments deficit lie in the simple fact that demand—*absorption*—exceeds production, so that firms, the government or households consume in excess of their incomes. A payments deficit *can be* growth-enhancing if the funds borrowed to finance that demand in excess of income is channelled to productive investments. In the medium- to longer-term, however, the costs of external imbalances need to be repaid. The stylized picture of external deficits suggests that often: (1) capital inflows increase either asset prices or private (luxury) consumption, or both, rather than productive investments, and (2) adjustment is abrupt, presenting substantial costs in terms of output and employment. It appears that even the US, which enjoys the tremendous benefit of not having to borrow in foreign currencies, is not immune to such a boom-bust cycle. Policy making needs to be aware of the risks of external imbalances.

## Unemployment and poverty

Macroeconomic policy should maintain the economy as close to full employment as possible. Economists consider some (frictional) unemployment necessary since it takes time for workers to move from one job to another, but significant underutilization of a country's capacity obviously represents a great waste of resources. One problem policymakers face is at what level they should start to be concerned with unemployment. As we discuss later, there is presumed to be a trade-off between unemployment and inflation, the link being that lower unemployment tends to give employees bargaining power for higher wages, which in turn are passed on to prices. In low employment conditions, inflation is a manifestation of excessive pressure on a number of resources, including labour, which can be addressed, e.g., by temporarily allowing immigration.

Many economists define full employment as the level of unemployment below which inflation would increase. One problem is that this number (sometimes referred to as the NAIRU, the non-accelerating inflation rate of unemployment) is an elusive variable. In 1993, the conventional wisdom in the United States was that the NAIRU was around 6.0 to 6.2 per cent. When unemployment fell well below that and inflation did not rise, it became clear that the economy was capable of operating at a much lower level of unemployment than the "inflation hawks" had said. There are important trade-offs that policymakers need to consider: lowering unemployment can increase inflation, and, perhaps even more importantly, fighting inflation can lead to higher unemployment and greater poverty.

Unemployment and underemployment are two of the most important sources of poverty and inequality; without a job, individuals in most developing countries are condemned to a life of poverty and exclusion. Unemployment also weakens workers' bargaining position, thereby lowering wages and further increasing inequity. There are, of course, also huge social costs of unemployment. But there are further reasons why unemployment may have a particularly strong impact on poverty and inequality. First, high unemployment typically hurts the least skilled people the most. There is a "job ladder", with the most skilled taking jobs from the less skilled in times of a job shortage. That is why the unskilled are most likely to experience bouts of unemployment.[7] Second, high unemployment pushes down wages, and this increases inequality even more. Third, in many countries, especially developing countries, unemployment insurance is non-existent or woefully inadequate, and most workers have only a small buffer of savings. Hence, after an extended period of unemployment, savings are consumed, and individuals generally lose any assets that have been collateralized.

It is clear that two key objectives—maintaining low unemployment and reducing poverty—typically complement one another. By the same token, some policies that promote growth also help to reduce poverty. But other policies might promote growth without reducing poverty or promote stability without stimulating growth. There are important trade-offs, especially when policymakers focus on intermediate variables. In the next section, we look at the main macroeconomic policy tools, the trade-offs associated with them, and their use in achieving long-term and short-term economic objectives.

## Fiscal, monetary and exchange rate policies

The three standard macroeconomic policy instruments that governments use to stabilize the macroeconomy are fiscal, monetary and exchange rate policies. Yet there are debates on the efficacy of each of these instruments. For example, some economists argue that fiscal and monetary policies are not effective in all countries. Others argue that they are important policy tools, though their effectiveness depends on

---

7   Furman and Stiglitz, 1998.

conditions in the economy. In addition how policies are pursued is important: different instruments have different implications for effectiveness, equity, development and growth.

Discussions of policy instruments are often further confused because governments have limited ability to pursue one policy independently of the others. For example, under a fixed exchange rate system, the exchange rate chosen by the government might not be sustainable, given the chosen fiscal and monetary policies. This is especially true with open capital markets, since monetary or fiscal policy choices can cause capital to leave or enter the country, putting pressure on the fixed exchange rate.

In the discussion below we look at the effectiveness of each of these policies. We also discuss the importance of policy coordination and how this affects basic policy choices, including the institutional framework for policymaking.

## Fiscal policy

Much of the fiscal policy debate has come to focus on the need for developing countries to maintain tight fiscal policy. One widespread view is that fiscal deficits should be avoided because they "crowd out" private investment, can lead to a loss of investor confidence, and are inflationary. Fiscal policy can be an effective tool for stimulating an economy facing an economic slowdown[8].

Yet, even those who believe in the efficacy of fiscal policy in developed countries recognize that developing countries face significant impediments to relying on fiscal policy during economic downturns (which is when they should engage in deficit spending). Many governments find it difficult or expensive to borrow the funds necessary to finance government spending, while countries that are able to borrow risk running up excessive debt burdens that could be difficult to repay in the future—especially when the funds are not well invested.

### Sources of fiscal revenues and policy constraints

### Borrowing constraints

One of the main reasons the IMF was founded in 1944 was to help countries in depressed conditions finance deficits for economic expansion. The founders recognized the interdependence of nations, which means that a downturn in one country can have adverse effects on others. They also recognized that capital markets are imperfect, and some countries, especially those that are heavily indebted and need funds the most, are sometimes unable to borrow at all. The modern theory of capital

---

8   Note that this section addresses only the *cyclical component* of fiscal policy, meaning the ways in which government can use tools at hand to counteract a slowdown. The section does not discuss the question of the appropriate level of *permanent* government involvement in the economy, which might be of particular relevance for developing countries, i.e., with regard to State-owned enterprises.

markets, with asymmetric information and costly enforcement, explains why such credit rationing can occur.[9] When it does, countries are forced to engage in pro-cyclical fiscal policy: they are forced to cut their deficits during economic slowdowns, exacerbating the recession.

Countries that depend on multilateral loans and foreign aid for financing also tend to be constrained to follow pro-cyclical policies—even when multilateral lending itself is counter-cyclical. The conditionality generally attached to public sector loans often has the same effect of creating pro-cyclical behaviour. Most conditionality includes nominal fiscal targets, meaning that during recessions, when tax revenues fall, countries are forced to cut expenditures to meet their targets. The pro-cyclicality due to conditionality is compounded by the pro-cyclical nature of aid.

## Aid delivery and absorption[10]

Since the Millennium Declaration was agreed upon by the UN General Assembly in 2000 and the Monterrey Consensus on Financing for Development in 2002, efforts have again been underway to muster support to increase development assistance to 0.7 per cent of developed country national income. In addition, the change in aid modalities has moved towards more direct budget support, often meaning that headline "aid" figures, in fact, involve debt relief.

The new environment poses challenges for both aid donors and recipients. Most people would naturally expect that an increase in aid would lead to an increase in spending. What few realize is that this is only one half of the equation—aid really only benefits the recipient economy when it is absorbed. In the best of times, coordination is needed between officials in the ministry of finance and the central bank. With budgetary support, this cooperation is of paramount importance.

Aid financing is like other foreign inflows: it impacts exchange rates, interest rates and domestic prices, as we discuss later in this note. The injections of liquidity, through the conversion of donor flows into domestic currency, can cause gyrations in interest and exchange rates, especially when flows are volatile. Donor flows may produce exchange-rate appreciation and, if sustained over a length of time, could lead to the kind of overvaluation phenomenon known as "Dutch disease", which we discuss later, following the section on exchange rate policies.

Predictability of aid flows over time is a precondition for their effective use. But aid flows, like other capital flows, tend to rise and fall with economic cycles in donor countries and policy assessments of the recipient countries, as well as shifts in donor policies. This volatility is exacerbated by the gap between commitments and disbursements. Empirical work suggests that the volatility of aid flows exceeds that of other macroeconomic variables, such as GDP or fiscal revenue. Moreover, donors tend to move in and out together, causing herding behaviour. The PRSP, PRGF and CPIA function like a rating signal for donors, and they react in a similar fashion to

---

9   Stiglitz and Weiss, 1981; and Eaton and Gersovitz, 1981.
10  This section is taken from Schneider, 2006.

signals by Bretton Wood institutions—in many ways, similar to the reactions of private creditors. When aid falls; it leads to costly fiscal adjustments in the form of increased taxation and spending cuts that reinforce the cyclical impact of declining aid flows. Similar to other capital flows, the volatility of aid flows also affects the balance sheets of the banking system and credit availability. We will discuss these issues and policy measures that countries can utilize to deal with volatile capital inflows later in this note.

A policy response is also needed at the international level to stretch out the period of the inflow in line with an underlying long-term development strategy. Donors should make commitments of assistance early in the budget cycle of the recipient, so that countries know how much they can reasonably expect and plan. Commitments should be for the medium term or longer, even if the outer years can only be indicative due to budgetary restrictions in donor countries. This will allow the central bank to manage the liquidity of donor flows to avoid sudden shocks due to erratic disbursements, and allow the Ministry of Finance to raise resources to meet short falls.

Policymakers need to look at the longer term as well, and answer some hard questions as they make decisions. If one expands public sector investment now, using aid, will the government be able to maintain that level of spending in the future, when the aid flows begin to slow? If not, is the initial spending wasted? Countries need to design policies to reduce aid dependency by maintaining and increasing domestic revenues in a sustainable fashion.

In summary, aid flows can be an important source of government funds. Donor and recipient countries in cooperation with multilateral institutions need to ensure that: (1) promised flows are delivered, (2) flows represent actual resources rather than debt relief, (3) aid is provided in a stable, reliable fashion so that (4) recipient countries can plan accordingly and manage the potential pitfalls of "Dutch disease".

## Public resource mobilization

The most effective way to fund government spending and reduce aid dependency is to mobilize domestic resources. The low levels of tax collection in many poor countries limits important government expenditures and forces countries to borrow or depend on aid flows to finance basic development needs. Given the volatility of external financing and the important role that public sector investment can play in long-term development, it is critical for governments to be able to raise domestic revenues. Only with increased tax revenues will countries be able to sustain long-term domestic investments and fiscal policy flexibility.[11]

Poor countries, on average, collect only about two thirds of the tax revenues as a percentage of GDP collected by richer countries.[12] Even some of the wealthier emerg-

---

11  Low levels of domestic resource collection limit the government's ability to use fiscal policy—the government cannot afford to lower tax rates during a recession and is unable to raise them during a boom.

12  Gordon and Li, 2005.

ing market countries, such as India, still have relatively low tax revenue to GDP. In most developing countries direct taxes, such as income taxes, contribute only a small percentage of total tax revenues. For example, tax collection on income, profits and capital gains in Latin America and Asia is one third to one half of collection levels in OECD countries.[13]

Most developing countries rely on indirect taxes for revenue. Many of the reforms of the 1990s and 2000s, which pushed an agenda of liberalization, shifted taxation to VAT from other indirect taxes, such as tariffs and other trade taxes. VAT is a tax on consumption, rather than investment, and many orthodox economists supported the shift to VAT because they believed it would distort incentives to invest less than other types of taxes. As such, VAT reform is in line with pro-business liberalization efforts. VAT, however, is also a tax on the formal sector, and therefore not as effective in countries with large informal sectors, where it operates like a tax on sales rather than a tax on value added. In fact, VAT can encourage firms to stay in the informal sector to avoid taxation, hindering the development of the formal sector.[14] VAT is a highly regressive tax, meaning that the poor pay more as a share of income than the wealthy. For the same reasons, lower income classes with higher spending propensities are taxed average rates. Multiple rates (such as higher taxes on luxury goods and lower or zero taxes on food and medicine) can be used to make VAT less regressive, though this requires additional administrative capacity.

Overall, the net result of the shift to VAT has been a reduction in revenues. A 2005 study by the IMF[15] found that VAT replaced less than 30 per cent of the revenues lost through the elimination of trade taxes. Revenues from VAT have often been lower than expected due to difficulties in administration and collection.

Rather than relying on one indirect tax, such as VAT, countries should try to diversify sources of tax revenues in a simple and transparent manner. Reducing exemptions and deductions that benefit the wealthy, such as exemptions from capital gains taxes or low taxes on financial income, would of course help to increase collection. Many economists have argued against capital gains taxes because they tax sources of investment, but in many developing countries, declaring income in the form of capital gains or dividends is a way to avoid other forms of direct taxation. In a second best world where income tax collection is difficult, taxing these sources of revenue can be an effective means of reducing evasion. Furthermore, there does not appear to be a clear link between direct taxation and growth rates. FitzGerald found that growth in Latin America is largely independent of tax rates; and even in OECD countries the relationship between growth and direct taxation is small and the causality unclear.[16]

Although the WTO has limited the ability to use trade taxes, there is still some scope within the WTO for some use of trade taxes as well. For example, taxes can tar-

13  FitzGerald, 2006.
14  Emran and Stiglitz, 2005.
15  Baunsgaard and Keen, 2005.
16  FitzGerald, 2006.

get luxury items that are imported; or a system of variable tariffs on agricultural and industrial goods can operate in a band within the WTO tariff bindings. (These and other trade-related taxes are discussed in the trade Policy Note in more detail.) Countries can also impose export duties to capture some of the gains from devaluation. Argentina, for example, imposed export duties that generated revenues of almost 2.5 per cent of GDP following the devaluation of the peso in 2001.[17]

To reduce evasion, countries can also try to design more "corruption-resistant tax structures" that rely on non-discretionary and readily observable tax instruments. One such measure is a tax on financial transactions. Countries such as Argentina, Brazil, India and the Republic of Korea imposed this type of a tax on bank debits. In Brazil, for example, the financial transaction tax collects about 1.5 per cent of GDP.[18] These taxes have the added benefit of providing information about firm transactions that can help authorities increase collection and find evading firms. The Republic of Korea has also implemented a similar programme to reduce the attractiveness of cash by offering a subsidy for credit cards. The goal is to shift transactions from cash to a medium that is traceable.[19] These types of taxes generally carry the risk that they might encourage firms to operate outside the formal banking sector, but in countries where banking services are relatively well developed, these taxes have proved to be effective. Furthermore, they play a counter-cyclical role by slowing financial transactions during financial booms and bubbles.

Other examples of non-discretionary "corruption-resistant taxes" include taxes that target consumption items, such as luxury cars or homes. Within these categories, collection agencies should focus on what is observable. So, for example, taxing property sales might be more effective than taxing property values. Taxes on luxury items would, again, serve to enhance counter-cyclical policymaking during boom periods.

Improving tax administration is also important for increasing collection. The United Republic of Tanzania's tax reform, for example, raised tax revenues by 47 per cent from 1998 through 2003.[20] The province of Buenos Aires' administrative reforms succeeded in increasing collection of direct taxes, such as car license fees (from 50 per cent to 90 per cent), real estate taxes (from 40 per cent to 70 per cent) and company income taxes. Other recommendations for improving tax collection and reducing corruption include improving information available to tax officials, sharing information between different departments (such as income, VAT, customs duties, etc.), and improving property and financial asset registries.

As mentioned above, income taxes have generally not collected significant amounts of tax revenue in most developing countries. Given the reliance on indirect taxation and the low level of direct taxation, collection of indirect taxes in developing countries is now comparable to collection levels in developed countries. Some economists argue that to significantly increase taxes further countries might now

---

17   Centrangolo, IPD Argentina tax case study, forthcoming.

18   Oliveira, IPD Brazil tax case study, forthcoming.

19   Jun, IPD Korea tax case study, forthcoming.

20   Culpeper and Kappagoda, 2006.

need to improve direct tax collection.[21] This would have the added benefit of increasing the progressiveness of tax collection in developing countries. In many developing countries, income taxes are currently not progressive in practice because the wealthy are able to take advantage of loopholes and other forms of tax evasion.[22] An increase in income tax collection could start by focusing on reducing these exemptions.

One argument often used against increasing direct taxation is that countries lack the administrative capacity to do so. Yet, before VAT taxes were instituted across developing countries, much of the policy debate was on whether developing countries would have the administrative capacity to implement VAT as well. To help countries build capacity, the international financial institutions mounted a successful campaign that provided technical assistance. FitzGerald has argued that similar international assistance to improve capacity for direct taxation could be equally effective.[23] But in the absence of such an effort, the example of the province of Buenos Aires shows that local policymakers can take steps to improve administration effectively.

Another important component to domestic resource mobilization is the extent of domestic savings and the development of local capital markets. With greater domestic savings, governments would not need to rely on foreign inflows. One of the reasons that the East Asian countries were able to grow as quickly as they did in the 1980s and 1990s was because they had a deep pool of domestic savings. Interestingly, in some Asian countries government policy was instrumental in stimulating the growth of domestic savings. In Japan, for example, the Government helped develop a postal savings bank network that gave citizens access to financial services and helped build the domestic savings base. The lack of sound financial institutions and financial services can make it difficult to mobilize savings. As the Asian example shows government policy can help reduce this obstacle.

More broadly, countries should aim to build deeper financial markets. One of the main risks to governments of financing their deficits through domestic capital markets is that it is often difficult for them to issue long-term paper in relatively new and thin markets. Governments thus face a trade-off between reducing currency risk (by reducing borrowing in international markets) and increasing the maturity mismatch (by increasing short-term borrowing in domestic markets to finance long-term projects).

Developing long-term capital markets is, of course, a long-term goal, but there are things governments can do to encourage their development. Many analysts point to the importance of regular and predictable auctions, standard instruments, a secondary market, a safe banking sector and macroeconomic stability. The lessons of Latin America and Asia in the 1990s and early 2000s have also shown that one of the most important steps in building domestic capital markets has been the development of local pension funds. Chile was a pioneer in this area, and in several other countries, such as Mexico, the growth of local pension funds has stimulated

---

21   FitzGerald, 2006.

22   Birdsall and Torre, 2001.

23   FitzGerald, 2006.

## Box 2.  Taxation of multinational corporations

Some of the biggest loopholes in developing countries are for large multinational corporations. Tax competition between countries to attract investment has eroded the taxation of foreign companies. Many developing countries have used tax holidays to attract foreign investment. But instead of having positive long-term effects on economic growth, tax holidays have often led to competition among countries, bringing revenue for all countries down in a race to the bottom. Furthermore, tax holidays give foreign investors an unfair advantage relative to domestic investors, and can lead to domestic firms demanding equivalent tax relief, reducing revenue collection further. Tax holidays also exempt all of a company's profits, irrespective of the profitability of the investment. When profits are high, investors would most likely have invested, whether or not there was a tax holiday being offered. On the other hand, companies that need tax holidays to ensure profitability often shift to another location once the holiday is over.

A second difficulty in tax collection on multinational corporations results from international tax havens. International tax havens allow multinationals to shift corporate profits to other jurisdictions. Tax havens have made it difficult to close many of the tax loopholes without a coordinated international action, but it is important for policymakers to be aware of the impact on tax revenues. FitzGerald has estimated that, after taking into account under-reporting, the effective tax rate on foreign investment in developing countries is only around 4 per cent (much lower than the 25 per cent officially reported). Tax havens have made it difficult to close many of the tax loopholes without a coordinated international action, but it is important for policymakers to be aware of the impact on tax revenues. One estimate[a] is that tax losses to developing countries, due to shifting profits and assets held abroad, are as high as $100 billion annually.

a  Cobham, 2005.

demand for long-term lending, as we will discuss later in this note under public-sector liability management.

### The effectiveness of fiscal policy

We now turn our focus to the effectiveness of fiscal policy. Assuming countries can borrow: is fiscal policy generally effective—or should it be avoided because it adds to inflationary pressures and crowds out private investment? Later in this note we will discuss low-cost stimuli and other fiscal measures that countries with limited ability to borrow can use to stimulate the economy.

In Keynesian analysis, government expenditures (or tax cuts) lead to an increase in GDP that is a *multiple*[24] of the original expenditure. Most of the money paid by

---

24  In the most simple macroeconomic model, where savings are the only "leakage" of aggregate demand (i.e., the additional income of an individual or household that is not spent), the *multiplier* is $1/s$, where $s$ is the savings rate. More generally, all leakages have to be included: not only private savings but also taxes and imports.

the government is re-spent, and the more that is re-spent, the greater the multiplier. If savings rates are low, as they often are in very poor countries, then the proportion of funds going into consumption will be high, the multiplier will be very large, and public expenditures will be particularly effective. By contrast, in East Asia, where savings rates have been very high, multipliers have been somewhat smaller.

When households and firms are credit and cash constrained (as there often are in developing countries), the multiplier can be even stronger: if those households and firms had more money they would spend it. For example, if the government provides better unemployment benefits, it is likely that the unemployed will spend all or almost all of the benefit. When they spend the money, some of it will go to individuals (landlords, storeowners, etc.) who will not spend all of it, but the important point is that in developing countries the multiplier can be quite high.

It is important to differentiate between the effects of deficits when the economy is in recession and when the economy is at full employment; the latter case is when deficits are more likely to have an adverse effect. Crowding-out (and inflationary) arguments are then persuasive because the size of the "pie" is fixed. When the economy is operating at capacity, increased government expenditures must come at the expense of reduced consumption or reduced investment somewhere else in the economy, and such policies can be beneficial if the government pursues redistribution or attempts to foster socially desirable investments. On the other hand, crowding-out is *not* inevitable when the economy is *below* full employment. The size of the pie can increase so that government expenditures can rise without private investment decreasing. Or, in the case of tax cuts, consumption can increase, without investment decreasing.

Private investment is crowded-out by government spending through interest rates. Either an increase in demand for goods and services leads to higher interest rates – essentially via central bank reaction—or the increase in government demand for loanable funds pushes up the interest rate. Thus, *the crowding-out argument implicitly assumes that Central Banks cannot take offsetting actions to lower interest rates.* Moreover, the empirical evidence on these theoretical links between government spending and interest rates (and their effect on investment) is, at best, tenuous.

Another concern about government borrowing is that the debt will be monetized, meaning the borrowing will be financed by, in effect, printing money, triggering inflation.[25] Even when interest rates are close to zero and there are limits on the ability of monetary authorities to lower interest rates further (a Keynesian-type liquidity trap[26]), central banks can at least undo the higher interest rates resulting

---

25   There are some models in which inflation can set in even when the economy has not reached full employment. Typically, this is because of structural rigidities; to the extent that these are important, full employment needs to be redefined to include them, and government policy needs to be directed at removing the structural rigidities.

26   In a liquidity trap, the public holds onto money supplied to the economy rather than investing or spending. A liquidity trap could occur when the economy is in recession and interest rates are low, so that the expected return on investments are also low. If the recession is accompanied by deflation, there is an added incentive for consumers to hold spending on consumption.

from government deficits. Moreover, in a small open economy, there is another reason why interest rates might not rise and there will not be crowding-out: an inflow of capital can prevent a rise in interest rates, as we will discuss below.

Finally, private sector responses may actually have the opposite effect —and enhance the effects of fiscal policy. There may be "crowding-in". For instance, higher government expenditures might stimulate the economy and improve the economic situation so much that there is room for more investment. Similarly, an increase in government investments that complements private investment (for example, spending on infrastructure) can increase returns in the private sector and stimulate private investment and the economy as a whole.

The success of China's expenditures during the East Asian crisis provides a case in point. Part of the reason for China's success was that current expenditures drew upon a set of strategic investment plans that focused on improving infrastructure. The improved infrastructure increased the returns to private investments. This, in turn, encouraged productive investments that stimulated China's long-term growth. India's experience with stabilization and adjustment, following its external debt crisis during the early 1990s, was somewhat different. Yet, it also provides clear evidence of complementarities between public investment and private investment, which suggests crowding-in rather than crowding-out.[27]

An additional reason why some economists also argue that governments need to maintain tight fiscal policy is to maintain investor confidence. According to this view, government spending leads to lower private investment because investors see the rising deficits, lose confidence in the economy and decide not to invest. Only resolute government action to counter the deficit can restore confidence, increase investment and quickly restore the economy to health.

However, there is little empirical research supporting this view, while there is overwhelming evidence that cutting government expenditures leads to lower GDP in both developed and developing[28] countries. Expenditure reductions in Argentina and East Asia in the 1990s did not have the positive effects predicted by the "confidence model", but instead produced the negative effects predicted by the more standard Keynesian models. The direct effect of a cut in government expenditure on GDP appears to be much stronger than the confidence effect.

The impact of tight fiscal policy on investor confidence depends in large part on the type of investors a government hopes to attract. *Short-term* investors and creditors are often more interested in the size of the fiscal deficit than in other variables. The most important issue for these investors is government's ability to repay its debt in the near term. To the extent that government saves money by cutting the fiscal deficit, it will have more funds to pay back creditors in the short run—even if this hampers long-term growth. But these are precisely the type of investors who heighten market volatility, rather than sustain long-term growth.

---

27   Nayyar, 2000.
28   Cooper, 1992, and Taylor, 1993.

*Long-term investors* look beyond the deficit to a range of variables. Policies that lead to long-term sustainable growth will naturally lead to greater confidence in the economy and more investment. If countries borrow to finance productive investments that will generate returns in excess of the interest rate charges, then growth will be enhanced. Investors will recognize the economy's increased strength and should have more confidence in it.

## The pro-cyclical bias of fiscal policy

Tax revenues rise during periods of economic growth when incomes rise, and fall during recessions when incomes fall and spending needs rise. Theoretically, external financing should diversify sources of income, but imperfections in capital markets and cycles of foreign aid have meant that capital flows have tended to be pro-cyclical, exacerbating the pro-cyclical bias of fiscal accounts.

There is widespread evidence that fiscal accounts are highly pro-cyclical in the developing world.[29] In Latin America, for example, out of 45 episodes of cyclical swings in 1990-2001, 12 were neutral, 25 were pro-cyclical and only 8 counter-cyclical.[30] So, the broader problem faced by developing countries is the strong incentives for fiscal policies to behave in a pro-cyclical way. This effect is compounded by the pro-cyclical performance of public sector revenues in the context of high GDP volatility.

The costs of pro-cyclical fiscal policies are high. During upswings, abundant financing may lead authorities to start some projects that have low social returns. During downswings, cuts in spending may mean that investment projects are left unfinished or take much longer to execute than planned, thereby raising their effective cost. In turn, extended cuts in public sector investment may have long-term effects on growth.[31] In general, "stop-go" cycles significantly reduce the efficiency of public sector spending.

There are also pro-cyclical patterns associated with granting government guarantees to the private sector, which have become increasingly important in the developing world. An example is public-sector guarantees for private-sector investments in infrastructure (such as minimum revenue or profit guarantees, or explicit coverage of interest or exchange rate risks). Another example is explicit and implicit guarantees issued to financial agents and depositors in the financial system. Both implicit and explicit guarantees have three elements in common: (*a*) they are not always transparent; (*b*) they encourage *private* spending during booms (public-sector spending is in the form of an implicit "insurance premium" incurred during periods of euphoria, indicating that accrued public-sector spending during such periods is underestimated); and (*c*) disbursements (cash spending) are incurred during crises, increasing borrowing requirements and crowding out other public-sector spending.

---

29  Kaminsky, et al., 2004.

30  Martner and Tromben, 2003.

31  Easterly and Servén, eds., 2003.

## Alternative fiscal policy measures

### Fiscal policy accounting: structural and primary deficits

A primary aim of economic policy in developing countries should be to avoid the pro-cyclical bias in fiscal policy. This can be consistent with the establishment of rules that guarantee long-term sustainability of the fiscal account, such as targets for the public sector deficit and/or maximum debt-to-GDP ratios. (The definition of such rules is not an easy task, however, as demonstrated by the recent debates over the European Stability and Growth Pact.)

In particular, a focus on the *current* fiscal deficit (measured during the recession) is clearly inappropriate. Rather, it is essential to estimate "the *structural* deficit", which evaluates what the budget would be without cyclical fluctuations[32] in a "normal" (full employment) situation. For example, when tax revenues fall during a recession, the current fiscal deficit will worsen, but the structural full employment deficit will not be affected, and the government will not be forced to tighten fiscal policy further to meet its deficit target. If necessary, the institutions could play a role in financing any *current* fiscal deficit that arises. To the extent that cyclical swings reduce the efficiency of public sector spending, it may make sense to determine structural targets on the basis of an essentially long-term criterion: the balanced supply of public and private goods.

Managing structural accounts, however, assumes considerable fiscal capacity beyond what most least developed countries have established, so that this tool is more appropriate for middle-income countries. Estimating structural fiscal positions in economies subject to external shocks is not an easy task as it may involve long-term GDP trends as well as trends of other crucial economic variables, such as commodity prices. Chile, for example, has adopted such structural accounting in recent years, relying on the evaluation by a panel of economists with mixed persuasions to advise on the trends of the crucial variables involved in the estimation.

It also makes sense for developing countries to focus on the *primary* deficit, the fiscal deficit minus interest payments. Interest rates can be extremely volatile and are often outside the control of developing countries. What is more, public debt that has accumulated over a long period of time means that a large fiscal deficit will persist for quite some time after correctives have been introduced. In highly indebted countries, much of the variability of the overall fiscal position depends on events outside the country (on emerging market interest rates around the globe). Countries need to focus on what they can control. The primary deficit shows more clearly whether an observed change makes the situation better or worse. The IMF agreed to focus on the primary deficit for the first time in its loan to Brazil in 2002.[33] A focus on the

---

32  For countries that were neutral, the structural fiscal deficit remained unchanged through the improvement or deterioration of fiscal accounts. See ECLAC, 1998*b*, and Ocampo, 2002 and 2005*b*, on which the analysis that follows relies.

33  The IMF did not, however, allow Brazil to use the primary structural deficit as a target, which would have been an even more appropriate measure.

primary deficit does not require extensive administrative capacity, so that least developed countries should also be able to use the primary deficit as a measure of the fiscal accounts—assuming the international institutions help to finance the additional interest costs implicit in the full fiscal deficit.

## Management of public-private partnerships

Deficit targets discussed above should be complemented by adequate mechanisms to manage public-sector guarantees. Deficit targets create a strong incentive for governments to promote private (rather than public) sector investment in infrastructure to circumvent the targets, even when there is no economic reason to do so. A major problem in relation to these guarantees is that they generate significant distortions in public sector accounting. The contingency costs of such projects for the State are not usually accounted for, and do not show up in current expenditures. Such guarantees imply that the government acts as an insurer of risks that the private investor might incur. The "insurance premium equivalent" of such guarantees should be regularly estimated and budgeted, with the corresponding resources transferred to special funds created to serve as a backup in the event that the corresponding contingencies become effective. The estimated contingent liabilities should also be added to the public sector debt. A 1996 Colombian law forces the government agency incurring the risk to make a provision in an "insurance" fund whose resources can be used if guarantees become effective.

The absence of any regular accounting of government guarantees for private sector infrastructure projects generates an incentive to prefer such infrastructure projects, even if they are not less costly to the government in the long run. Such public sector guaranteed private infrastructure investments might become a useful way to circumvent stringent fiscal deficit targets. The nature of fiscal targets should be chosen to avoid these problems.

There is a similar issue in accounting for State-owned enterprises, which we discuss in more detail later in this note. These accounting practices distort the incentives authorities face. Accounting for State-owned companies as part of the consolidated budget constrains expenditures on investments and gives developing countries the incentive to privatize these companies to reduce the fiscal deficit, even when there is no real economic reason to do so.

## Automatic stabilizers: fiscal stabilization funds

Due to the inevitable time lags in the decision-making process, *automatic* stabilizers may sometimes be preferable to discretionary changes. Progressive taxation, which reduces the impact of taxation on the poor during a recession, can be less destabilizing than other forms of taxation. (The shift toward VAT has moved countries away from progressive taxation, which may lead to the tax system being a less effective automatic stabilizer.) Well-designed social safety nets that protect vulnerable groups during crises, preferably as part of permanent social protection systems, and fiscal stabilization funds are other important instruments in this regard.

Fiscal stabilization funds, which sterilize temporary public-sector revenues, should be a central tool for counter-cyclical policy. The experience gained from the management of stabilization funds for commodities that have a significant fiscal impact (the National Coffee Fund of Colombia, the copper and petroleum funds in Chile and the oil funds in several countries)[34] can be extended to develop broader fiscal stabilization funds.[35] A similar example is foreign-exchange reserves, which provide "self-insurance" against sudden interruptions in external financing (as well as reduced currency appreciation).

The point of a stabilization fund is to put funds aside when the economy is booming, to be used when the economy is in recession. However, economists disagree on when a country should be building funds and when it should be spending them. For example, in 2005, the province of Mendoza in Argentina was growing at or above the national average and running a fiscal surplus. Many economists recommended that Mendoza save the surplus above current expenditures in an anti-cyclical stabilization fund. However, the governor of Mendoza pointed out that unemployment at the time, while lower than elsewhere in Argentina, was still high, at between 7 and 8 per cent. In his view, it made more sense to invest the surplus in employment generating activities, since the economy was still significantly below full employment.

There are two criteria that can help determine when the surplus should be spent, rather than saved. The first is based on expectations about the future. If the economy is growing today and a slowdown is expected, it would make sense to save a significant portion of the surplus. Employment would be lower today, but resources would be available to support more employment generation tomorrow when the economy slows down. The second is based on the expected returns of each project. Is government spending going into investment and job creation or consumption? To the extent that funds go into consumption, they are unlikely to lead to future growth, and it would be wiser to put the surplus into a fund. To the extent that funds go into investment, the returns could be high for both current employment and future growth, due to the multiplier and crowding-in effects discussed earlier.

The major policy implication of the previous analysis is, however, that international financial institutions should help countries build stabilization funds that can be used as counter-cyclical tools.

## Counter-cyclical tax policies, low-cost stimuli and other fiscal policy alternatives

To the extent that stabilization funds sterilize the additional revenues generated by a commodity or capital boom, they make fiscal policy cycle *neutral* at most, as the additional revenues due to increased demand go into reserves. A complementary instrument, of clear *counter*-cyclical character, would be to design flexible tax rates, particularly to manage sharp private sector spending cycles. The best candidate is

---

34 See an evaluation of some of these experiences in Davis, et al., 2003.
35 ECLAC, 1998*b*.

obviously a tax on the source of the spending boom. This is the traditional argument for taxing exports subject to temporary price surges, which has served as the basis for the design of commodity stabilization funds.

A similar argument can be used to justify an increase in the tax on capital inflows during booms, as this is the major source of private sector spending upswings today. It is interesting to note that this argument is in addition to the arguments associated with the greater monetary autonomy that a tax on capital flows provides, which will be discussed. An argument can also be made for temporary hikes of VAT rates during private-spending booms and reductions of VAT rates during downswings.[36]

Countries unable to borrow to finance a tax reduction during a downturn still have some fiscal policy tools that can be used to stimulate the economy. Two such policy tools are "expenditure and tax shifting" and "low cost stimuli". "Expenditure and tax shifting" increases taxes on those who are less likely to reduce expenditures, and cuts taxes on those more likely to increase expenditures, thereby stimulating the economy. Increasing the progressivity of taxation (as discussed under automatic stabilizers) does precisely this. As noted, giving a tax cut to low-income individuals is likely to stimulate the economy more per dollar of tax cut simply because poorer people are more credit and cash constrained. Spending more money on goods produced at home and less on goods from abroad will similarly help stimulate the economy.

Countries facing limitations on borrowing need to focus on policies that have a bigger impact for a limited amount of expenditure, called *low-cost stimuli*. For example, a temporary sales tax cut can have a far larger effect than a temporary income tax cut. The importance of cash flows and credit constraints suggests some other examples of low-cost stimuli. As discussed above, increasing unemployment benefits for low-income workers has been particularly effective because virtually all such workers are credit—and cash—constrained. (In many countries an increase in aid to regional governments and localities during recessions is also more likely to have a bigger stimulus effect, since subnational governments are often subject to balanced budget fiscal frameworks, or have more limited access to financing and have to cut expenditures or increase taxes without such aid.)

Public investment expenditures may have a double effect. First, there is the immediate stimulation to the economy. Second, if the public investments are complementary to private investments, as discussed above, increasing government spending will increase the returns to private investment, fuelling additional investment.

Other low-cost stimuli focus on firms. The prototypical low-cost stimulus is the "*incremental* investment tax credit". An incremental investment tax credit provides a tax credit on increases in investments (e.g., the tax credit might apply to investments over 80 per cent of the previous year's investment). The incremental investment tax credit lowers the *marginal cost of investment*; just as an ordinary investment tax credit would (the government, in effect, picks up a fraction of the cost of the machine or other investment). At least in standard models, it has the same stimulative effect of a full investment tax credit, but the cost to the government is

36  Budnevich and Le Fort, 1997.

markedly less because the credit does not apply to the bulk (or the "base") of an investment. (This, incidentally, is why U.S. businesses have been distinctly uninterested in this kind of tax credit.)

A *temporary* incremental investment tax cut can be even more effective in providing short-run stimulus to the economy. A temporary investment tax credit lowers the price of investing today relative to investing in the future. This is like a temporary "sale" on investment goods, and will encourage current investment (although partly at the expense of future investment). However, if markets are imperfect and firms' available cash (or net worth) limits their investment, the incremental investment tax credit (whether permanent or temporary) will not be as effective. When fewer funds are available, investment is stimulated less.[37]

Another low-cost stimulus is carry-forward or carry-back tax treatment. The government can extend the period of loss carry-forward (when tax deductions are not taken in the current year, but are used to reduce tax liabilities in future years) or carry-back (when deductions are used to reduce tax liabilities in earlier years). This has the positive effect of increasing economic efficiency[38] and makes the losses fully creditable, to the extent that firms engage in investment. These policies might boost investment for yet another reason: in effect, they increase the extent of government risk-sharing. Since the ability and willingness of firms to bear risk limits their willingness to invest, better risk sharing between government and firms enhances investment. The government can also provide direct credit to firms for investment (though obviously, it is important that this be well designed, so that the government is able to recover principal and interest.)

In short, developing countries often have difficulties borrowing, which can impair their ability to engage in fiscal policy. But there are alternative fiscal policy tools, including tax structure, stabilization fund (insurance) policies and new instruments that can minimize the pro-cyclical nature of fiscal policy and give the government some means to engage in counter-cyclical policy.

## Monetary policy

Economists have long debated whether fiscal or monetary policy instruments offer the more suitable tools to conduct countercyclical policies. Keynes famously argued that monetary policy can be like "pushing on a string," and therefore, as discussed in previous sections, fiscal policy plays a crucial role in demand management.

Over the past three decades, conservative economists have argued that fiscal policy—due to the presumably negative impact of budget deficits—should be restrained, and monetary policy conducted by central banks has to be of primary

---

37  This suggests that an optimally designed tax system might have different provisions for large and small firms; large firms would be confronted with a net investment tax credit, small firms with a tax credit of the conventional form.

38  Auerbach, 1991, and Auerbach and Bradford, 2002, argue that limitations on loss carry-forward and carry-back are among the major distortions in the tax system.

importance. While a measured policy approach and informed use of a variety of tools appear to be most beneficial, the debate on monetary policy focuses on its *effectiveness*.

## The effectiveness of monetary policy

Recent experiences confirm both the strengths and limitations of monetary policy. In general, economists view monetary policy as more effective in restraining an over-heated economy than in expanding an economy in deep recession. Monetary policy, for example, has not been effective in stimulating growth in countries experiencing deflation (such as Japan).[39] In the United States, lowering interest rates from 2001 to 2003 did little to stimulate investment, but did induce the financial sector and households to increase their debt burdens.[40] The reduced mortgage payments and the improved financial position of households enabled consumers to sustain their spending even as their stock market wealth diminished enormously.

The impact of monetary policy in developing countries is likely to differ from the impact in the United States and other advanced industrial countries. Monetary policy has its most direct impact through the banking system. In countries with more developed banking sectors the effects of monetary policy can be more significant in developing countries than in developed countries since firms have less access to non-bank sources of finance and tend to rely more on bank lending. In many least developed countries, though, the banking sector is extremely undeveloped, and most firms rely on self-finance. In these circumstances, the impact of monetary policy on the economy is limited. The narrower the impact of monetary policy, the greater the costs associated with using it, since a few sectors are forced to bear the brunt of adjustment. Those sectors may face greater volatility, as interest rates rise and fall in an attempt to stabilize the economy.

Under conventional closed economy analysis, lowering interest rates leads to increased investment and higher growth. Recent research points to additional channels through which changes in interest rates either reinforce or counteract the conventional effects. First, there are several channels through which lowering interest rates may stimulate consumption further than the conventional analysis implies. Changes in the interest rate represent a redistribution of income between creditors to debtors. Distribution matters: debtors may have a higher marginal propensity to consume than creditors. If firms and households are credit constrained, lowering interest rates may mean that firms will have more money for investment and households will have more money for consumption. In addition, there may be wealth, or balance sheet effects. The value of assets such as stocks and real estate increases with lower interest rates; and the increased wealth may induce households to consume more.

---

**39**   Bank of Japan, 2003.
**40**   Stiglitz, 2003*b*.

Similarly, under conventional closed economy analysis, raising interest rates to slow an overheated economy leads to lower growth. Due to wealth effects, the value of assets will fall with higher interest rates, reinforcing the conventional effects. Because different firms own different assets, firms' net worth will be affected differently, often in ways that even informed investors may find difficult to ascertain. The interest rate increases thus also give rise to uncertainty, further dampening economic activity. Large increases in interest rates also weaken government finances when the stock of outstanding public debt is significant as a proportion of GDP. The consequent rise in interest payments on public debt can reduce the government's fiscal flexibility. All of these effects reinforce the response of the economy to monetary tightening to dampen the economy and restrain inflation.

On the other hand, recent research also suggests additional reasons why monetary policy might be *ineffective*. In particular, Greenwald and Stiglitz emphasize that *credit*, and not the money supply, matters for the level of economic activity. The banking system is central in determining the supply of credit. Even if the interest rate on treasury bills falls, banks may be reluctant to lend more when they believe their balance sheets are weak, or when they perceive the risk of lending to be very high (and therefore, can achieve high, safer returns by lending to the government).[41]

This is further complicated in an open economy by the impact of capital flows. Standard analysis does not explicitly deal with capital inflows, to the extent that it assumes that their effects can be fully sterilized through monetary policy. But this analysis overlooks the impact of capital flows on the supply of credit. Capital flows affect the resources available to households and firms, and even affect the lending activity of banks.

One reason why it is difficult to disentangle the effects of monetary policy on an open economy, particularly one with flexible exchange rates, is that the impact on capital flows is hard to predict. The general view is that, *other things being equal*, an increase in a country's real income generated by expansionary macroeconomic policies is likely to induce capital inflows. So too, *other things being equal*, an increase in the interest rate—associated with, say, a contractionary monetary policy—will induce capital inflows and lead to an exchange rate appreciation (and, alternatively, a lower interest rate will result in capital outflows, and a weaker exchange rate). But other things are never equal, particularly due to the complex interaction between interest rates and capital flows.

In an open economy, lower interest rates can lead to capital outflows and a weaker exchange rate. This, combined with the weakened balance sheets that often result from exchange rate devaluations, may limit credit availability, and could attenuate, or even reverse, the normal impact of lower interest rates on aggregate demand. Any attempt by policymakers to counteract the drop in demand by lowering interest rates further will be partially self-defeating, as the lower interest rates will induce

---

41 There is a kind of liquidity trap, resulting not from the high elasticity of demand for money, but from a low elasticity of the supply of bank credit.

even more capital outflows. *In other words, open capital markets limit the effectiveness of monetary policy.*

On the other hand, there are important medium- and long-term effects of the weaker exchange rate that can reinforce the usual effect of lower interest rates. The weaker exchange rate increases the competitiveness of exporting and import competing industries leading to increased output and encouraging domestic technological development, as we discuss in more detail under exchange rate policies. This effect often occurs with a lag, so that in the short term the effect may not be obvious. At times, however, the impact is immediate, as was the case in the Russian Federation following the 1998 devaluation, as discussed below.

Higher interest rates may attract capital inflows, increasing the credit supply and leading to higher investment, limiting or reversing the usual effect. In addition, there are two medium-term effects of raising rates. First, when the central bank raises rates, it usually raises short-term rates, attracting short-term speculative capital. These flows often go into consumption or real estate, rather than into long-term productive investment. The implication is that the short-term boom is exacerbated, without a long-term positive impact on growth. Second, the increased inflows also lead to currency appreciation. This can slow the economy in the medium to long term as export and import-substitution industries become less competitive. The capital inflows can lead to changes in the structure of production that stymie medium- to long-term growth, while the higher rates do little to limit the short-term bubble.

Furthermore, the capital inflows repeatedly turn into outflows. In the mid-1990s in Thailand, speculative inflows of capital led to a real estate bubble. When the bubble burst in 1997, so did expectations of high and sure returns. The inflows stopped, and capital started rushing out of the country. In the late 1990s, Latin America was characterized by significant vulnerabilities due to high debt, high current account deficits and currency overvaluation that had accumulated during the period of booming capital inflows. In 1998, a change in global sentiment towards emerging markets led to capital outflows.

Standard recipes for dealing with a crisis call for central banks to reduce interest rates and for governments to stimulate the economy by increasing expenditures and/or cutting taxes. But countries with open capital markets often find it difficult to do either. Rather than lowering interest rates in a downturn—especially a downturn associated with a crisis—countries with open capital markets often raise interest rates to stop capital outflows. Again, the effectiveness of monetary policy is severely restricted.

Nonetheless, in recent years, many economists in advanced industrial economies have advocated greater reliance on monetary than fiscal policy for stabilization. They argue that the political processes required to change taxes or expenditure levels are too slow, and that monetary authorities can act in a timelier manner. The limitations of monetary policy, noted above, as well as the limitations on the use of fiscal policy discussed earlier, suggest the need to find innovative means to use both in the face of the severe volatility that characterizes developing countries.

## Monetary policy instruments

Historically, most central banks used direct methods, such as regulations and controls, to manage the money supply. In the late 1970s and mid-1980s, most industrialized countries moved toward indirect instruments, which work mainly through market interventions. Many developing economies followed suit as part of the push toward becoming "emerging markets" in the 1990s. The monetary policy standard since has become *inflation targeting* via *interest rate adjustments*. The central bank uses indirect measures, such as open market operations, to set (short term) interest rates close to its policy rate.

The Central Bank of New Zealand, for example, switched from direct to indirect measures in 1985. They concluded: "In its earlier years, in particular, [direct controls] provided effective monetary control ... [but] the system made the allocation of credit a complex and inefficient process, biasing the flow of credit towards long-standing and existing borrowers".[42]

Yet, New Zealand's experience with indirect measures has been mixed. The same central bank report notes that "higher interest rates will often attract foreign buyers of New Zealand dollars, pushing up the exchange rate, and shifting some—sometimes much—of the adjustment burden onto the export sector, regardless of whether any inflation pressures were apparent in that sector ... With only one instrument to adjust—interest rates—these imbalances are frustratingly inevitable: a single interest rate means one interest rate for all regions and one interest rate for all sectors."

In this section, we examine standard monetary policy instruments and revisit the question of whether alternative monetary policy tools can be designed to improve monetary policy effectiveness, while learning from the weaknesses of the direct mechanisms used in the past.

### Indirect monetary policy instruments

Standard indirect interventions include open-market operations, changes in reserve requirements and central bank lending facilities. Most developed countries use *open market operations* as their main monetary policy tool to influence the interest rate, and thus, the ultimate target, inflation. Open market operations can be more difficult to conduct in countries with illiquid public debt markets. A second monetary tool is the *discount rate*. The discount rate is the interest rate the central bank charges commercial banks for loans, which are usually short-term in nature. Some central banks use the discount rate as a signal; for others, especially those with less developed markets in which open market operations are not very effective, it is the main instrument of monetary policy. The central bank can also use the discount window to act as a lender of last resort during liquidity shortages.

A third method for managing the money supply is through *reserve requirements*. Reserve requirement stipulates that banks hold a percentage of their total reserves

---

42  Reserve Bank of New Zealand, 2000.

with the central bank. Reserve requirements are generally not used significantly as monetary policy tools in most industrialized countries. However, reserve requirements can be a useful instrument, especially when targeted to specific sectors, as discussed below.

## Direct mechanisms and other microeconomic measures

Monetary policy is a blunt tool: raising interest rates affects all sectors of the economy, those experiencing bubbles, as well as those experiencing fragile recoveries or still in recession. Rather than relying on interest rates, authorities can use other measures to target specific sectors of the economy. In this regard, there are three issues that are particularly important for developing countries: how to target bubbles; ways to encourage credit when constraints are specific to certain sectors of the economy; and ways to encourage bank lending when credit constraints are more general.

Direct measures can be extremely useful in developing countries that want to maintain economic growth, but worry about excessive investment in a particular sector. When bubbles exist, central banks can raise reserve requirements on loans to the sectors affected, such as real estate or equity markets. This mechanism could have been effective at limiting some of the build-up in bubbles prior to the Asian crisis. Similarly, many economists urged Greenspan to increase the margin requirement on leverage for stock exchange transactions during the technology boom in the United States. Increases in taxes on capital gains can also be used to dampen speculative booms. Unlike higher interest rates and open-market operations, which entail issuing central bank bills that carry the higher interest rate, these types of direct mechanisms have the added benefit that they do not carry large fiscal costs.

When the banking system is inefficient, these measures can be particularly useful. Whereas indirect instruments generally require a well-developed money market, direct measures are relatively easy to implement. Many developing countries are in a position where administrative controls still work fairly well—far more effectively than traditional channels of monetary policy. The administrative measures China employed in 2004 and 2005, for example, seem to have been relatively effective in curtailing the real estate boom. Had the Government relied on interest rate increases, it would have squelched investments in factories and other job creation at the same time (or even before) it had tamed the speculative boom.

When credit rationing exists, as it does in most developing countries, what is relevant is not loan demand, but loan supply; authorities need to implement policies to induce banks to increase lending. For example, changing regulatory policies, such as capital adequacy requirements and other banking regulations, can impact credit availability. When inflation is due to supply shortages in sectors of the economy experiencing credit constraints, authorities can look to innovative ways to ensure that credit reaches these sectors, rather than raising interest rates and slowing the economy as a whole. Development banks are one tool that can help direct credit to areas in need. Recent research has focused on isolating market failures and constraints on growth and on using market mechanisms, rather than discretion, to determine those sectors in need.[43]

More generally, in many developing countries, banks often have excess liquidity. Instead of lending, they find it more attractive to buy government bonds—or even to buy the bonds of foreign governments or corporations. This is particularly important during crises: banks view lending to private firms as too risky just when the economy needs additional private credit to avoid a credit crunch. There are a variety of ways that governments and monetary authorities can, in such circumstances, encourage banks to lend. For instance, they can tax excess reserves, or impose taxes on capital gains from currency changes (to discourage banks from, in effect, engaging in foreign exchange speculation). They can take more explicit regulatory actions, such as not allowing banks to hold net foreign exchange assets (either loans or bonds). They can go so far as actively to discourage banks from purchasing government bonds (e.g., by limiting the amount of excess reserves than can be held in the form of government bonds, or by increasing the risk rating of such bonds).

Restrictions and regulations on capital flows are another important set of tools that can give central banks additional independence in monetary policy, as discussed later in detail. During booms, capital account regulations give monetary authorities the ability to raise interest rates without attracting excessive foreign capital inflows. During downturns, central banks can lower rates without precipitating a massive outflow of capital. Prudential regulations can also be used for this purpose.

### The macroeconomic dimensions of prudential regulations

Changes in banking regulations have more macroeconomic implications than is usually accepted (their effects tend to be ignored in most macroeconomic analysis). Banks use microeconomic risk management to reduce the risks associated with the individual characteristics of borrowers, and prudential regulations have been designed to encourage banks to manage these risks. But it is more difficult to reduce risks associated with the common factors that all market agents face, such as the effects of macroeconomic policies and the business cycle. In recent years, increasing attention has been placed on risks that have a clear *macroeconomic* origin, and ways to use prudential regulations as a tool for macroeconomic policy.

Traditional regulatory tools, including both Basle I and Basle II standards, have a pro-cyclical bias.[44] In these systems, banks have to provision capital against loan delinquency or short-term expectations of future loan losses. Since expectations of losses are low during economic expansions, these systems are not effective in hampering excessive risk-taking during booms. Sharp rises in loan delinquencies during economic slowdowns (or crises) increase bank losses, or force them to increase provisions

---

43 Rodrik, forthcoming.

44 In relation to Basle II, see Griffith-Jones and Persaud, forthcoming. Since credit ratings are also pro-cyclical, basing risk on such ratings, as proposed by Basle II, is also a pro-cyclical practice.

for those losses, reducing their capital and their lending capacity. This may trigger a "credit squeeze" and exacerbate the downswing in economic activity.[45]

Given the central role that all these processes play in developing countries' business cycles, the crucial policy issue is how to introduce a counter-cyclical element into prudential regulation and supervision.[46] Banking authorities can, for example, engage in forbearance: they can allow banks to continue to operate undercapitalized. (Banks are allowed to continue to operate in such circumstances; regulators need to monitor the banks to prevent them from undertaking excessively risky loans or looting the bank, i.e., moral hazard problems.[47])

The Spanish system of forward-looking provisions, introduced in December 1999, is a major policy innovation in addressing the pro-cyclical elements of prudential regulation. According to this system, provisions are made when loans are *disbursed* based on *expected* (or "latent") losses. Such "latent" risks are estimated on the basis of a full business cycle, and are not based on the current economic environment.[48] This system implies that provisioning follows the criteria that are traditionally used by the insurance industry (where provisions are made when the insurance policy is issued) rather than by the banking industry (where they are made when loan payments come due).

In the Spanish system, provisions[49] are accumulated in a fund[50] that grows during economic expansions and is drawn upon during downturns. As long as the fund has adequate resources, banks should not need to make additional provisions for new loan losses during a recession. Although growth and drawing down of the fund has counter-cyclical dynamics, it actually just counteracts the cyclical pattern of bank lending. The system is, strictly speaking, "cycle-neutral" rather than counter-cyclical, but it is certainly superior to the traditional pro-cyclical provisioning for loan losses.

Strictly counter-cyclical prudential provisions should complement such a system. These criteria could include holding excess provisions against loan losses when authorities think that there is a disproportionate growth of credit (relative to some benchmark), or limits on lending to sectors characterized by systematic (economy-wide) risks, such as the construction sector. Alternatively, direct restrictions on credit growth, or restrictions on new lending to certain risky activities, could be used. The regulations also could be supplemented by more specific regulations aimed at control-

---

45  For this reason, the sudden introduction of strong regulatory standards during crises may worsen a credit squeeze. Although authorities must adopt clearly defined rules to restore confidence, the application of stronger standards should be gradual.

46  See Ocampo, 2003*a*, on which the analysis that follows relies.

47  Akerlof and Romer, 1993.

48  Fernández de Lis, et al., 2001.

49  Under this system, provisions are estimated using either the internal risk management model of the financial institution or the standard model proposed by Banco de España. The latter establishes six categories, with annual provisioning ratios that range from 0 per cent to 1.5 per cent.

50  The fund is combined with traditional provisions for non-performing assets or for borrowers under stress, and with recoveries of non-performing assets.

ling currency and maturity mismatches (including those associated with derivatives), such as limits on foreign currency–denominated loans to the domestic non-tradable sectors. Insofar as developing countries are likely to face more macroeconomic volatility, there may be an argument for requiring higher capital/asset ratios, but provisioning against loan losses is probably a better solution.[51]

In addition, prudential regulation needs to ensure adequate levels of liquidity for financial intermediaries so that they can handle the mismatch between the average maturities of assets and liabilities. Such a mismatch is inherent in the financial system's essential function of transforming maturities, but it generates risks associated with volatility in deposits and/or interest rates. Reserve requirements, which are strictly an instrument of monetary policy, provide liquidity in many countries, but their declining importance makes it necessary to find new tools.

An alternative system could be one in which liquidity or reserve requirements are estimated on the basis of the net maturity of a financial institution's balance sheet based on its asset and liability structure. The valuation of assets used as collateral for loans also presents problems when those assets exhibit price volatility because, in many cases, prices used to value collaterals may be significantly higher than ex post prices. Limits on loan-to-value ratios and/or rules to adjust the values of collateral for cyclical price variations could avoid some of these problems.

We should emphasize that any regulatory approach has clear limits and costs that cannot be overlooked. Prudential supervision is a discretionary activity susceptible to abuse. Experience also indicates that even well regulated systems in industrial countries are subject to periodic episodes of euphoria, when risks are underestimated. The 2001 crisis in Argentina is a case in which an ostensibly foolproof currency board and a financial sector characterized by dominance of multinational banks proved unsustainable, and mounting foreign debt clearly failed to protect the domestic financial system from the effects of currency and other macroeconomic shocks.

## Exchange rate policy

When other instruments for stimulating the economy are limited (as they typically are in developing countries), a weak exchange rate can be an effective instrument for economic growth and job creation. Weak exchange rates increase the attractiveness of exporting by making the country's products cheaper abroad, and help domestic industries that compete with imports (import-substitution industries) by making foreign goods more expensive relative to domestic goods. Exchange rate policy, then, is not simply a tactical matter of getting-prices-right, but may turn out to be a strategic matter of a deliberately undervalued exchange rate, maintained over a period of time, to provide an entry into the world market for differentiated manufactured goods.[52] Several Asian countries have used such strategic exchange rate policy to

---

51   See Rojas-Suárez, forthcoming.
52   Frenkel and Taylor, 2006.

promote manufactured exports. Similarly, the build-up of the Chilean boom of the 1990s was clearly preceded by a weak exchange rate policy in the late 1980s and early 1990s.

A competitive exchange rate is seen today as an essential ingredient of dynamic growth and employment in developing countries.[53] It allows domestic firms to benefit from rapid growth in international trade and attracts international firms searching for the best location for their worldwide sourcing of their goods. This may also have positive spillovers for domestic technological development, and lead to a process of learning how to produce with the best technologies available, and with the best marketing tools for the global economy. Furthermore, a competitive exchange rate means that spillovers of export production on other domestic sectors are enhanced, as exporters find it more attractive to buy the inputs and services they need domestically. In a world of reduced trade barriers, import-competing sectors see a competitive exchange rate as their major (and perhaps only) source of protection.

This is the reverse of what sometimes happens with currency appreciation. A couple of decades ago, this issue was dealt with in the literature on "Dutch disease", also referred to as the resource curse. This literature analysed the long-term losses that a boom in the availability of foreign exchange could have, due to a discovery of natural resources or a capital surge. More recently, there has been a growing debate on the impact of "Dutch disease" on foreign aid, discussed below. The essential insight is that the booming inflows of foreign exchange lead to a real exchange rate appreciation that could permanently hurt other tradable sectors—exports as well as import-competing sectors—and could entail the permanent loss of technological and other spillovers from those sectors. Such "de-industrialization" (as this effect is sometimes called) implies that booming inflows of foreign exchange may be a mixed blessing.

There are, however, risks associated with devaluation. Devaluations can lead to inflation, since, for example, imports become more expensive. Second, there can be balance sheet effects. When a country (or the firms within the country) has borrowed and lent in foreign currencies, devaluations change the value of the country and firms' overall balance sheets. This effect, for example, was particularly important in Indonesia during the Asian crisis. Many companies were unable to repay their large foreign currency liabilities after the currency devaluation raised the value of their debt in local currency terms, leading to widespread bankruptcies throughout the economy.

### Impact of devaluation

### Impact on aggregate demand and growth

As we have noted, currency devaluations should boost export and import-competing sectors and raise income and output. The effect of devaluations on imports can, in some cases, be immediate. For instance, in the Russian and Argentinean devalu-

---

**53**  See a recent defence of this view (with a particular emphasis on employment) in Frenkel, 2004.

ations, there was large and rapid substitution of imports with domestic products, leading to improvements in the trade deficit and large rebounds in output. Yet often, the effects on exports and some import-competing sectors take time to materialize. Furthermore, devaluations can also have short-term contractionary effects on aggregate demand.[54] This may lead to what is usually referred to as a "J-curve": an initial contractionary effect of a devaluation followed by a longer period in which the expansionary effects prevail.

There are several reasons why the effect of the devaluation on exports and import-competing sectors often occurs with a lag. It takes time for exporters to find new markets, and some of the more permanent effects may require that producers retool their businesses. Furthermore, if firms believe that the real devaluation is only temporary because of inflation, the devaluation will produce only limited new investments in exports or import-competing industries. Before firms are willing to invest, they need to be convinced that the increase in profitability that results from the devaluation will be sustainable.

There are also several reasons why the initial effect of devaluations may be contractionary. The first arises from the adverse effect the devaluation may have on real wages. If increases in wages lag the increase in prices of imported and exported consumer goods, aggregate demand and output will fall as consumers' purchasing power falls. (A similar effect is produced if the money supply is slow to adjust to higher prices.) When domestic firms face credit constraints and have trouble borrowing, the short-term contractionary effects of a devaluation can be especially large. Export-oriented and import-substitution firms might not have the capital to pay for imported intermediate or capital goods, and may find it difficult to invest and increase capacity to meet the new demand.

Finally, devaluations also entail significant redistribution, especially in the short run. Exporters benefit, while importers lose. Debtors in foreign currencies lose while those who own net assets in foreign currencies benefit. Also, as we have seen, wages may lag. The losers often become vocal opponents of devaluation, while the long-run benefits to the economy derived from devaluation (increased exports and greater sales of import substitution goods) may be harder to see in the short run.

Overall, the consensus is that normally the positive effects on exports and import-substitution industries outweigh the negative effects, so that devaluations are expansionary in the medium to long run. Furthermore, governments can act to reduce or offset some of these adverse effects by implementing heterodox policies, such as providing additional trade credit or temporary investment tax credits for domestically produced investment goods.

## Impact on inflation

In general, the magnitude and durability of the effects of a weakening currency depends on its impact on inflation and the net effect on the real exchange rate. We

---

54  Díaz-Alejandro and Velasco, 1988, ch. 1, and Krugman and Taylor, 1978.

begin our analysis by looking at the direct impact of exchange rate changes on prices. If we assume the exchange rate weakens, the devaluation will lead to higher prices of imported and exported goods. Imports become more expensive in local currency terms, as do exported goods, since firms generally receive a higher price in foreign markets in local currency terms.

The magnitude of the inflationary impact is likely to depend on the proportion of imported goods in the economy, especially intermediate and capital goods. When imported goods are large, the devaluation can lead to increased costs of production in many industries. This may be a "once and for all" effect: the higher prices of tradable goods are reflected in the domestic price indices at once, with no further impact on prices. But it could also lead to an inflationary spiral.

Whether inflationary worries are justified depends in large part on expectations, the structure of the economy (i.e., the import content of output, the extent of indexation, such as cost-of-living clauses in nominal contracts), and on how the government and other economic actors respond to exchange rate movements. For example, workers may react to the initial inflationary effect by demanding higher wages.

It appears that when there is sufficient slack in the economy (when unemployment, for instance, is high enough), devaluations have generally *not* given rise to sustained inflation, at least in recent years. We saw marked exchange rate devaluations without inflationary spirals in East Asia, Argentina and Brazil after the East Asian and Latin American crises in the 1990s. The same was true for India, following its external debt crisis earlier in the 1990s. Expectations depend, at least in part, on history. Recent history has shown that there is no reason that even large devaluations will be followed by episodes of sustained inflation. This means that, going forward, it is less likely that devaluations will give rise to indexation and inflationary expectations.

Overall, the benefits to growth from exchange rate stability and competitiveness typically outweigh the costs associated with mild inflation. The impact of devaluation, however, also depends on how monetary authorities respond to any resulting inflation. If the monetary authorities respond by raising interest rates (as they might, following strict inflation targeting rules), the devaluation's positive impact—the economic expansion of exports and import-competitive sectors and its possible spillovers to the rest of the economy—will be reduced. Raising rates to respond to the threat of increased inflation posed by a currency devaluation is problematic, even when combating inflation is a goal. (The key question, as discussed above, is whether the devaluation leads to a one-time increase in prices, or whether it will lead to further price rises and an increase in the rate of inflation.)

## Real balance sheet effects

When a country (or the firms within the country) have borrowed and lent in foreign currencies, devaluations will change the value of the country's and the firms' overall balance sheets. These balance sheet effects can have the effect of making exchange rate policies pro-cyclical: instead of experiencing the expected gains from increased competitiveness, the country can experience an economic slowdown due to increased bankruptcies and a credit contraction.

As we have noted, the value of foreign currency liabilities rises in relation to domestic assets following devaluations. Debtors, for example, might have more difficulty repaying loans to foreign creditors. This effect was particularly important in Indonesia during the Asian crisis. Many companies were unable to repay their large foreign currency liabilities after the currency devaluation raised the value of their debt in local currency terms. The increased bankruptcies that result can have adverse effects on growth and output throughout the economy.

If a country is a net foreign debtor, a devaluation will generally make the country worse off. The value of the country's liabilities will increase, and the weaker balance sheet of indebted firms will depress consumption and investment. (This is one reason the Asian crisis was so severe.) If a country is a net creditor, it will be better off, on average, because foreign denominated assets will be worth more. But even if the country is a net creditor overall, some firms will be net debtors, and the economic consequences of their losses might more than offset the benefits to the better off firms. So the impact of a currency devaluation will depend heavily on assessment of the balance sheets of domestic firms, households and the government. Moreover, because creditors generally do not know the exact balance sheet of each firm to whom they lend, and firms do not know the balance sheet of each firm with which they interact, large devaluations give rise to extreme uncertainty.

If a country has large sovereign external borrowings, a currency devaluation will raise the government's cost of borrowing and increase its risk of default—sometimes so much so that countries are afraid to let their currencies weaken. The increased cost means that governments may have to cut back real domestic expenditures, so the *net* effect of the devaluation might be negative: the cutbacks in government expenditures might exceed the increase in net exports.

These balance sheet effects point to the importance of governments managing their foreign liability exposure. Furthermore, a good institutional framework can help minimize private balance sheet effects of devaluations. Prudential regulations in place prior to the devaluation can limit the amount of banks' (and indirectly, firms') foreign currency exposure. If the country has good bankruptcy laws—say modelled after chapter 11 of the U.S. bankruptcy code, which allows fairly rapid corporate reorganizations—the costs on the country can be limited.[55]

In order to design effective economic policies, we need to appraise the situation of each particular country. If a country is a *net* debtor in foreign currency, the devaluation will generally have negative balance sheet effects. If a country is a net creditor, it will generally have positive balance sheet effects. These balance sheet effects then need to be weighed against the benefits of a weaker exchange rate on growth and development discussed earlier. Initial conditions matter. The structure

---

55  Stiglitz has argued for a "super chapter 11"—an even more expedited restructuring process which would come into play in the event of a macroeconomic disturbance. See Miller and Stiglitz, 1999.

of balance sheets matters; the institutional framework matters; the choice of currency regime matters.

## The debate on exchange rate regimes

### Fixed and floating rate regimes

Under a fixed (or pegged) rate regime, policymakers target the exchange rate and monetary authorities intervene in the foreign exchange market by buying or selling international reserves to maintain the peg. In doing so, they severely limit their ability to pursue monetary and fiscal policies (e.g., lowering rates generally leads to capital inflows, putting pressure on the peg). Under a flexible, or pure floating, exchange rate regime, the government does not need to buy or sell reserves. The exchange rate is endogenous (or determined by the market), but authorities influence it through fiscal or monetary policies. The effectiveness of monetary (and fiscal) policies in open economies is still limited by the effects of capital flows (as discussed above), though less so than with a fixed rate.

Most countries do not maintain either a pure fixed or floating regime. Rather, they engage in some type of managed or "dirty" float. In these intermediate regimes, authorities intervene periodically (sometimes according to specified rules) by buying and selling international reserves, as in the fixed rate system. But they have somewhat more flexibility than if they operated under a pure fixed rate, and the effectiveness of monetary and fiscal policies is somewhere in between the two extreme cases.

In choosing an exchange rate regime, developing countries are faced with a trade-off between their need for stability and their need for flexibility. The demand for stability comes from its positive impact on investment, as well as the need to avoid pro-cyclical balance sheet effects of exchange rate fluctuations. The demand for flexibility comes from the need to have some degrees of freedom to manage trade and capital account shocks. The relative benefits of flexibility versus stability are determined by both the external environment and objective factors. For example, increased international instability (e.g., the breakdown of the dollar standard, a period of turmoil in world finance for emerging markets or a world recession) will increase the relative benefits of flexibility, whereas a period of tranquillity (e.g., the heyday of the Bretton Woods system or a period of stable world economic growth) will increase the relative advantages of stability.

The relevance of these conflicting demands is not captured by the call to choose polar exchange rate regimes—i.e., either "hard pegs" (e.g., currency boards or even dollarization or euroization) or totally flexible exchange rates. Rather, the defence of polar regimes is based on the argument that any attempt to manage the conflicting demands on exchange rate policy is futile and should be given up altogether.

Hard pegs introduce built-in institutional arrangements that provide for fiscal and monetary discipline, and avoid the balance sheet effects of exchange rate fluctuations, but at the cost of eliminating monetary policy autonomy. Under this type of regime, adjustment to overvaluation (however that might occur) is painful, and may lead to low growth rates. When the currency becomes overvalued, domestic prices and wages need to fall for the country to regain competitiveness. More price flexibility, which in this case means deflation (and recession) during crises, generates severe adjustment problems; of particular concern is the rapid increase in real debt burdens generated by deflation. It may also generate a short-term bias in bank lending, which is necessary to reduce nominal portfolios rapidly during periods of monetary contraction. One of the alleged advantages of the hard peg was that it was supposed to be speculation proof. But the experiences of currency boards in Argentina in 1994-1995 and 1998-2001, Hong Kong Special Administrative Region of China in 1997 (and, for that matter, of the gold standard in developing countries during the late nineteenth and early twentieth centuries) indicate that this has not been the case.

When a currency is overvalued, it is often not a question of whether the fixed rate should be maintained, but when and how it will be devalued. It is preferable to devalue gradually than to have a crisis (in which there is often overshooting). Slow, or creeping, devaluations also avoid major price shocks. In addition, raising interest rates to maintain the currency may have even more adverse effects on the economy than the devaluation itself. The questions that policymakers need to address are: what are the costs and benefits of interventions in foreign exchange markets, and when are these interventions sustainable.

On the other hand, the volatility associated with freely floating exchange rate regimes increases the costs of trade and reduces the benefits of international specialization. As developing countries are largely net importers of capital goods, exchange rate uncertainty also affects investment decisions.

## Interventions in the foreign exchange market

Maintaining an undervalued exchange rate is considerably easier than maintaining an overvalued exchange rate, but it has costs, too. To maintain an undervalued exchange rate, governments can lower interest rates (to discourage capital inflows) or can intervene in the exchange rate market directly by buying dollars and selling the local currency. Maintaining an undervalued exchange rate through direct intervention produces a build-up of international reserves. This has a long-term benefit: it protects the country against future capital account volatility (it acts as a "war chest"). But buying up international reserves has costs. The central bank has to sell domestic currency to buy the reserves, and this increases the money supply. To keep the money supply within limits, authorities may choose to "sterilize" the monetary effect of the foreign exchange intervention by selling domestic assets and buying the additional currency from the market.

The mechanisms generally used (e.g., open market operations) are somewhat costly as they involve issuing central bank bonds, which pay interest, to absorb the excess liquidity. Furthermore, these interventions may lead to higher interest rates, raising the overall cost of government funding. The higher rates might attract more capital, overheating the economy and forcing even larger reserve accumulations. Raising reserve requirements on banks is a less costly means to sterilize, but may lead to higher credit costs and to financial disintermediation (in which banks use unregulated mechanisms to channel liquid funds).

There can be an additional cost to purchasing foreign currency reserves at an undervalued exchange rate: if the currency does eventually revalue, then the value of the foreign reserves will drop relative to domestic GDP. The question is whether and when the costs of sterilization can become too great to maintain and outweigh the benefits of a weak exchange rate. Sterilization is especially costly for countries with relatively high interest rates and high levels of government debt. In the late 1990s, the Hungarian Central Bank, for example, felt that sterilization had become too expensive and let its exchange rate strengthen. On the other hand, the costs of letting a currency strengthen are often greater than the costs of maintaining reserves. For extended periods China has maintained an exchange rate that some have argued has been undervalued. Unlike Hungary, China has maintained its capital account restrictions, giving it more leeway to manage its money supply.

While it is possible for a country to maintain an undervalued exchange rate for extended periods of time, it is far more difficult for it to maintain an overvalued exchange rate, even for short periods of time. Direct intervention in the currency market is unsustainable. If the devaluation is expected to occur in the not too distant future, a speculative attack will be mounted now. The standard prescription to stem exchange rate depreciation is to raise interest rates to attract capital into the country. Two questions have been raised concerning this conventional policy prescription: does it work, and are the benefits worth the costs? The evidence[56] suggests a mixed record at best. In the case of East Asia, the interest rate increases, even combined with huge bail-outs, did not stem the large exchange rate depreciations.

The cost of raising interest rates to defend the currency depends on the structure of the economy, but can be high, as we saw during the Asian crisis. There are real balance sheet effects, similar to the effects of currency devaluation. For firms with outstanding short term debts, high interest rates affect their balance sheets. The high rates reduce the value of long-term assets (including real estate). In many cases, firms are unable to meet their interest obligations on domestic debt in local currency. This has a ripple effect through the economy, as economic problems in one firm get pushed to the firms they trade with. Banks' balance sheets are weakened and new lending falls.

In short, raising interest rates has similar adverse effects on balance sheets, bankruptcies and economic activity to devaluing the exchange rate. But there are differences. First, the effects of raising interest rates are more pervasive, since many firms—especially small and medium-sized enterprises at the heart of developing countries—only borrow domestically. Relatively few, mostly large firms, borrow internationally, and many of these are in export sectors, so that in the event of a devaluation, they gain from the improvement in their profitability what they lose on their balance sheet. Second, a policy of attempting to stave off devaluations by raising interest rates contributes to a moral hazard problem—it lessens the incentives to buy

---

**56**  Furman and Stiglitz, 1998.

insurance against exchange rate fluctuation or to borrow in the local currency, thereby reducing government room for manoeuvre. Third, there are high long-run costs to raising interest rates, as discussed earlier. Finally, appropriately designed monetary and regulatory policies can restrict firm exposure to foreign exchange rates; it is more difficult (and costly) to design monetary policies that restrict exposure to interest rate fluctuations. Firms would have to restrict their short-term borrowing (and there are even risks to long-term borrowing, since it has to be renewed).

In addition to trying to maintain an overvalued or undervalued exchange rate, government intervention in the currency market is often used to *smooth* exchange rate variations. Many developing countries are particularly concerned about the volatility of the *real* exchange rate and try to avoid what they judge as either excessive real depreciations or appreciations. Most countries also intervene to smooth short-term volatility. This form of intervention is especially useful in countries with illiquid markets, where one large foreign currency payment can cause the currency to jump. The reasons to avoid real exchange rate fluctuations are clear. Temporary real exchange rate appreciation can have especially large long-term costs if entry into tradable sectors has fixed costs (fixed capital investments or fixed costs of building a clientele in foreign markets), especially in the presence of capital market imperfections. The absence of a complete set of futures and risk markets provides another reason for government intervention; in these circumstances, the market equilibrium would not be efficient, even when expectations are fully rational.

## Intermediate regimes

The frequency of "dirty floats", or floating rate regimes with limited flexibility,[57] shows how authorities in the developing world often opt for striking a balance between the conflicting demands they face. Intermediate exchange rate regimes can take several forms: (*a*) quasi-fixed exchange rate regimes with large central bank interventions in foreign exchange markets; (*b*) managed exchange rates, such as crawling pegs and bands; and (*c*) dirty floats, in which monetary authorities intervene in the market from time to time. All these regimes can be understood as including an element of "real exchange rate targeting" in the design of macroeconomic policy, and many or most of them are often combined with some form of capital account regulations, we discussed below. To the extent that smoothing out real exchange rate fluctuations has a counter-cyclical effect, "real exchange rate targeting" turns out to be complementary with the objective of smoothing real (output) volatility.

One of the advantages of intermediate regimes is that flexibility *can be graduated*, depending on the relative benefits of stability versus flexibility that we have analysed. This implies that any intermediate regime has an embedded "exit option". (Of course, even a peg has an exit option, but as the Argentine experience showed, the cost of that exit was high.) Also, if some degree of exchange rate flexibility is available before an external crisis hits, it would provide scope for avoiding the real interest rate

---

**57**  Reinhart and Rogoff, 2004

overshooting that seems to characterize the transition away from a fixed exchange rate regime in developing countries.

There are still risks associated with intermediate regimes. The scope for monetary autonomy is still limited. First, as with fixed rate regimes, intermediate options are subject to speculative pressures if they do not generate credibility in markets. Defending the exchange rate may be costly, as discussed earlier in this chapter. This is particularly true of any pre-announcement (of the rate of the crawl, of a band or of a specific exchange rate target). Second, macroeconomic autonomy still depends on the effectiveness of capital account regulations as a macroeconomic policy tool, as discussed below. Third, similar to fixed rate regimes, intermediate regimes will generally require sterilized intervention in foreign exchange markets, which can be costly. Finally, interventions in the foreign exchange market always face the difficult choice of distinguishing between a real (permanent) shock and a temporary aberration in the exchange rate caused by random fluctuations in market sentiment.

In short, no exchange rate system is risk free. Different regimes have different benefits and costs. Like all economic policies, the choice of currency regime involves trade-offs. The optimal choice will depend on the objectives of the authorities, and on the macroeconomic, institutional and political characteristics of the country in question.

## Microeconomic measures

In addition to direct management of the exchange rate, microeconomic interventions can be used to impact relative prices. For example, microeconomic policies can be used to change the composition of demand towards non-tradables and away from imports. Tax policies that encourage more spending on domestically produced goods and less on goods produced abroad will help to stimulate the economy, and, at the same time, strengthen the currency. In many developing countries, most luxury consumption goods are imported. A high sales tax on such goods discourages these imports. Government expenditures can also be weighted towards domestically produced goods.

### Box 3.  Managing "Dutch disease"

Foreign aid used to finance domestic expenditures can contribute to overvaluation of the exchange rate, making domestic exporters and import competing industries less competitive, through the effect known as the 'Dutch disease'. Assuming that significant foreign exchange inflows will have a macroeconomic effect, this note concentrates on potential policy responses.

    The general view is that countries should intervene in the exchange market to keep the currency from appreciating, and sterilize inflows to minimize the inflationary impact of the increase in domestic money supply. If aid flows go into long-term productive investments, the productivity gains from the investment can compensate for the strengthening of the nominal exchange rate. In addition, if inflows are used to purchase imported goods, the effects of the increased aid on the exchange rate will be limited.[a] However, there are real questions of whether, on average, the increase in aid will be invested in projects that generate improved productivity significant enough to compensate for the loss in competitiveness due to the exchange rate strengthening, especially in the short to medium term. Furthermore, countries often need aid to finance social spending and basic services for the poor that will not be productivity enhancing, at least in the short run.

Policymakers can try to constrain exchange appreciation by buying foreign exchange inflows (and building up reserves) in conjunction with sterilization. With limited amounts of aid, this can be an effective strategy. But intervention has costs and is not always sustainable. The build-up in international reserves has opportunity costs, and sterilization raises domestic interest rates.

Furthermore, sterilization generally involves issuing treasury bills to absorb the excess liquidity. *In other words, the increase in aid has the perverse effect of leading to a build-up in domestic debt.* It is ironic that just as the international community has moved to replace loans with grants in an attempt to avoid developing country debt crises, the policy framework used to manage these inflows is leading to a new build-up in debt. Yet, aid inflows can be crucial for development and poverty reduction in poor countries; policymakers need to think about alternative frameworks to manage these inflows.

One possible alternative is for the central banks to choose not to sterilize the inflows; instead, they would allow the inflows to be monetized. All policies have trade-offs: borrowing from the market through open market operations leads to higher interest rates, which can crowd out investment; monetizing can lead to inflation. But, as we have discussed, relatively low inflation does not necessarily have high costs. When a country is in a recession and in need of investment, monetizing could be an option. (Of course, the central bank would need to monitor the inflation rate to make sure it does not become excessive. In addition, monetization can be done in conjunction with accounting frameworks and safeguards to monitor the increase in money supply fully.)

An alternative policy stance would allow the exchange rate to strengthen somewhat and to look to policies to counteract the effect of the strengthening exchange rate on competitiveness. Exchange rates, like interest rates, are blunt instruments, affecting all sectors of the economy. One goal of alternative policy instruments is to target sectors subject to credit constraints. In the case of appreciating exchange rates, authorities can similarly target sectors of the economy hurt by exchange rate strengthening (to try to compensate them for the loss of competitiveness). In theory, tariffs could be used to adjust specific relative prices, though WTO and other trade treaties have reduced the ability to impose tariffs. But tax incentives, reduced interest loans (though these too may be subject to WTO), or reduced reserve requirements can have similar effects. The government needs to look to alternative microeconomic instruments to counteract the impact of the strengthening exchange rate.

Ultimately, the choice of policy response to "Dutch disease" effects will depend on country-specific circumstances, but the macroeconomic framework of intervention and sterilization is not the only policy alternative. Policymakers can manage the trade-offs of the effects on interest rates, exchange rates and inflation through intervention in the currency market, sterilization, monetization and heterodox policies to target those sectors impacted most by a loss of competitiveness.

---

a   McKinley, 2005.

## Monetary and exchange rate policy rules
## and institutional design

The choice of exchange rate regime is closely related to the broader question of what monetary policy rules the central bank should follow, and the institutional design of the central bank itself. There are three distinct but related questions: whether the central bank should follow monetary policy rules, such as fixing the currency or inflation targeting, or whether it should follow discretionary policies; whether the mandate of the central bank should focus on inflation or whether it should include other policy variables, such as growth and employment; and whether the central bank should be independent.

### Rules versus discretion and inflation targeting
### versus foreign exchange targeting[58]

In the 1980s, the orthodox rule prescribed money supply growth at a constant rate. Then, it became clear that the demand function for money was unstable and hard to predict, especially in developing countries, and the money supply rule lost favour. Many developing countries chose to target the exchange rate since it was viewed as a simple and transparent indicator. But the exchange rate crises in the mid- to late 1990s led to a shift to flexible exchange rate regimes, and today inflation targeting[59] is the preferred monetary rule.

Most Keynesian economists believe that central bankers should be allowed to use more discretion than allowed by strict rules. Because strict inflation targeting rules do not distinguish between inflation fuelled by expectations and inflation fuelled by VAT increases or external shocks (such as food or other supply shortages, oil price rises or exchange rate devaluations) it can lead to pro-cyclical policies. For example, inflation targeting can lead to exchange rate targeting or contractionary monetary policies during devaluation, counteracting the exchange rate effect on competitiveness. Inflation targeting often incorporates two widely used pro-cyclical policies: anchoring the price level to a fixed exchange rate during periods of foreign exchange inflows and counterbalancing the inflationary effects of devaluation with contractionary monetary policies during periods of outflows. Strict inflation targeting can therefore generate more output volatility than monetary policy goals that take into account other objectives such as reducing the output gap.[60]

The key problem faced by the authorities during booms is that capital surges exert expansionary aggregate demand effects that are enhanced by downward pressure on interest rates and/or exchange rate appreciation. Any attempt by policymakers to counteract these aggregate demand effects through contractionary monetary poli-

---

**58**  This section is based on Ocampo (forthcoming), as well as Stiglitz, et al., 2007.

**59**  With inflation targeting, the central bank targets a publicly announced level of inflation. Central banks that do not use explicit inflation targeting might target the money supply or the exchange rate to fight against inflation.

**60**  Svensson, 2000.

cies will be partly self-defeating, as the higher interest rates will induce additional capital inflows, and thus additional appreciation pressures. During crises, the reduction of capital inflows will have a direct effect on aggregate demand, which will be combined with a mix of devaluation and interest rate hikes. Any attempt to avoid the latter by using expansionary monetary policy will encourage a stronger devaluation. Thus, if authorities consider that the exchange rate fluctuations generated by boom-bust cycles are too strong to start with, they may be encouraged to use pro-cyclical monetary policy to smooth out those fluctuations. In other words, contrary to the traditional argument about the additional degrees of freedom for monetary policy (discussed below) provided by floating exchange rates, such a regime may, in fact, lead to pro-cyclical monetary policies. The only way to guarantee adequate degrees of freedom for counter-cyclical monetary policies may thus be to give up free floating, free capital mobility or both.

A second issue to consider in choosing monetary regimes is the efficiency or stability of the inflation-targeting rule. This is more complicated than can be addressed in this note, but we will discuss it briefly. It concerns, for instance, the extent to which (and the circumstances under which) conventionally measured changes in inflation provide a good indicator of whether employment is above or below the full employment level. There is, in addition, a more fundamental question surrounding inflation targeting: whether a policy structure—in which monetary authorities focus on inflation and fiscal authorities focus, for instance, on external balance—is a good way of achieving the ultimate objective of full employment with external balance.

Under inflation targeting, the government or monetary authority announces a target for the inflation rate, and the monetary authorities commit to achieve this target. Inflation targeting divides responsibilities between government and a monetary authority, so that each policymaker focuses on a single objective. The problem is that dividing responsibilities reduces coordination.

The nature of the response to excess aggregate demand *should* depend on an analysis of the source of the disturbance. A rule that simply looks at the magnitude of the inflation rate is not likely to provide for a quick adjustment of the economy to the new equilibrium. Monetary authorities cannot detach themselves from the broader objectives of macroeconomic policy, such as full employment and external balance. They must coordinate the appropriate response to the specific source of disturbance with the fiscal authorities. Dividing responsibilities between the two authorities in a simple way, as assumed in the "inflation targeting" rule, is not an effective way to manage macroeconomic policy. Inflation targeting does not provide a smooth convergence to an equilibrium with both external and internal balance, since to achieve full employment and external balance, it is crucial to coordinate monetary, fiscal and exchange rate policies.

## Central bank mandate

Many countries have narrowed the mandate of the central bank to fight inflation. In the United States, however, the Federal Reserve's mandate is not only to ensure price stability, but also to promote growth and full employment. A Bank of England survey of 94 central banks found that only 26 per cent had monetary stability as their only objective; 70 per cent had monetary stability combined with other goals; 3 per cent had no statutory goals; 1 per cent had only non-monetary stability as a goal.[61]

There is some evidence[62] that independent central banks with an inflation target do achieve lower levels of inflation—it would be striking if they did not. But inflation is only an intermediate variable. The significant question is whether economies with this institutional structure achieve better performance in real terms: growth, unemployment, poverty, equality. There is little evidence that independent central banks focusing exclusively on price stability do better in these crucial respects.[63] As mentioned above, a sole focus on price stability might lead to greater instability in financial variables. Simple theoretical models suggest the following: with shifting demand and supply curves (common during crises like those in many developing countries in the 1990s), an attempt to stabilize prices can easily destabilize output; price adjustments are meant to buffer quantity adjustments, and reducing the scope for price adjustments (in the process of fighting inflation) is likely to result instead in quantity adjustments.[64]

Central banks make decisions that affect every aspect of society, including rates of economic growth and unemployment. Because there are trade-offs, these decisions can only be made as part of a political process, as discussed in the next section.

### Independent central bank

An independent central bank has been promoted as the most appropriate institutional arrangement to separate monetary policymaking from the political process. There are, however, two main criticisms of this approach.

The first criticism is that the arrangement can undermine democratic governance. Citizens consider few issues more important than the quality of macroeconomic management. By delegating authority over the economy to an independent central bank, the government is being held accountable for something over which it does not have authority. Moreover, we have seen that macroeconomic management entails trade-offs, with different decisions affecting the well-being of different groups. Such decisions are necessarily political. Delegating them to technocrats who are "independent" from the government undermines democratic accountability.

---

61  Mahadeva and Sterne, 2000.

62  Alesina and Summers, 1993.

63  Stanley Fischer, 1996. See also Posen, 1998.

64  There is a line of research which suggests that that is not the case, and has attempted to explain this seeming anomaly. Goodfriend and King, 2001, for example, argue that maintaining price stability guarantees that the economy always operates at its potential output. This result arises from the simplistic assumption that they incorporate only one type of shock in their model. Gaspar and Smets, 2002, argue that central banks should focus on price stability because of the time-inconsistency problem associated with output stabilization, because of the difficulty in assessing potential output, and because it facilitates agents' learning.

While economists and politicians have long discussed the desirability of independent central banks, they have spent much less time considering the importance of *representativeness* (or lack thereof) of these banks. The two concepts are distinct. The problem in many countries is that the governing body of the central bank is typically not representative of society and its broader interests. Governments more sensitive to democratic processes argue that they, and not the central bank, should set targets, such as inflation targets, because the decision involves trade-offs, such as the trade-off between unemployment and inflation. But even a government specified inflation target does not depoliticize the conduct of monetary policy. The central bank is responsible for reaching the target, and missing it still can have costs that not everyone in society bears equally. Independent central banks also undermine effective macroeconomic policy coordination, management and implementation.

## Capital market interventions and other policy options for open economies

So far, in this note, we have focused on fiscal, monetary and exchange rate policies. We have also presented several heterodox measures as alternatives or enhancements to these. One of the most important set of economic tools available to policymakers is capital account controls and regulations. In this section, we will consider some additional microeconomic tools for macroeconomic management, focusing on capital market interventions.

### Interventions in capital markets

In the face of market failures in financial markets, pro-cyclical capital flows and limited room to manoeuvre for macroeconomic policy, capital market interventions can be used to serve multiple purposes. First, they can stabilize short-term volatile capital flows. Second, they can give policymakers additional instruments that allow them more effective and less costly macroeconomic stabilization measures. Third, effective capital account regulations can promote growth by reducing the volatility of financing and the volatility of real macroeconomic performance. Finally, they can also discourage long-term capital outflows. Of all the objectives of intervention listed, discouraging long-term capital outflows is perhaps the most difficult. Yet interventions can be effective, even if controls are partially circumvented. The most critical issue today is not whether market interventions are desirable in theory, but whether, in practice, policymakers can design interventions whose benefit to an economy outweigh the ancillary costs.

### Price and quantity based controls on inflows and outflows

There are different types of capital account regulations. Capital controls include quantity and price-based regulations, both of which can be administered on either

inflows or outflows. In addition, some countries use indirect regulations, such as prudential regulations on financial institutions or regulations on investments of pension
funds, which have implications for capital flows. Thus, a broader concept of capital
account restrictions is useful to understand the complementary use of, and overlap
among, different forms of regulation.

Traditional quantity-based capital restrictions (administrative restrictions and
controls) continue to be widely used by developing countries, including key countries such as China and India, despite the gradual liberalization of their capital accounts. These regulations are used to target either inflows or outflows on domestic
or foreign residents. Regulations that affect domestic residents include restrictions
on currency mismatches (only companies with foreign exchange revenues can borrow abroad), end-use limitations (borrowing abroad is allowed only for investment
and foreign trade), minimum maturities for borrowing abroad, limitations on the
type of agents that can raise funds abroad through ADRs[65] and similar instruments,
prohibition on borrowing in foreign currencies by non-corporate residents and, in
some countries, overall quantitative ceilings. Limitations on non-residents include
restrictions or a prohibition on their capacity to borrow in the domestic markets,
direct regulations of portfolio flows (including explicit approval and limitations on
the assets in which they can invest), sectoral restrictions on FDI and minimum stay
periods.

Other countries, such as Chile and Colombia, implemented price-based interventions on inflows (an unremunerated reserve requirement, equivalent to a tax on
inflows). Argentina introduced a similar mechanism in the mid-1990s. Such measures aim to discourage inflows or outflows by raising associated costs. Price-based
interventions are often mixed with some quantity-based interventions. For example,
Malaysia introduced a tax on outflows during the Asian crisis, after a short period
in which it used quantitative controls, but still maintained quantity restrictions on
currency mismatches by not allowing domestic agents without foreign exchange revenues to borrow abroad. Similarly, Chile maintained a one-year minimum maturity
on most capital inflows, and Colombia directly regulated the inflows and investments of foreign investment funds throughout the 1990s.

Economists have a strong preference for price-based, as opposed to quantity-
based, interventions. Price-based interventions are flexible, non-discretionary and
thus less susceptible to bureaucratic manipulation, and in line with market incentives. But the case for price-based interventions is far from clear. Theoretical work
in economics has shown that sometimes quantity-based restrictions can reduce risk
more effectively than price interventions.[66]

---

65  ADRs or American Depositary Receipts are negotiable certificates issued by U.S. banks
for shares of foreign stocks. ADRs are issued in U.S. dollars and are traded on U.S. stock
exchanges.
66  See Weitzman, 1974, for a general discussion. In the context of trade interventions, see Dasgupta and Stiglitz, 1977.

Most economists also prefer regulating inflows to outflows. There are several reasons for this. First, regulating inflows helps prevent crises, which should be the ultimate goal of policymaking. Second, regulating inflows involves less uncertainty and more transparency: creditors know the cost of regulations before they invest. But, again, the arguments against regulating outflows are not clear-cut. For example, restrictions on outflows may be the only way to solve a collective action problem or coordination market failure. When markets exhibit herding behaviour (and creditors and investors pull their funds out of a country during a crisis because they are afraid that others will pull their funds out first), restrictions on outflows may be the only instrument available to avoid a downward recessionary spiral. Markets generally overshoot in these circumstances, so the restrictions are welfare enhancing.

The empirical evidence shows that all types of instruments can have positive effects, depending on the circumstances under which each mechanism is applied. Policymakers in China, India and Malaysia were able to use quantitative capital account regulations to achieve critical macroeconomic objectives, including prevention of maturity mismatches, attraction of favoured forms of foreign investment, reduction in overall financial fragility and insulation from speculative pressures and contagion effects of financial crises—leading to greater economic policy autonomy.[67]

There is some evidence that regulations on capital inflows in Chile, Colombia and Malaysia[68] proved useful in inducing better debt profiles, restraining asset bubbles and improving the macroeconomic trade-offs faced by authorities. In the latter case, they achieved a variable mix between reducing overall inflows and generating a higher domestic interest rate spread that allowed for a more restrictive monetary policy to work during periods of booming capital inflows. However, the macroeconomic effects, including on asset prices, depended on the strength of the regulations and tended to be temporary in the case of the unremunerated reserve requirements used by Chile and Colombia, which operated more as "speed bumps" than as permanent speed restrictions. In contrast, effective quantity-based controls on inflows adopted by Malaysia in 1994 proved to be much stronger in terms of stopping the massive capital surge that the country had experienced in the early 1990s. Thus, when immediate and drastic action is needed, quantitative controls may be more effective.

The experience of Malaysia illustrates the fallacy of another argument often put forward: that controls on outflows "deter future inflows of all kinds".[69] This argument was used to criticize Malaysia's controls when they were established in 1998. But even before the tax was lifted in 2001, Malaysia started attracting additional inflows. Investors are forward looking, and Malaysia's positive fundamentals (its current account surplus, high savings ratio, moderate external liabilities with a low share of short-term debts, large international reserves and strengthening stock market) drew these additional funds into the country.[70]

---

67  Epstein, Grabel and Jomo, forthcoming.

68  Ocampo and Palma, forthcoming.

69  Only firms that relied on borrowing directly from foreign banks would be unaffected.

70  *The Economist*, 2003.

The capital account interventions discussed above all work by essentially seg-menting domestic markets from international markets. There is another category of restrictions called "soft controls" that aim to segment the market directly.

## Soft controls: encouraging market segmentation

Soft controls can require domestic funds, such as social security or pension funds, to invest their assets in domestic markets and can prohibit or limit investment abroad. These restrictions reduce the funds' potential to generate pro-cyclical disturbances. Soft controls have an additional positive effect of creating a local demand for domes-tic securities and helping to develop the local capital markets, and build a domestic capital base.

This kind of control might become particularly relevant in the future because of the growth of privately managed pension funds in many developing countries, espe-cially in Latin America. In Chile (the pioneer in this area), such funds are equivalent to 70 per cent of annual GDP. Most countries place limits on the extent to which domestic funds can invest abroad, and have experienced new sustained growth in domestic markets, in large part because of the increased demand for local securities from domestic pension funds. Once again, the Chilean experience demonstrates the stimulating role of pension funds on the development of domestic capital markets. But it also demonstrates how pension funds can generate macro-instability when the markets are not segmented and funds are allowed to invest abroad.[71]

Some economists oppose these soft controls because they limit the ability of domestic funds to diversify their assets. This is true, but all economic policies involve trade-offs. Building a local capital market and domestic capital base is essential, and its benefits far outweigh the costs of controls. To the extent that domestic institu-tional investors add to the pro-cyclical nature of open capital markets, they impose an externality on the entire population. Soft controls can help turn this negative process into a positive one for long-term growth.[72]

## Indirect interventions in capital account transactions through prudential regulations

In addition to direct quantity-based and priced-based regulations, governments can use a variety of indirect measures to control (or at least influence) capital account inflows and outflows. The most critical use of regulations is to avoid currency mis-matches in the balance sheets of financial and non-financial agents.

---

71  Zahler, 2003.

72  Government regulations allowing for swaps—an exchange of assets, say, between the pen-sion funds of one country and that of another—could help diversify risk, without putting any pressure on the exchange rate, and without subjecting countries to pro-cyclical capital flows.

Prudential regulations on the banking system are one such tool. Numerous countries forbid, or strictly limit, banks from holding currency mismatches on their balance sheets. To avoid domestic financial dollarization/euroization, many countries also forbid financial institutions from holding deposits from domestic residents in foreign currencies, or limit the nature and use of such deposits. Bank regulators can also prohibit domestic banks from lending in foreign currencies to firms that do not have matching revenues in those currencies. For a more subtle approach, they can impose higher risk-adjusted capital adequacy requirements or additional liquidity and/or loan-loss provisioning (reserve) requirements on foreign currency loans made to domestic agents who lack matching revenues. In countries with deposit insurance, the government can impose higher insurance premiums on banks that have riskier practices. These softer regulations would discourage (but not eliminate) the indirect foreign exchange exposure of banks. To reduce the maturity mismatch of non-financial firms, regulators could similarly set higher capital, liquidity or prudential requirements for short-term lending by domestic financial institutions.

Since banks traditionally mediate much of the capital flow in an economy, regulation of the financial sector has a significant economic impact. However, unless regulations focus adequate attention on the exposure of non-financial firms, the impact of the financial sector can be vitiated. For example, regulations that simply forbid banks from holding dollar-denominated liabilities might encourage firms to borrow directly from abroad. So banks must examine the entire asset and liability structure of the firms to which they lend (which they should do, in any case). Regulations can also be designed to target borrowing abroad by non-financial firms directly. These might include rules on the types of firms that can borrow abroad (for example, only firms with revenues in foreign currencies) and establishes prudential ratios for such firms. Regulations might also include restrictions on the terms of corporate debt that can be contracted abroad (minimum maturities and maximum spreads, for example) and public disclosure of the short-term external liabilities of firms.

There can be problems administering these provisions because corporations will have an incentive to circumvent the rules by using derivatives. To address this, governments should require full disclosure of all derivative positions.[73] Foreign-denominated debt can also be subordinated to domestic currency debt in bankruptcy proceedings. An alternative (or complementary) approach is for governments to create adverse tax treatment for foreign-denominated borrowing, especially when it is short term. For example, countries that have a corporate income tax with tax-deductible interest payments might exclude foreign-denominated debt from the tax deduction or make the interest payments only partially tax deductible.[74]

These alternative measures rely on a combination of banking regulations and complementary policies aimed at non-financial firms. The direct capital account

---

73 To do so, the government would need to add all the longs (investments) and shorts (borrowings) to get the net position and ascertain the actual extent of foreign-denominated borrowing.

74 For an analysis of these issues, see World Bank, 1999, and Bhattacharya and Stiglitz, 2000.

regulations discussed earlier might be simpler to administer than such a system. They may work better because they are aimed at the actual source of the disturbance—pro-cyclical capital flows. For developing countries with strong administrative capabilities and a derivatives market, though, a combination of direct and indirect measures can succeed in restricting flows and helping to limit circumvention.

---

### Box 4.   Accounting frameworks

Accounting frameworks not only provide a description of the economy, but also influence policy. Some of these issues were addressed in the discussion of fiscal policy. This section will explore accounting frameworks currently used by developing countries, and discuss measurement and interpretation issues so that they can be more effective tools of economic policy.

Most countries maintain accounts of their budget or fiscal positions (similar to cash flow statements for firms). The budget numbers are often used to serve several purposes. They provide a measure of government borrowing requirements, and a signal concerning the government's balance sheet position. Ideally, there should be separate accounting frameworks for each of these uses. In reality, most governments use accounting frameworks that are a melange; they provide only incomplete indicators for any of the questions of interest.

For example, an accounting framework can suggest there is excess aggregate demand (inflation) when there is not. Borrowing for investment has a different impact on economic well-being than borrowing for consumption, and should be recognized as such in the accounts. A *balance sheet* would measure assets and liabilities and net worth (the value of assets minus liabilities), and make this distinction clear. In the first case, assets would increase in tandem with liabilities; in the second case, they would not.

One of the problems with this approach is that differentiating between true investments and consumption expenditures is not always clear cut. For example, we typically treat expenditures on education as current expenditures (consumption), but they are really investments in human capital. Health-care expenditures on children should also be considered an investment, while health expenditures on the aged should probably not. But such issues could at least be addressed with an appropriate framework.

Some of the most striking examples of accounting failures include: excluding foreign aid from government budgets; consolidating borrowing by government-owned enterprise with the rest of the budget; accounting for privatization; and responding inappropriately to budget deficits that increase after the privatization of social security. Even the standard measure of economic success, current gross domestic product (GDP), often suggests that the economy is doing better (sometimes much better) than it really is. We discuss a few of these examples in more detail below.

### GDP measurement problems

GDP is the value of all goods and services produced in a country (measured as government spending, consumption, investment and exports minus imports). The problem is that GDP can rise even as citizens become poorer because the government might be selling national assets to foreigners, borrowing abroad or using up its scarce natural resources.

A better measure of overall welfare is gross national product (GNP). GNP includes income earned by domestic residents on investments abroad and subtracts income earned by foreigners on investments made within the country. Even better is net national product (NNP), which subtracts depreciation of the country's capital goods. Measures of national output that take into account the depletion of natural resources, the degradation of the environment and the assumption of risks are even better measures of well-being.

### Fiscal accounting for State-owned enterprises

Another example is the way developing countries are sometimes forced to account for expenditures of State-owned companies. As the IMF has now acknowledged, it has long treated borrowing by government-owned corporations in Latin America differently from the way this borrowing is accounted for in Europe. In Latin America, there is a consolidated public sector deficit which categorizes this borrowing as an increase in the government deficit. In Europe, borrowing by public sector firms is not consolidated with that of the public administration. This means that the budget numbers for Europe and Latin America are not really comparable—a Latin American country in a similar situation to that of a European country will appear to have a larger deficit. Investment by public sector firms also implies that the public sector is accumulating assets, but such assets are not included in the accounts, which generally refer to flows rather than balance sheets. Such differences in accounting practices give countries the incentive to privatize State-owned companies, even when there is no economic reason to do so. Even when there is a reason to do so, it would be preferable to use receipts from such asset-sales to repay public debt. But conventional accounting frameworks do not provide credit for doing so.

### Other examples of fiscal accounting distortion: stabilization funds, land reform and bank recapitalization

There are still other examples of accounting distortions. Some countries, such as Chile, have created rainy day, or stabilization, funds, designed to save surplus funds so they can be spent during an economic downturn. But if the budget treats these expenditures like any other form of deficit spending, it could look as though a country has exceeded the fiscal spending targets negotiated with the IMF. Not wanting to appear profligate could discourage countries from using the self-financed deficit spending that they need for recovery.

Brazil is a country with enormous inequalities in income, wealth and the distribution of land. Land reform holds the promise of increasing efficiency, growth and equality. But inappropriate accounting frameworks are impeding land reform. In one of the better designed land reform programmes, the government borrows money to buy land from rich landowners, using its ability to buy privately owned land to turn it into public land to force sales at fair market value. It then lends money to small peasants so they can buy the land. If the government charges an appropriate interest rate on the loans, there is no real fiscal burden on the government. Of course, there is some probability the peasants will default on the loans, but in that case the government repossesses the land and then resells it.[a] Traditional fiscal

---

a The only loss is the actuarial value of the loss in rental payments during the interim—between the period when the loan goes into default and the time the land is resold—presumably a small fraction of the value of the underlying transaction itself.

**Box 4.   Accounting frameworks** (*continued*)

accounting, however, treats the government borrowing to buy land as a liability; it does not acknowledge the mortgage that the government receives as an asset, no matter what the interest paid. Because the liabilities, but not the assets, are recognized, land reform shows up as deficit spending. Given the IMF's strict deficit targets, land reform becomes essentially impossible. Land reform must compete with all other expenditures even though it would be entirely, or almost entirely, self-financing with an appropriate accounting framework.

In short, fiscal accounting frameworks affect government policy and have enormous political consequences. Avoiding the wrong incentives that accounting practices generate may require an entirely different set of rules than those used in current fiscal programmes. In particular, it may be better to target the current fiscal balance of the public administration (through a structural "golden rule", by which expenditures should be financed by government savings, or a structural primary surplus), as discussed earlier, together with the consolidated debt of the public sector, including all contingent liabilities.

## Public sector liability management in developing countries

If domestic debt markets are thin, governments might be tempted to finance expansionary fiscal policies through borrowing abroad. But this exposes them to greater future risk as a result of exchange rate changes, and undermines the role of exchange rate changes as part of the adjustment process. One reason East Asian countries did so well for so long is that their high savings rate enabled governments to invest at a high rate without borrowing from abroad. It appears that public expenditures generally encouraged, rather than crowded out, private sector investments. (Indeed, the extent of the East Asian crisis was largely a result of capital market liberalization, which was something they need not have done, given their high savings rate.) For countries with high external borrowings, one medium-term goal is to develop local capital markets so they can borrow in their own currency and encourage domestic savings.

If foreign capital markets were well functioning, developing countries would be able to borrow abroad in their own currency (or in a market basket of currencies highly correlated with their own currency). "Ideal" markets would enable the transfer of exchange rate risks to developing country lenders who can bear the risk more easily.[75] There have been a few instances in which this happened, but by and large developing countries have to bear the brunt of the risk of exchange rate and interest rate fluctuations. What matters is not so much the source of the funds, but the risk associated with the debt, and given that foreign borrowing entails the imposition of these high risks, countries should limit their exposure.

Severe currency and maturity mismatches in public sector debt structures are an important problem in many developing countries. Most long-term debt is denominated in foreign currencies, while domestic debt is generally short term. Yet, with

---

**75**   See ECLAC, 1998*a*, ch. VIII.

the exception of a few public sector firms, the public sector produces services for the domestic economy (non-tradables) and public sector investments are long term.

The maturity structure of public sector *domestic* liabilities is also extremely important, as has been revealed in several financial crises. The basic reason for this is the highly liquid nature of public sector securities, which facilitates asset substitution and capital flight. When most debt is short term, the country will continually have to borrow to roll over their debts. With high gross borrowing requirements in periods of pessimism, the interest rate will have to increase to make debt rollovers attractive. Higher interest rates will then feed into the budget deficit, contributing to the rapid increase of debt service and the accumulation of indebtedness. In addition, rollovers of domestic private sector liabilities may be viable only if the government assumes the risks of devaluation or future interest rate changes, and this, in turn, generates additional sources of instability. This was the case prior to the Mexican crisis of 1994 and the Brazilian crisis of 1999, when fixed-interest bonds were swiftly replaced by variable-rate and dollar-denominated securities. Colombia, which has slightly longer-term debt (it has a tradition of issuing public sector securities with a minimum one-year maturity), did not experience a substitution of similar magnitude during its 1998-1999 crisis.[76]

Although the fact that government revenues are largely related to domestic prices suggests that governments should borrow in their domestic currency, there are two reasons why this rule should not be strictly followed. The first has to do with macroeconomic management. The government should manage its external public sector debt to compensate for the highly pro-cyclical pattern of external private capital flows. For example, during phases of reduced private capital flows, the public sector can be one of the best net suppliers of foreign exchange, thanks to its preferential access to external credit, including credit from multilateral financial institutions.

The second reason relates to the depth of domestic bond markets, which determines the ability to issue longer-term domestic debt securities. Well-functioning markets require the existence of secondary markets and market makers that provide liquidity for these securities. In the absence of these preconditions, the government faces a trade-off between maturity and currency mismatches. It may make sense to have a debt mix that includes an important component of external liabilities, despite the associated currency mismatch. In the long run, the objective of the authorities should be to deepen the domestic capital markets. Due to the lower risk levels and the greater homogeneity of the securities it issues, the central government has a vital function to perform in the development of longer-term primary and secondary markets for domestic securities, including the creation of benchmarks for private sector debt instruments. The existence of a government bond enables the market to separate out sovereign risk from firm risk more easily, and some assert that this facilitates corporate borrowing.

To be sure, there is nothing that is risk free. The domestic currency debt market may affect short-term capital inflows. The domestic government debt market can

---

**76**  Ocampo, 2003*a*.

give foreigners easy access to short-term investment instruments, increasing capital surges during booms and adding to capital outflows during crises. A liquid treasury bill market provides investors the ability to sell the currency short, making it easier for speculators to bet against the exchange rate. But these concerns are probably not sufficiently important that they should induce governments not to borrow domestically (when they otherwise would have). There are different types of capital account regulations that can be used to address these risks. For example, authorities can ban foreigners from being allowed to buy short-term instruments; it can mandate that foreigners hold long-term securities for over a year, or it can provide incentives for foreigners not to speculate.

Another problem is posed by the decentralized nature of most governments: many (or even most) subnational administrations and public sector firms expect to be bailed out in case of a crisis. This gives rise to an important moral hazard problem. Specific legal limits and regulations are required, including clear rules on public sector indebtedness, direct mechanisms of control of foreign borrowing, and rules establishing minimum maturities and maximum spreads at which public sector entities can borrow. These rules should apply not only to the central administration, but also to autonomous public sector agencies and subnational governments.[77]

## Conclusion: microeconomic interventions and other heterodox measures

As discussed throughout this note, there are many heterodox interventions that developing countries can use to stimulate their economy such as tax, banking and other regulatory policies. This list of micro-interventions is not meant to be exhaustive. The point is a simple one: there is no reason to limit attempts to stabilize the economy to the standard macroeconomic interventions.

The claim is sometimes made that such microeconomic interventions should be avoided because they lead to distortions; however, there are several responses to this objection. First, in developing countries especially, there are limits to the effectiveness of the standard instruments; the losses from "Harberger triangles" (losses in efficiency, from, say, tax interventions) pale in comparison with those arising from the underutilization of a country's resources. Moreover, developing countries are rife with market inefficiencies; even in developed countries, capital markets are characterized by imperfections, many associated with inherent limitations caused by imperfect information. Those who argue against these microeconomic interventions assume the economy is well described by a perfectly competitive model with perfect information and no distortions—an assumption inappropriate for even developed countries,

---

77  One way foreign lenders can reduce the risk of lending in local currency is through diversification. Domestic creditors generally have a concentrated risk in their own currency, but foreign creditors can take advantage of the low correlations between emerging market local markets and reduce the risk of any one local currency investment. See Dodd and Spiegel, 2005.

but particularly irrelevant for the developing world. Well-designed microeconomic interventions can increase the efficiency of the economy at the same time that they contribute to economic stability.

## References

Akerlof, George, and Paul Romer (1993). "Looting the economic underworld of bankruptcy for profit", *Brookings Papers on Economic Activity*, vol. 2, pp. 1-73.

Alesina, Alberto, and Lawrence Summers (1993). "Central Bank independence and macroeconomic performance: Some comparative evidence", *Journal of Money, Credit and Banking*, vol. 25, No. 2, pp. 151-162.

Auerbach, Alan (1991). "Retrospective capital gain taxation", *American Economic Review*, vol. 81, No. 1, pp. 167-178.

Auerbach, Alan, and D. Bradford (2002). "Generalized cash-flow taxation", NBER Working Paper, 8122.

Baker, Dean, and Mark Weisbrot (2002). "The role of social security privatization in Argentina's economic crisis", Washington, D.C.: Center for Economic and Policy Research.

Bank of Japan (2003). "Japan's deflation and policy response", based on a speech given by Kazuo Ueda, Member of the Policy Board, at the Meeting on Economic and Financial Matters in Nara City, Nara Prefecture. 24 April 2003.

Barro, Robert (1997). *Determinants of Economic Growth: A Cross-Country Empirical Study*. Cambridge, Mass.: MIT Press.

Baunsgaard, Thomas, and Michael Keen (2005). "Tax revenue and (or?) trade liberalization", Working Paper 05/112, IMF, Washington D.C. http://www.imf.org/external/pubs/ft/wp/2005/wp05112.pdf.

Ben-David, Dan, and David Papell (1998). "Slowdowns and meltdowns: postwar growth evidence from 74 countries", *Review of Economics and Statistics*, vol. 80, pp. 561-571.

Bhattacharya, Amar, and Joseph Stiglitz (2000). "The underpinnings of a stable and equitable global financial system: from old debates to a new paradigm", Annual World Bank Conference on Development Economics 1999. Washington, D.C.: The World Bank.

Birdsall, Nancy, and Augusto de la Torre, with Rachel Menezes (2001). "Washington contentious: economic policies for social equity in Latin America", Washington, D.C.: Carnegie Endowment for International Peace. http://www.carnegieendowment.org/pdf/files/er.Contentious.pdf.

Boskin Commission Report (1999). "Toward a more accurate measure of the cost of living", *Final Report to the Senate Finance Committee from the Advisory Commission to Study Consumer Price Index*. http://www.ssa.gov/history/reports/ boskinrpt.html.

Bruno, Michael (1995). "Inflation growth and monetary control: non-linear lessons from crisis and recover", Paolo Baffi Lectures on Money and Finance. Rome: Bank of Italy, Edizioni dell'elefante.

Bruno, Michael, and William Easterly (1996). "Inflation and growth: in search of a stable relationship", *FRBSL*, vol. 78, No. 3, pp. 139-146.

_____(1998). "Inflation crises and long-run growth", *Journal of Monetary Economics*, vol. 41, No. 1, pp. 3-26.

Bruno, Michael, Stanley Fischer, Elhanan Helpman, Nissan Liviatan and Leora Meridor, eds. (1988). *Lessons of Economic Stabilization and its Aftermath.* Cambridge, Mass.: The MIT Press.

Bruno, Michael, Guido Di Tella, Rudiger Dornbusch and Stanley Fischer, eds. (1991). *Inflation Stabilization: The Experience of Israel, Argentina, Brazil, Bolivia, and Mexico.* Cambridge, Mass.: The MIT Press.

Budnevich, Carlos, and Guillermo Le Fort (1997). "Fiscal policy and the economic cycle in Chile", *CEPAL Review,* vol. 61.

Buiter, Willem (2003). "James Tobin: an appreciation of his contribution to economics", NBER Working Paper, 9753.

Centrangolo, Oscar (forthcoming), "Argentina", IPD Argentina tax case study (2005). In *IPD Tax Task Force Volume,* Roger Gordon and Joseph E. Stiglitz, eds.

Chirinko, Bob (1993). "Business fixed investment spending: modeling strategies, empirical results, and policy implications", *Journal of Economic Literature,* vol. 1, No. 4, pp. 1875-1911.

Cobham, Alex (2005). "Tax evasion, tax avoidance and development finance", Working Paper 129, Queen Elizabeth House, Oxford, September. http://www.qeh.ox.ac.uk/pdf/qehwp/qehwps129.pdf.

Cooper, Richard (1992). *Economic Stabilization and Debt in Developing Countries.* Cambridge, Mass.: The MIT Press.

Culpeper, Roy, and Nihal Kappagoda (2006). *Domestic resource mobilization, debt sustainability and the Millennium Development Goals.* Ottawa: The North-South Institute.

Dasgupta, Partha, and Joseph Stiglitz (1977). "Tariffs versus quotas as revenue raising devices under uncertainty", *American Economic Review,* vol. 67, No. 5, pp. 975-981.

Davis, Jeffrey, Rolando Ossowski, James Daniel and Steven Barnett (2003). "Stabilization and savings funds for nonrenewable resources: experience and fiscal policy implications", in *Fiscal Policy Formulation and Implementation in Oil-producing Countries,* Jeffrey Davis, Rolando Ossowski and Annalisa Fedelino, eds. Washington, D.C.: International Monetary Fund.

Díaz-Alejandro, Carlos, and Andrés Velasco (1988). *Trade, Development and the World Economy. Selected Essays of Carlos F. Díaz-Alejandro.* Oxford: Basil Blackwell.

Dodd, Randall, and Shari Spiegel (2005). "Up from sin: a portfolio approach to salvation", in *The IMF and World Bank at 60.* Ariel Buira, ed. London: Anthrem Publishers.

Easterly, William, and Luis Servén, eds. (2003). *The Limits of Stabilization: Infrastructure, Public Deficits, and Growth in Latin America.* Palo Alto, California: Stanford University Press and World Bank.

Eaton, Jonathan, and Mark Gersovitz (1981). "Debt with potential repudiation: theoretical and empirical analysis", *The Review of Economic Studies,* vol. 48, No. 2, pp. 289-309.

ECLAC (Economic Commission for Latin America and the Caribbean) (1998a). *Cincuenta años de pensamiento en la CEPAL: Textos seleccionados.* Santiago: Fondo de Cultura Económica y CEPAL.

_____(1998b). *The Fiscal Covenant: Strengths, Weaknesses, Challenges.* Santiago: ECLAC.

*The Economist* (2003). "A place for capital controls", 3 May, p. 16.

Emran, Shahe, and Joseph Stiglitz (2005). "On selective indirect tax reform in developing countries", *Journal of Public Economics,* vol. 89, pp. 599-623.

Epstein, Gerald, Ilene Grabel and Jomo K. S. (forthcoming). "Capital management techniques in developing countries: managing capital flows in Malaysia, India, and China", in *IPD Capital Market Liberalization and Development*. J. A. Ocampo and J. Stiglitz, eds. Oxford: Oxford University Press.

Fernández de Lis, Santiago, Jorge Martínez and Jesús Saurina (2001). "Credit growth, problem loans and credit risk provisioning in Spain", in *Marrying the Macro- and Microprudential Dimensions of Financial Stability*. BIS Papers, 1 March.

Ffrench-Davis, Ricardo, and Guillermo Larraín (2003). "How optimal are the extremes? Latin American exchange rate policies during the Asian crisis", in *From Capital Surges to Drought: Seeking Stability for Emerging Markets*. Ricardo Ffrench-Davis and Stephany Griffith-Jones, eds. London: Palgrave/Macmillan.

Fischer, Andreas (1996). "Central bank independence and sacrifice ratios", *Open Economies Review*, vol. 7, pp. 5-18.

Fischer, Stanley (1996). "Why are central banks pursuing long-run price stability?", in *Achieving Price Stability*, proceedings of a symposium sponsored by the Federal Reserve Bank of Kansas City in Jackson Hole, Wyoming, 29-31 August, 1996.

FitzGerald, Valpy (2006). "Tax reform in a globalized world", presented to the UNDESA/FONDAD Policy Space for Developing Countries in a Globalized World Conference, New York, 7-8 December 2006.

Frenkel, Roberto (2004). "Real exchange rate and employment in Argentina, Brazil, Chile and Mexico". Paper prepared for the Group of 24, Washington, D.C.

Frenkel, Roberto, and Lance Taylor (2006). "Real exchange rate, monetary policy, and employment", in *Policy Matters: Economic and Social Policies to Sustain Equitable Development*, J. A. Ocampo, Jomo K. S. and Sarbuland Khan, eds. New York, N.Y.: United Nations.

Furman, Jason, and Joseph Stiglitz (1998). "Economic crises: evidence and insights from East Asia", *Brookings Papers on Economic Activity*, vol. 2, pp. 1-114.

Gaspar, Vitor, and Frank Smets (2002). "Monetary policy, price stability and output gap stabilization". *International Finance*, vol. 5, No. 2, pp. 193-211.

Goodfriend, Marvin, and Robert King (2001). "The case for price stability", NBER Working Paper, w8423.

Gordon, Roger, and Wei Li (2005). *Tax Structures in Developing Countries: Many Puzzles and a Possible Explanation*. UCSD and University of Virginia.

Griffith-Jones, Stephany, and Avinash Persaud (forthcoming). "The pro-cyclical impact of Basle II on emerging markets and its political economy", in *IPD Capital Market Liberalization and Development*. J. A. Ocampo and J. Stiglitz, eds. New York: Oxford University Press.

Hubbard, Glenn (1998). "Capital-market imperfections and investment", *Journal of Economic Literature*, vol. 36, No. 1, pp. 193-225.

Jorgenson, Dale, and Eric Yip (2001). "Whatever happened to productivity growth?", *New Developments in Productivity Analysis, Studies in Income and Wealth*, vol. 63, pp. 509-540.

Jun, Joosung (forthcoming). "The tax-expenditure linkage in Korea", IPD Korea tax case study. In *IPD Tax Task Force Volume*. Roger Gordon and Joseph E. Stiglitz eds. http://www0.gsb.columbia.edu/ipd/pub/Jun_Presentation.pdf.

Kaminsky, Graciela, Carmen Reinhart and Carlos Végh (2004). "When it rains, it tours: pro-cyclical capital flows and macroeconomic policies", NBER Working Paper, 10780.

Keynes, J. M. (1936). *General Theory of Employment, Interest and Money*. London: Macmillan.

Krugman, Paul, and Lance Taylor (1978). "Contractionary effects of devaluations", *Journal of International Economics*, vol. 8, No. 3, pp. 445-456.

Levine, Ross, and David Renelt (1992). "A sensitivity analysis of cross-country growth regressions", *American Economic Review*, vol. 82, No. 4, pp. 942-963.

Levine, Ross, and Sara Zervos (1993). "What have we learned about policy and growth from cross-country regressions", *American Economic Review*, vol. 83, No. 2, pp. 426-430.

Lutz, Matthias (1999). "Unit roots versus segmented trends in developing countries output series", *Applied Economic Letters*, vol. 6, pp. 181-184.

Mahadeva, Lavan, and Gabriel Sterne, eds. (2000). *Monetary Policy Frameworks in a Global Context*. New York: Routledge.

Marfán, Manuel (2005). "Fiscal policy, efficacy and private deficits: a macroeconomic approach", in *Beyond Reforms: Structural Dynamics and Macroeconomic Vulnerability*. J. A. Ocampo, ed. Stanford: Stanford University Press and ECLAC.

Martner, Ricardo, and Varinia Tromben (2003). "Tax reforms and fiscal stabilization in Latin America", in Tax Policy, Banca d'Italia Research Department, Public Finance workshop.

McKinley, Terry (2005). "Why is the Dutch disease always a disease? The macroeconomic consequences of scaling up ODA". UNDP International Poverty 42 Centre Working Paper No. 10, Brasilia. http://www.undp-povertycentre.org/newsletters/WorkingPaper10.pdf.

Miller, Marcus, and Joseph Stiglitz (1999). "Bankruptcy protection against macroeconomics shocks: the case for a 'super chapter 11'". World Bank Conference on Capital Flows, Financial Crises and Policies.

Nayyar, Deepak (1997). "Themes in trade and industrialization", in *Trade and Industrialization*. Deepak Nayyar, ed. Delhi: Oxford University Press.

_____(2000). "Macroeconomic reforms in India: short-term effects and long-run implications", in *Adjustment and Beyond: The Reform Experience in South Asia*. Wahidudin Mahmud, ed. London: Palgrave.

Neary, Peter, and Joseph Stiglitz (1983). "Toward a reconstruction of Keynesian economics: expectations and constrained equilibria", *Quarterly Journal of Economics*, vol. 98, pp. 199-228.

Ocampo, J. A. (2002). "Developing countries' anti-cyclical policies in a globalized world", in *Development Economics and Structuralist Macroeconomics: Essays in Honour of Lance Taylor*. Amitava Dutt and Jaime Ros, eds. Aldershot: Edward Elgar, 2002.

_____(2003a). "Capital account and counter-cyclical prudential regulation in developing countries", in *From Capital Surges to Drought: Seeking Stability for Emerging Markets*. Ricardo Ffrench-Davis and Stephany Griffith-Jones, eds. London: Palgrave/Macmillan.

_____(2003b). "International asymmetries and the design of the international financial system", in *Critical Issues in Financial Reform: A View from the South*. Albert Berry, ed. New Brunswick: Transaction Publishers.

_____(2004b). "Lights and shadows in Latin American structural reforms", in _Economic Reforms, Growth and Inequality in Latin America: Essays in Honor of Albert Berry_. Gustavo Indart, ed. Aldershot: Ashgate.

_____(2005b). "A broad view of macroeconomic stability". IPD Conference Background Papers.

_____(forthcoming). "Latin America and the world economy in the long twentieth century", in _The Great Divergence: Hegemony, Uneven Development and Global Inequality During the Long Twentieth Century_. Jomo K. S., ed. New Delhi: Oxford University Press.

_____and G. Palma (forthcoming). In _IPD Capital Market Liberalization and Development_, J. A. Ocampo and J. Stiglitz, eds. Oxford: Oxford University Press.

Oliveira, Jose (forthcoming). "The Brazilian tax structure", IPD Brazil tax case study. In _IPD Tax Task Force Volume_. Roger Gordon and Joseph E. Stiglitz eds.

Posen, Adam (1998). "Central bank independence and disinflationary credibility: a missing link?", _Oxford Economic Papers_, vol. 50, pp. 335-359.

Reinhart, Carmen, and Kenneth Rogoff (2004). "The modern history of exchange rate arrangements: a reinterpretation", _Quarterly Journal of Economics_, vol. 119, No. 1, pp. 1-48.

Reserve Bank of New Zealand (2000). _Alternative Monetary Policy Instruments_. http://www.rbnz.govt.nz/monpol/review/0096420.pdf.

Rodrik, Dani (2008). "A practical approach to formulating growth strategies", in _From the Washington Consensus Towards a New Global Governance_. Narcís Serra and Joseph Stiglitz, eds. Oxford: Oxford University Press.

Rodrik, Dani, Andres Velasco and Ricardo Hausmann (forthcoming). "Growth diagnostics", in _From the Washington Consensus Towards a New Global Governance_, Narcís Serra and Joseph Stiglitz, eds. Oxford: Oxford University Press.

Rojas-Suárez, Liliana (forthcoming). "Domestic financial regulations in developing countries: can they effectively limit the impact of capital account volatility?", in _IPD Capital Market Liberalization and Development_. J. A. Ocampo and J. Stiglitz, eds. New York: Oxford University Press.

Romer, Paul (1987). "Crazy explanations for the productivity slowdown", in _NBER Macroeconomics Annual_. Stanley Fischer, ed. Cambridge, Mass.: NBER.

Schneider, Benu (2006). "Aid delivery, management and absorption". UNDESA, mimeograph.

Shapiro, Carl, and Joseph Stiglitz (1984). "Equilibrium unemployment as a worker discipline device", _American Economic Review_, vol. 74, No. 3, pp. 433-444.

Shigehara, Kumiharu (1992). "Causes of declining growth in industrialized countries", _Policies for Long-Term Economic Growth_. Wyoming: Federal Reserve Bank of Kansas City.

Stiglitz, Joseph (1998). "Knowledge for development: economic science, economic policy, and economic advice", in _Annual World Bank Conference on Development Economics_. Boris Pleskovic and Joseph Stiglitz, eds. Washington: World Bank, pp. 9-58.

_____(2003a). "Whither reform? Towards a new agenda for Latin America", _Revista de la CEPAL_, vol. 80, pp. 7-40.

_____(2003b). _The Roaring Nineties_. New York: W. W. Norton & Company.

Stiglitz, Joseph, and A. Weiss (1981). "Credit rationing in markets with imperfect information", _American Economic Review_, vol. 71, No. 3, pp. 393-410.

Stiglitz, Joseph, J. A. Ocampo, Shari Spiegel, Ricardo Ffrench-Davis and Deepak Nayyar (2006). *Stability with Growth.* Oxford: Oxford University Press.

Svensson, Lars (2000). *Does the P\* Model Provide any Rationale for Monetary Targeting?* NBER Working Paper No. 7178. NBER.

Tanzi, Vito, and Howell Zee (2001). *Tax Policy for Developing Countries.* International Monetary Fund.

Taylor, Lance (1988). *Varieties of Stabilization Experience: Towards Sensible Macroeconomics in the Third World.* Oxford: Clarendon Press.

_____(1993). *The Rocky Road to Reform: Adjustment, Income Distribution and Growth in the Developing World.* Cambridge, Mass.: The MIT Press.

Tobin, James, and William Brainard (1977). "Asset markets and the cost of capital", in *Economic Progress, Private Values and Public Policy: Essays in Honor of William Fellner.* Richard Nelson and Bela Balassa, eds. Amsterdam: North-Holland. pp. 235-262.

Weitzman, Martin (1974). "Prices vs. quantities", *Review of Economic Studies*, vol. 41, No. 4, pp. 477-491.

World Bank (1999). *Global Economic Prospects and the Developing Countries, 1998-99—Beyond Financial Crisis.* Washington, D.C.: World Bank.

Zahler, Roberto (2003). "Macroeconomic stability under pension reform in emerging economies: the case of Chile", *Proceedings of the Seminar on Management of Volatility, Financial Globalization and Growth in Emerging Economies.* Santiago: ECLAC.

# Financial policies

## C. P. Chandrasekhar

## Introduction: objectives

Successful development is not just the growth of productivity and per capita GDP, but also ensuring that the pattern of growth is inclusive, delivers broad-based improvement in the quality of life and contributes to human development. A national development strategy, which includes policies that apply to and take account of the specific features and role of individual sectors, must tailor those policies to achieve the objectives of both growth and human development. This Policy Note discusses the financial policies that can be used to influence, complement and regulate the activities of financial agents to realize these twin objectives.

The financial sector can serve as a significant catalyst to growth by agglomerating the savings of different agents of varying economic strength and allocating them between competing demands for funds. Given the incremental output that can be obtained from a unit of investment, growth in any period depends on the share of national income devoted to investment. Many factors influence the incentives to invest and, therefore, the level and structure of intended investments. However, some or a substantial share of those intentions may remain unrealized, even when potentially viable, because of lack of access to the capital needed to finance such investments or the insurance needed to guard against unforeseen risk. This has obvious implications for growth.

It also affects the realization of human development objectives. Access to financial markets is influenced by the perceptions of creditors, financial investors and insurers regarding the reputation and risk profile of their clients and the adequacy of the collateral they can provide. Hence, it is the poorly endowed and the poor who are most often denied access to these markets, reducing the contribution they make to growth as well as the benefits derived from it. Thus, the challenge of inclusiveness is substantial in the case of the financial sector, making this a crucial objective to be addressed when seeking to plug gaps in the structure of the sector, guide the behaviour of its actors and influence the outcomes of its operations.

Financial sector operations have differential impacts across groups, regions and individuals, even in times of financial stringency and/or crisis that result from devel-

\* The author would gratefully like to acknowledge comments on earlier drafts of this paper from Jomo K. S., Jan Kregel, Isabel Ortiz and Sylvie Illana Cohen (UNDESA); Paul Ladd and Kamal Malhotra (UNDP); Randall Dodd (FPF); Khay Jin Khoo and Harry Shutt, and Joseph Stiglitz (Columbia University).

opments within the financial sector itself. As discussed below, features specific to the financial sector and its activities make it prone to fragility and crisis. As and when such fragility arises and results in partial or systemic crisis, its effects are not merely damaging to growth, but also impact on those with limited or no access to the financial sector in the first place and are least able to deal with these effects. Those suffering financial exclusion are not insulated from the effects of financial fragility. Intervention to identify and ameliorate fragility and pre-empt crises is a must.

Finally, since the financial sector includes institutions and agents involved in mediating the flow of foreign capital and savings into the country, their practices have implications for the volume and pattern of foreign capital inflow. If the volume, structure and maturity of such flows are not regulated, they could increase external vulnerability and trigger currency and financial crises, as illustrated by periodic episodes of such crises in a number of developing countries. Financial policies must also deal with these potential dangers.

This Policy Note identifies policies that can help transform financial agents and markets into instruments of inclusive growth, while ensuring that their presence and/ or operations do not render the system fragile and crisis-prone in the long run.

Four broad motives should guide the design of such policies:

1.  To ensure availability of finance at costs commensurate with prospective returns to key sectors, projects and agents from a development point of view.
2.  To ensure the financial structure does not exclude important sectors of the economy or large sections of the population when such access is required to finance viable productive investment and emergency consumption needs.
3.  To minimize the risk that the behaviour of financial agents could result in losses for savers holding financial assets or deposits.
4.  To pre-empt financial practices that lead to closure of financial firms and increased fragility of the financial system, and that result in macroeconomic instability.

## Need for and constraints on financial intervention

Policies of intervention are justified because markets often:

-   Do not deliver the results needed to advance the objectives of growth and equity, and
-   Contribute to widening the distance between actual outcomes and desired goals.

Financial policies are needed because financial markets are not like those for other goods and services. A loan or an insurance contract is not a contemporaneous trade, but a payment made by one party in lieu of an actual or contingent return in the future (Stiglitz, 1991).

Information is central to the functioning of financial markets. Savers need information on the viability and practices of financial intermediaries; intermediaries need information on the health and motivations of entities they lend to; and borrowers need information on the options they have when seeking credit.

In practice, information tends to be incomplete and asymmetric in distribution. This has important implications:

- Borrowers are heterogeneous in terms of the probability of default, but banks cannot perfectly judge the probability of default of each borrower. Lending then cannot be determined by the choice of the best project but must involve screening based on incomplete information.
- Incomplete and asymmetric information also makes monitoring difficult. This could, for example, encourage managers to divert profits to managerial perks and investment in management and skills that strengthen their own market position, rather than serve the interests of lenders and equity investors.
- Conventionally, such problems are seen as increasing the possibilities of adverse selection, moral hazard and financial fragility.[1]

Confronted with such problems banks may ration credit and financial investors may hold back credit or equity investment. They may also simultaneously raise interest rates to provide for higher risk, resulting in the exclusion of some borrowers and the inclusion of investors in risky projects that promise high returns.

Financial markets are also prone to failure because of the public goods characteristics of information which agents must acquire and process (Stiglitz, 1993; Rodrik, 1998). Once gathered, information can be used by all simultaneously, and it is difficult completely to prevent others from accessing that information without paying a price. Individual shareholders tend to refrain from investing money and time in acquiring information about managements, hoping that others would do so instead and knowing that all shareholders, including themselves, benefit from the information garnered.

As a result there may be inadequate investment in information and poor monitoring, leading to risky decisions and malpractice. Financial firms wanting to reduce or avoid monitoring costs may just follow other, possibly larger, financial firms in making their investments, leading to what has been observed as the "herd instinct" characteristic of financial players. This not only limits access to finance for some agents, but could lead to over-lending to some entities whose failure could have systemic effects. The prevalence of informational externalities aggravates some of these problems. Malpractice in a particular bank leading to failure may trigger fears among depositors in other banks, resulting in a run on deposits there.

---

1   To quote Arestis, 2005: "Adverse selection refers to cases when selection is likely to produce adverse results. In the market for loans, for example, the problem refers to borrowers who may not be able to repay their loans; they use the loans for excessively risky investments, but lenders do not know about them due to lack of information. Moral hazard describes a situation where the borrower acts 'immorally'—that is, in a way that is not in the best interest of the lenders who possess incomplete information. For example, depositors due to incomplete information cannot observe the high risks banks may undertake, which encourages unscrupulous behaviour."

Finally, disruptions may occur because expected private returns differ from social returns in many activities. This could result in a situation where the market undertakes unnecessary risks in search of high returns. Typical examples are lending for investments in stocks or real estate. Loans to these sectors can be at extremely high interest rates because the returns in these sectors are extremely volatile and can touch extremely high levels. Since banks accept real estate or securities as collateral, borrowing to finance speculative investments in stock or real estate can spiral. This activity thrives due to the belief that losses can be transferred to the lender through default, and lenders are confident of government support in case of a crisis. This could feed a speculative spiral that can lead to the collapse of a bubble and bank failures.

As a result of all this, financial markets are characterized by features that almost inevitably result in the deviation of actual results from desired outcomes. Some combination of regulation to correct for potential market failure and creation of special institutions is therefore necessary. However, while government intervention is an appropriate response, shaping the nature of that intervention may not be easy. Governments may be the best agents for dealing with problems of incomplete markets and coordination failure, but the problems of screening clients and monitoring managers, even if government servants, remain. Moreover, decision makers as individuals may be driven by private incentives and can use the excuse of pursuing social goals to cover up bad judgement or malpractice. Political favouritism and corruption may take their toll.

For example, many development banks set up to direct credit to specific sectors or target groups have lent money to projects that were neither commercially nor socially profitable or to have inadequately executed their mandate. Even a seemingly successful development bank like BNDES has been faulted for lending mainly to large enterprises. Sometimes such occurrences are the result of bad judgement. But the issue of authority or straightforward corruption, resulting in State organizations becoming the site for private accumulation by redistributing wealth from the government and/or the poor to the rich and/or a powerful elite, has also played a role.

However, given the arguments that warrant intervention in the first instance, a return to the market may not be the best alternative. While choosing the appropriate mix between intervention and the market is necessary, the problems of public governance can in the final analysis be resolved only through the creation of transparent and participative institutional structures, allowing public monitoring of the monitors through parliament and other democratic bodies.

## Defining the ambit of a financial strategy

Given the objectives laid out earlier, the financial policies that need to be formulated are those that:

- Determine the contours of the financial structure (in terms of markets, institutions and instruments);
- Regulate the activities of financial agents and entities; and

- Utilize elements of the structure to realize pre-specified goals.

This definition of the ambit of "financial policy" explicitly excludes those financial interventions that are not sectoral but macroeconomic in nature, and are dealt with in "Macroeconomic and growth policies" in this series of Policy Notes. For example, the government can be considered the grand financial intermediary in any economy, inasmuch as it absorbs, through taxation, a part of the money incomes and, through borrowing, draws on the savings of the private sector, part of which is transferred to entities needing funds for investment purposes. Through these means the government can seek to ensure the realization in the financial realm of desired rates of savings and a desired allocation of that savings. However, the government is not a financial intermediary, and is normally not an agent seeking to make a profit from the difference between the cost of funds and the returns on subsequent transfers. Hence, the extent to which the government can and should resort to such "intermediation" is not considered the ambit of financial, but fiscal, policy. While there is a need to coordinate fiscal and financial policies, they are conceptually and practically different.

Similarly, the credit-creating behaviour of the banking system as a whole and the interest rate structure it adopts in practice are not treated as strictly "financial sector" concerns, but monetary policy issues. This Policy Note restricts consideration of financial policies to those directly affecting the behaviour of financial entities, though such behaviour is circumscribed by the central bank's "monetary policy". However, there is no sharp line separating monetary policy from financial policy. This is also true of policies relating to inflows of funds from abroad as recorded in the capital account of the balance of payments in the form of debt, portfolio inflows and foreign direct investment. While these are determined by the capital account policies of the government, some or all of these flows tend to influence the functioning of the financial system and the liquidity available.

The above discussion suggests that the fiscal and monetary policy of the government and its policies with respect to cross-border flows of foreign and domestic capital are prior to and should influence and shape its financial sector policies. This need not be the sequence in practice. Very often, governments begin by making changes in their financial sector policies, which in turn necessitate adjustments in their monetary and fiscal policy stance (box 1). Therefore, the discussion here has implications for efforts to establish an appropriate macroeconomic policy framework.

## Is more better?

Often, when designing policies of financial intervention, governments are advised that financial development as measured by the extent of *financial deepening* (the ratio of financial to material wealth) and/or the degree of *financial intermediation* (the share of financial assets of financial institutions in the value of all financial assets) is an unqualified good. This implies that any scheme of intervention that restrains the proliferation of financial markets, institutions and instruments is inappropriate.

However, there is no reason to expect a linear and positive relationship between financial deepening and increased financial intermediation, on the one hand, and growth and equity, on the other. Financial deepening and increased financial intermediation have their uses when economies develop and become more complex, but they are not virtues in themselves. In all economies, the value of financial proliferation depends on its ability to ease transactions, facilitate investment and direct financial resources to the projects that yield the best social returns. This implies that there are financial systems and policies that shape these characteristics in ways most appropriate for each country at specific stages of development. Autonomously evolved financial systems may not be the most appropriate, since they can reflect the imperfections and inequities of the economic base from which they emerge (box 2). This is of relevance since private financial intermediaries are controlled by entities that risk a small volume of their own capital to leverage large volumes of "outside" savings that they are then responsible for allocating. *This makes it imperative that governments act to ensure that resources mobilized by financial intermediaries are put to the best possible use from a social—and not purely private—point of view and that financial systems are relatively safe for investors.*

## Finance for growth through development banking

The objective then should be to ensure that the processes of financial expansion occur in the context of a policy regime that can use that expansion as the instrument to realize a wide range of goals such as faster and more broad-based growth and human development. In particular, the delivery of credit to targeted clients, in adequate amounts and at an appropriate interest rate, is crucial. This is because in developing countries, especially the poorer among them, banking, broadly defined, constitutes the principal segment of the formal financial sector.[2] Further, even though availability of credit in itself cannot be expected to spur investment in a supply-leading manner, wherever the inducement to invest and, therefore, demand for credit, exists, lack of access can prevent the full realization of the potential for investment and growth.

### Realizing target credit-deposit ratios

Thus the first objective of policy should be to ensure that credit is available for all bankable projects which have attracted investor interest. A fundamental problem with the inevitable process of financial intermediation by banks and other financial institutions is the mismatch between the maturity (pre-specified period of lock-in) and liquidity (possibility of encashment) characteristics of the liabilities of financial intermediaries and of the loan-demands they face. As a result, financial firms may hold back on credit provision and show a preference for "investment" in gilts, such as

---

2  This segment includes not only commercial banks, but also cooperative credit institutions, specialized development banks aimed at supporting investments in large and medium industry, small-scale enterprises and agriculture, specialized refinance institutions and, more recently, microfinance institutions.

## Box 1.   Financial liberalization and macroeconomic policy

Over the last two to three decades, many developing countries, intent on attracting foreign capital flows, have liberalized policies governing the presence and activities of foreign financial firms in their domestic financial sectors. One likely consequence that has received considerable attention is an increase in financial fragility and the likelihood of currency and financial crises. The impact on fiscal and monetary policy has received less attention.

Consider a country that succeeds in attracting large inflows of foreign capital after financial liberalization. If the economy is unable immediately to absorb these flows, there is an excess supply of foreign exchange in domestic markets that could lead to an appreciation in the value of the domestic currency, which in turn adversely affects export competitiveness.

To deal with this, central banks often purchase dollars (say) and accumulate them as reserves. This increases the demand for foreign exchange and moderates the pressure on the domestic currency to appreciate. However, this also increases the foreign exchange assets of the central bank; its corollary is an increase in its liabilities, implying an increase in money supply. To "sterilize" the effects of its increased holding of foreign exchange assets, the central bank often chooses to reduce its holding of domestic credit instruments. Since this consists largely of government debt, the net result is a reduction in the holding and accretion of government debt with the central bank.

To accommodate this need to reduce domestic currency assets enforced by the increase in foreign currency assets, three supportive policies are pursued:

- the fiscal deficit of the government is sought to be pruned, to reduce its overall borrowing requirement;
- to the extent that the government chooses to borrow it is forced increasingly to rely on higher cost credit from the "open market" rather than borrowing from the central bank, and
- the central bank is sought to be insulated from fiscal developments by making it autonomous of the government in the sense that it need not respond positively when subjected to additional credit demands from the government.

However, the central bank is not truly "autonomous" since it is forced to purchase autonomous flows of foreign exchange into the country to prevent currency appreciation. As and when it exhausts its available stock of government securities through sterilizing sales, it will find that its assets and liabilities, hence the volume of money supply, are influenced by movements of foreign capital. This loss of control over the supply of money implies a loss of monetary sovereignty.

government securities, rather than in the provision of credit. This tendency could be aggravated by collateral demands by overcautious lenders which prospective borrowers may not be able to meet. In sum, there could be a process of credit rationing that implies an inadequate degree of aggregate credit provision.

Any growth-oriented financial policy regime must therefore ensure an adequate degree of credit availability. An important instrument in realizing that objective is the specification of target credit-deposit ratios, that imply an adequate degree of intermediation from a development point of view, to be achieved by the banks. This would also put pressure on banks to reduce their intermediation costs to accommo-

## Box 2. Unregulated financial sectors can be inappropriate

In practice, there are a number of reasons why autonomously evolved and unregulated financial sectors can be inappropriate from a developmental point of view. For example, informal financial structures in backward and predominantly agrarian economies reflect the unequal distribution of assets and economic power and, because of the interlinking of land, labour and credit markets, operate in ways that result in usurious moneylending inimical to productive investment. Similarly, autonomously evolved financial structures that reflect a high degree of interconnectedness between an oligopolistic industrial sector and a numerically small set of financial intermediaries are known to result in an excessive concentration of credit and in investment choices influenced by considerations that put at risk the savings of uninformed depositors. According to Díaz-Alejandro, 1986, "between 1975 and 1982, Chile went from a financially shallow economy, where inflation had wiped out the real value of debt, to an excessively financially deep economy where creditors owned a very large share of real wealth, a clear case of 'too much debt and too little equity'". This was because linkages "between banks and firms, which were hardly arms' length, were responsible for the high use of debt by private firms. In Chile by late 1982 private firms were more indebted than State enterprises; within the private sector, extreme indebtedness was found among those that controlled banks". By late 1982, the two largest business groups in Chile controlled the principal insurance companies, mutual funds, brokerage houses, the largest private company pension funds and the two largest private commercial banks. Many banks had lent one quarter or more of their resources to affiliates. Such concentration of credit in related enterprises not only results in exclusion of other potential borrowers, but also in lending driven by criteria other than economic or even social returns and in overexposure that can lead to default.

date lower spreads associated with larger lending. Macroeconomic circumstances, such as recessionary conditions, may on occasion constrain lending by the banks. If this is the case, then low credit-deposit ratios should be treated as a signal for the adoption of policies to revive the economy, since banks cannot be made to bear the burden of circumstances beyond their control.

## Creating long-term credit

Commercial banks, which mobilize finance through savings and time deposits, acquire liabilities that are individually small and protected from income and capital risk, are of short maturity and are substantially liquid in nature. On the other hand, the credit required for most projects tends to be individually large, subject to income and capital risk and substantially illiquid in nature. Consequently, commercial banks conventionally focus on providing working capital credit to industry. This is collateralized by firms' inventories of raw materials, final products and work in progress. Though this can involve provision of credit in relatively large amounts, with significant income and credit risk and a degree of illiquidity, it implies a lower degree of maturity and liquidity mismatch than lending for capital investment. This makes banks less suited to lending for capital investment.

As noted elsewhere (United Nations, 2005), left to themselves, private financial markets in developing countries usually fail to provide enough long-term finance to undertake the investments necessary for economic and social development. As a result, firms in developing countries often hold a smaller portion of their total debt in long-term instruments than firms in developed countries. Private institutions may fail to provide such finance because of high default risks that cannot be covered by high enough risk premiums because such rates are not viable. In other instances, failure may be because of the unwillingness of financial agents to take on certain kinds of risk or because anticipated returns to private agents are much lower than the social returns in the investment concerned (Stiglitz, 1994).

This creates a shortfall in funds for long-term investments. One way to deal with this problem is to encourage the growth of equity markets. This is attractive because, unlike in the case of debt, risk is shared between the financial investor and the entrepreneur. This enhances the viability of the firm in periods of recession. However, the evidence shows that even in developed countries equity markets play a relatively small role in mobilizing capital for new investments.

To cover the shortfall in funds required for long-term investment, developing countries need to and have created *development banks* with the mandate to provide long-term credit at terms that render such investment sustainable. According to an OECD estimate quoted by Eshag, 1983, there were about 340 such banks in some 80 developing countries in the mid-1960s. Over half of these banks were State-owned and funded by the exchequer; the remainder had mixed ownership or were private.

Handicapped by colonial legacies, international inequalities and various systemic biases, these kinds of institutions are a "must" for developing countries. Any national strategy of modernization in a mixed-economy framework must provide for the establishment of institutions of this kind. However, it is best to create separate development banks to provide long-term capital at near-commercial rates and "policy banks" to provide credit to special areas such as agriculture or the small-scale sector where interest rates have to be subsidized and grace periods have to be longer. This allows different criteria to be applied to the evaluation of the performance of these banks, with profitability a more important consideration in the case of the former.

Since development banks play a role normally bypassed by commercial banks and as they are funded by the State (with deep pockets), there is always the possibility that lending to projects that are neither commercially viable nor socially profitable may occur for reasons other than errors of judgement. Governance mechanisms to ensure transparent procedures, adequate disclosure and participative monitoring involving oversight by democratically elected bodies are crucial. Such mechanisms should not be diluted or passed up on the grounds that they undermine managerial autonomy.

## Ensuring sectoral distribution

Growth requires not just an adequate volume of credit but an appropriate distribution of such credit. For example, certain sectors—infrastructure being the most obvious—are characterised by significant "economy-wide externalities". That is, their presence is a prerequisite for and a facilitator of growth in other sectors. But the infrastructure sector is usually characterized by lumpy investments, long gestation lags, higher risk and lower profit. Banks would be wary of lending to such projects, given the maturity and liquidity mismatch involved. Such reticence would be greater in economies with a predominantly private banking system. If private—rather than social—returns drive the allocation of financial savings, these sectors would receive inadequate capital, even though their capital-intensive nature demands that a disproportionate share be diverted to them. Given the "economy-wide externalities" associated with such sectors, inadequate investments in infrastructure obviously constrain the rate of growth. Hence, specialized policy development banks are needed, with sources of finance other than deposits by small savers (box 3). While such institutions can be funded by the government or the central bank, government guarantees on borrowing by these entities is needed if adequate capital is to be mobilized.

Development banks of this kind can help address the fact that local industrialists may not have adequate capital to invest in capacity of the requisite scale in more capital-intensive industries characterized by significant economies of scale. They help promote such ventures through their lending and investment practices, and often provide technical assistance to their clients. Given the inadequate development of equity and long-term debt markets in developing countries, these institutions soon account for an important share of external finance for the private sector.

## Leveraging capital provision to influence investment decision and performance

The need for a growth-oriented financial policy to extend credit to special sectors such as infrastructure is an important component of a larger requirement in economies with predominantly private investment decision makers: the need to ensure that the pattern of production is geared to maximizing growth. In economies with an important role for private agents in investment decision-making, market signals determine the allocation of resources for investment and, therefore, the demand for and allocation of savings intermediated by financial enterprises. This can result in "short-termism" of various kinds, resulting in inadequate investment in sectors with significant "external" effects and long-term potential from the point of view of growth. In addition, the private-profit driven allocation of savings and investment could direct investment to capital- and import-intensive sectors, adversely affecting the balance of payments and the employment elasticity of output growth in the process. This could constrain the pace of growth, as well as the pursuit and efficacy of the poverty reduction effort.

Realizing a growth-oriented pattern of production of goods and services requires the State to guide the allocation of investment. Since independent and atomistic decision makers cannot have the economy-wide and "social" seeing power to undertake such coordination and targeting, the State must play a role in overcoming market failure resulting from inadequate coordination. One way to do this is to use the financial sector as an instrument for investment coordination and targeting. Even in developing countries that choose outward-oriented strategies or are forced to choose a more mercantilist strategy of growth based on rapid acquisition of larger shares in segments of the world market for manufactures, the relevant segments have to be identified by an agency other than individual firms. Experience indicates that the State has the capacity to assess and match global opportunities and economy-wide capabilities.

Hence, though its financial policies, the State must ensure an adequate flow of credit at favourable interest rates to these entities so that they cannot only make investments in frontline technologies and internationally competitive scales of production, but also have the means to sustain themselves during the long period when they expand market share. The State must not merely play the role of investment coordinator; it needs to use the financial system to direct investment to sectors and technologies at appropriate scales of production. Equity investments and directed credit are important instruments in such a State-led or State-influenced development trajectory.

Executing this role requires leveraging lending to influence investment decisions and monitoring the performance of borrowers. Financial institutions in backward countries have to undertake entrepreneurial functions, such as determining the scale of investment, the choice of technology and the markets to be targeted by industry, and extension functions, such as offering technical support to the farming community. Stated otherwise, financial policies may not help directly to increase the rate of savings and ensure that the available ex ante savings are invested, but they can be used to influence the financial structure so as to ensure that lending leads to productive investment that accelerates growth and makes such lending sustainable.

Development and commercial banks can also monitor corporate governance and performance on behalf of all stakeholders, rather than rely on the system of indirect monitoring resulting from the discipline exerted by the threat of takeover in stock markets ostensibly prevalent in the United States and the United Kingdom. The effectiveness of the latter option is limited. Moreover, it is not available in most developing countries where equity markets are poorly developed and most firms are not listed.

In practice, development banks do not always leverage their capital-provision role to intervene effectively in management in all contexts. In some countries, despite a significant role as providers of finance, development banks adopt a passive role with respect to technological or managerial decisions of private borrowers, avoiding a role that such institutions are expected to play. This is also the loss of an opportunity, not only to exploit the economies of scale associated with investment in knowledge skills of certain kinds, but also to coordinate investment decisions in systems dominated by private decision-making.

**Box 3.   Development finance in Viet Nam**

In Viet Nam, the Government has continued with targeted lending for specific purposes even after the adoption of financial liberalization policies. This involved the creation of a special Development Assistance Fund (DAF) in 2000, separate from the commercial banking system, which had as its objectives: (i) the provision of subsidized State loans for medium- to long-term investments in priority sectors such as infrastructure, heavy industry and public services, (ii) provision of interest-rate support and investment guarantees for chosen projects and (iii) provision of short-term export promotion credit. Support in these forms can go to both private and State-owned enterprises, taking account of both commercial and policy criteria, such as encouraging investment in underdeveloped areas, preferential sectors, and projects related to health, education, culture and sport. The DAF has branches in all 61 provinces, with a registered capital of five billion dong (US$ 326.8 million). Before 2002, the Office of the Prime Minister determined allocation of funds. Funds came from the Social Insurance Fund, the Sinking Fund, the Viet Nam Postal Service Savings Company (VPSC),[a] the Government budget, loan repayments and official development assistance (ODA). Since 2002, the DAF has been expected to mobilize its own resources. It continues to draw funds from the sources mentioned above, through negotiation. If funds come from the Government budget, this usually involves issuance of investment bonds.

Outstanding credit from the DAF in 2001 to 2002, and loan disbursements in 2002 and 2003 grew much faster than total domestic credit to the economy. As a result disbursements through the DAF amounted to an increasing share of domestic credit, reaching 24 per cent in 2002, equal to 3.3 per cent of GDP. Over time, the DAF has emerged as the largest financial intermediary in Viet Nam for channelling domestic and foreign funds to investment activities (Weeks, et al., 2003).

---

a  VPSC was established in 1999. In 2002, it already had 539 to 600 branches all over the country, and has been a good and fast-growing venue to mobilize rural savings. There are around half a million deposit accounts with outstanding deposits at D3.8 billion (around US$ 250 million).

## Role for differential interest rates

Since one of the objectives of these actions is to guide investment to chosen sectors, the rate of interest on loans to favoured sectors may have to be lower than even the prime lending rate offered to the best borrowers, judged by creditworthiness. That is, differentials in interest rates supported with subsidies or enabled by cross-subsidization is part of a directed lending regime.

Financial policies were an important component of the strategic policies pursued by countries like the Republic of Korea and Taiwan Province of China on the way to competitive success (Wade, 1991; Amsden, 1989). These included interest rate differentials and bank financing of private investment, resulting from the channelling of corporate finance through a still largely regulated banking system.

Table 1 summarizes some of the main financial policy options that can be used to accelerate growth.

**Table 1.   Some salient financial policy options to promote growth**

| Policy | Objective | Dangers | Requirements |
|---|---|---|---|
| Target credit-deposit ratios | Ensuring banks create adequate credit from deposits they garner, rather than invest in secure instruments such as government securities or in commercial paper and rationing credit | a. Indiscriminate lending to meet target resulting in adverse selection<br>b. Low spreads adversely affecting profitability | a. Clear guidelines on screening of clients<br>b. Emphasis on social return rather than profitability in performance assessments<br>c. Flexibility to determine interest rates to permit cross-subsidization<br>d. Refinance on concessionary terms for lending to specific target groups |
| Create and/or strengthen development banks | Fill the shortfall in funds available for long-term investment from banks | Lending to projects that are neither commercially viable nor socially profitable | a. Adoption of alternative performance criteria<br>b. Implementation of transparent procedures and participative governance mechanisms |
| Separate development banks from "policy banks" | a. Allows defining the objectives of the institution clearly, such as providing long-term credit as opposed to directed credit at concessional rates<br>b. Allows for implementation of different performance criteria | The opportunity to cross-subsidize different segments may be passed up | Systems to evaluate the appropriate degree of concessionality and volume of subsidy for policy banks in different areas |

**Table 1.   Some salient financial policy options to promote growth** (*continued*)

| Policy | Objective | Dangers | Requirements |
|---|---|---|---|
| Directed lending for sectors characterized by externalities, especially "economy-wide" externalities | Ensuring growth | Same as for policy banks | a. Provision of government guarantees for borrowing by these entities<br>b. Creating specialized development banks/vehicules for the purpose |
| Leverage capital provision to influence investment decisions and monitor performance | a. Overcome "coordination failures" and "short-termism"<br>b. Ensure investments incorporate best-practice techniques, of appropriate scale<br>c. Influence pricing and marketing policies, especially for global markets<br>d. Monitor corporate governance and performance | a. Possibility of "government failure" leading to wrong decisions<br>b. Possibility of wrong decisions influenced by conflicts of interest, corruption, etc. | Implementation of transparent procedures and participatory governance mechanisms |
| Differential or discriminatory interest rates | Realize the objectives of directed credit and render the programme viable | Same as above | a. Possibility of cross-subsidization<br>b. Provision of interest subsidies<br>c. Implementation of transparent procedures and participative governance mechanisms |

# Financial policies to promote equity and human development

When countries frame policies that determine their financial structures and influence the behaviour of domestic financial agents, the concern is not just with accelerating growth. Just as important is the need to ensure that such development is broad-based. An obvious prerequisite for this is that the coverage of lending, supervisory and developmental services of the financial sector must be near comprehensive. The creation of an inclusive financial sector, defined as one that provides "access to credit for all 'bankable' people and firms, to insurance for all insurable people and firms and to savings and payments services for everyone" (United Nations, 2006), should be among the prime objectives of financial policy.

In practice, there is only limited access to the financial sector in many developing countries. According to recent estimates (United Nations, 2006), an average of 89.6 per cent of the population in the 15 countries of the European Union have a bank or postal savings account. The comparable figure for the United States is 91.0 per cent. In contrast, in a set of 10 developing countries or major cities in such countries, the figure varied from as low as 6.4 per cent to a maximum of 47 per cent (table 2). This is a matter of concern since, "access to a well-functioning financial system can economically and socially empower individuals, in particular poor people, allowing them to better integrate into the economy of their countries, actively contribute to their development and protect themselves against economic shocks" (United Nations, 2006). As the World Economic and Social Survey 2005 (United Nations, 2005) noted: "This lack of access to finance has become a matter of wider development-related concern because deeper and more inclusive financial systems are linked to economic development and poverty alleviation".

**Table 2. Populations with a savings account in selected developing countries/locations**

| Botswana | 47.0 | Mexico City | 21.3 |
|---|---|---|---|
| Brazil (urban) | 43.0 | Namibia | 28.4 |
| Colombia (Bogotá) | 39.0 | South Africa | 31.7 |
| Djibouti | 24.8 | Swaziland | 35.3 |
| Lesotho | 17.0 | United Republic of Tanzania | 6.4 |

*Source*: United Nations, 2006.

Access to credit for women is worse than for men. Studies have shown that women entrepreneurs often face problems of gender bias, which can severely hamper women seeking small business credit. This happens despite evidence that women generally have a higher loan repayment rate than men. Women also tend to lack the collateral needed for loans, often due to social and legal disadvantages such as lower wage incomes or limitations on property ownership (UNCTAD, 2001).

Inadequate region-, class- and unit-wise allocation is often the outcome of allocation driven purely by considerations of private profit rather than social returns. Credit allocation driven by private returns can aggravate the inherent tendency in markets to concentrate investible funds in the hands of a few large players in sectors delivering high private profits and to direct savings to already well-developed centres of economic activity. Besides resulting in excess exposure to certain sectors and segments, this concentration of financial flows militates against broad-based development (box 2). Consequently, financial policies are often designed to ensure adequate flows of capital to less developed areas of the economy and to disadvantaged sections of the population.

Thus, financial exclusion is not just a matter of inadequate access for individuals, but for whole sectors such as agriculture or small-scale industry. As a result of such exclusion, financial flows can be mechanisms that significantly aggravate the biased developmental outcomes of the unequal distribution of assets. This occurs because the divergence between private returns and social returns varies across sectors, and private returns tend to be higher in sectors (say, real estate and the stock market) where social returns are low. It also occurs because financial intermediaries concentrate in their hands household savings, which tend to be a relatively high share of total savings in the system. If the allocation of these savings is governed by the private predilections of those who control or manage these intermediaries, the bias in allocations can be substantial and not necessarily always socially efficient.

Further, in poor countries, where the pattern of effective demand is significantly influenced by the extent of inequality, market signals could direct credit to capital- and import-intensive sectors, the expansion of which may have limited effects on employment, incomes and poverty reduction.

As a result of such tendencies, a number of weaknesses afflict the banking system in developing countries, including those with relatively more developed financial systems, such as India (box 4). They include:

- Poor population coverage as measured by the ratio of bank branches, deposits and credit to the population;
- Urban concentration;
- Significant inequities in the sectoral allocation of credit; and
- Excessive control over banks by industrial and commercial interests.

## Ensuring financial inclusion

It is because of these outcomes associated with the operation of "self-organized" financial systems, that financial policies aimed at ensuring financial inclusion must be an important component of a national development strategy. In developing countries adopting a mixed economy framework with significant private initiative and investment, the financial sector has to play a major role in a system of "inclusive finance" by channelling credit at reasonable interest rates to units and agents, so as to ensure a degree of intersectoral, rural-urban, region-wise and asset size-wise balance

## Box 4.  Financial exclusion in India pre-nationalization

Features of financial exclusion were visible in India before the nationalization of major banks in 1969 and the promotion of a policy of social reorientation.

First, the coverage of the branch network was unduly low compared with the size of the population—an average of one branch office for 65,000 persons, whereas the developed country norm was one branch per 8,000 population.

Second, the urban orientation of the banking system was obvious. At the end of June 1969, there were just 1,832 (or 22.2. per cent) out of 8,262 bank branches located in rural areas. This spread was only achieved because of the accelerated branch banking policy of the State Bank of India, which operated 629 branches in rural areas.

Third, concentration was excessive even in urban areas. As of April 1969, there were 617 towns without any commercial bank branch; of these, 444 were not served by any bank at all. Five metropolitan cities (Bombay, Calcutta, Delhi, Madras and Ahmedabad) accounted for 46 per cent of total bank deposits and 65 per cent of total bank credit as at the end of 1967.

Fourth, the most disconcerting aspect of the banking structure was the sectoral distribution of bank credit. The share of agriculture in total bank advances in 1951 was 2.1 per cent; it had declined to 0.2 per cent by 1965-1966. On the other hand, the share of industry in bank credit increased from 30.4 per cent in 1949 to 52.7 per cent in 1961 and further to 62.7 per cent in March 1966.

Finally, the financial stake of the shareholders in banks was almost negligible. For major banks, paid-up capital constituted just about 1 per cent of total bank deposits (ICBP, 2006).

in credit disbursal. In particular, it is necessary to ensure that financial flows reach sectors and sections that would otherwise be bypassed or neglected.

### Bank branching

A basic requirement for such financial inclusion is widely accessible deposit and credit facilities, through banks, post offices and other institutions. While the post office can play a partial role, increasing the number and spread of bank branches is crucial. Most developing countries are underserved in terms of the number of bank branches per thousand of the population. Governments should adopt a scheme of branch licensing to ensure branching in underserved areas or specify a ratio of branching in well-served and underserved areas, or of urban to rural branches, for example, that must be maintained.

### Preventing credit migration

Bank branching in underserved areas, while helpful in mobilizing deposits in institutions belonging to the formal financial sector, is no guarantee of balanced regional credit dispersion. Deposits mobilized in rural areas or backward regions can be used by geographically diversified banks to provide credit to clients in urban areas or more developed regions. More extensive bank branching must be accompanied with guidelines to prevent excessive credit migration from less to more developed areas in the country (box 5).

## Preventing credit concentration

Given the incompleteness of information available to lenders, the adage that "nothing succeeds like success" would tend to hold. Agents with a longstanding relationship with a bank, a good track record and significant financial strength may be favoured with a disproportionate share of credit. This could lead to large individual loan contracts for such clients and to the accommodation of multiple applications from the same client. A concomitant would be the exclusion of other bankable and needy projects. While large, creditworthy borrowers should not be overly discriminated against, measures are needed to prevent their past success being a barrier to access for others. A simple way to deal with this likelihood is to institute a "credit authorization scheme", requiring banks to obtain prior authorization from a designated body to grant credit above a particular level to any single party so as to align credit policy more closely with developmental objectives. The other is to set strict limits on credit provided to interlinked firms controlled by a single authority, which also helps reduce risk due to failures of a single set of agents.

## Directed credit

Central to a framework of inclusive finance are policies aimed at pre-empting bank credit for selected sectors like agriculture and small-scale industry. Pre-emption can take the form of specifying that a certain proportion of lending should be directed at these sectors. In addition, through mechanisms such as the provision of refinance facilities, banks can be offered incentives to realize their targets. Directed credit programmes should also be accompanied by a regime of differential interest rates that ensure demand for credit from targeted sectors by cheapening the cost of credit. Such policies have been and are still used in developed countries as well (box 6).

---

**Box 5.  Preventing credit migration**

The United States passed the Community Reinvestment Act in 1977, which requires banks to provide credit to neighbourhoods in which they raise funds from deposits. This is enforced through the collection of data that banks are required to file, by postal zone, on the source of their deposits and the destination of their loans, leases and other lines of credit. Other banking laws prohibit banks from denying credit on the basis of race, ethnicity and gender. This explicit prohibition against discrimination, enforceable by bank regulators and by private lawsuits to recover damages, helps promote lending to those members of society. These banking laws promote the policy of inclusive finance, and they are supported on the grounds that discrimination is wrong and that banks should not drain savings from any area but instead be responsible for mobilizing savings into credit for investment and consumption.

## Box 6.   FarmerMac:  farm credit system in the United States

A lesson for developing countries from developed country experience can be found in U.S. financial policy for assuring adequate credit flows to its agricultural sector. The Federal Farm Loan Act of 1916 established a nationwide Farm Credit System—a network of credit cooperatives—that has proved to be a reliable source of funding for farmers, ranchers and aquatic producers during good times as well as bad. This includes 12 regional farm land banks whose original capital was supplied mostly by the Government. Two related Government-owned funding corporations raised money from capital markets by issuing bonds. These funds are lent to the network of credit banks and credit cooperatives at interest rates that reflect the Government's low cost of borrowing. In turn these funds are lent to rural producers and homeowners. It has proved to be low cost, stable and non-cyclical.

Credit pre-emption, aimed at directing debt-financed expenditures to specific sectors, can also be directly exploited by the State. In many instances, besides a cash reserve ratio, the central bank requires a part of the deposits of the banking system to be held in specified securities, including government securities. This ensures that banks are forced to make a definite volume of investment in debt issued by government agencies. Such debt can be used to finance expenditures warranted by the overall development strategy of the government, including its poverty alleviation component. Beyond a point, however, these roles have to be dissociated from traditional commercial banks and located in specialized institutions.

### Institutional safeguards

The need to ensure inclusion may be accepted by line officials, managers and directors, but the motivation to realize these objectives may not exist, resulting in slippages. Institutional mechanisms to ensure cognition and pursuit of this objective when making lending decisions are crucial. One form such a mechanism can take is a statutory requirement to constitute commercial bank boards with representation for different stakeholders, including sectors normally neglected in credit provision, so as to monitor and ensure financial inclusion.

### Supply-leading role

Finally, it is not enough for institutional mandates to ensure "financial inclusion", merely to accept it as an objective, and wait for credible borrowers to arrive. Small, inexperienced and poor borrowers may neither be familiar with the borrowing options they have nor have the capacity to design and frame a project in ways that can render it successful and creditworthy. Inclusive banking, therefore, requires institutions that take on a supply-leading role, identifying potential entrepreneurs with bankable projects, helping them through the phases of project preparation and credit appraisal, and ensuring successful and timely implementation. The relationship should not end there either. Rather, the lending institution should use the leverage provided by its support to monitor the functioning of small and medium-scale businesses to render them productive and financially sustainable.

## A case for public ownership

Inclusive finance of this kind inevitably involves the spread of formal financial systems to areas where client densities are low and transaction costs are high. Further, to ensure sustainable credit uptake by disadvantaged groups, interest rates charged may have to diverge from market rates. This regime of differential or discriminatory interest rates may require policies of cross-subsidization and even government support to ensure the viability of chosen financial intermediaries. Intervention of this kind presumes a substantial degree of "social control" over commercial banks and development banking institutions.

It implies that "social banking" involves a departure from conventional indicators of financial performance such as costs and profitability and requires the creation of regulatory systems that ensure that the "special status" of these institutions is not misused. In sum, "inclusive finance" as a regime is defined as much by the financial structure in place as by policies such as directed credit and differential interest rates. In particular, it involves a substantial measure of social regulation of banking.

If instruments of social control of the kind discussed above prove inadequate to ensure compliance with financial inclusion guidelines, governments can use and have used public ownership of a significant section of the banking/financial system to ensure the realization of developmental and distributional objectives. If an overwhelmingly dominant banking system has to play a role in directing savings and rendering the financial structure inclusive, the question of ownership and/or regulatory structure of the banking industry has to be addressed.

This was recognized by governments in many countries in Europe, where banking development in the early post-Second World War period took account of the vital differences between banking and other industries. Recognizing the role the banking industry could play, many countries with predominantly capitalist economic structures thought it fit either to nationalize their banks or to subject them to rigorous surveillance and social control. France, Italy and Sweden are typical examples in this respect. Overall, even as late as the 1970s, the State owned as much as 40 per cent of the assets of the largest commercial and development banks in the industrialized countries (United Nations, 2005). An example of a more recent successful transition to inclusive finance through nationalization of a significant part of the banking system is India post-1969 (box 7).

The declared objectives of public presence in and social regulation over banking are:

- To ensure a wider territorial and regional spread of the branch network;
- To ensure better mobilization of financial savings by the formal sector through bank deposits; and

## Box 7.  Public ownership and inclusive finance in India

India's achievements with regard to financial sector development after bank nationalization have been remarkable. There was a substantial increase in the geographical spread and functional reach of banking, with nearly 62,000 bank branches in the country as of March 1991, of which over 35,000 (or over 58 per cent) were in rural areas. Along with this expansion of the bank branch network, steady increases were recorded in the share of rural areas in aggregate deposits and credit. From 6.3 per cent in December 1969, the share of rural deposits in the total rose to touch 15.5 per cent by March 1991 and the rural share of credit rose from 3.3 per cent to 15.0 per cent. More significantly, with the target credit-deposit (C-D) ratio set at 60 per cent, the C-D ratios of rural branches touched 64-65 per cent on the basis of sanctions. Sectorally, a major achievement of the banking industry in the 1970s and 1980s was a decisive shift in credit deployment in favour of the agricultural sector. From an extremely low level at the time of bank nationalization, the credit share of the sector grew to nearly 11 per cent in the mid-1970s and to a peak of about 18 per cent (the official target) at the end of the 1980s (ICBP, 2006).

- To reorient credit deployment in favour of hitherto neglected or disadvantaged sections by reducing control by a few private entities.

Public ownership of banks also serves a number of overarching objectives:

- It ensures the information flow and access needed to pre-empt fragility by substantially reducing any incompatibility in incentives driving bank managers, on the one hand, and bank supervisors and regulators, on the other.
- By subordinating the profit motive to social objectives, it allows the system to exploit the potential for cross subsidization and to direct credit, despite higher costs, to targeted sectors and disadvantaged sections of society at different interest rates. This permits the fashioning of a system of inclusive finance that can substantially reduce financial exclusion.
- By giving the State influence over the process of financial intermediation, it allows the government to use the banking industry as a lever to advance the development effort. In particular, it allows for the mobilization of technical and scientific talent to deliver both credit and technical support to agriculture and the small-scale industrial sector.

This multifaceted role for State-controlled banking allows credit to lead economic activity in chosen sectors, regions and segments of the population. It amounts to building a financial structure in anticipation of real sector activities, particularly in underdeveloped and under-banked regions of a country.

## Financial innovation for development

### Policy banking

Financial inclusion requires not just social control over commercial banks, but the creation of special institutions such as "policy-oriented" development banks, cooperative credit organizations and specialized rural financial agencies. It may also require prescribing specific quantitative targets for managers of these institutions.

Fundamentally, policy banking is required because, as noted above, private lenders are only concerned with the returns they receive. On the other hand, the total return to a project includes the additional surplus (or profit) accruing to the entrepreneur, and the non-pecuniary social returns accruing to society. The projects that offer the best return to the lender may not be those with the highest total expected return. As a result, good projects get rationed out, necessitating measures such as development banking or directed credit (Stiglitz, 1994).

In practice, financial intermediaries seek to match the demand for credit by adjusting not just interest rates, but also the terms on which credit is provided. Lending gets linked to collateral, and the nature and quality of that collateral is adjusted according to the nature of the borrower as well as supply and demand conditions in the credit market. Depending on the quantum and cost of funds available to the financial intermediaries, the market tends to ration out borrowers to differing extent. In such circumstances, borrowers rationed out because they are considered risky may not be the ones that are the least important from a social point of view.

Policy banks are expected to focus on specific sectors such as the small-scale industrial sector, providing them with long-term finance and working capital at subsidized interest rates with longer grace periods, as well as offering training and technical assistance in areas like marketing. Similarly, agricultural development banks, most of which are State-backed and funded, advance credit at subsidized rates to the agricultural sector, in particular to small and marginal farmers without the means to undertake much-needed investments. Given their low credit rating, these farmers are excluded from the normal lending of commercial banks and are forced to rely on "informal" sources, such as professional moneylenders, landlords and traders, at interest rates far exceeding those charged by commercial banks.

These institutions must not be seen as a drain on the exchequer, except when they do not function according to accepted norms. Directed credit has positive fiscal consequences. In contrast to subsidies, such credit reduces the demand on the government's own revenues. This makes directed credit an advantageous option in developing countries faced with chronic budgetary difficulties that limit their ability to use budgetary subsidies to achieve a certain allocation of investible resources.

To deal with these problems, countries must incorporate the following in their national development strategies:

(i)   Create and/or strengthen policy banks to provide credit to specified clients (often in targeted quantities) at interest rates which they can reasonably pay given their expected returns;

(ii)    Make it incumbent on policy banks to intervene in the functioning of the entities to which they lend, with nominee directors on the board, backed by technical and managerial expertise in the development bank's offices;

(iii)   Allow for the possibility that policy banks can encourage commercial banks, normally concerned with short-term lending for working capital purposes, to undertake long-term lending as well. They can do this by offering guarantees as well as refinance facilities at reasonable rates against long-term loans provided by commercial banks for specific purposes. By reducing default and liquidity risks for the commercial banks, such facilities enable them to play a role in the market for long-term funds;

(iv)    Provide policy banks with forms of financial support—such as long-term funds from the central banks (financed out of their "profits"), long-term loans or equity contributions from the government, loans from multilateral and bilateral agencies guaranteed by the government, and concessions such as the grant of tax-free status—to ensure the viability of these institutions and the efficacy of their operations. This is necessary because, given the role that development banks are expected to play, it is difficult for them to compete with commercial banks and other financial intermediaries to mobilize funds from the market. The cost and short-term maturities of such liabilities make it difficult to realize the objectives for which these institutions are established in the first instance;

(v)     Ensure that development banks leverage their lending to monitor their clients and direct them to adopt technologies, marketing and managerial practices that would render them viable.

## Cooperatives

Another channel to deliver credit as part of a system of inclusive finance is cooperative banks incorporating of members from the target community, set up with State aid and supported by State subsidy. Cooperatives have a long history and have been extremely successful in many contexts. They have also played an important role in developed country contexts, as illustrated by the credit union movement in the United States (box 8).

### Box 8.   Credit unions in the United States

Credit unions played an important role in development in the United States. Credit unions are member-owned organizations that offer higher interest rates on savings and charge lower interest rates on loans compared with commercial banks. The credit unions return any profit to their members at the end of each year, and they operate as non-profits, paying no taxes on earnings that are retained or paid out to members. This tax-exempt status helped the expansion and growth of credit unions, despite the competition from commercial banks.

Cooperative banks were promoted based partly on the view that the systems and procedures of traditional banks were determined by the needs of urban industrial and business financing, making them inadequate agencies for covering the last mile in rural areas. Their methods are not always appropriate for banking with the poor, which involves intensive relationship banking that permits the use of social collateral. Dependent largely on documentation-based appraisal, they are inadequate in environments where lending needs to be based more on trust and production-related appraisals. This makes cooperative banks, constituted with target group members, much better vehicles for delivering credit to small and marginal farmers, and those who have little or no productive assets. A cooperative bank component to a system of inclusive finance is, therefore, imperative.

However, while formally cooperatives are democratic institutions with participatory management and peer-group monitoring, in practice local class hierarchies and patronage structures result in their managements being dominated by powerful rural interest groups. Since their constitution and structure makes them less accountable to oversight agencies in the formal banking sector, there can be significant failures of governance. This substantially influences their lending decisions, leading even to diversion of credit away from the region. In India, for example, cooperative banks are known to have financed dubious investments in metropolitan stock markets leading to substantial losses.

Moreover, since these institutions are convenient vehicles for governments to channel their development budgets and subsidies, they become the conduit for leakages of expenditures targeted at disadvantaged groups. They also serve as conduits to distribute political patronage, often resulting in politicians dominating the boards of cooperative banks.

Such problems do not warrant dispensing with cooperatives and the role they can play. Governments must enact laws aimed at ensuring the participatory nature of managements of cooperative banks and preventing conflicts of interest from marring the managements and their practices. They should also create special regulatory institutions to monitor these institutions to ensure proper use of funds and the sustainability of their finances.

### Microfinance institutions (MFIs)

Conventional development banks and cooperatives may not be adequate as a source of finance for the poorest. Hence, an often advocated strategy for ensuring inclusion is the promotion of microcredit through microfinance institutions. Microfinance has been defined as the provision of diverse financial services (credit, savings, insurance, remittances, money transfers, leasing) to poor and low-income people. The case for microfinance is based on the understanding that:

- Even if a policy of inclusive banking is adopted, the likelihood that the really poor will be touched by the formal banking system, including cooperatives, is low;

- Thus, the poorest will be deprived of credit or be dependent on informal sources at interest rates that limit their resort to credit in emergencies;
- Access to individual and household level microcredit may be crucial to ensuring earning opportunities for the majority, since wage employment in agriculture and small businesses cannot meet the scale of demand for livelihood opportunities, especially in the rural areas; and
- They permit the creation of self-help groups, often constituted by women, and can be a potent means for social mobilization and women's empowerment.

Thus, microfinance should be promoted as a complement to formal finance and a substitute for informal sources of credit in urban and rural areas. However, it is necessary to address problems confronted by the microfinance movement across the developing world.

There has been an explosion of microcredit programmes since the 1990s, implemented under various institutional arrangements, run by NGOs as well as, increasingly, government organizations, often supported by bilateral and multilateral donor assistance and advice (box 9). Many of these experiments have been successful in displacing exploitative, informal private sector creditors, meeting demands for credit to finance consumption and emergency expenditures and, in some cases, even small investments.

There is much praise of the pro-poor consequences of many of these programmes. These are targeted at specific sectors with a preponderance of the poor, provide credit without collateral on the basis of peer group guarantees, and, on occasion, combine credit with other technical services. In Bangladesh, for example, microcredit has been seen as the favoured alternative means of credit delivery to the poor. That country was a leader in attempting to use microcredit as a solution to the credit access problem for the poor created by financial liberalization, with the Grameen Bank becoming a model for similar experiments elsewhere in the developing world. The average annual disbursement of loans from these programmes is estimated to be over Taka 5000

---

**Box 9.   The spread of microfinance**

At the end of 2004, there were 3,044 MFIs in developing countries making microloans to over 92 million clients. Of these, 66.5 million were classified as among the "poorest" people, 55.6 million of them women. Though concentrated in Asia, which accounts for 88 per cent of all reported loan clients in developing countries, significant numbers of MFIs operate elsewhere: 994 in Africa, 388 in Latin America and the Caribbean and 34 in the Middle East. While MFIs may lend very small amounts, they can be very large organizations. Eight individual institutions and three networks each served one million or more clients. Adding the 41 individual institutions that served between 100,000 and a million clients would account for almost 84 per cent of all poor clients served. The rest were serviced by the remaining 3,000 MFIs, the overwhelming majority serving fewer than 2,500 clients each.

Extracted from: United Nations, 2006.

crores (US$ 0.9 billion), far exceeding the total rural operations of the nationalized banks and specialized banking institutions taken together. Impressed by the growth of the movement, the Government has even attempted to centralize flows of micro-credit through a public sector organization created for the purpose, the Palli Karma Sahayak Foundation (PKSF) (Osmani, et al., 2003).

With hindsight, it is clear that, despite successes, there are a number of problems that plague microfinance in developing countries. Besides differences in the actual extent of coverage of the rural poor and contribution to poverty alleviation, some common problems are:

- Excessively high rates of interest, making successful lending for productive investment near impossible;
- Inability to reach, in a financially viable way, the really poor;[3]
- Donor dependence; and
- Financial non-sustainability.

Part of the reason for the high interest rates is the extremely high transaction costs associated with microfinance ventures. As is widely recognized (United Nations, 2006), the cost of disbursing, managing and collecting instalment payments on many tiny loans, often at frequent intervals, is significantly more costly than for fewer loans of larger amounts. In addition, reaching poor clients requires more staff time and personal interaction, implying additional costs. Staff time is increased because of illiteracy, the need to explain borrower and lender responsibilities and obligations, and the travel distances over poor infrastructure. Further, banking for the poor is a high-risk activity, given the vulnerability and high failure rates of units/activities set up by such borrowers.

Promotion of microfinance, despite these higher transaction costs, is warranted because MFIs can provide the close supervision and support to borrowers that mainstream financial institutions cannot afford. They serve as microdevelopment banks, offering extension services to the poor, and as an effective instrument to bring the illiterate rural poor into the cash economy and to impart some managerial and financial discipline to them. It is the lack of such discipline which perpetuates the view that lending to the poor is a mere "handout", based on instances of failure or lack of sustainability of traditional State- or donor-financed rural credit schemes operated through banks.

However, it would be utopian to believe that this role of MFIs can be extended to a level where they provide credit for all viable projects on a self-financing basis.

---

3  In addition, as United Nations, 2006, notes: "As crucial as the microcredit revolution has been, it has not provided the full range of credit products needed by poor people. The one-size-fits-all working capital loan entails inflexible terms, rigid loan cycles and amounts that are only suitable for microbusinesses with high turnover or those that produce regular weekly or monthly cash flows. The inflexibility of the product limits its usefulness to people who operate businesses with irregular cash flows, or require higher (or lower) amounts to support their businesses. Customers may use the inappropriate credit product, may not qualify for it, or may simply decide not to borrow".

The higher transaction costs have to be covered by some combination of higher-than-market interest rates and interest subsidies. The larger the subsidy and lower the interest, the higher the possibility that microcredit can be used for financing projects involving fixed investment. But, since microcredit is also used for non-productive purposes, the presence or extent of the subsidy should be calibrated according to the purpose for which credit is sought. Peer group monitoring can help with such calibration. This will also serve to discourage excess borrowing for non-productive uses. To exploit these potential features of microfinance for social benefit, the State and the donor community should consider supporting it with subsidies. If no subsidies and transfers from the State or other donors are available to render microfinancial services a feasible source of capital for productive investment, successfully scaling up of donor-driven experiments will prove difficult.

Microfinance has to be viewed as a form of small-scale development banking—requiring heavy effective subsidies even while charging relatively high interest rates—rather than as having any connection with commercial banking. Backed by some donors, commercial banking institutions, seeing MFIs as a potential source of competition, have sought to dilute this role of microfinance as a complementary, separate channel of provision of finance with its own requirements. They have promoted the view that MFIs should, over a period of time, graduate into more diversified non-bank financial companies or serve as delivery mechanisms for the formal financial system in a new form of "agency banking". Thus, commercial financial providers have begun to offer certain services to this market and some banks have opened full-service microfinance operations. Not surprisingly, many NGO MFIs, lacking adequate resources, often resort to bank loans, and many have borrowed to an extent that threatens their viability. To repeat, microfinance and microcredit institutions must be seen as complementary to, but separate from, formal financial institutions and not embryonic forms of formal financial institutions.

But MFIs can learn from formal institutions and adopt certain kinds of professional practices. For example, many MFIs are not sufficiently equipped to undertake proper risk assessment, and need to be trained to do so. Often, reporting systems are also not adequate, which is a problem because of the lack of accountability of many microfinance groups. State support for improving management and accounting practices must therefore be provided.

The problems afflicting microfinance institutions notwithstanding, the evidence does suggest that the poor can be served successfully with appropriate organizational and managerial innovations, despite the higher cost of small-scale transactions. There is also evidence that the use of information and communications technology can bring down the costs of many of the transactions and the cost differential involved in serving poor customers (United Nations, 2006). Moreover, while many microfinance providers are, or have been, subsidized in one form or another, there are a number which operate independent of subsidy and are self-sustaining.

Nevertheless, while efforts to improve the system of microcredit as a second channel must continue, there is no alternative to strengthening the formal credit system to deal with the challenges faced in predominantly rural developing economies with a high incidence of poverty. The aim of financial intervention is not to prevent the creation of a modern financial sector. Rather, its primary aim is to expand the reach of the formal financial sector, so as to enable the State to use the financial structure as an instrument of development. It is for this reason that development practitioners increasingly call for a paradigm shift involving a change from an emphasis on microfinance to one on inclusive finance (United Nations, 2006).

Table 3 summarizes some of the main financial policy options that can be used to realize a process of more broad-based and equitable growth.

## Learning from historical experience

Policies to ensure the flow of financial savings to key sectors from a development point of view did not originate in developing countries. Financial structures in late-industrializing countries like Germany and Japan emerged or were fashioned to deal with the difficulties associated with late industrialization. Capital requirements for entry in most areas were high, because technology for factory production had evolved in a capital-intensive direction from its primitive industrial revolution level. Competition from established international producers meant that firms had to be supported with protection and finance to survive long periods of low capacity utilization during which they could seek a foothold in domestic and world markets and become competitive producers. Not surprisingly, late industrializers created strongly regulated and even predominantly State-controlled financial markets aimed at mobilizing savings and using the intermediary function to influence the size and structure of investment. Despite their differences, the *hausbank* system in Germany, the lead bank system in Japan and the financial system in the Republic of Korea epitomized this feature. Their financial systems were characterized by directed credit policies and differential interest rates, and the provision of investment support for the nascent industrial class in the form of equity, credit and low interest rates.

Based on the roles played by Crédit Mobilier in France and the "universal banks" in Germany, Gerschenkron (1962) argued that the creation of "financial organisations designed to build thousands of miles of railroads, drill mines, erect factories, pierce canals, construct ports and modernise cities" was hugely transformative. Financial firms based on the old wealth were typically rentier in nature and limited themselves to floatations of government loans and foreign exchange transactions. The new financial firms were "devoted to railroadisation and industrialisation of the country" and, in the process, influenced the behaviour of old wealth as well.

The function played by these institutions is noteworthy. The banks, according to Gerschenkron, substituted for the absence of a number of elements crucial to industrialization: "In Germany, the various incompetencies of the individual entrepreneurs were offset by the device of splitting the entrepreneurial function: the German investment banks—a powerful invention, comparable in economic effect to that of the steam engine—were in their capital-supplying functions a substitute for the insufficiency of the previously created wealth willingly placed at the disposal of entrepreneurs. But they were also a substitute for entrepreneurial deficiencies. From

Table 3. Some salient financial policy options to promote equality

| Policy | Objective | Dangers | Requirements |
|---|---|---|---|
| Set bank branching targets, especially for underserved areas | Provide wide access to banking facilities as part of a strategy of inclusive finance | | a. Possibility of cross-subsidization<br>b. Provision of State financial support |
| Guidelines to prevent excessive credit migration from less to more developed areas in the country | Ensure credit created based on deposits from backward or rural areas is not all diverted to developed or urban regions | Allocation to unviable projects for lack of demand from creditworthy borrower | a. Possibility of cross-subsidization<br>b. Provision of State financial support |
| "Credit authorization scheme" to monitor grant of credit limits above a particular level to any single party | Prevent concentration of credit in few borrowers | | Identify an appropriate regulatory agency |
| Limits on credit to interlinked firms controlled by a single authority | Prevent concentration of credit in few borrowers | | |
| Pre-emption of bank credit for selected sectors like agriculture and small-scale industry:<br>a. Specify that certain proportion of lending be directed at these sectors<br>b. Provide credit at interest rates lower than market interest rates | a. Ensure access to hitherto neglected sectors<br>b. Keep cost of credit at levels where demand is forthcoming, given potential returns in these sectors | Adverse effects on bank profitability | a. Adoption of alternative performance criteria<br>b. Possibility of cross-subsidization<br>c. Provision of State financial support |
| Provide representation for all stakeholders in bank boards | a. Ensure access to hitherto neglected sectors<br>b. Ensure transparency and participative governance | | |

**Table 3. Some salient financial policy options to promote equality** (*continued*)

| Policy | Objective | Dangers | Requirements |
|---|---|---|---|
| Financial institutions to play supply-leading role:<br>a. Identifying potential enterpreneurs with bankable projects<br>b. Helping them through phases of project preparation and credit appraisal<br>c. Ensuring successful and timely implementation, and<br>d. Use leverage from credit provision, to monitor functioning | Deal with some of the demand-side problems resulting in poor credit off-take | Credit allocation based on corruption and favouritism | Implementation of transparent procedures and participatory governance mechanisms |
| Provide for or strengthen public ownership of banks/development banks | a. Overcome obstacles to "social banking"<br>b. Increase compatibility of objectives of regulators and bankers so as to strengthen regulation | Credit allocation based on corruption and favouritism | Implementation of transparent procedures and participatory governance mechanisms |
| Create separate "policy banks" as opposed to general purpose development banks | a. Ensure clarity of objectives<br>b. Prevent misuse of policy banking requirement to justify poor performance<br>c. Monitor and ensure proper utilization of government support or subsidies | | |

| | | | |
|---|---|---|---|
| Encourage creation of and rejuvenate pre-existing cooperative banks | a. Ensure mobilization of local savings<br>b. Ensure participation in the allocation of credit<br>c. Develop a channel suitable for directing credit and financial support to smaller borrowers | Cooperatives can become instruments for local vested interests and vehicles for political patronage | Bring cooperative banks within the ambit of a special regulatory framework which monitors management and performance |
| Launch and/or encourage the microfinance movement | a. Reach the really poor<br>b. Ensure social mobilization<br>c. Develop a channel to reach extension services needed for microenterprises | a. High transaction costs and interest rates that limit lending for productive purposes<br>b. Financial non-sustainability<br>c. Donor dependence<br>d. Poor governance | a. Treat microfinance as a case of small-scale development banking<br>b. Provide subsidies to support lower interest rates in lending for productive purposes<br>c. Use information technology to reduce transaction costs<br>d. Bring MFIs within ambit of the same special regulatory framework which monitors management and performance in cooperative banks |

their central vantage points of control, the banks participated actively in shaping the major—and sometimes even not so major—decisions of the individual enterprises. It was they who often mapped out a firm's paths of growth, conceived far-sighted plans, decided on major technological and locational innovations, and arranged for mergers and capital increases" (Gerschenkron, 1968).

From a development point of view, this experience implies that financial institutions must not only serve to direct credit at pre-specified interest rates, but must adopt a pro-active role in the decision-making of the entities they finance. To do so, they need to mobilize the best talent—technological expertise, managerial competence and marketing skill—to facilitate the conversion of savings channelled to farms, firms and individuals into investment in productive and socially high-yielding assets.

When serving this role, financial intermediaries move up the scale from being a mere pool of savings, as they are conventionally seen, to being a pool of knowledge and expertise, allowing them to overcome the coordination failures that afflict atomistic decision makers in market-based systems.

## Autonomy and regulation

### Pre-empting financial fragility

Besides pursuing the objectives of growth and equity, financial policies should be geared to ensuring the stability and sustainability of the financial system. Failures in financial markets affect not only the institution concerned, but other sectors of the economy. In some instances, this could have systemic effects. Thus, when speculative bubbles lead to financial crises, they squeeze liquidity and result in distress sales of assets and deflation with adverse impact on employment and living standards. To prevent such effects, governments often resort to costly bailouts, which also have implications for growth and equity.

Failure can never be abolished, but regulation can help to reduce the recurrence of crisis. The best model of regulation remains the framework adopted in the United States in response to the wave of bank failures during 1920-1932. Its anchor was the Banking Act of 1933 (the Glass-Steagall Act), which imposed a strong regulatory framework that developed to have five dimensions:

- First, it created the Federal Deposit Insurance Corporation (FDIC) for federal insurance of deposits. From the point of view of the small depositor, all banks became identical and completely secure, regardless of their balance sheets.
- Second, it set limitations on interest payments on deposits. Interest was prohibited for demand deposits and ceilings introduced for time and savings deposits. With these controls, the principal financial intermediaries could not attract depositors with higher interest rates, so that there was no direct imperative to invest in assets offering high returns that are also risky and prone to default.

- Third, together with the McFadden-Pepper Act of 1927, Glass-Steagall provided for entry barriers that limited "excessive" competition resulting from the previous regime of free banking. It reinforced the individual states' authority to restrict inter-state banking and limit bank holding companies and other instruments of concentration.
- Fourth, it restricted the operations of banks. There were restrictions on investments that banks could make, principally limiting them to loan provision and to purchases of government securities. There were prohibitions on the activities of banks or their affiliates, with a ban on underwriting securities and serving as an insurance underwriter or agency, and commercial activities. The restrictions also included a 10 per cent limit on outstanding exposure to a single borrower and limits on lending to sensitive sectors like real estate.[4] This was clearly aimed at ensuring that the moral hazard associated with deposit insurance did not lead to risky investments and at pre-empting the practice of financing losses elsewhere in the financial sector with bank equity.
- Finally, a system of regulating solvency was put in place, involving periodic examination of bank financial records and informal guidelines relating to the ratio of shareholder capital to total assets.

This model served the United States extremely well for over three decades. Macroeconomic developments in the 1970s and after launched a period of accelerated "financial innovation", requiring its revision, but it remains substantially relevant for developing countries. Governments must seek to remain as close to this model as possible.

Insofar as circumstances warrant a deviation, there must be special provisions to deal with the risks involved. These should include:

- Restrictions on banks lending to firms or investing in securities in which the owners/directors of the bank have an interest;
- Restrictions on the volume of lending to and proportionate exposure to sensitive sectors like the stock and real estate market; and
- Monitoring and reduction of high spreads between deposit rates and lending/investment returns, which provide evidence of limited competition or excessively risky investments.

Such provisions can moderate the tendency to undertake unnecessary risks in search of high returns. Typical examples are lending for investments in stocks or real estate. Loans to these sectors can be at extremely high interest rates because the returns in these sectors are extremely volatile and can touch extremely high levels. Since banks accept real estate or securities as collateral, borrowing to finance speculative investments in stock or real estate can spiral. This type of activity thrives because

---

4 Real estate loans secured by first liens could not exceed total savings deposits of a bank or, if greater, its unimpaired paid-up capital and surplus.

of the belief that losses if any can be transferred to the lender through default, and lenders are confident of government support in case of crisis. This could feed a speculative spiral that can in time lead to a collapse of the bubble and bank failures.

These kinds of tendencies need to be curbed also because they affect real investment. As the maximum returns to productive investment in agriculture and manufacturing are limited, there is a limit to what borrowers would be willing to pay to finance such investment. Thus, despite the fact that social returns to agricultural and manufacturing investment are higher than for stocks and real estate, and despite the contribution such investment can make to growth and poverty alleviation, credit at the required rate may not be available.

### Financial sector supervision and regulation

In addition to such measures, governments must implement strict regulations with regard to accounting standards, disclosure norms and governance structures. They should also put in place institutions responsible for prudential regulation of markets, involving a mix of monitoring of individual transactions, ensuring adoption of appropriate risk-management systems, routine scrutiny of company accounts, enforcement of guidelines to prevent conflict of interest and assessment of company adherence to capital adequacy norms. It must be noted that these forms of regulation do not fully insure against fragility. Advocates of freer and more open financial markets claim that capital adequacy norms and prudential regulation can deal with these problems. However, instances of increased and periodic financial failure suggest otherwise, as does the growing evidence of conflicts of interest, accounting fraud and market manipulation even in the well-developed and ostensibly transparent and well-regulated United States market.

Market-based financial systems are fragile and prone to failure, and regulation cannot fully redress this. Systems of social regulation and control have the advantage that regulation is built into the very structure that serves to promote development. But even then, since government-appointed agents are responsible for supervision, monitoring and scrutiny, the perennial question as to who will monitor the monitor remains. Particular agents may misuse their position, indulge in favouritism and/ or corruption, and government regulation may fail. The ways of dealing with this problem is not merely to return to the market with all its deficiencies, but to evolve institutional mechanisms to monitor agents in the public sector. Central elements of such mechanisms must be participatory governance and accountability to democratically constituted bodies.

## On liberalizing financial systems

The policy conclusions emerging from the above discussion are not just relevant from the point of view of pro-actively framing financial policies, but should also serve to correct or stall policies that militate against the objectives of growth, equity and financial stability.

In recent years, however, processes of financial liberalization in developing countries have challenged many of the features of financial systems that are favourable from a developmental point of view. These processes are justified on the grounds that the interventionist financial policies adopted by developing countries to accelerate growth, improve distribution and avoid fragility have resulted in "financial repression", involving low and even negative interest rates and distortions that divert financial flows away from the best, high-return projects (McKinnon, 1973; Shaw, 1973).

There are a number of ways in which interventionist policies are seen to have adversely affected growth (Fry, 1997). To start with, low interest rates resulting from regulation are seen to affect adversely the level of savings, and therefore investment, by encouraging current consumption. Second, low interest rates offered by financial intermediaries are seen as encouraging direct investments by savers rather than through intermediaries. Given the scale economies associated with the pooling of resources and the greater ability of financial intermediaries to identify the best projects and monitor the functioning of borrowers, this process is seen to reduce the efficiency of investment allocation. Third, since interest rates are low, the number of projects looking for funding tends to be large, resulting in the possibility that some or many low-quality projects are funded at the expense of better projects. To boot, on average, projects tend to be more capital intensive because of the lower costs of capital, with adverse employment effects. That is, low interest rates could result in inferior investment choices. Finally, since returns to lenders are low and often fixed, their lending practices are not driven by potential yields of projects financed, but influenced by extraneous factors such as political pressures, loan size or private benefits to bankers.

The adverse effects of these factors on growth, it is argued, are made worse as "repressive" financial policies limit the extent of financial deepening and intermediation. This is seen as inimical to development, based on the view that there is a strong positive relationship between financial deepening/intermediation and growth (Levine, 1997).

A logical corollary of the financial repression argument is that interest rates should be freed, financial markets and institutions liberalized and markets allowed to determine the allocation of credit. As has been pointed out by a number of economists (Stiglitz and Weiss, 1981; Arestis, 2005), the conceptual bases of these arguments are questionable. In particular, they are based on the assumption that liberalization delivers "competitive" financial markets, in which financial institutions compete to attract savings and identify the best borrowers. However, competitive markets do not always deliver the desired results. This is because what matters is not the number of firms that accept deposits but their willingness to offer credit, and this may be limited for other reasons even when there are a large number of banks in a country (box 10).

In practice, liberalization delivers unanticipated results. As early as 1985, Díaz-Alejandro, 1986, detailed why efforts in Latin America in the 1970s to follow the recommendations of the financial repression literature and "free domestic capital markets from usury laws and other alleged government-induced distortions" had "yielded by 1983 domestic financial sectors characterized by widespread bankrupt-cies, massive government interventions or nationalization of private institutions (to save financial firms and pre-empt adverse effects), and low domestic savings".

Rather than encouraging greater competition, there was a strengthening of oli-gopolistic power through the mergers of financial intermediaries or association of fi-nancial intermediaries and non-financial corporations. Financial intermediaries that were a part of these conglomerates allocated credit in favour of companies belonging to the group, which was by no means a more efficient allocation than could have oc-curred under directed-credit policies of the government.[5]

Further, financial liberalization did not result in intermediation of financial as-sets with long-term maturities, with deposits and loans of less than six months' dura-tion dominating. The Southern Cone experience of the late 1970s and early 1980s suggests that deregulation did not lead to stable interest rates, that interest rates on the whole could remain very high and way above "reasonable estimates of the socially optimal shadow real interest rate".

Finally, despite short booms in stock markets, there was little mobilization of new capital or capital for new ventures. In fact, small investors tended to withdraw from markets because of allegations of manipulation and fraud, and erstwhile areas of long-term investments supported by State intervention tended to disappear. While financial liberalization did encourage new kinds of financial savings, total domestic savings did not increase in many cases, and expansion of available financial savings was the result of inflow of foreign capital.

Despite the repetition of this experience across the developing world since the early 1970s, many developing countries have opted for similar policies, either ne-cessitated by conditionalities imposed by donors when countries turn to them for emergency balance-of-payments finance, or voluntarily in the hope of attracting large capital flows into their economies. That is, there is a strong correspondence between unavoidable or voluntary dependence on capital flows and processes of financial lib-eralization.

These processes militate against the adoption of financial policies appropriate for development and even dismantle financial structures that are suitable from a de-velopment point of view, as discussed above. There are three broad effects from the process of financial liberalization:

- It opens the country to new forms and larger volumes of international financial flows, in order to attract part of the substantially increased flows of financial capital to the so-called "emerging markets" since the late-1970s;
- To facilitate these inflows, it liberalizes, to differing degrees, the terms gov-erning outflows of foreign exchange in the form of current account invest-ment income payments and capital account transfers for permitted transac-tions; and

---

5  In India, nationalization of the bigger private commercial banks in 1969 was partly moti-vated by the need to prevent the diversion of household savings to companies linked to the banks or their directors.

> **Box 10. Financial strategies can lead to credit rationing**
>
> In India, following financial sector reforms, the credit-deposit ratio of commercial banks declined substantially from 65.2 per cent in 1990-1991 to 49.9 per cent in 2003-2004, despite a substantial increase in the credit-creating capacity of banks through periodic reductions in reserve ratios. This may have been the result of a decline in demand for credit from credit-worthy borrowers. However, one fact appears to question this argument: the decrease in the credit-deposit ratio has been accompanied by a corresponding increase in the proportion of risk-free government securities in the banks' major earning assets, i.e., loans and advances, and investments. The investment in government securities as a percentage of total earning assets for the commercial banking system as a whole was 26.1 per cent in 1990-1991. But it increased to 32.4 per cent in 2003-2004. This points to the fact that lending to the commercial sector may have been displaced by investments in government securities offering relatively high, near risk-free returns (Chandrasekhar and Ray, 2005).

- To attract these flows, it transforms the structure of the domestic financial sector and the nature and operations of domestic financial firms such that it makes the financial system resemble that adopted over the last three decades at much higher levels of development in countries like the United States and the United Kingdom.

It is now widely accepted that the first two of these, involving liberalization of controls on inflows and outflows of capital respectively, have resulted in an increase in financial fragility in developing countries, making them prone to periodic financial and currency crises. Analyses of individual instances of crises have tended to conclude that the nature and timing of these crises had much to do with the shift to a more liberal and open financial regime. What is more, crises rarely lead to controls on capital inflows and reduced dependence on them. Rather, adjustment strategies emphasize further financial liberalization, resulting in a history of periodic financial failure.

But what requires special attention are the structural effects (elaborated in box 11) of liberalization on the ability of countries to use the financial system as an instrument in a national development strategy. As might be expected from the above discussion, the empirical experience with financial liberalization is that it results in:

- Declining credit-deposit ratios or reduced credit provision;
- "Diversion" of credit to sensitive sectors, such as the stock market and real estate, as well as to consumer finance;
- Greater emphasis on "investments" in instruments such as government securities or certificates of deposit issued by corporations;
- A preference for commissions and fee-based incomes rather than returns from interest rate spreads;
- An unwillingness of banks to perform their role as the principal risk bearers in the system, with a market preference to use innovative instruments to transfer credit risk to institutions and investors less equipped to assess such risks; and

## Box 11.    The structural consequences of financial liberalization

There are a number of aspects and consequences of financial liberalization as implemented in practice. To start with, it involves reducing or removing controls on interest rates or rates of return charged or earned by financial agents. This encourages competition between similarly placed financial firms to attract depositors, on the one hand, and entice potential borrowers, on the other. Competition not only takes non-price forms, but leads to price competition that squeezes spreads and forces firms to depend on volume to profit. This often leads to diversification of activity away from socially relevant but privately less profitable areas.

The second feature of financial liberalization is that it removes or dilutes controls on the entry of new financial firms, subject to their meeting pre-specified norms with regard to capital investments. This aspect of liberalization inevitably applies to both domestic and foreign financial firms, and caps on equity that can be held by foreign investors in domestic financial firms are gradually raised or done away with. Easier conditions of entry do not automatically increase competition in the conventional sense, since liberalization also involves freedom for domestic and foreign players to acquire financial firms and extends to permissions provided to foreign institutional investors, pension funds and hedge funds to invest in equity and debt markets. This often triggers a process of consolidation that creates or restores a nexus between large oligopolistic players and financial intermediaries with attendant implications.

Thirdly, liberalization involves a reduction in controls over investments that can be undertaken by financial agents. Financial agents can be permitted to invest in areas they were not permitted to enter previously. Most regulated financial systems seek to keep separate the different segments of the financial sector such as banking, merchant banking, mutual funds and insurance. Agents in one segment were not permitted to invest in another for fear that conflicts of interest could affect business practices adversely. Financial liberalization breaks down the regulatory walls separating these sectors, leading, in the final analysis, to the emergence of so-called "universal banks", or financial supermarkets. The consequent ability of financial agents to straddle multiple financial activities implies that the linkages between different financial markets tend to increase, with developments in any one market affecting others to a far greater degree than previously. Besides increasing the probability of failure, this influences lending and investment practices in ways unsuited to broad-based national development.

Fourth, liberalization involves relaxation of the rules governing the kinds of financial instruments that can be issued and acquired. Financial instruments allow agents to share financial gains and risks to differing degrees, where the gains are incomes and asset price appreciation and the risks are default on interest payments and amortization, interest rate changes or depreciation of asset values. These assets can be issued directly by those looking for capital for productive investments, or by intermediaries expecting to obtain part of the incomes in return for bearing part of the risk. This aggravates the tendencies noted above.

Fifth, in many contexts, liberalization involves withdrawal of the State from financial intermediation, with the conversion of "development banks" into regular banks and privatization of the publicly owned banking system, on the grounds that their presence is not conducive to the dominance of market signals in the allocation of capital.

Sixth, financial liberalization eases conditions for the participation of both firms and investors in the stock market by diluting or removing listing conditions, by providing freedom in the pricing of new issues, by permitting greater freedom to intermediaries such as brokers, and by relaxing conditions on borrowing against shares and investing borrowed funds in the market.

Finally, rather than regulation through direct intervention, liberalization involves shifting to a regime of voluntary adherence to statutory guidelines with regard to capital adequacy, accounting norms and related practices, with the central bank's role being that of supervision and monitoring.

- A greater degree of financial exclusion, with a growing concentration of credit and investment in a few favoured sectors and its direction to larger clients.

A set of country studies in sub-Saharan Africa by Cornia and Lipumbia, 1999, for UNU/WIDER found that a decade or more of financial liberalization notwithstanding, the removal of financial repression had not increased the volume of credit available to the small-scale urban sector and to rural areas. This has occurred, despite the fact that the number of private banks had grown, and the share of credit allocated to the private sector had increased while that of the public sector had decreased. What is more, real lending rates had risen sharply while deposit rates had declined and spreads had soared markedly. As a result, savings and investment rates had not increased. The increase in the number of banks had not markedly reduced the concentration of bank deposits and assets. Most of the loans continued to be of short-term maturity, financing mainly trade. Long-term finance for agricultural and industrial development was not available. The majority of the population working in smallholder farms and small and medium-scale enterprises had no access to credit. And, with limited supervision from understaffed central banks and weak regulatory frameworks, the rapid creation of new financial institutions had been accompanied by greater instability and a rise in the number of bank failures. The results of the policies seem to be the same when applied to both small and large as well as less and more developed among developing countries.

Since market forces mediate the realization of these outcomes, financial liberalization policies, often adopted on the grounds that the financial proliferation resulting from such liberalization is an unqualified good, can result in an aggravation of the problem of financial exclusion (box 12).

As Mkandawire, 1999, notes, Ffrench-Davis' argument for Latin America has resonance in the African case when he argues that "what is needed is an institutional framework that encompasses a vigorous long-term segment of the financial market, in order to finance productive investment. In addition, low- and medium-income sectors, which typically suffer from the social segmentation of the capital market, need easier access to capital. They need this market to deal with contingencies, to invest in training and to promote the development and modernization of productive activities" (Ffrench-Davis, 1994).

**Box 12.   Financial liberalization and financial exclusion**

The experience of a small, land-locked least developed country like Nepal illustrates how financial liberalization can result in financial exclusion. After the liberalization of Nepal's financial system, the evidence (Deraniyagala, et al., 2003) points to an eight-fold increase in deposit mobilization by the banking sector during the 1990s (from Rs 22 billion in 1990 to Rs 181 billion in July 2001).[a] Deposit mobilization by finance companies also increased substantially. As a ratio to GDP, bank deposits increased from 19 per cent in 1985 to 43 per cent in 2001. Deposits with non-bank financial institutions also increased from 0.5 per cent of GDP in 1995 to 4.6 per cent in 2001. The consequent increase in financial intermediation is reflected in the fact that the ratio of financial assets to GDP rose from 29.3 per cent in 1985 to 32.5 per cent in 1990 and a huge 84.3 per cent in 2001. Financial deepening and increased financial intermediation obviously increased credit provided by the financial system substantially. Commercial banks' credit to the private sector rose from 8.7 per cent of GDP in 1985 to 29.4 per cent in 2001.

   This process was not accompanied by adequate provision of credit to the poverty-sensitive sectors. Of the credit provided by commercial banks in 2001, only 9 per cent went to the agricultural sector, although 80 per cent of the country's population was involved in cultivating some land and 50 per cent derived their incomes from agriculture, making it extremely important in terms of livelihoods and poverty reduction. On the other hand, credit to industry increased from 18.8 per cent in 1985 to 45 per cent in 2001. Part of this increase reflected a shift from the commercial sector, whose share fell from 44 to 33 per cent over the same years, but a shift away from agriculture was also responsible. Further, small borrowers must have suffered discrimination as 85 per cent of formal sector lending is based on collateral. The evidence indicates that despite financial consolidation, not more than a fifth of borrowing households in Nepal are covered by institutional finance.

   This trend is not surprising as liberalization has seen the rise to dominance of the private financial sector. The ratio of private sector credit to total credit rose from 68.5 per cent in 1985 to 76.2 per cent in 1990 and to an overwhelming 92.5 per cent in 2001.

---

   a   Some caution must be exercised when interpreting these figures. There is reason to believe
       that a substantial part of what was occurring was a transfer of savings and credit provision
       from the informal to the formal credit system.

Finally, greater freedom to invest, including in sensitive sectors such as real estate and stock markets, ability to increase exposure to particular sectors and individual clients, and increased regulatory forbearance, all lead to increased instances of financial failure. In addition, by institutionally linking different segments of financial markets by permitting the emergence of universal banks or financial supermarkets, the liberalization process increases the degree of entanglement of different agents within the financial system and increases the impact of financial failure of entities in any one segment of the financial system on agents elsewhere in the system.

   The implication for governments is clear. If the intention is to put in place financial policies that promote growth, privilege stability and ensure inclusion, an emphasis on financial liberalization as a panacea for problems in the functioning and impact of the financial sector should be abjured.

## Foreign savings and their implications

Financial liberalization is often driven by the desire of developing country governments to attract large volumes of foreign capital inflows, especially purely financial flows. It is often argued that access to foreign savings in the form of capital flows reduces the pressure on developing country governments to extract and allocate domestic savings, reducing the need for intervention that may go awry. Access to foreign finance—in the form of grants, debt and foreign portfolio and direct investment—relaxes the constraints domestically available real resources set on the potential rate of growth of the system. Foreign exchange, being a "fungible" asset, can be used to alter the structure of domestic supply through imports. Depending on how foreign exchange resources are deployed, they can overcome domestic supply constraints, such as a wage-goods, or a capital goods, constraint, by resorting to imports. On the financial side, these resources reduce the need to use measures such as taxation to restrain the consumption of particular commodities by particular groups, in order to mobilize surpluses needed to finance long-term development. Further, inasmuch as foreign "savings", in the form of foreign aid or foreign borrowing, are accessed directly by the State they can be allocated in line with the preferences of the State and in keeping with its strategy of development.

However, for most developing countries, the volume, pattern and direction of foreign capital flows cannot be chosen, but are exogenously given by the political choices of donor governments, the lending strategies of multilateral agencies, the preferences of private creditors and investors and the state of play in international financial markets. While some of the more developed among developing countries can attract flows of the kind they want some of the time, that flexibility is predicated on creating a facilitating environment for autonomous capital flows which often reduces policy space and involves a loss of control.

Foreign finance is not costless. While grants can be considered as pure transfers, their volume is small and their share has been declining over time. Other forms of capital flows have the following costs and implications:

- First, as with domestic debt, foreign debt carries a pre-specified profile of interest payment commitments. If the deployment of these resources does not result in a rate of nominal output growth greater than the nominal rate of interest, resources must be diverted from elsewhere to meet these costs, or further debt has to be contracted to meet payment commitments.
- Second, these commitments must be met in foreign exchange, necessitating the transformation of domestic resources into foreign exchange. To the extent that there are specific constraints on the possibilities of transformation through trade, reliance on foreign savings can increase external vulnerability.
- Third, access to foreign finance very often comes with conditionalities that limit the policy space of the government—that is, relying on foreign finance to finance a development strategy may reduce the strategic options available to a government, including options relating to financial policy. Official

flows are conditional upon the pursuit of specified monetary, fiscal or other policies. Private flows are implicitly conditional upon minimizing government intervention and the pursuit of market-friendly policies.

- Fourth, accessing foreign finance through the foreign direct investment route may involve a net foreign exchange outflow in the medium or long term, since cumulative flows in the form of repatriated dividends, royalty payments and technical fees tend to far exceed the actual inflow of foreign equity and reinvested profit share of foreign investors and the foreign exchange earned by net exports of the concerned firm.

- Fifth, reliance on debt and portfolio flows from private commercial banks and investors may require changing financial sector policies and embracing financial openness in a way that reduces the ability of the government to use the financial structure as an instrument in a national development strategy.

- Finally, reliance on private flows may increase dependence on capital inflows that are more volatile, resulting in an increase in external vulnerability and increasing the threat of a currency/financial crisis.

Given these factors, governments cannot assume that their access to foreign savings will remain at peak levels attained in the past or will grow at rates recorded in the past. A substantial degree of volatility must be provided for. This implies that excessive dependence on foreign savings to finance current expenditures or investments in sectors producing non-tradables should be abjured, so also should the soft option of making foreign savings a substitute for domestic savings.

## Capital flows and financial fragility

The fact that not all countries receive significant inflows of private capital, which tend to be concentrated in a few developing countries, is not necessarily a disadvantage. The East Asian crisis of 1997 and the large number of crises that have followed in countries such as the Russian Federation, Turkey, Brazil and Argentina have also focused attention on other dangers associated with an excessive reliance on fluid finance. Some of these dangers are:

- First, notwithstanding all talk of efficiency of financial markets, the structure of the financial system appears to be such that banks and financial institutions from developed countries are not merely prone to over-exposure in individual markets, but to exposure reflective of unsound financial practices. A combination of moral hazard generated by an implicit guarantee from the State that the financial system will be bailed-out in periods of crisis, the herd instinct characteristic of imperfect financial markets, and the competitive thrust for speculative gains on funds garnered from profit-hungry investors, all result in a situation where lending to, and financial investments in, particular countries continued well after evidence of high-risk exposure had exceeded warranted limits. The corollary is that supply-side factors are likely to result in high volatility in financial flows to developing countries, with a surge in such flows followed in all likelihood by a sudden collapse.

- Second, a sudden and whimsical turnaround in flows can set off currency speculation in the host country which can have extremely severe consequences for the exchange rate. Once the speculative fever begins, three factors appear to drive down the exchange rate. One, a collapse in investor confidence results in a panic withdrawal of funds invested in equity shares and bonds and also prevents the rollover of short-term debt by multinational banks. Two, a scramble for dollars on the part of domestic banks and corporations with imminent dollar commitments, the domestic currency costs of which are rising in the wake of depreciation. Three, an increase in speculative operations by domestic and international traders cashing in on currency volatility.

- Third, with completely unbridled capital flows, it may not be possible for a country to control the amount of capital inflow or outflow, and both movements can create undesirable consequences. For example, a country suddenly chosen as a preferred site for foreign financial investment can experience huge inflows which in turn causes the currency to appreciate, thus encouraging investment in non-tradables rather than tradables, and altering domestic relative prices and therefore incentives. Simultaneously, unless the inflows of capital are simply (and wastefully) stored up as accumulated foreign exchange reserves, they must necessarily be associated with current account deficits. In other words, once there is completely free capital flows and completely open access to external borrowing by private domestic agents, there can be no "prudent" macroeconomic policy; overall domestic balances or imbalances will change according to the behaviour of capital flows, which will themselves respond to the economic dynamics that they have set into motion.

- Fourth, when the surge in capital flows is reversed, a massive liquidity crunch and a wave of bankruptcies result in severe deflation, with attendant consequences for employment and the standard of living. Asset prices collapse, paving the way for international acquisitions of domestic firms at low prices denominated in currencies that have substantially depreciated. Such acquisitions are, however, encouraged, since they are often the only means to restructure and revive cash-strapped corporations. A crisis triggered by finance capital becomes the prelude to conquest by international capital in general, with substantial changes in the ownership structure of domestic assets without much green-field investment.

- Finally, the East Asian crisis brought home the fact that financial liberalization can generate crises in so-called "miracle economies" as well.

## Managing external debt and capital flows

Given these features, countries formulating a national development strategy need to:

(i)     Make a realistic assessment of potentially available foreign savings and their likely composition and direction;

(ii)    Assess the domestic and foreign exchange costs of relying on these inflows;

(iii)   Choose an appropriate volume and composition of such inflows;

(iv)    Design policies to restrict flows to that magnitude and structure; and

(v)     Ensure that foreign capital inflows are not a substitute for domestic savings, but an additional contribution to investment.

These choices establish the external frame in which an appropriate domestic financial policy is pursued.

Managing inflows requires capital controls, or measures that manage the volume, composition, or allocation of international private capital flows. They can target either inflows or outflows and can be market-based (incentive-based) or involve strict quantitative limits. Special reserve requirements for capital flowing in are an example of a market-based control. On the other hand, quantitative capital controls involve outright bans or quotas on certain investments such as the purchase of equity by foreign investors.

However, as Epstein, et al., 2003, argue, it can be difficult to draw a clear line between prudential domestic financial regulation and capital controls. For example, domestic financial regulations that limit the maturity range or specify reporting requirements for inflows may influence the composition of international capital flows to a country. Thus, prudential domestic financial regulations are another type of capital management technique.

Based on an examination of the diverse capital management techniques (table 4) employed by countries during the 1990s, Epstein, et al., 2003, argue that:

• Capital management techniques can enhance overall financial and currency stability, buttress the autonomy of macro and micro-economic policy, and bias investment towards the long term.

• The macroeconomic benefits of capital management techniques outweigh the often scant evidence of their microeconomic costs.

• Capital management techniques work best when they are coherent and consistent with a national development vision.

• There is no single type of capital management technique that works best for all developing countries.

**Table 4.     Types and objectives of capital management
              techniques employed during the 1990s**

| Country | Types of capital management techniques | Objectives of capital management techniques |
|---|---|---|
| Chile | **Inflows**<br>• FDI and PI: 1-year residence requirement<br>• 30 per cent URR<br>• Tax on foreign loans: 1.2 per cent per year<br>**Outflows**: No significant restrictions<br>**Domestic financial regulations**: strong regulatory measures | – Lengthen maturity structures and stabilize inflows<br>– Help manage exchange rates to maintain export competitiveness<br>– Protect economy from financial instability |
| Colombia | Similar to Chile | Similar to Chile |
| Taiwan POC | **Inflows**<br>(a) Non-residents<br>• Bank accounts only for domestic spending, not financial speculation<br>• Foreign participation in stock market regulated<br>• FDI tightly regulated<br>(b) Residents<br>• Regulation on foreign borrowing<br>**Outflows**<br>• Exchange controls<br>**Domestic financial regulations**<br>• Restrictions on lending for real estate and other speculative purposes | – Promote industrialization<br>– Help manage exchange for export competitiveness<br>– Maintain financial stability and insulate from foreign financial crises |
| Singapore | **"Non-internationalization" of Singapore $ inflows**<br>**Outflows**<br>*Non-residents*<br>• Financial institutions cannot extend S$ credit to non-residents if they are likely to use for speculation<br>• If they borrow for use abroad, must first swap into foreign currency<br>**Domestic financial regulations**<br>• Restrictions on creation of swaps, and other derivatives that can be used for speculation against Singapore $ | – To prevent speculation against Singapore $<br>– To support "soft peg" of S$<br>– To help maintain export competitiveness<br>– To help insulate Singapore from foreign financial crises |

**Table 4.    Types and objectives of capital management techniques employed during the 1990s** (*continued*)

| Country | Types of capital management techniques | Objectives of capital management techniques |
|---|---|---|
| Malaysia (1998) | **Inflows**<br>• Restrictions on foreign borrowing<br><br>**Outflows**<br>(*a*) Non-residents<br>• 12-month repatriation waiting period<br>• Graduated exit levy inversely proportional to length of stay<br>(*b*) Residents<br>• Exchange controls<br><br>**Domestic financial regulations**<br>(*a*) Non-residents<br>• Restrict access to ringgit<br>(*b*) Residents<br>• Encourage to borrow domestically and invest | – To maintain political and economic sovereignty<br>– Kill the offshore ringgit market<br>– Shut down offshore share market<br>– To help reflate the economy<br>– To help create financial stability and insulate the economy from contagion |
| India | **Inflows**<br>*Non-residents*<br>• Strict regulation of FDI and PI<br>**Outflows**<br>(*a*) Non-residents<br>• None<br>(*b*) Residents<br>• Exchange controls<br>**Domestic financial regulations**<br>• Strict limitations on development of domestic financial markets | – Support industrial policy<br>– Pursue capital account liberalization in an incremental and controlled fashion<br>– Insulate domestic economy from financial contagion<br>– Preserve domestic savings and foreign exchange reserves<br>– Help stabilize exchange rate |
| China | **Inflows**<br>*Non-residents*<br>• Strict regulation on sectoral FDI investment<br>• Regulation of equity investments: segmented stock market<br>**Outflows**<br>(*a*) Non-residents<br>• No restrictions on repatriation of funds | – Support industrial policy<br>– Pursue capital account liberalization in incremental and controlled fashion<br>– Insulate domestic economy from financial contagion<br>– Increase political sovereignty<br>– Preserve domestic savings and foreign exchange reserves<br>– Help keep exchange rates at competitive levels |

| Country | Types of capital management techniques | Objectives of capital management techniques |
|---|---|---|
| China | • Strict limitations on borrowing Chinese Renminbi for speculative purposes<br>(b) Residents<br>• Exchange controls<br>**Domestic financial regulations**<br>• Strict limitations on residents and non-residents | |

*Source*: Epstein, et al., 2003.

Even when it comes to attracting foreign direct investment, countries should, at the minimum, seek to ensure that foreign exchange investment in and export revenues from these units balance the foreign exchange out-go on account of royalties, technical fees, dividends and imports. This is a long-term safeguard against external vulnerability. A maximal objective of foreign direct investment management should be that the employment created as a result of the investment does not fall short of the employment displaced by the activities of the unit concerned.

## Conclusions

In sum, the premises on which governments should design financial policies as part of a national development strategy are that:

- Actually existing markets cannot and do not correspond to any ideal that delivers optimal outcomes that no one wants to change;
- Far more than markets for most other goods and services, financial markets are characterized by features that deliver outcomes that can adversely affect growth and aggravate inequities in the sectoral, regional, group and individual distribution of the benefits of growth;
- The structure and behaviour of financial systems that are not socially controlled and regulated is such that they do not advance the objectives of growth and financial inclusion; and
- Financial markets left to themselves are prone to failure leading to closure of financial firms, losses for consumers and clients, and systemic fragility with adverse macroeconomic implications.

Therefore, intervention is needed to ensure:

- Availability of credit to viable projects in crucial sectors at sustainable rates;
- Access to financial markets for all; and
- The soundness and stability of the financial system.

A range of policy options is available to meet each of these objectives. The specific mix of policies that governments choose will and should vary with the relative importance of specific objectives in their own national context, the degree of development and diversification of the financial system, and the area of control or degree of manoeuvrability of the government concerned. However, the aim should be to move over time to a best-practice combination of financial policies that advance the objectives of growth, equity and human development.

It must be noted that the use of any set of policy instruments implies a certain presence and role for the State. This raises the issue of government failure, resulting not just from errors of judgment, but also from pursuit of individual rather than social objectives by government agents, favouritism and corruption. Thus policies must be implemented in a framework that is transparent, requires full disclosure and is subject to monitoring by bodies that are democratically constituted.

## References

Amsden, Alice (1989). *Asia's Next Giant: South Korea and Late Industrialisation.* New York: Oxford University Press.

Arestis, Philip (2005). "Washington consensus and financial liberalisation", *Journal of Post-Keynesian Economics*, vol. 27, No. 2.

Chandrasekhar, C. P., and Sujit Kumar Ray (2005). "Financial sector reform and the transformation of banking: some implications for Indian development", in V. K. Ramachandran and Madhura Swaminathan, eds., *Agrarian Studies 2: Financial Liberalization and Rural Credit in India.* New Delhi: Tulika Books.

Cornia, Giovanni, and Nguyuru Lipumba, eds. (1999). "The impact of the liberalization of exchange rate and financial markets in sub-Saharan Africa", *Journal of International Development*, Special Issue, vol. 11, No. 3.

Deraniyagala, Sonali, Yubaraj Khatiwada, Shiva Sharma, Rathin Roy and Ashwini Deshpande (2003). *Pro-poor Macroeconomic Policies in Nepal.* New York: The Asia-Pacific Regional Programme on the Macroeconomics of Poverty Reduction UNDP.

Díaz-Alejandro, Carlos (1986). "Goodbye financial repression, hello financial crash", *Journal of Development Economics*, vol. 19, No. 1, pp. 1-24.

Do Qui Toan, Le Thanh Tam, Nguyen Thi Viet Nga and Dinh Lam Tan (2001). "Credit", in *Living Standards During and Economic Boom.* Dominique Haughton, Jonathan Haughton, Nguyen Phong, eds. Hanoi: UNDP and Statistical Publishing House.

Epstein, Gerald, Ilene Grabel and Jomo K. S. (2003). "Capital management techniques in developing countries: an assessment of experiences from the 1990s and lessons for the future". Paper prepared for the Group of 24 Technical Meetings available at http://www.g24.org/tgpapers.htm (accessed March 2006).

Eshag, Eprime (1983). *Fiscal and Monetary Policies and Problems in Developing Countries.* Cambridge: Cambridge University Press.

Ffrench-Davis, Ricardo (1994). "The macroeconomic framework for investment and development: the links between financial and trade reforms", in *The New Paradigm of Systemic Competitiveness: Toward More Integrated Policies in Latin America.* C. Bradford, ed. Paris: OECD.

Fry, Maxwell (1997). "In favour of financial liberalisation", *The Economic Journal*, vol. 107, No. 442.

Gerschenkron, Alexander (1962). *Economic Backwardness in Historical Perspective: A Book of Essay.* Cambridge, Mass.: The Belknap Press of Harvard University Press.

_____ (1968). *Continuity in History and Other Essays.* Cambridge, Mass.: The Belknap Press of Harvard University Press.

ICBP (2006). *Report of the Independent Commission on Banking and Financial Policy.* New Delhi.

Levine, Ross (1997). "Financial development and growth: views and agenda", *Journal of Economic Literature*, vol. 35, No. 2.

McKinnon, R. I. (1973). *Money and Capital in Economic Development.* Washington, D.C.: Brookings Institution Press.

Mkandawire, Thandika (1999). "The political economy of financial reform in Africa", *Journal of International Development*, vol. 11, No. 3.

Osmani, S. R., Wahiduddin Mahamud, Binayak Sen, Hulya Dagdeviren and Anuradha Seth (2003). *Pro-Poor Macroeconomic Policies in Bangladesh.* New York: The Asia-Pacific Regional Programme on the Macroeconomics of Poverty Reduction UNDP.

Robinson, Joan (1952). "The generalisation of the general theory", in *The Rate of Interest and Other Essays.* London: Macmillan.

Shaw, Edward (1973). *Financial Deepening in Economic Development.* New York: Oxford University Press.

Stiglitz, Joseph (1991). "Governments, financial markets and economic development", *NBER Working Paper No. 3669.* Cambridge, Mass.: National Bureau of Economic Research, www.nber.org/papers/w3669.pdf.

Stiglitz, Joseph (1994). "The role of the state in financial markets", *Proceedings of the World Bank Annual Conference on Development Economics 1993* (Supplement to the World Bank Economic Review and World Bank Research Observer). Washington, D.C.: World Bank.

Stiglitz, Joseph, and Andrew Weiss (1981). "Credit rationing in markets with imperfect information", *American Economic Review*, vol. 71, No. 3.

UNCTAD (2001). *Improving the Competitiveness of SMEs in Developing Countries*, UNCTAD/ ITE/TEB/Misc.3, Geneva: UNCTAD.

United Nations (2005). *World Economic and Social Survey 2005: Financing for Development*, Department of Economic and Social Affairs, New York.

_____ (2006). *Building Inclusive Financial Sectors for Development*, New York: Department of Economic and Social Affairs and United Nations Capital Development Fund, New York.

Wade, Robert (1991). *Governing the Market: Economic Theory and the Role of Government in East Asian Industrialisation.* Princeton: Princeton University Press.

Weeks, John, Nguyen Thang, Rathin Roy and Joseph Lim (2003). *The Macro-economics of Poverty Reduction: The Case Study of Viet Nam*, New York: United Nations Asia-Pacific Regional Programme on the Macroeconomics of Poverty Reduction.

# State-owned enterprise reform

Ha-Joon Chang*

## Introduction: public investment and economic development

Public investment has to play a key role in any pro-poor national development strategy, including the achievement of the Millennium Development Goals (MDGs).

Markets are powerful mechanisms to promote economic development, but they often fail to produce the economic dynamism and the social justice that sustainable economic development requires.

As a "one-dollar-one-vote" system, markets are not likely to meet the basic needs of the poor adequately. For example, 20 times more money is spent on research on slimming drugs than on research on malaria, a disease that kills more than a million people every year. If we want broad-based and politically sustainable development, we need to find mechanisms that can meet the basic needs of everyone.

Moreover, there are "public goods" that are likely to be under-provided by individuals acting purely on market incentives. Law and order, basic infrastructure, primary health, basic education and scientific research are examples of such public goods. The classic mechanism to provide such goods is through taxation and public provision.

Without appropriate regulation, markets encourage short-term profit-seeking at the cost of the long-term investments that are necessary for sustainable economic development. It is no coincidence that investment rates have fallen markedly in developing countries over the last two decades, following the liberalization and the opening up of their financial markets. Actions that are necessary in this regard include prudential regulation, appropriate counter-cyclical macroeconomic policy, financial market rules that discourage speculation, taxation and other policies that encourage long-term investment.

* The author would like to thank Rathin Roy, Senior Public Finance Advisor, Bureau for Development Policy, UNDP, and Jenik Radon, Columbia University and an international attorney with Radon and Ishizumi, for their important inputs into the paper, and Jomo K. S. for providing important guidance in shaping the paper. Khay-Jin Khoo has provided not only extensive editorial advice but also many important substantive comments. Joseph Stiglitz provided incredibly detailed and enlightening comments. The author also would like to thank, in alphabetical order, Barbara Barungi, Luba Fakhrutdinova, Ben Fine, Adil Khan, Kamal Malhotra and Isabel Ortiz for their very helpful comments on the earlier drafts of the paper.

In correcting for the deficiencies of the market, public investment can, and should, play a key role, especially in relation to long-term development. Long-term development requires investments in a range of physical and human capabilities. Public investment programmes can increase physical capabilities by investing in capital equipment and physical infrastructure (e.g., transport, telecommunications). They increase human capabilities by investing in health, education, training and scientific research capacity. Appropriately targeted public investment programmes—educational expenditure targeted at poor children or infrastructure built to help a poor region export its products—may also contribute to alleviating poverty and thus to economic and social development in the long run.

Public investment is also a critical instrument to enhance private sector activities through the "crowding in" effect.[1] Over the last two decades, there has been a tendency to presume that all public investment "crowds out" private investment. However, "crowding out" becomes a significant possibility only when the economy is near full employment. In most countries with underutilized resources or increased resources obtained through aid, we can expect public investment to "crowd in" private investment. Public investment can further enhance economic development, especially if they are made in areas that complement private sector investment (e.g., road facilities for major export crop region, investment in the training of engineers for a newly expanding industry, investment in the basic inputs industries that are too risky for the private sector).

Despite all its potential benefits, public investment has fallen in many developing countries (Roy, 2006). Public investment as a share of GDP in the developing countries fell from the peak of 10 per cent in the early 1980s to just over 5 per cent in 2000. The fall was particularly dramatic in Latin America, where it fell from 8-9 per cent in the late 1970s to under 3 per cent in 2000. This dramatic fall was not least because of the IMF conditionalities. The strong emphasis put on stabilization over other goals (growth, employment, development) has meant that countries had the incentive to cut investment of all kinds. At the same time, budget-balancing conditionality had no distinction between current and capital expenditures, thus making governments cut public investment rather than current expenditures, the reduction of which is politically more difficult.

All our concerns about falling public investment, of course, do not mean that everything has been fine with public investment. In many developing countries, poor management of public investment has been a serious problem, and ways need to be found to improve public investment management. This Policy Note addresses this issue.

This Policy Note covers two main areas of public investment management. The first is the management of State-owned enterprises (SOEs). The second is the management of natural resources. It aims to provide practical policy suggestions but it is preceded by discussions of the theories underlying the key policy debates in this area, presented in a user-friendly way.

---

1   See Roy, 2006, for an up-to-date and comprehensive discussion on the issue.

For a policymaker who is anxious to get into action, the theoretical discussions may seem like an unnecessary detour. However, we provide the discussions in the belief that an understanding of the theories underlying policy debates is the best way to improve policy capabilities. If the policymaker understands the underlying theories, he/she can apply the reasoning to a range of different situations.

## Managing State-owned enterprises (SOEs)

Before starting the main discussion, it is useful to state some major theoretical and empirical findings relating to SOEs. This is done in the belief that it is useful for the reader to see the "big picture" before getting into the details.

First of all, there is no clear theoretical case either for or against SOEs. Pervasive informational asymmetries and "bounded rationality" (Simon, 1983) necessitate "hierarchical" arrangements (i.e., firms) rather than "contractual" arrangements (i.e., markets). Furthermore, the Sappington-Stiglitz Fundamental Privatization Theorem shows that the performance of private sector firms is superior to that of SOEs only under stringent and often unrealistic conditions.

Second, it is important to note that the problems faced by large SOEs and large private sector firms are often very similar. As large and complex organizations that have multiple and overlapping layers of hierarchy, they both suffer from complex "agency problems", or "principal-agent problems". When discussing the problems of SOEs, many people often implicitly assume that private sector firms are perfectly controlled by their owners, thus assuming away their agency problems. If we compare idealized private sector firms with real life SOEs, it is not surprising that the former come out on top.

Third, even at the logical level, full-scale privatization, the solution often recommended by supporters of today's economic orthodoxy, is only one possible way to deal with the problems of SOEs. The government may sell a significant portion of the shares of an SOE but retain a majority share or at least a controlling stake (say, 30-40 per cent) in it. Moreover, as will be explained later, SOE performance can be improved without any sale of shares but through organizational reform, an increase in competition and political-administrative reforms.

Fourth, given the ambiguity of the theoretical findings, it is important to pay attention to real world outcomes. There are undoubtedly many SOEs that are inefficient, undynamic and corrupt. However, there is no clear systematic evidence that SOEs are burdens on the economy.[2] Furthermore, there is a certain degree of "selection bias" in the empirical materials relating to SOEs in the sense that poorly performing SOEs tend to get discussed more. It is natural that people talk more about problem cases, but this gives the wrong impression of the prevalence of poor SOE performance.

---

2  See Chang and Singh, 1993, for detailed reviews of the literature.

## The case for SOEs

Despite popular perception, encouraged by the business media and contemporary conventional wisdom and rhetoric, SOEs can be efficient and well-run. This may sound like a trivial statement, but it is very important to start our discussion with this point, given the depth of prejudice against SOEs.

Singapore Airlines, often voted the best airline in the world, is an SOE, 57 per cent owned by the Government holding company, Temasek Holdings, whose sole shareholder is the Singapore Ministry of Finance (see box 1). The highly respected Bombay Transport Authority of India is also an SOE. World-class companies like the Brazilian regional jet manufacturer EMBRAER, the French carmaker Renault and the Korean steelmaker POSCO all initially succeeded as SOEs, with the State still exercising critical influence in the case of EMBRAER and Renault (see box 2).

Many countries achieved economic success with a large SOE sector. In addition to Singapore Airlines, the Singapore Government owns enterprises not just in the "usual" sectors like telecommunications, power (electricity and gas), transport

---

**Box 1.   Singapore's SOE sector**

Singapore's domestic SOE sector comprises two main components: Government-Linked Companies (GLCs) and Government Statutory Boards. GLCs are entities in which the wholly owned Government holding company, Temasek Holdings, directly holds a controlling share as well as subsidiaries and associates of those entities. Statutory Boards include the Public Utilities Board, Economic Development Board, Housing and Development Board, etc. Over time, the Government of Singapore has converted many Statutory Boards into GLCs.

Temasek Holdings directly owns majority shares in the following enterprises: 100 per cent of Singapore Power (electricity and gas) and of PSA International (ports), 67 per cent of Neptune Orient Lines (shipping), 60 per cent of Chartered Semiconductor Manufacturing (semi-conductor), 56 per cent of SingTel (telecommunications), 55 per cent of SMRT (rail, bus, and taxi services), 55 per cent of Singapore Technologies Engineering (engineering), and 51 per cent of SemCorp Industries (engineering). It also directly owns a controlling stake in the following enterprises: 32 per cent of SembCorp Marine (shipbuilding) and 28 per cent of DBS (the largest bank in Singapore).

Singapore's SOE sector, measured in terms of its share in national investment, is nearly three times that of the Republic of Korea, which has an average-sized SOE sector. According to a 1995 World Bank report, the weighted average of the share of the SOE sector in GDP in the 40 developing countries it studied was 10.7 per cent during 1978-1991. The corresponding figure for the Republic of Korea was 9.9 per cent. The World Bank study unfortunately did not provide data on Singapore. However, in 1993, the Ministry of Finance estimated that "the public sector and GLCs ... account for about 60 per cent of our GDP". In 2001, the Department of Statistics estimated that GLCs accounted for 12.9 per cent of GDP in 1998, with the non-GLC public sector accounting for another 8.9 per cent, giving a total public sector/GLC share of 21.8 per cent. The Department of Statistics used a tighter definition of GLC as those companies in which the government has an effective ownership of 20 per cent or more.

*Sources:* Temasek website (http://www.temasekholdings.com.sg/), Shin, 2005; World Bank, 1995, Table A.1; Singapore Ministry of Finance, 1993; Singapore Department of Statistics, 2001.

(rail, bus, and even taxi) and ports, but also in sectors like semiconductors, ship-building, engineering, shipping and banking. It has one of the largest SOE sectors in the world (see box 1 again). Taiwan Province of China achieved its economic "miracle" on the basis of a large SOE sector and with little privatization (see box 3). Throughout most of the second half of the twentieth century, countries like Austria, France, Norway and West Germany had large SOE sectors and performed well. Especially in France, SOEs were often at the forefront of industrial modernization.

Conversely, many unsuccessful economies have small SOE sectors. Even before the large-scale privatization of the 1990s, Argentina's SOE sector was less than half the average of 40 developing countries featured in a World Bank study (World Bank, 1995, table A.1). Between 1978 and 1991, Argentina's SOE sector accounted

---

**Box 2. EMBRAER, Renault and POSCO: world-class firms with SOE origins**

**EMBRAER**

EMBRAER (Empresa Brasileira de Aeronáutica), the Brazilian manufacturer of "regional jets", was established as an SOE in 1960, with 51 per cent Government ownership. Until the mid-1980s, it did very well thanks to a shrewd management strategy that astutely targeted niche markets, emphasis on export that permitted longer production runs and strong support from the Brazilian air force.

However, by the end of the 1980s, Government investments in the aerospace industry was greatly reduced, due to the new Constitution of 1988, which extinguished many forms of support to the industry, and due to the lack of interest in the defence area following the end of the cold war. The failure of its CBA 123 Vector project, combined with the crisis in the aviation industry in general caused by the oil price increase of 1990, plunged EMBRAER into a deep financial crisis.

EMBRAER was privatized in 1994. However, the Brazilian Government still owns the "golden share" (1 per cent of capital) in the company, which allows it to veto certain deals regarding military aircraft sales and technology transfer to foreign countries.

EMBRAER is now the largest regional jet manufacturer in the world and the third largest aircraft manufacturer of any kind, after Airbus and Boeing.

*Sources*: Embraer website (http://www.embraer.com/english/content/empresa/history.asp); Wikipedia online encyclopedia (http://en.wikipedia.org/wiki/Embraer); Goldstein, 2002.

**Renault**

The French carmaker Renault was established as a private company in 1898. It was nationalized in 1945 for having been "an instrument of the enemy"—its owner, Louis Renault, was a Nazi collaborator—and became an SOE.

Under State ownership, Renault did very well until the 1970s, producing a series of successful models, such as CV4, Dauphine, Renault 4, Renault 8 and Renault 5. In the 1980s, it ran into trouble. However, it has been doing very well since its restructuring in the mid-1990s. Privatization was an important, but not the sole, element in this restructuring.

Renault's privatization is an excellent example of a successful gradualist approach to privatization. In 1994, the French State started selling the shares, but kept a 53 per cent share.

> **Box 2.   EMBRAER, Renault and POSCO:**
> **world-class firms with SOE origins** (*continued*)
>
> In 1996, the French State relinquished its majority share, reducing its holdings to 46 per cent. However, 11 per cent of the shares was sold to what the company website calls "a stable core of major shareholders", essentially financial institutions partly controlled by the French State. Since then, the share of the French Government has been gradually reduced to 15.3 per cent in 2005, although it remains the largest single shareholder. Moreover, an important part of this reduction in State share is explained by the acquisition of 15 per cent of its shares in 2002 by Nissan, in which Renault has owned the controlling stake (first 35 per cent, now 44 per cent) since 1999. Thus, the French State remains the dominant force in Renault.
>
> *Sources*: Renault company official website (http://www.renault.com); Wikipedia on-line encyclopedia (http://en.wikipedia.org/wiki/Renault).
>
> **POSCO**
>
> In 1967, the Government of the Republic of Korea applied for a loan to build the country's first modern steel mill to an international consortium that included the World Bank. The application was rejected on the grounds that the project was not viable.
>
>      This was not an unreasonable decision. The country's biggest export items at the time were fish, cheap apparels, wigs and plywood. The Republic of Korea did not possess deposits of either key raw material—iron ore and coking coal. Furthermore, the cold war meant it could not even import them from nearby China. They had to be brought all the way from Australia. To cap it all, the Government of the Republic of Korea proposed to run this as an SOE. There could not be a more perfect recipe for disaster, so it was thought.
>
>      The Government of the Republic of Korea borrowed from some Japanese banks and set up the steel mill as an SOE, called Pohang Steel Company (POSCO), in 1968. POSCO started production in 1973. The company remained an SOE until 2000. Its first chairman, Tae-Joon Park, under whose leadership POSCO became a world-class firm, was a political appointee; he was an ex-army general personally close to the country's then President (former) General Chung-Hee Park.
>
>      POSCO made profits right from the start, although this initially required tariff protection and subsidies. This success was partly due to Government policy to let the company be profit oriented. However, this result would not have been possible without the cutting edge technology POSCO imported from New Nippon Steel, the leading Japanese steelmaker, and the strenuous efforts the company made to master it.
>
>      POSCO became the most efficient steelmaker in the world in the mid-1980s and remained so until the late 1990s, when it was overtaken by Bao Steel, a Chinese SOE. It is now the fourth largest steel producer globally.
>
> *Sources*: Amsden, 1989; POSCO company official website (http://www.posco.co.kr/homepage/docs/en/company/posco/s91a1010010m.html); Wikipedia online encyclopedia (http://en.wikipedia.org/wiki/POSCO).

for only 4.7 per cent of GDP, against the 40-developing-country average of 10.7 per cent and the Republic of Korea's 9.9 per cent. The SOE sector in the Philippines, another widely recognized case of "development failure", was even smaller. During the same period, at 1.9 per cent of GDP, it was just over one fifth that of the Republic of Korea (9.9 per cent) and less than one fifth of the 40-country average of 10.7 per

**Box 3. Privatization, Taiwan Province of China style**

Taiwan Province of China (hereafter, Taiwan PoC) achieved its economic miracles with a large SOE sector. During the miracle years of the 1960s and the 1970s, the SOE sector's share in the economy increased from 14.7 per cent in 1951 to 15.9 per cent in 1961 to 16.7 per cent in 1971 before coming down slightly to 16.0 per cent in 1981. Although the Taiwanese Government allowed the private sector to grow, the SOE sector occupied the "commanding heights" of the economy, controlling the banking sector and the key upstream inputs industries, such as steel and petrochemicals.

Taiwan PoC started privatizing in a serious way only in 1996, relinquishing majority shares in SOEs in banking, insurance, petrochemicals, transportation and a few other industries. However, Taiwan PoC's privatization has been a very controlled one, as the Government still has a controlling stake (average of 35.5 per cent) and accounts for 60 per cent of board members in the 18 privatized SOEs. The Taiwanese Government is allowed to own the "golden share" (i.e., the veto over important decisions) when privatizing SOEs in defence or public utilities.

*Source*: CEPD, 2002.

cent (World Bank, 1995, table A.1). Despite this, Argentina and the Philippines are commonly touted as economies that failed because of large public sectors.

In addition to the above real life examples going against the conventional wisdom of "private, good; public, bad", there are respectable theoretical justifications for the existence of SOEs. These are explained below and summarized in box 4.

The most frequently cited reason is the case of natural monopoly. This refers to a situation in which the technical requirements of an industry are such that only one supplier may exist. When a natural monopoly exists, the supplier is able to extract high monopoly profits by charging high prices. A natural monopolist can also exploit suppliers by bargaining their prices down, if it happens to be a monopsonist (sole buyer) for some inputs. Such positions result not only in unequal distribution of economic surpluses, but also in economic inefficiency, as the monopolistic firm produces (or buys, in the case of the monopsonist) less than the socially desirable amounts of output. Under such circumstances, there is a strong case for an SOE to be set up and regulated to prevent abuse of such a natural monopoly.

Another justification for SOEs is capital market failure, where private sector investors refuse to finance projects that have high returns in the long run but carry high risks in the short term. For example, the Government of the Republic of Korea set up the steelmaker POSCO as an SOE, as the risk was considered too high by the private sector (see box 2). If the venture subsequently proved so successful, why did the private sector fail to finance it? This is because capital markets have an inherent bias towards short-term gains and do not like risky, large-scale projects with long gestation periods. One obvious solution to capital market failure is for the government to set up a development bank that finances risky, long-term ventures, rather than to set up and run productive SOEs itself. However, in most developing countries, there is a shortage of entrepreneurial talent in the private sector so, even with

**Box 4.  Justifications for SOEs**

- **Natural monopoly**: In industries where technological conditions dictate that there can be only one supplier, the monopoly supplier may produce at less than socially optimal level and appropriate monopoly rents.
  *Examples*: railways, water, electricity.

- **Capital market failure**: Private sector investors may refuse to invest in industries that have high risk and/or long gestation period.
  *Examples*: capital-intensive, high-technology industries in developing countries, such as aircraft in Brazil or steel in the Republic of Korea.

- **Externalities**: Private sector investors do not have the incentive to invest in industries which benefit other industries without being paid for the service.
  *Examples*: basic input industries such as steel and chemicals.

- **Equity**: Profit-seeking firms in industries that provide basic goods and services may refuse to serve less profitable customers, such as poor people or people living in remote areas.
  *Examples*: water, postal services, public transport, basic education.

the development bank, the necessary venture may not be set up. In this case, setting up SOEs may be a more effective way to address capital market failure than setting up a development bank.

The example of POSCO illustrates another classical justification for SOEs; namely, the problem of externalities. POSCO, under Government direction, did not abuse its monopoly position to make extra profits; instead, it passed on its productivity gains to buyers of its products, thus benefiting the rest of the economy. The "social" return to the Government of the Republic of Korea's investment in POSCO—or the return to the whole economy—was therefore higher than the "private" return—or the return to the company alone. Such discrepancies between private and social returns, known as externalities in economic jargon, is another reason for setting up an SOE.[3]

Fourth, SOEs may be set up to address equity concerns, broadly defined. For example, if left at the mercy of profit-seeking firms, people living in remote areas may be denied essential services like post, water and transport. In such cases, an SOE is an easy way to ensure universal access to essential services for all citizens. Another example is privately run pensions or health insurance systems may refuse to admit "high-risk" cases, usually poorer people. Running such systems as SOEs would ensure that the most vulnerable groups get vital social security.

In theory, all of the above justifications for SOEs, with the exception of moral concerns, can be addressed by private enterprises operating under an appropriate regulatory regime and/or tax-and-subsidy scheme, which equates private and social costs/benefits. For example, the government may subsidize private sector firms that

---

3  The most important class of externalities for the purpose of economic development is the "learning externalities", that is, the knowledge spill-over from new industries to the traditional sectors. For a general theoretical exposition of this point, see Greenwald and Stigtliz, 2006.

are engaged in activities with high externalities (e.g., R&D). For another example, the government may license private sector firms to operate "essential services" (e.g., post, rail, water) on the condition that they provide universal access (the "equity" concern). Therefore, it may appear that SOEs are not necessary.

However, this ignores one crucial point. Regulation or tax/subsidy regimes involve contractual agreements—explicit, in the case of direct regulation, or implicit, in the case of tax/subsidy regimes—that are costly to manage.

Outside the ideal world of economics textbooks, it is impossible to specify all contingencies for which the contents of a contract—for example, the level of the regulated price ceiling or the amount of subsidy—may need to be revised. Such contractual revisions usually involve a lot of negotiation and even legal disputes, all of which can incur substantial costs, known as "transaction costs" in economic jargon. This is the 1991 Nobel Economics Laureate Ronald Coase's classic explanation of why not everything is done by the market and firms exist.

Of course, the savings on transactions costs made by choosing SOEs over private sector provision under government regulation and/or tax-and-subsidy schemes have to be set against the "organizational costs" of SOEs. Most importantly, the lower degree of transparency of the firm-type arrangement compared to more contractual arrangements may make the former more susceptible to political influence ("capture") and, worse, outright corruption.[4]

However, even considering the "organizational costs", the existence of transaction costs means that it is often much less costly to set up an SOE and deal with unexpected contingencies through internal government directives than to set up some contract-based regime—regulation and/or taxes/subsidies—to address such concerns. This argument is particularly relevant for activities that SOEs normally engage in, where market price signals are non-existent (e.g., natural monopoly) or unreliable (e.g., externalities). It is particularly relevant for developing countries whose governments lack legal capabilities even more than they lack administrative capabilities.

## The case against SOEs—and its limitations

Despite the theoretical justifications for SOEs and the many examples of well-performing SOEs, many SOEs are not well run. Why? The most popular explanation contains two elements: the principal-agent problem and the free-rider problem, both based on the assumption of self-seeking individuals.

An SOE is, by definition, run by managers who do not own the firm. Given the self-seeking nature of humans, the argument goes, no SOE manager will run the firm as efficiently as an owner-manager would run his own firm. This problem would not

---

4  The fact that SOEs have often been the worst offenders in terms of safety and environmental standards in many countries is due at least partly to this reason. Given this consideration, it is important to subject SOEs to the same set of clearly specified regulatory standards as private sector firms, whether they are supervised by issue-specific regulatory agencies (e.g., environmental regulatory agency, work safety regulatory agency) or by SOE-specific agencies (e.g., specialized SOE supervisory body, relevant ministries, government audit agency).

exist if the citizens, who are the owners (principals) of SOEs, can perfectly monitor the SOE managers (their agents). However, because it is inherently difficult to verify (although managers know) whether poor enterprise performance is due to shirking by the managers or circumstances beyond their control, monitoring by principals will always remain imperfect, resulting in inefficient management. This is called the principal-agent problem.

Moreover, individual citizens do not have the incentive, and means, to monitor the SOE managers. Instead, the costs that an individual owner (citizen) incurs in monitoring SOE managers are solely his or hers, while the benefits of improved management accrue to all owners. Thus, individually, the citizens have no incentive to monitor the SOE managers, which means that, in the end, no one monitors them. This is the so-called free-rider problem.

While the principal-agent and free-rider problems are real, and can be very important in explaining poor SOE performance, they also apply to large private enterprises with dispersed ownership. If the private enterprise is run by hired managers and if numerous shareholders own small fractions of the company, the hired managers will also have an incentive to put in sub-optimal (from the shareholders' point of view) levels of effort, while individual shareholders do not have enough incentive to monitor the hired managers. In other words, the monitoring of hired managers is a "public good", whose provision is a problem for both SOEs and private sector firms.

In fact, under certain circumstances, it may be easier to monitor SOEs than to monitor private sector firms with dispersed ownership. On the one hand, the public, comprising taxpayers whose contributions will be squandered if SOEs are inefficiently managed, has at least as great an incentive to discipline errant SOE managers as do shareholders in the private sector. On the other hand, the centralized governance structure within which SOEs operate makes it easier to monitor them. In the SOE sector, there is often one, or at most a few, clearly identifiable agencies responsible for monitoring SOE performance, e.g., relevant ministries, public holding companies, government audit board, dedicated SOE supervisory agency, whereas dispersed shareholders of private enterprises cannot take concerted actions unless there are some shareholders that are large enough to unilaterally provide the "public good" of monitoring.[5] Indeed, we may say that governments are set up to solve "public good problems", of which monitoring of hired managers (of SOEs) is an example.

More importantly, the fact that many companies, both private and State-owned, are well managed despite dispersed ownership suggests there is more to the good management of an enterprise than giving individuals the right material incentives.

Individual self-interest is not the only thing that drives humans. People working in an enterprise are motivated not simply by "selfish" things like their own salaries and power but also by loyalty to the enterprise, a sense of obligation to their colleagues, commitment to workmanship, honesty, dignity, a work ethic and many other moral values. When it comes to SOEs, there may be additional motives that

---

5   The takeover mechanism may provide another disciplinary device.

need to be taken into account, such as nationalism, dedication to public service, concern for social justice, pride in working for a "leading" company and so on. These motives matter and we ignore them at our peril (for further discussion, see box 5).

If there is relatively little difference between the internal workings of SOEs and those of private enterprises with widespread ownership, can there be other factors that differentiate them?

One obvious candidate is the so-called soft budget constraint that SOEs are typically subject to, due to their status as public enterprises. The argument is that, being part of the government, SOEs are able to secure additional finances if they make losses and get rescued with public money if they are threatened with bankruptcy. In this way, it is argued, SOEs can act as if the limits to their budgets are malleable, or "soft".

The term "soft budget constraint" was coined by the famous Hungarian economist, Janos Kornai, to explain the behaviour of socialist enterprises under central planning, but it can be applied to SOEs in capitalist economies too. For example, the existence of "sick enterprises" in India that never go bankrupt is the most frequently cited example of the soft budget constraint of SOEs.

It is true that politically generated or politically sustained soft budget constraints encourage lax management, and therefore need to be "hardened". However, it should also be noted that the soft budget constraint is not simply a consequence of the ownership status of SOEs. If they are politically important enough, e.g., large employers or politically sensitive industries such as armaments or hospitals, private firms can also have soft budget constraints, although it may be reasonable to argue that an SOE will find it easier to get political support than a private enterprise.

### Box 5.   Non-selfish motives in enterprise management

A good way to see the limits to the contractual approach based on self-interested individuals in understanding enterprise management is the fact that "working to rule" is a widely used method of industrial action. If everything could be specified in a contract, working-to-rule could never be a method of industrial action, as the workers would be doing exactly what they should be doing. Enterprises run as they do, only because people put in efforts that go beyond their contractual obligations.

As the 1978 Nobel Economics Laureate Herbert Simon once remarked, if human beings were as selfish as depicted in orthodox economics textbooks, it would be impossible to run any company. In such a world, companies would collapse under the burden of monitoring and bargaining costs (transaction costs).

Moreover, if non-selfish motives did not matter, there would be no difference between good and bad managers. All a manager has to do is to specify contractually the employees' duties and to design an effective, but obvious, incentive system, using individual rewards and punishments. However, non-selfish motives matter and good managers are those who can induce his/her workers to do extra through mechanisms that cannot be contractually specified—it is impossible to specify contractually that an employee should be, say, "loyal to the company" or "take pride in his work".

Interestingly, many government bail outs of large private sector firms have been made by avowedly free-market governments (see box 6).

Having acknowledged the existence of soft budget constraint, it has to be emphasized that it does not have to make the managers of SOEs lazy. Why?

If professional managers, whether they are running an SOE or a private enterprise, know they will be severely punished for poor management, say, have their salaries cut or even lose their jobs, they will not have the incentive to mismanage their firms (Chang, 2000). Indeed, if we believe in unadulterated self-seeking, what matters to the managers is their personal welfare, and not whether their company survives thanks to government bail outs. If they know they will be sanctioned for poor management, the possibility of government bail outs for their firms is unlikely to induce mismanagement.

Therefore, even if we acknowledge the greater likelihood of soft budget constraints for SOEs, its adverse impact on SOE efficiency will be reduced insofar as SOE managers are held accountable for SOE management.

Our discussion in this section shows that public ownership, in itself, whether due to ownership dispersion or political influence, is not an inevitable reason for poor performance by SOEs. All the key arguments against SOEs—the principal-agent problem, the free-rider problem and the soft budget constraints (summarized in box 7)—apply to large private sector firms with dispersed ownership.

## Is privatization a solution to SOE problems?

Despite the absence of any peculiar barriers to good SOE performance, it is the case that, as a group, SOEs have under-performed private enterprises in many countries.

---

**Box 6.    Soft budget constraints for large private sector firms**

In the late 1970s, the bankrupt Swedish shipbuilding industry was rescued through nationalization by the country's first right-wing Government in 44 years, despite the fact that the Government came to power with a pledge to reduce the size of the State.

In the early 1980s, the troubled U.S. carmaker Chrysler was rescued by the Reagan administration, which was at the vanguard of neo-liberal market reforms at the time.

Chile was plunged into a financial crisis in 1982, following its premature and ill-designed financial liberalization in the late 1970s. Faced with the crisis, the Pinochet Government, which had come to power in bloodshed in the name of defending the free market, rescued the entire banking sector with public money.

In Greece, the SOE sector is filled with former inefficient private firms, which were nationalized, thus bailed out, because of their political importance. It is no surprise that the Greek SOE sector has performed poorly.

These examples show that "soft budget constraints" exist not only for SOEs but for private sector firms that are "too big to fail". The above examples, except for Greece, show that avowedly pro-market Governments are no exceptions when it comes to bailing out politically and economically important private sector firms in trouble.

*Source:* Chang and Singh, 1993; Chang, 2000.

> ### Box 7.  Arguments against SOEs
>
> - **The principal-agent problem:** SOEs are not run by their owners. Unable to monitor them perfectly, the owners cannot tell how much of performance is due to managerial failure or external factors. This allows the managers to put in sub-optimal efforts.
> - **The free-rider problem:** SOEs have numerous owners (all citizens). No individual owner (citizen) has the incentive to monitor the SOE managers as the benefits from monitoring will accrue to all owners while the costs are borne by the individuals who do the monitoring.
> - **The soft budget constraint:** Being part of the government, SOEs are able to secure additional financial assistance if their performance lags. This leeway makes the SOE managers lax in their management.

For this reason, privatization has been touted as a means for squeezing better performance out of SOEs. Unfortunately, such a solution presents a conundrum. At its root, it appears that if a government has the capacity and capability to conduct a good privatization, it probably also has the capacity to operate good SOEs; whereas, if a government does not have the capacity to operate good SOEs, it likely also lacks the capacity to conduct a good privatization. This section examines this issue in some detail and two boxed items provide some guidance on the matter.

From the 1980s until recently, privatization was widely considered to be the main, or even the only, way to improve SOE performance.[6] The financial muscle of donor governments, the World Bank and the IMF made sure that this view was put into practice in the developing and transition economies.

While the conviction with which privatization has been pushed has diminished in recent years, not least because of the accumulating evidence that it has often failed to deliver on the promises, privatization is still considered the obvious solution to the problems associated with SOEs.

Privatization is definitely an option to consider for policymakers interested in improving the performances of their SOEs. However, as discussed in the next section, there are many ways to improve SOE performance without privatization. Moreover, it is wrong to assume, as is often done, that the choice is between fully privatized and fully State-owned enterprises. There are many intermediate "third way" solutions. The government can sell some of the shares of an SOE while retaining majority control or a controlling stake (see the cases of Renault in France in box 2 or of many Taiwanese SOEs in box 3).[7] Such "partial" privatization may be done in order to raise revenues, but it is also done in order to gain access to key technologies or key markets through partnership with a major foreign company. Some governments have utilized the so-called "golden share" to retain control over key matters (e.g., control over key

---

6   See World Bank, 1995, for the most representative statement of this view.

7   There is no clear definition of the "controlling share", but a shareholding that is above 30-40 per cent is normally considered "controlling". Depending on shareholding patterns, the controlling share could be significantly lower than that (see the case of Renault in box 2).

technology, M&A) while selling almost all its stake (e.g., see the case of EMBRAER in Brazil in box 2). There are also possibilities of "cooperative corporatization", where the government could sell an SOE to a "cooperative" of private sector firms, such as selling airports to a "cooperative" of airlines (Stiglitz, 2006).

Even if we ignore all the "third way" options using the intermediate organizational forms mentioned above, privatization involves a number of serious practical problems that limit its effectiveness. Thus seen, privatization should be undertaken only when the conditions are right, as explained below and summarized in box 8.

First, experience shows that privatization of profitable SOEs makes little difference to their performances, so the government should focus on privatizing unprofitable SOEs. Unfortunately, the private sector is not very interested in buying unprofitable SOE. Therefore, in order to generate private sector interest in a poorly performing SOE, the government often has to invest heavily in it and/or restructure it.[8] This raises a dilemma—if SOE performance can be thus improved while in State ownership, why privatize in the first place? Indeed, there is evidence that gains in productivity in privatized enterprises usually occur before privatization through anticipatory restructuring. This suggests that restructuring is more important than privatization. Therefore, unless it is politically impossible to restructure an enterprise without a strong government commitment to privatization, a lot of problems in the SOEs may be solved through restructuring without privatization.

Secondly, the very process of privatization involves financial expenditure, which can be a significant problem for cash-strapped developing country governments. The valuation of an SOE and the flotation of its shares on the stock market are costly exercises, especially if they have to be managed by expensive international accounting firms and investment banks—often inevitable for developing countries that do not have such firms domestically.

Third, privatization processes in many countries have been riddled with corruption, with a large part of the potential proceeds ending up in the pockets of a few insiders rather than in the State coffers. The corrupt transfer is sometimes effected illegally, through bribery, but often legally, e.g., government "insiders" acting as consultants in the process. This is ironic, given that one frequent argument against SOEs is that they are rife with corruption. However, the sad fact is that a government that is unable to control or eliminate corruption in SOEs is not suddenly going to have the capacity to prevent corruption when it is privatizing them. Indeed, the corrupt have an incentive to insinuate themselves into the privatization process and to push through privatization at all costs, because it means they do not have to share the bribery with their successors and can "cash in" all future bribery streams. It should also be added that privatization will not necessarily reduce corruption, for private sector firms can be corrupt too. False accounting and insider trading became huge problems even in the relatively well-regulated United States during the "Roaring Nineties".[9]

---

8   Moreover, it is not always possible for the government to recoup the value of the additional investments that were made for restructuring.

9   The term is from the title of Stiglitz, 2003a.

## Box 8.   Privatization checklist

**Factors in favour of privatization**

- The SOE is in a potentially competitive industry, but competition cannot be increased without privatization for political reasons.
- The domestic capital market is relatively well developed, making it easy to sell the SOE shares.
- The government at the relevant level (national, state, local, etc.) has adequate regulatory capabilities.
- There are domestic firms that can value and arrange the sale of the SOE at adequate price.
- The government is considered relatively clean.
- Only one or a few SOEs are going to be sold at any one time and, if more than one, at sufficient intervals.
- Organizational reforms in the SOEs are impossible for political reasons.
- The SOE in question is performing certain non-essential functions at considerable cost to its current efficiency and future growth, and it is not politically feasible to establish institutions that may perform those functions better.

**Factors against privatization**

- The SOE is in a natural monopoly industry.
- The SOE is in a potentially competitive industry, and competition can be increased without privatization.
- The SOE is providing an essential service for which universal access is crucial (e.g., water, electricity, urban transport, postal service, railways).
- The government at the relevant level (national, state, local, etc.) lacks adequate regulatory capabilities.
- The prospective buyers are already politically influential, which means that the "soft budget constraint" is likely to persist, even after privatization.
- Valuation and sales of the SOE have to be arranged through foreign firms that charge high fees.
- The government is considered relatively corrupt.
- The political decision makers want to sell a lot of SOEs at the same time or sell them at short intervals.
- The economy has a severe foreign exchange shortage, which makes large-scale privatization a convenient way out.
- The prospective buyer is a foreign SOE.
- It is politically feasible to make organizational reforms in the SOEs.
- Political compromises can be struck that are necessary for setting up new institutions to take over certain non-essential functions that the SOE has been performing at considerable cost to its efficiency and future growth.

Fourth, privatization can put an excessive burden on the regulatory capabilities of the government, especially if done on a large scale. When the SOEs concerned are natural monopolies, privatization without appropriate regulatory capability can make things worse, as it may replace inefficient, but restrained public monopoly with inefficient and unrestrained private monopoly. The problem of regulatory capability is particularly serious with local governments. In the name of political decentralization and of "bringing service providers closer to the people", the World Bank and donor governments have recently pushed for breaking up SOEs into smaller units on a geographical basis, and leaving the regulatory function to the local governments. This looks very good on paper, but given the reality of inadequate regulatory capabilities of local governments, it has, in effect, often resulted in regulatory vacuums (see Kessler and Alexander, 2003).

Fifth, the timing and the scale of privatization matters. For example, trying to sell many enterprises within a relatively short period—the so-called "fire sale" approach—weakens the government's bargaining power, thus lowering the proceeds it gets. As another example, trying to privatize when the stock market is down, other things being equal, will lower the proceeds of privatization. In this sense, setting a rigid deadline for privatization—which the IMF often insists on and which some governments have also voluntarily adopted—is a bad idea, as it will force the government to privatize regardless of market conditions. If the government gets the scale and the timing of privatization wrong, the prices paid for the enterprises will not be as high as they could have been had the government taken a more pragmatic approach and waited more patiently for the best deals.[10]

Sixth, privatization should be done for the "right" reason. It should be done for the purpose of improving enterprise performance, rather than as a means to raise money ("selling the family silver"). For example, in many Latin American countries in the 1990s, large-scale privatization was conducted as a means to raise large amounts of foreign exchange in a short period of time. The proceeds were then used to reduce external debt, finance consumption binges (of mainly imported goods) and/or to prop up an unsustainable exchange rate. Such "abuses" of privatization proceeds are to be avoided.

Seventh, SOEs in developing countries, especially in Latin America, were often sold to foreign SOEs. For example, the State-owned Spanish airline, Iberia, bought a number of State-owned Latin American airlines, while the State-owned Spanish telephone company, Telefonica, bought a number of State-owned Latin American telephone companies. If public ownership and management is the problem, it is

---

10  Countries have sometimes used "creative accounting" to exaggerate the extent of privatization in an attempt to circumvent IMF conditionality on privatization. For example, a government can lower its ownership share of an enterprise below 50 per cent, while having a State-run pension fund, or government-controlled financial entities own 2 per cent, thus effectively retaining control. The picture is even more complicated in the case of public-private partnerships. According to the IMF, "[n]o internationally acceptable accounting standard has been developed so far to reflect varying degrees of risk transfer from the government to the private sector, and country practices differ substantially in this area" (IMF, 2004). Further, many countries include privatization receipts as budget revenues. This is against international practice and dangerous. Privatization receipts are capital receipts and are "one-offs". You can only privatize an airport once. Including these as revenue receipts can overstate resources available to that government.

rather strange to sell one SOE to another, albeit foreign, one. The only argument for such a practice is that the government will be less compelled to grant politically motivated soft budget constraints to SOEs of foreign countries. However, very often, the foreign SOEs have even greater political leverage than domestic ones, due to their sheer size and the international political clout wielded by the national governments that own them.

Eighth, care needs to be taken to get the privatization contracts right. There are a number of issues involved here. One such issue is that of breach of contract by the purchaser of the privatized SOE. The firm can extract profits and then simply walk away, when they turn negative, leaving the government to deal with the problem.[11] This may not be a problem in some cases, such as radio spectrum, where the underlying asset is not destroyed by the termination in services. However, if it involves assets that require maintenance (e.g., water system, roads), it can lead to the deterioration, or even destruction, of the assets involved. Therefore, privatization contracts should include expedited procedures for reclaiming the assets when there is a breach of contract. A related issue is that of performance requirements. One challenge here is to use the right performance indicator—for example, profitability may not be the best performance measure in a contract for essential services like water. Another challenge is to find a way to prevent companies (should they be multinational) from undermining performance requirements (e.g., investment requirement) by using, for example, transfer pricing.

As can be seen, the list of conditions necessary for privatization to succeed is rather lengthy (see box 9). Many of these conditions are not met in reality, especially in developing countries. Not surprisingly, many privatization attempts have failed.

## Alternatives to privatization

If public ownership per se is not the only, or even the most, important reason for inefficient performance, privatization cannot be an effective cure for the problems of SOEs. Moreover, as seen above, there are many practical problems involved in privatization. Hence, it may be fair to say that privatization should be considered as one of the last, rather than the first, means to address poor SOE performance.

Below, we discuss three groups of policy alternatives to privatization—organizational reforms, increasing competition and political-administrative reforms. These are explained below and summarized in box 12 at the end of this section.

### Organizational reforms

First, the goals of the SOEs should be critically reviewed. Very often, SOEs are charged with serving too many goals—for example, meeting social goals (e.g., affirmative action for women and minorities), employment generation, industrialization and provision of basic services. There is nothing inherently wrong with an SOE serving multiple goals,

---

11 For some examples, see Kessler and Alexander, 2003, p. 15.

**Box 9.   Conditions necessary for successful privatization**

A poorly thought out privatization may cause more problems than it solves, resulting in more corruption and a greater rich-poor divide, exacerbating social tensions, enriching a select few and creating a system that defies future reform.

Privatization should not occur in the absence of an appropriate legal, regulatory and institutional framework, especially if the entities being considered for privatization are engaged in activities requiring regulation and oversight, such as activities with significant environmental or health impacts.

Assuming such a framework is in place, below is a brief checklist of the essential requirements for successful privatization:

- A clear, transparent and comprehensive strategy, including a timetable setting forth to-be-achieved milestones:
  - A commercial strategy
  - An industry strategy (one size does not fit all)
  - A regulatory and institutional strategy
  - A legal strategy
  - An educational/training strategy
  - A social impact assessment
  - Anti-corruption strategy.
- Expertise and skills
  - Negotiation experts, financial experts, legal experts
  - Policy oversight of the experts (experts do not necessarily view the big picture as they focus on the functional expertise).
- A well-worked-out sales plan
  - Set up a separate agency to oversee, supervise and implement, possibly reporting directly to the highest levels of the government
  - Consider pros and cons of different approaches (e.g., auctions, direct sales)
  - Consider societal impacts (e.g., deprivation of some, enrichment of others)
  - Establish contractual sales terms as well as buyer commitments
    - Should require a proposed business plan from the purchaser
    - Should provide for default on provisions of sales agreement commitments (failure to meet conditions should even result in return of privatized property)
    - Need to know true identity of buyer and the source of funds
    - Where appropriate, domestic purchasers should be encouraged (e.g., special loans, management and skill support).

*Source*: Jenik Radon.

but this can adversely affect enterprise performance, if the goals and the relative priority among them are left unclear. Therefore, each SOE should have clear goals, with explicit weights given to each goal. It would also be helpful to minimize the number of goals and provide guidelines for reconciling potentially contradictory goals.

The second important element of organizational reform involves improving the quality of information regarding SOE performance and enhancing the ability of the monitoring agency to process and act on that information. In some countries, the agencies that supervise SOEs lack even the most basic information (e.g., balance sheets). Therefore, it is vital that such information be generated, and clear lines and schedules of reporting be specified, adhered to and meaningfully used in order to monitor and improve performance without the government engaging in external micro-management. At the same time, the supervisory authorities' ability to obtain, process and effectively use information should be improved. Making more information available, without increasing the ability to process and utilize it, is of little use.

Third, the incentive systems for those who work for SOEs need to be improved. A system of clear and effective incentives should be designed to reward the managers and employees for improvements in efficiency, productivity and consumer satisfaction (see box 10). However, "incentives" here should not necessarily be narrowly interpreted as meaning individual materialistic incentives. They should include various types of non-materialistic and non-individualistic motives (see above).

Fourth, the establishment of a single, competently staffed agency dedicated to SOE supervision could also improve monitoring. In some countries, SOEs are monitored by multiple agencies. In practice, this can often mean that they are not meaningfully supervised by any agency. Alternatively, it can put an unreasonable demand on the SOE managers by subjecting them to almost constant inspection (see the case of the Republic of Korea in box 10). Consolidation of monitoring responsibilities into a single agency could increase monitoring efficiency either by making it impossible for the agency to "pass the buck" or by liberating the SOE mangers from excessive inspection. However, in consolidating the monitoring responsibilities, it is necessary to ensure that there are adequate checks and balances on such an all-powerful agency.

Fifth, reducing the number of SOEs may also help improve the monitoring of SOEs, given that the government only has a limited ability to monitor and reform SOEs. Liquidations, mergers and even privatization of some less essential SOEs (say, tourist hotels) may be helpful in improving the performance of other, more essential, SOEs (say, water and gas companies) by releasing the government's monitoring and reforming resources.

## Increasing competition

Beyond organizational reforms, increasing competition can be important in improving SOE performance. SOEs are often in activities where there is a natural monopoly, and increasing competition is either impossible or socially unproductive. However, there are cases when competitive pressure can be increased with positive results.

Indeed, in many countries, SOEs compete vigorously with private sector firms in activities that are not natural monopolies (see box 2). For example, in France, Renault, which was State-owned until 1996, faced direct competition from the private firm Peugeot as well as from foreign producers. Even when they were virtual monopolies in their domestic markets because of trade protection and subsidies, SOEs like EMBRAER and POSCO were required to export and therefore had to compete internationally.

Even SOEs in natural monopolies can be given some competitive stimulus because all products and services are at least partially substitutable. For example, during

**Box 10.    Organizational reform of the SOE sector:
the case of the Republic of Korea**

In 1984, the Government of the Republic of Korea reformed its system of evaluating the SOEs. It was meant to address the criticisms against the country's SOE sector, which had been performing well on the whole but still could be improved. The thrusts of this reform were more managerial autonomy, an improved performance evaluation system and a better incentive structure.

To provide more managerial autonomy, Government control over budget, procurement and personnel management was reduced. For example, previously all procurements for SOEs had to be made through the Office of Supply, but under the new provision the central executive officer of an SOE had an option to purchase from outside sources directly or to commission the purchase to the Office of Supply. To eliminate political influences in the managerial appointment, the new system banned appointing outsiders for senior executive positions.

Another change was concerning inspection. Previously, the Government had monitored the SOEs very tightly through various audits and inspections conducted by the Board of Audit and Inspection and the relevant ministries. As a result, an enormous amount of time and energy of SOE managerial staff were spent in preparing for such inspections. For example, the Korean Electricity Company underwent eight Government inspections, lasting for 108 days, in 1981 alone. Under the new system, the Board of Audit and Inspection was authorized as the sole inspection agency for the SOEs, thus lessening the burden of inspection both on the side of the ministries and on the side of the SOE managers.

The reform also introduced a new evaluation system, to which bonus payments for the employees of the enterprise were linked. The performance was evaluated with multiple criteria, including both quantitative measures (70 per cent weight) like private profitability, public profitability and productivity, on the one hand, and qualitative measures (30 per cent weight) like R&D expenditure, long-term corporate planning, organizational improvements, product quality, improvement in the managerial system. And the profitability measure chosen was pre-tax, pre-interest payment profit, reflecting the idea that essentially non-value-adding activities like tax-saving and loan recruitments, although not actively discouraged, should not enter performance evaluation.

After the reform, there were noticeable changes in managerial attitude, which lead to a universal adoption of long-term corporate planning, which not all SOEs had been practicing before the reform. Operating profit was up 50 per cent in 1984 and up 20 per cent in 1985. The R&D/sales ratio increased from 1.0 per cent to 1.2 per cent between 1984 and 1985. There were also reports of noticeable improvements in product (goods and services) quality.

*Source*: Chang and Singh, 1993.

the 1980s, the State-owned railway of Britain faced rather intense partial competition from privately owned bus companies in some market segments.

Competition does not always have to come from the private sector. Where feasible, competition can be increased by setting up another SOE. In 1991, the Republic of Korea set up a new SOE, Dacom, specializing in international calls, whose competition with the existing dominant telephone SOE, Korea Telecom, greatly contributed to increasing efficiency and service quality throughout the 1990s.

In theory, it is also possible to "simulate" competition by artificially dividing up a natural monopoly industry into regional units and reward/punish them according to their relative performances. This may be accompanied by privatization, as in the case of the British railway system, but it can be done under State ownership.[12] This method, known as "yardstick competition", unfortunately does not work very well, especially in developing countries where the regulators are not fully capable of administering complicated performance-measurement formulas. Moreover, in the case of network industries (e.g., railways), the potential benefit from simulated competition among regional units should be set against the increased costs of coordination failure due to the fragmentation of a network—as in the case of the disastrous failure of the British railway privatization programme which created dozens of regional operators who, in fact, competed very little, if at all.

### Political and administrative reforms

In some countries, SOEs are used as a mechanism to address problems that could have been better addressed by other means, because the "first best" solutions are politically difficult to implement. In such cases, it may be desirable, although certainly not easy, to make it possible to go for the "first best" policies through political and concomitant institutional reform.

For example, SOEs may be instructed to retain unnecessary workers despite making losses, because the government does not have an unemployment insurance programme nor can it create more "productive" jobs through public works programmes. In this case, a better solution would be to create a political environment where the government does not have to worry about generating "fictitious" employment because it has good unemployment insurance and public works programmes. Setting up these programmes, however, may need political reforms, because they require a political consensus for higher taxes and government deficit spending (when necessary).

To be effective, political reforms must be accompanied by administrative reforms. Unless the bureaucrats monitoring the SOEs are competent in doing their job, creating the political space for them is not going to produce results.

Administrative reform requires a number of different elements. Improving the relative pay of civil servants will allow the government to recruit better people and also reduce corruption. Civil servant training also needs to be improved, although the training required is more of a generalist kind, rather than technical training in economics (see box 11). A campaign to inculcate a public service ethos into civil serv-

---

12 A natural question that arises at this point is whether the government privatize a monopoly before breaking it up. This is sometimes done in the belief that the government will receive more money (part of the monopoly rents). However, it is a costly (to the economy) way of getting revenue. Privatizing before the monopoly is broken up results in a special interest to preserve the monopoly. Moreover, the government often receives little in return, since the bidder attaches considerable risk to the monopoly being broken up in the future, and so will highly discount the future monopoly profits. The author thanks Joseph Stiglitz for raising this important point.

### Box 11.    Improving the quality of the economic bureaucracy

A high-quality economic bureaucracy is necessary for the success of economic policy, including the management of SOEs and the management of natural resource rents. Indeed, a good economic bureaucracy is required for good post-privatization regulation; without such regulation, privatization cannot succeed either.

A good economic bureaucracy cannot be built overnight, but it is possible to build one within a relatively short span of time, if there is political will and economic investment. For example, the quality of the bureaucracy of the Republic of Korea was so poor that, until the late 1960s, bureaucrats of the Republic of Korea were sent to Pakistan and the Philippines for extra training! However, thanks to continuous administrative reform and investment in bureaucratic training, it came to be considered among the best in the developing world by the early 1980s.

What makes for a high-quality economic bureaucracy? In popular perception, a high-quality economic bureaucracy is one staffed with people with advanced training in economics or management. However, the East Asian countries provide some interesting, if not necessarily generalizable, examples that suggest that this may not be the case.

Most of the elite economic bureaucrats in Japan have been lawyers by training. The Republic of Korea also has had a high proportion of lawyers running the economic bureaucracy. In Taiwan PoC and China today, the elite economic bureaucrats have been mostly engineers by training. These lawyers and engineers did acquire some training in economics, but the economics training was often of the "wrong" kind until the 1980s. For example, until the 1980s, Marxists dominated Japanese economics faculties, and Schumpeter and List were widely taught. Above all, until recently, the economics training in these countries was not of such high quality, going by international standards. The fact that the bureaucracy in India, a country with arguably among the best economics training in the world, has not been equally successful in guiding its economy also suggests that specialized training in economics may not be so crucial to the creation of a high-quality economic bureaucracy.

In the end, and somewhat counter-intuitively, the competence needed for good economic bureaucrats seems to be that of a generalist, rather than that of an economist in the conventional sense, as Johnson, 1982, pointed out in his classic work on Japan. This suggests that the least developed countries intent on developing a good economic bureaucracy should put more emphasis in recruiting people of generally high calibre, rather than looking for specialists in economics and other related subjects.

*Source*: Chang, 2004a; Johnson, 1982.

ants will be useful, if it is accompanied by a decent pay scale: many civil servants are willing to work for the good of the nation without parity with private sector pay, but there is a limit to what their good intentions can bear or afford.

All this takes time, but we do not need to believe in the currently popular view that developing country governments with poor administrative capabilities should not try to do anything "difficult". A poor country does not need to, indeed cannot, start its economic development with a fully formed economic bureaucracy. More importantly, bureaucratic capabilities can be increased within a relatively short period of time (see box 12).

## Box 12.   What makes a good SOE?

The theories of enterprise performance and real life examples discussed above allow us to state principles that are likely to lead to successful SOEs. Many of these principles also apply to running successful private firms.

**At the enterprise level,**

- Clearly define non-profit objectives
  - There is nothing wrong with SOEs having non-profit objectives, such as guaranteeing universal access to basic social services. Indeed, in many cases these are their raison d'être. However, these objectives need to be clearly defined and their trade-offs with profit objectives clarified.
- Given the non-profit objectives, establish a management strategy that is profit-oriented but from a long-term point of view.
  - Once the trade-off with non-profit objectives is made clear, management strategy should focus on running a profitable enterprise, given the constraints. However, in developing countries, where long-term investment in capability building is crucial, it is important that profitability is defined from a long-term point of view.
- Adopt the latest possible technologies
  - As seen in the case of POSCO (box 2), adopt the latest possible technologies, provided that there are technological capabilities to cope with them (with appropriate invesment in enhancing technological capabilities).
- If in the tradable sector, promote exports
  - Exports reduce costs by allowing longer production runs, thus spreading the costs of product development and of dedicated machinery, and higher capacity utilization. Exports also expose firms to higher product standards. Exports should be promoted whenever feasible, even though it should be combined with protection and subsidies in the beginning.
- Invest in human resources
  - Ultimately, good enterprises require good people to run them. Invest in training at all levels, from the managers and research scientists down to the level of ordinary workers.
- Improve the incentive system
  - Good work should be rewarded and poor performance punished. However, the rewards need not be individually oriented material rewards. Group incentives are sometimes better, while non-material benefits matter.

**At the level of the government,**

- Create a dedicated supervisory agency if possible
  - Create a dedicated agency to supervise the SOEs, if possible. Often the supervisory responsibility for SOEs is diffused across many ministries and other government agencies, resulting either in neglect or, conversely, supervision overload.
- Reduce the number of SOEs when appropriate
  - Reducing the number of SOEs through liquidation, mergers or even privatization of some non-essential SOEs may reduce the demand on monitoring resources.
- Improve information
  - Establish a good accounting system. Improve the flow of information to the supervisory agencies by requiring regular and detailed reporting by the SOEs.

**Box 12.   What makes a good SOE?** (*continued*)

- Increase competition where feasible
    - Many SOEs operate in natural monopolies, where increasing competition is not feasible. However, competition can be increased outside those industries by allowing new entries of private firms and SOEs.
- Avoid political appointments to managerial positions
    - Political appointments tend to harm performance. Although the case of POSCO (box 2) shows that political appointees can be good mangers, too, this is an exception to the rule.
- Reform politics so that SOEs do not need to take on non-essential functions
    - SOEs are sometimes used as a mechanism to address problems better addressed by other means, which are unavailable for political reasons. Political reforms can lead to the creation of such means (e.g., public works programme or unemployment insurance) releasing the SOEs from the unnecessary burden.
- Improve the quality of the economic bureaucracy
    - Without a competent economic bureaucracy, creating the necessary political space is useless. The government should improve pay, invest in training and encourage the public service ethic of the economic bureaucrats (see box 11).

## Managing natural resource rents

Most people agree that non-renewable, mainly mineral, natural resources should be treated differently from other sources of wealth (see box 13). This is because such resources are not created by the efforts of those who own the land that produces them. Moreover, their extraction will render them unavailable to others, including later generations.[13] This is why many mineral resources are publicly owned in most countries, which means that countries with larger mineral resources tend to have larger SOE sectors. Additional material on, especially non-renewable, natural resource management and development can be found in the annex I.

Fewer people take the same view on renewable natural resources, but in most countries exploitation of certain renewable resources, e.g., forestry or fisheries, is publicly regulated for reasons of sustainability, while in others at least parts of such resources are publicly owned. Therefore, the management of natural resources shares certain important characteristics with the management of SOEs.

---

13  In order to take this problem into account, attempts have been made to construct "Green GDP". The intuition is that, "[j]ust as a firm's accounting frameworks take into account depreciation of its assets, a country's accounting framework should take into account depletion of its natural resources and deterioration of its environment. Just as a firm's accounting frameworks consider assets and liabilities, so should a country's, noting whether there are increases in liabilities. A country that sells off its natural resources, privatises its oil company, and borrows against future revenues, may experience a consumption binge that raises GDP, but the accounting framework shows that the country has actually become poorer." (Stiglitz, 2005).

**Box 13.   What makes natural resources different?**

Natural resources, especially minerals and energy,
- Are depleteable, non-renewable assets
  - Therefore need to be compensated for the asset as such, taking account of
    - Changes in value over time due to market conditions
    - "Replacement" cost of its value, as the resource itself cannot be replaced
- Are location specific
- Are permanent assets, i.e., they take a relatively long time to develop.

In many nations natural resources belong to the State by law
- Private property owners do not have rights to them simply by the fortuitous fact that such resources are located beneath their property.
- Mere location of a natural resource within a nation can make a nation wealthy.

The development of natural resources has a wide-ranging impact
- Natural resource development does not happen in isolation
  - It impacts on local communities, neighbouring communities and the nation
    - Impacts can be both positive and negative
    - Impacts are social, including health and labour, environmental and political
      ◊ Determining the impacts is critical
    - Extensive externalities
      ◊ If the externalities and their costs are not defined, hence not covered by the development, the true cost of development is being subsidized
  - Recommendation:
    - Have a developer commit to defining the externalities (by what they are and what they are not) and fully guarantee the costs thereof
    - They are the experts and they should know.

*Source*: Jenik Radon.

## Appropriating natural resource rents

The challenge of managing renewable resources is even greater than in the case of non-renewable resources. In the case of renewable resources, good management can make the difference between depletion and sustainability, whereas not even the best management can make non-renewable resources last forever.

However, even in the case of non-renewable resources, outcomes can be very different, depending on policies adopted in relation to the mode of resource rent appropriation, management of price volatility, and the management of the so-called "Dutch disease".[14]

---

14   "Dutch disease" refers to a situation where the sudden discovery and/or increase in the price or rate of extraction of a natural resource leads to increased export earnings, which then leads to the appreciation of the local currency, weakening the export competitiveness of other products.

**Box 14.   Designing and selling contracts
              for natural resource exploration**

Designing and selling the rights to exploit natural resources is not a simple matter. Depending on how the rights are designed and sold, the benefits a country derives from the sale could be markedly different.

In terms of contract design, it is crucial that the contract is transparent so that it reduces the chance of corruption. Most important is to make companies "publish what they pay", although making transparent the amount produced and the use of the received funds is also important. The home governments of natural resource companies can also help by allowing only published payments to be tax deductible.

In terms of selling the rights, selling large rights in quick succession or allowing one firm to come in ahead of others should be avoided. The first course of action is likely to reduce prices progressively in subsequent sales, as even the largest firms have limited appetite for risk. The second course of action gives the first firm informational advantages in subsequent auctions, thus making the others bid less in the knowledge that, if they beat the first firm in the auction, it is because they bid too much.

Different forms of auction produce different results. Bonus bidding, where the company willing to pay the largest up front bonus wins the contract, will discourage bidders because they have to bid without having full knowledge of the cost of production. Bonus bidding is especially of concern in developing countries, where there is more risk of expropriation, or of future governments changing the terms of the contract. It is also important to estimate the implied interest rate of bonus payments, as it is rather like a loan. In contrast, royalty bidding, where competitors bid on the fraction of revenue (royalties) they give to the government, carries less risk and generates more competition and therefore more revenue for the government.

*Source*: Stiglitz, 2005.

The option most frequently recommended to developing country governments in relation to natural resource rent appropriation is to sell off exploitation rights and to live off the proceeds that accrue. Those who advocate this view emphasize that developing countries lack the ability to extract the resources efficiently and to manage the resulting rents prudently.

This option may be sensible in theory, especially in the short run, but in practice it requires two critical conditions if the potential benefit is to be realized. First, the developing country government should design and sell the contracts for natural resource exploitation in the right way. Second, there should be no corruption involved in the rights sales process or in the process of revenue appropriation. These conditions are often absent in developing countries (see box 14 on how these conditions may be improved).

More importantly, this is not a very good option in the longer run. Contrary to the popular claim of a "resource curse",[15] renewable and non-renewable natural

---

15   "Resource curse" refers to the fact that many resource-rich countries have experienced low
     growth and unequal income distribution, despite the fact that abundant resources should

resources can create numerous forward and backward linkages, and thus become engines of growth. For example, forestry resources can create forward linkages into paper and furniture, and backward linkages into logging machinery and earth-moving equipment. In turn, the furniture industry can create backward linkages into metalworking (e.g., nails, hinges) and chemicals (e.g., paint).

That natural resources do not have to be a "curse" is demonstrated by the examples of several developed countries that have turned their resource endowments to their advantage. Examples include the United States (numerous minerals, forestry, fisheries), Canada (numerous minerals, forestry, fisheries), Australia (numerous minerals), Sweden (iron ore, forestry), Finland (forestry) and Norway (oil and gas). Even in the developing world, there are countries like Malaysia (forestry, tin, oil and gas), Indonesia (oil and gas) and Botswana (diamonds) that have managed their natural resources rather well and not allow them to become "curses".

Given the potential forward and backward linkages that natural resources can create and contribute to economic development, a developing country government should find ways to create national capabilities to exploit natural resources productively in the long run. For example, because foreign oil companies did not want to transfer key technologies related to drilling for or refining of oil to the host nation, the Brazilian Government has invested heavily and successfully to develop such capabilities through an SOE, Petrobras.

Even if it decides to sell off the exploitation rights, care should be taken to find the right forms of contracts—licenses, joint venture, production-sharing arrangements (for the respective merits and problems of these forms, see Radon, 2005). In addition, the rights should be made renewable after a relatively short period of time (10 or 20 years), so that the situation can be reviewed in light of the development of national capabilities, whose development trajectories are difficult to predict with precision. Moreover, in the event of award or sale of rights to a foreign company, the sales process and the resulting contracts should be designed to effect a transfer of technological, managerial or even production capabilities by the foreign company. This may be achieved through a joint-venture agreement with a national, usually public, company and/or through explicit requirements for various types of capability transfers, e.g., transfer of technologies, managerial training and worker training, so that the country is better able to exploit the resources with its own capabilities in the future, if it so chooses.

## Investing the rents

More important, especially in the long run, than the method of rent appropriation is the way the rent is invested. In this regard, the following quote from Joseph Stiglitz, 2003*b*, is highly instructive.

---

help growth and also enable countries to redistribute income without having to impose distortionary taxes (thus possibly lowering growth). For a quick, user-friendly introduction to the issues surrounding the "resource curse", see Stiglitz, 2005.

"One can think of natural resources, oil, as a capital good. It is a capital good. It is a capital good that is below the ground. And what you're doing when you sell oil is taking the wealth of the country and moving it from below the ground to above the ground. Now as you move it from below the ground to above the ground, the question is whether the country is wealthier or poorer as a result. The answer depends on what you do with that money. If you just spend it on consumption, then you are poorer. You had wealth and you no longer have that wealth—that wealth has disappeared. If you take it from below the ground and bring it above the ground and you convert that oil into roads, or capital goods, then you could become wealthier, if those capital goods that you replaced the oil with are highly productive. It is like a portfolio allocation problem: you covert from one form of capital to another form of capital and if in that process you make it into a more productive form of capital, you're wealthier."

## Investing in financial assets

The easiest option in relation to investment of natural resource rents is to invest them in financial assets, probably through a dedicated fund, and to live off the returns from them (see box 15). Norway's Petroleum Fund (now called the Government Pension

### Box 15.  National resource funds

A good natural resource fund should have the following features:

- Clear purpose
  - Should be a combination of the short and long term
  - Should be set forth in statutes, possibly even anchored in the constitution with barriers to easy modification, such as requiring a citizen referendum
  - Should be established as a trust
- Clear policy and strategy on the use of funds specifying the time perspective and the types of uses
- Supervision by an independent board, made up of persons appointed by the executive, legislature and civil society, with staggered terms, not overlapping with national or local elections, and with its structure anchored in law
- Expertise to advise on economic impact
- Skilled fund managers
- Transparency, with publication of accounts and independent audit.

A good natural resource fund should not be:

- An extension of the budget, although it can be a supplement to the budget if prescribed by clear rules
- A petty cash machine for government, including executive
- A substitute for a normal tax regime.

Best practice examples of fund management are Norway (box 14), Chile, Alaska (United States) and Alberta (Canada).

*Source*: Jenik Radon.

Fund) is the best-known example of this kind (see box 16). Given the volatile nature of natural resource prices, these funds may also be used by countries as "stabilization funds" that allow them to smooth their income and expenditure.

Especially when the resource rents have suddenly increased, investment in foreign financial assets is an attractive option in the short run for two reasons. First, an economy's absorptive capacity cannot be increased quickly, so the rents are likely to be invested in low-yielding projects. Moreover, keeping the money outside the country will help reduce the pressure for currency appreciation, thus alleviating the "Dutch disease".

However, the safe financial assets (e.g., United States Treasury bonds) are not likely to give high returns, while investing in high-risk financial assets, especially in foreign financial markets, is the last thing a developing country should do, especially considering their lack of financial expertise. More importantly, financial investments are unlikely to enhance the productive capabilities of the national economy. This may not be a huge problem for an advanced economy like Norway, but it is a serious one for developing countries, where investments in capability building are still necessary.

To sum up, investment in financial assets is often the "safest" option with regards to the management of natural resource rents. However, in the long run, developing countries need to invest in building productive capabilities. If so, the option

---

**Box 16.   The Petroleum Fund of Norway**

In 1990, Norway established the Petroleum Fund (oljefondet)—called the Government Pension Fund (Statens pensjonsfond) since January 2006—in order to invest parts of the large surplus generated by the oil sector, mainly taxes of companies but also payments for licenses to explore. It was set up to counter the effects of the forthcoming decline in income and to smooth out the disrupting effects of highly fluctuating oil prices. It is administered by the Norwegian Central Bank.

The Fund has rightly maintained a relatively conservative investment strategy. Its official website states its objective as "high return subject to moderate risk in order to contribute to safeguarding the basis of future welfare, including national pensions". Consequently, it was only in 1998 that the fund was allowed to invest in equity (but only up to 50 per cent of its portfolio). It was not until 2002 that it was allowed to invest in non-governmental guaranteed bonds.

Since 2004, the Fund has acted under strict ethical guidelines. As a result, on 5 January 2006, arms-related companies such as Boeing, Northrop Grumman and Honeywell International BAE Systems were removed from its portfolio. In June 2006, WalMart was similarly removed from its portfolio for ethical reasons.

It is predicted that revenues from the petroleum sector, at over NOK 1.48 trillion (US$ 245 billion), is now at its peak and will decline over the next decades. It is currently similar in size to the California public employees pension fund (CalPERS), the largest public pension fund in the United States.

*Source*: Norwegian Central Bank website (http://www.norgesbank.no/nbim/pension_fund/); wikipedia online encyclopedia (http://en.wikipedia.org/wiki/The_Petroleum_Fund_of_Norway).

of investing in financial assets should mainly be used as a short-term measure when faced with a large and sudden increase in resource rents.

### Investing in general capability building

Natural resource rents can be invested in building the "general" capabilities of the economy. For example, they could be invested in improving health, basic education or general physical infrastructure, thereby enhancing overall capabilities in the economy, rather than those of specific industries.

Investing in general capabilities is likely to be a politically safe option, as few would object to such investment at least in theory. For the poorer developing countries, which need more investment in basic capabilities, it is probably also an economically necessary option as well. However, it is a limiting strategy for most developing countries that already have established much of those general capabilities. At their stages of development, they need more targeted investments in specific capabilities. As soon as we move beyond basic education or the most basic of the infrastructure, there is no such thing as investments in "general" capabilities. We do not educate engineers in abstract nor do we build roads in abstract; we have to decide whether we are going to train chemical engineers or electronic engineers, while we need to make up our minds as to whether the next highway will be built between the textile city and the port or between the forestry region and the port.[16]

Therefore, except in the poorest countries, only a small part of the natural resource rents should be devoted to investments in general capabilities, and the rest should be channeled to developing specific capabilities that are deemed necessary for economic upgrading for the future.

### Investing in related diversification

Another option is to invest the natural resource rents by diversifying into areas related to the natural resource bases. So, for example, Sweden successfully diversified from its forestry resources into paper-making, furniture, and then, into paper-making and furniture-making machinery, and eventually into high-quality furniture design and life-style services (as exemplified by the case of the famous flat-pack furniture company, IKEA). It has also successfully diversified from its iron ore deposits, into an iron and steel industry, and then to various steel-based products including ships, cars and armaments. As another example, Malaysia had spectacular success in diversify-

---

16  The contrast between "general" and "specific" capabilities is somewhat less severe in the case of human capabilities. Once, for example, a road is built, it is there and cannot be moved. However, if people initially invest in acquiring better learning capabilities ("learning to learn"), it may give them higher returns to their investment in subsequent investments in the acquisition of specific capabilities that they need in order to get a job. However, even with enhanced learning capabilities, there is only so much specific knowledge one person can learn in his/her lifetime, so the worker is likely to be locked into certain areas of knowledge, once he/she chooses his/her initial career.

ing from raw palm oil into refined palm oil, with moderate success in diversifying from rubber into tyres (see box 17 for details).

Related diversification is of course a "natural" choice that is also forward-looking. Some activities "naturally" lead to certain others, which either provide inputs to them or buy from them. Albert Hirschman's classic Linkage Approach and Wassily Leontief's Input-Output Approach are built on this very insight.

However, for most natural resources, the scope for related diversification is simply limited—there is only so much one can diversify from coffee or fish. There are some resources that have much greater potential for related diversification—iron ore, forestry or oil. However, even for them, at least some degree of unrelated diversification is needed, if related diversification is to proceed to the top of the value chain. For example, iron ore is "related" to the automobile industry, which uses a lot of steel plates, but the development of the automobile industry requires many other industries that are "unrelated" to iron ore (e.g., electronics, glass, rubber and paint, just to name a few). Therefore, even those natural resources with a high potential for related diversification are likely to be stuck at low value-added activities, unless those unrelated industries are also developed.

While the potential for related diversification should be exploited to the full, in the longer run there has to be a shift to unrelated diversification into technologically dynamic areas. Moreover, unrelated diversification is often necessary to maximize the scope for related diversification.

### Box 17.   Resource-based diversification: the Malaysian case

Under British colonial rule, Malaysia was a major producer of tin and rubber. After independence in 1957, Malaysia attempted to diversify away from tin and rubber but even as late as 1970 the two commodities still accounted for nearly 60 per cent of the country's exports.

From the 1970s, the Government encouraged diversification from tin and rubber. "Horizontal" diversification into other primary commodities was tried. For example, palm oil and cocoa production was encouraged with crop-specific subsidies. Exports of hardwoods and newly discovered oil and gas also grew. "Vertical" diversification was also encouraged, especially from rubber and palm oil.

Malaysia's attempt to diversify from rubber into tyre manufacturing was not very effective because it failed to demand export success in return for the protection granted to (foreign-owned) tyre manufacturers. This contrasts with the export success of the tyre industry of the Republic of Korea, a country that produces neither rubber nor oil (the raw material for synthetic rubber). The Republic of Korea's export success in tyres was possible because tough export requirements on the protected (domestically owned) tyre manufacturers made them attain scale economies quickly.

In contrast to the tyre industry, Malaysia has had spectacular success in diversifying from crude palm oil into refined palm oil by imposing a higher export duty on crude palm oil in the mid-1970s, thus attracting massive investments in palm-oil refining capacity. Since the mid-1980s, Malaysia has been the world leader in palm oil refining technology.

*Source:* Jomo and Rock, 1998.

### Investing in unrelated diversification

Natural resource rents also need to be invested in "unrelated diversification". There is only so much related diversification and upgrading that one can do even for a very widely used resource like wood or iron ore, as we pointed out above. Therefore, in order to achieve sustainable long-term development, countries need to use their natural resource rents in order to diversify into unrelated industries that are the most technologically dynamic.

Nokia, the Finnish company famous for mobile phones, offers the best example of a successful unrelated diversification out of natural resources (see box 18 for further details). Nokia started as a logging company, but later diversified into rubber, electric cables and telephone exchanges, and more recently into electronics and mobile telecommunications. Interestingly it took the electronics company of the Nokia group 17 years before it made any profit, suggesting that unrelated diversification often involves a long gestation period.[17]

Unrelated diversification is of course the most difficult option, with a long gestation period. It also needs a good long-range industrial planning, which may be difficult to manage for the poorest developing countries that lack administrative capabilities, although such capabilities can be built relatively quickly, contrary to the conventional wisdom (see box 11 above).

However, as we can see from the Nokia example, unrelated diversification into technologically dynamic industries can bring the highest return, albeit after a long gestation period. Therefore, efforts should be made to move away from the natural–resource–based industries in the long run through unrelated diversification. However, given its long gestation period, it is necessary in the short- to medium-run to supplement this option with other options that yield more immediate returns.

### Choosing the right policy mix

Investments of natural resource rents in (related or unrelated) diversification should be based on a coherent development strategy. Its execution may be done through SOEs (in which case, the points made previously need to be heeded) or by using the rents to provide subsidies (directly or indirectly through tariffs and other forms of trade protection) to private sector firms setting up in new industries (for this, see the Policy Notes on investment and technology policy in this series).

The appropriate mix of the different strategies for using resource rents—financial investment, investment in general capability building, investment in related diversification, investment in unrelated diversification—will differ across countries, but it is likely to involve all four options, with their relative importance varying

---

17  Our emphasis on the long-term perspective should not be interpreted as saying that, given sufficient time, everything will succeed, and therefore that we can back any venture. It is important to know when to accept failure and cut losses. There is no clear rule on this, but at least after the first few years of "teething", one would expect a venture to show a trend improvement in performance if it is to justify continued support.

## Box 18.    From logging to mobile phones: the story of Nokia

The Finnish company, Nokia, is today known as the maker of ultramodern mobile phones. However, it was founded as a logging company in 1865.

The shape of the modern Nokia group started emerging when Finnish Rubber Works Ltd. (founded in 1898) bought the majority shares in Nokia in 1918 and in Finnish Cable Works (founded in 1912) in 1922. Finally in 1967 the three companies were merged to form Nokia Corporation. Some Finnish observers summarize the nature of the merger by saying that the name of the merged company (Oy Nokia Ab) came from wood processing, the management from the cable factory and the money from the rubber industry.

Nokia's electronic business, whose mobile phone business forms the core of the company's business today, was set up in 1960. Even until 1967, when the merger between Nokia, FRW and FCW took place, electronics generated only 3 per cent of Nokia group's net sales. The electronics arm lost money for the first 17 years, making its first profit only in 1977.

The world's first international cellular mobile telephone network, NMT, was introduced in Scandinavia in 1981 and Nokia made the first car phones for it. Nokia produced the original hand-portable phone in 1987. Riding on this wave, Nokia rapidly expanded during the 1980s by acquiring a series of electronics and telecommunications companies in Finland, Germany, Sweden and France. Since the 1990s, Nokia's leading business has been mobile phones.

By the 1990s, Nokia became the leader in the mobile telecommunications revolution and an icon of globalization. The facts that Finland used to classify all firms with more than 20 per cent foreign ownership as "dangerous" until 1987 or that its electronics arm had played havoc with the sacred "shareholder value" by making losses for the first 17 years were conveniently forgotten by the globalization enthusiasts.

*Sources*: Steinbock, 2001; Chang, 2004*b*; Nokia official website: http://www.nokia.com/ link?cid=EDITORIAL_3913.

across countries and changing over time, even in the same country. The pros and cons for each option and the recommended policy actions in relation to each option are summarized in box 19.

For example, in the very early stage of development, financial investment and investment in general capability building may be more important, while the other two routes will become more important as the economy develops. Similarly, the relative importance of related and unrelated diversifications may alternate, as countries may first need unrelated diversification to jump to a new stage, while a period of consolidation of new industries through related diversification may be necessary after it enters a new industry.

## The political economy of natural resource rents management

One major concern regarding the management of natural resources is the apparently greater susceptibility of natural resources to corruption.

Some have argued that mineral resources are usually concentrated in their natural locations (so-called "point resources") and therefore easy to "steal" or "loot" (i.e., have high "lootability"). They argue that high lootability makes the prevention of

## Box 19.   Options for natural resource management

### Option 1.   Sell off the exploitation rights

*Pros:*

- May be the only option if the country lacks productive capacities in the extreme.

*Cons:*

- Weak administrative capacities make it difficult to conclude a good deal with foreign investors.
- Likely to create more room for corruption.
- Low return in the long run.

*Recommended policy actions:*

- The sales process should be transparent in order to prevent corruption.
- Contracts should be made renewable after a relatively short period (say, 10 years) so that they can be re-negotiated according to the changes in the country's capabilities.
- Contracts should be designed in order to ensure capability transfers.

### Option 2.   Invest in financial assets

*Pros:*

- Especially good option when rents have suddenly increased, as it can get around the problem of the lack of absorptive capacity and may also mitigate "Dutch disease".

*Cons:*

- The safe assets are not likely to give high returns, while investing in high-risk financial assets is the last thing a developing country should do.
- Does not enhance the productive capabilities of the national economy.

*Recommended policy actions:*

- Should be used as a short-term measure when faced with a large and sudden increase in resource rents.

### Option 3.   Invest in general capability building

*Pros:*

- Likely to be a politically safe option.
- For the poorer developing countries, it is probably an economically necessary option as well.

*Cons:*

- A limiting strategy for most developing countries that have already established much of those general capabilities.

*Recommended policy actions:*

- Except in the poorest countries, only a small part of the resource rents may be devoted to this option. The rest should be channeled to developing more industry-specific capabilities.

### Option 4.   Invest in related diversification

*Pros:*

- A "natural" choice that is also forward-looking.

*Cons:*
- For many natural resources, the potential for related diversification is limited (e.g., coffee).
- Even those few resources with much greater potential for related diversification—iron ore, forestry or oil—may become stuck at low value-added activities, unless complemented by unrelated diversification.

*Recommended policy actions:*
- The potential for related diversification should be exploited to the full.
- Needs careful coordination with unrelated diversification to maximize the scope.
- In the longer run, a shift to unrelated diversification into technologically dynamic areas is necessary.

**Option 5.  Invest in unrelated diversification**

*Pros:*
- The most productive strategy in the long run, if diversified into the technologically most dynamic industries.

*Cons:*
- Most difficult to manage.
- Long gestation period.

*Recommended policy actions:*
- This should be the ultimate goal, but given the long gestation period, it is necessary to combine it with other options that yield more immediate returns.

corruption and of private attempts at rent-capture (through politics and violence) much more difficult. In contrast, they point out, agricultural resources—say, coffee or cocoa—tend to be more dispersed (so-called "diffuse resources"), requiring sustained work to generate income, making looting more difficult.

While there is some truth to this argument, we should not take the natural characteristics of resources as a given. Depending on the political and administrative capabilities of the State, agricultural resources can also be concentrated to a very high degree, while a government made up of honest people and well monitored by civil society may make looting of even very geographically concentrated resources difficult. Nature is not destiny.

African marketing boards are probably the best-known mechanism used to concentrate agricultural resources. Less well known but equally important is the fact that countries like Taiwan Province of China and the Republic of Korea were able almost completely to concentrate their rice output. This was achieved through mandatory sale of rice to the State-controlled Agricultural Cooperative, whose control over the supply of chemical fertilizers and the irrigation system made it virtually impossible for farmers to "opt out". In contrast, through the Petroleum Fund and the welfare State within a "clean" political system, Norway has been able to distribute its oil rents equitably (see box 14).

Thus, lootability is more a consequence of politics and institutions than an immutable natural characteristic of the natural resource concerned. There is nothing inevitable about the so-called "resource curse". If there is nothing pre-destined about the lootability of particular resources and the likelihood of corruption surrounding them, it becomes possible to think of ways to design a natural resource rent management system that is less corrupt, with more equitable and sustainable consequences.

The first thing to do is to design a system of allocating the rights to exploit natural resources that is less prone to corruption. This requires that the system be transparent and simple, so that outsiders can easily monitor it. It would be better if the system is subject to relatively frequent review, so that wrong decisions can be promptly corrected.

At the same time, it is a good idea to create a transparent single fund for resource rents, rather than leaving them diffused in lots of different little pots. This will make it easier to monitor the use of such rents, thereby ensuring its developmental and equitable deployment, as well as preventing abuse.

With a reasonable degree of transparency in the system and proper auditing as well as accountability mechanisms, a single fund will be much easier to monitor. This can be enhanced by consolidating monitoring responsibilities in a single supervisory agency, as discussed above in relation to SOE management.

Preventing abuse, corruption and fraud is not easy. Joseph Stiglitz, 2003*b*, has pointed out that cheating on resource rents is widespread and not easy to detect, even in countries like the United States. However, strenuous effort must be made to ensure that wealth belonging to everyone, including future generations, in the country is not appropriated by a small minority.

# Annexes

## Annex I.    Natural resource management
            and development

In view of the apparent difficulties with natural resource management and development, this annex provides some guidance on these matters, focusing particularly on non-renewable resources.

---

**Annex box 1.    Natural resource SOEs**

Natural resource SOEs are, or should be, managers and trustees of a valuable national non-renewable asset.

However, natural resource SOEs are risky ventures, subject to outright failure for reasons of:
- heavy exploration and development costs
- heavy capital investment
- market swings in commodity prices
- competitive pressures from other producers
- availability of experts and skilled services.

While natural resource SOEs do not themselves have to be the operators, they do have to be:
- national wealth creators/ transformers
- the supervisors or operational watchdogs
- the policy and strategic directors
- responsible to the nation and the impacted communities.

At the same time, it should be clearly recognized that the SOEs are not themselves the regulators, and therefore need to be regulated.

A natural resource SOE requires a sophisticated organization with:
- clear policy and plans addressing:
  - strategic, operational and commercial concerns
  - investment
  - technology concerns and management
  - social and environmental impact concerns
- skilled personnel
- ability to separate regulatory concerns, e.g., environment, health and safety, from the non-regulatory, e.g., commercial, ones.

Examples of well-run natural resource SOEs are Statoil of Norway and Saudi Aramco of Saudi Arabia.

*Source:* Jenik Radon.

## Annex box 2.  Managing the exploration and development of natural resources

The following is a list of some critical issues with regards to the exploration and development of natural resources.

1. Data/information
   - Need exploration data: this is costly
   - Need market data
     - E.g., what is the prospective market, profile, etc.

2. Exploration
   - Expensive, with risk of no commercial discovery.

3. Development
   - Expensive and long term by definition.

4. Negotiation: the key to pursuing exploration and development
   - Need "partners"
     - Whether as real partners, as service providers, etc.
   - Need to negotiate everything
     - All types of agreements: exploration, development, service, marketing
   - Negotiation is a skill
     - Not everyone can negotiate effectively
   - The devil is in the details
     - Outsourcing of certain responsibilities/tasks is unavoidable (engagement of experts)
       - Negotiation
       - Legal
       - Technical, including environmental, etc.
       - Financial
       - Remember: experts are expensive and often you get what you pay for
         ◊ Make sure experts are free of conflicts of interest, i.e., truly independent; find out who their clients are
   - Terms: compensation, operation, termination, etc.
     - Need compensation for the asset (i.e., the natural resource)
     - Different types of compensation
       - E.g., upfront fees, royalties, profit taxes, windfall profit taxes
         ◊ Industry finds it unacceptable but a windfall profit tax should be considered, e.g., tied into market prices
           ¤ All companies base investment decisions on an expected internal rate of return; excess returns are an unexpected bonanza
     - Regulatory issues
       - Should be set forth in statutes and regulations, not in agreements
         ◊ If the legal system is inadequate, refer to other legal systems
   - Type of agreements (not all will be done internally by SOE)

- Exploration, development, production
  - Production sharing
  - License
  - Joint venture
- Marketing, distribution
- Service
- Note: each form is different, has a different purpose and has different results
  - Remember: potential partners to such agreements are often multinational companies with extensive experience and knowledge, are financially strong and professionally staffed
    - ◊ Makes negotiation challenging
  - Each provision of an agreement must be negotiated
  - Service contracts are not popular with international companies as returns are too small
    - ◊ Challenge is to find companies willing to part with knowledge in return for service-type compensation
- Always make sure the ultimate parent company is contractually legally responsible, including through a guarantee
  - Accountability and responsibility stops only at the top and should not be limited to a subsidiary
  - Just because a provision is industry practice, does not make it right, fair or acceptable
    - ◊ Example: stabilization clauses which include provisions other than a fixed tax regime for a limited period of time
      - ¤ They make the present permanent
      - ¤ Limit the right of a nation to enact new legislation and regulation.

5. Supervision/management of operations
   - Exploration plans
   - Development plans
   - Termination and abandonment plans
   - Community/social impact studies/plans
   - Environmental impact studies/plans.

6. Access to capital
   - SOEs need to be able to borrow significant funds
   - Need to be able to give security.

*Source*: Jenik Radon.

## Annex 2.    The role of property rights
##                     in economic development*

There is great emphasis on the importance of property rights in recent orthodox discourse. The logic behind it is simple, but powerful.

It is argued that we have to give people the right to claim the fruits of their investments, to encourage them to invest and raise productivity. And in making such an argument, it is pointed out that such a right should be "private", because if something is collectively owned, no one would take care of it properly.

This idea is best expressed in the so-called "tragedy of the commons", where common grazing land with open access is over-grazed to everyone's detriment, because it is always in an individual's interest to let his/her cattle graze as much as possible, without regard to the sustainability of the grazing land.

The same logic is applied to SOEs, when it is argued that no citizen (as a principal) has the incentive to invest in monitoring the SOE managers (as his/her agents), because the gains from better management are shared by everyone, while the costs are borne by individuals.

However, there are numerous problems with this argument.

### The measurement problem

To begin with, unlike some other institutions (e.g., the bureaucracy or the fiscal system), the property rights system is a complex of a vast set of institutions—land law, urban planning law, tax law, inheritance law, contract law, company law, bankruptcy law, intellectual property rights law and customs regarding common property, to name only the most important ones.

And being made up of such diverse elements, it is almost impossible to "aggregate" these component institutions into a single institution called the property rights system.

Given the impossibility of aggregating all elements of a property rights system into a single measurable indicator, empirical studies tend to rely on subjective measures of the overall "quality" of the property rights system.

Many rely on surveys among (especially foreign) businessmen, "experts" (e.g., academics, chief economists of major banks and firms, etc.), or even the general public, asking them how they assess the business environment in general, and the quality of property rights institutions in particular.

Such measures are very problematic, as the survey results can be strongly influenced by the general state of business, rather than the inherent quality of the property rights system itself. For example, a lot of people who were quite happy to praise the good business environment in East and Southeast Asia suddenly started criticizing cronyism and other institutional deficiencies in these countries once the 1997 financial crisis broke out.

---

* This is drawn from Chang, 2007, forthcoming.

As with so much else, we need to be cautious in accepting the evidence allegedly showing that a "stronger" property rights system is better for economic development.

## The coverage problem

The discourse on property rights does not recognize all possible forms of property rights. It essentially recognizes only three types of property rights—open access, State ownership and pure private ownership, of which the last is deemed the best. However, there are other important forms of property rights.

Usually overlooked in the orthodox literature, there are genuinely communal property rights that allow no individual ownership but are based on clear rules about access and utilization. For example, in most rural communities, there exist communal rules for gathering firewood in communally owned forest; on the internet there exist rules regulating profits from open source software distributed under the General Public License (GPL).

Moreover, post-socialist developments in China have involved hybrid forms of property rights. For example, the TVEs (township and village enterprises) are de jure owned by local governments, but in most cases, operate with de facto, although legally unclear, control by powerful local political figures.

## Limits to the notion of "private" ownership

Much economic analysis starts from the assumption that all property rights are exogenously and clearly defined.

However, in reality, existing ownership rights are the product of previous social bargaining, and are constantly being altered because people are constantly attempting to create new property rights, expand the boundaries of existing property rights, eliminate existing property rights and defend their existing property rights against such encroachments.

As a result, most, if not all, ownership rights are "truncated" in a most complex manner, and there are very few examples of pure private ownership as envisaged in economics textbooks.

Ceilings or floors are imposed on the prices at which individuals may buy or sell. For example, rent control imposes price ceilings on real estate rentals, while the Common Agricultural Policy of the European Union establishes price floors, the minimum prices at which the EU guarantees purchase.

The ability to use assets or to transform them can also be limited. Zoning laws, which restrict the ways in which land can be used, are the best example of this. For another example, many regulated firms have only limited freedom to scrap their physical capital, to set prices or to decide on the geographical areas they want to serve.

Even when there are no such explicit restrictions, the uses to which a resource can be put are bound to be limited. For example, I may own a knife, but may not kill someone with it. Or you may own a certain machine, but you may not be allowed to operate it with the labour of a child under a certain age.

In other words, the delineation of property rights is not independent of what members of society believe to be legitimate rights and corresponding obligations. What is accepted as legitimate depends on the politics of the society concerned. For example, banning child labour may be seen as encroaching on employers' rights in one society, but not in another.

### Security of property rights and economic development

In the orthodox literature, it is presumed that stronger protection of property rights is always better. However, this cannot be true as a general proposition.

The fact that something, in this case protection of property rights, is good does not mean that more of it is always better. While it is probably true that very weak protection of property rights is bad, excessively strong protection may not be good either, as it can end up protecting obsolete technologies and outmoded organizational forms. If that is the case, there may be an inverse U-shaped relationship, where a system of protection that is too strong or too weak is not good. Alternatively, it may be that, as long as it is above a minimum threshold level, the strength of property rights protection may not matter too much.

Whatever the exact relationship between the strength of property rights protection and economic development, it is not likely to be linear.

Moreover, and more importantly from the point of view of economic development, the growth impact of a particular property right may not be constant over time.

A particular property right may become good or bad for society, depending on changes in the underlying technology, population, political balance of power or even ideologies.

Indeed, there are many examples in history where the preservation of certain property rights proved harmful for economic development, while the violation of certain existing property rights and the creation of new property rights were actually beneficial for economic development.

The best known example is probably the enclosure movement in England, which violated existing communal property rights by confiscating the commons, but contributed to the development of wool manufacturing by promoting sheep farming on the land thus confiscated. De Soto, 2000, documents how the recognition of squatter rights, in violation of the existing property rights of owners, was crucial in developing the American West. Land reform in Japan, the Republic of Korea and Taiwan PoC after the Second World War violated the existing property rights of landlords, but contributed to the subsequent development of these countries. Many people argue that the nationalization of industrial enterprises in France after the Second World War contributed to its industrial development, by transferring certain industrial properties from a conservative and non-dynamic industrial capitalist class to professional public sector managers with a penchant for modern technology and aggressive investments.

The examples could go on, but the point is that, if there are groups who are able to utilize certain existing properties better than their current owners can, it may be better for the society not to protect the existing property rights and to create new ones that transfer the properties in question to the former—bearing in mind that what is the "better" use is always debatable, not only from an economic but also from a political point of view. In this circumstance, too strong a protection of certain (existing) property rights may become a hindrance to economic development.[18]

## References

Amsden, Alice (1989). *Asia's Next Giant—South Korea and Late Industrialization*, New York and Oxford: Oxford University Press.

Chang, H.-J. (2000). "The hazard of moral hazard—untangling the Asian crisis", *World Development*, vol. 28, No. 4.

_____(2004*a*). "Institutional foundations for effective design and implementation of selective trade and industrial policies in the least developed countries: theory and evidence", in *The Politics of Trade and Industrial Policy in Africa: Forced Consensus*. C. Soludo, O. Ogbu and H.-J. Chang, eds. Trenton, New Jersey and Asmara, Eritrea: Africa World Press.

_____(2004*b*). "Regulation of foreign investment in historical perspective", *European Journal of Development Research*, vol. 16, No. 3.

_____(forthcoming). "Understanding the relationship between institutions and economic development: some key theoretical issues", in *Institutional Change and Economic Development*. H.-J. Chang, ed. Tokyo and London: United Nations University Press and Anthem Press.

Chang, H.-J., and A. Singh (1993). "Public enterprise in developing countries and economic efficiency", *UNCTAD Review*, 1993, No. 4.

De Soto, Hernando (2000). *The Mystery of Capital*. London: Bantam Books.

Goldstein, Andrea (2002). "Embraer: from national champion to global player", *CEPAL Review*, No. 77, August 2002. http://www.eclac.cl/publicaciones/SecretariaEjecutiva/0/LCG2180PI/lcg2180i-Goldstein.pdf.

Greenwald, Bruce, and Joseph Stiglitz (2006). "Helping infant economies grow: foundations of trade policies for developing countries", *American Economic Review*, vol. 96, No. 2.

IMF (2004). *Public Investment and Fiscal Policy*. Washington D.C.: International Monetary Fund.

Johnson, Chalmers (1982). *MITI and the Japanese Miracle*. Stanford: Stanford University Press.

---

18  This is, of course, the main insight from Marx's theory of social evolution, where a property rights system ("social relations of production") that was once good for the development of technologies ("forces of production") can become an obstacle to further developments of the very same technologies that it once helped to promote.

Jomo, K. S., and Rock, Michael (1998). "Economic diversification and primary commodity processing in the second-tier South-East Asian newly industrializing countries". UNCTAD Discussion Paper, No. 136. Geneva: United Nations Conference on Trade and Development.

Kessler, Tim, and Nancy Alexander (2003). "Assessing the risks in the private provision of essential services". Discussion Paper for G-24 Technical Group, Geneva, Switzerland, 15-16 September 2003. http://www.unctad.org/en/docs/gdsmdpbg2420047_en.pdf.

Radon, Jenik (2005). "The ABCs of oil agreements", in *Covering Oil: A Reporter's Guide to Energy and Development*. Anya Schiffrin and Svetlana Tsalik, eds. New York: Open Society Institute. http://www.revenuewatch.org/reports/072305.pdf.

_____ (2007). "How to negotiate your oil agreement", in *Escaping the Resource Curse*. Macartan Humphreys, Jeffrey Sachs and Joseph Stiglitz, eds. New York: Columbia University Press.

Roy, Rathin (2006). "Fiscal space for public investment: towards a human development approach". Paper prepared for the G-24 Technical Meeting, Singapore, 13-14 September 2006.

Sappington, David, and Joseph Stiglitz (1987). "Privatization, information, and incentives", *Journal of Policy Analysis and Management*, vol. 6, No. 4.

Singapore Department of Statistics (2001). "Contribution of government-linked companies to gross domestic product". Occasional Paper on Economic Statistics, No. 22.

Singapore Ministry of Finance (1993). "Interim report of the Committee to Promote Enterprise Overseas".

Shin, J-S. (2005). "Globalization and challenges to the developmental state: a comparison between South Korea and Singapore", *Global Economic Review*, vol. 34, No. 4.

Simon, Herbert (1983). *Reason in Human Affairs*. Oxford: Basil Blackwell.

Steinbock, Dan (2001). *The Nokia Revolution*. New York: AMACOM.

Stiglitz, Joseph (2003a). *The Roaring Nineties—A New History of the World's Most Prosperous Decade*. New York and London: W. W. Norton.

_____ (2003b). "Covering resource wealth". Presentation at the Initiative for Policy Dialogue/ Public Finance Monitor Center Workshop, 20 November, Baku, Azerbaijan. http:// www2.gsb.columbia.edu/ipd/bakutranscript.pdf.

_____ (2005). "Making natural resources into a blessing rather than a curse", in *Covering Oil: A Reporter's Guide to Energy and Development*. Anya Schiffrin and Svetlana Tsalik, eds. New York: Open Society Institute. http://www.revenuewatch.org/reports/072305.pdf.

_____ (2006). "An airport debacle worsened by greed and neglect", *Financial Times*, 22 August 2006.

United Nations (2008). *Public Enterprises: Unresolved Challenges and New Opportunities*. New York: UNDESA.

World Bank (1995). *Bureaucrats in Business—The Economics and Politics of Government Ownership*. New York: Oxford University Press.

# Investment and technology policies

Mushtaq H. Khan*

## Introduction

Governments in developing countries are responsible for important investments, e.g., in education and infrastructure. These investments require a view of the evolving structure of the economy—the design of an education system or a road network requires a vision of where the economy is likely to be a quarter century hence. But successful developing countries have had investment and technology policies that have gone far beyond this minimalist role. They have actively promoted particular sectors of the economy. Economic theory can justify such active intervention in terms of widespread "market failures". Markets in developing countries do not work as efficiently as they do in textbooks, and many opportunities of improving productivity, incomes and employment are missed as a result. However, the concept of market failure covers many (often quite complex) issues and policy has to identify not only the most pressing market failures but also the ones that can be feasibly addressed given the institutional and fiscal capacities of the government. It is not practical to expect hard-pressed developing country policymakers to carry out a comprehensive analysis to identify the market failures they can feasibly address in their countries. However, this note suggests that policymakers can follow some simple steps to identify a few of the most critical components of investment and technology policies appropriate for their context. In particular, if they start by investigating how *existing* technologies and sectors in their countries can be upgraded to improve productivity, create higher wage jobs and/or create greater employment, they are likely to identify a number of feasible steps they can follow to achieve relatively quick results. For many countries this may be a sufficiently challenging goal for investment and technology policies. In other countries with more advanced analytical and implementation capacities, a more detailed analysis of market failures and feasible responses may be appropriate.

* The author would gratefully like to acknowledge comments on earlier drafts of this paper from Jomo K. S., Assistant Secretary-General for Economic Development, United Nations; Joseph Stiglitz, Professor at Columbia University; José Antonio Ocampo, former Under-Secretary-General, UNDESA; Bernardo Kosacoff, Director, Economic Commission for Latin America (ECLAC); Khay Jin Khoo, Malaysia; Kamal Malhotra, UNDP; David O'Connor, Isabel Ortiz and Sylvie Illana Cohen, UNDESA.

## Overview: developing an investment and technology policy

This Policy Note will help policymakers and civil society develop policies appropriate for their context in a series of steps summarized in figure 1. The *first step* is to identify national priorities for investment and technology policy and the critical constraints and bottlenecks that may be preventing their achievement through a consultative exercise that interacts with other components of the national development strategy (NDS). This process will vary from country to country for a number of reasons. Data availability can vary widely, countries face different technological and investment bottlenecks, and have strengths and weaknesses in different areas. Key stakeholders may also disagree about the investment and technology policy priorities in different sectors like manufacturing, agriculture and services. Thus, at the outset, transparent procedures have to be used to identify priorities and bottlenecks at the country level, making the best use of available data and other resources, and taking into account local conditions.

In countries with limited administrative and planning capacities, the first step can be significantly simplified by focusing on *existing* economic sectors and subsectors and investigating if there are obvious areas where big gains can be made in terms of national priorities (employment growth, employment growth for women and other vulnerable sections of the population, wage growth, export earnings and so on) through achievable improvements in investment and technology upgrading. Backward and forward linkages with existing competitive sectors can also be investigated, as these are areas where new competitive advantage is most likely to be developed.

The *second step* in the policymaking process is to identify instruments and policy measures to address the most important constraints and bottlenecks that are preventing the achievement of the investment and technology upgrading goals identified in step 1. For instance, the aim may be to identify policies and instruments that can increase investments in critical sectors, or accelerate the adoption and adaptation of new technologies in these sectors. However, many reasonable policies may not be feasible in the context of particular countries given limitations in governance capacities to implement and enforce the policies adopted. These limitations have to be taken into account when designing policies and instruments. This takes us to the third step of this process.

The *third step* is to ensure that the policies and instruments discussed in step 2 can actually be implemented, given the governance and enforcement capacities available. Monitoring and implementation of policies and instruments have often been unsatisfactory in developing countries because of political constraints that prevent the correction of policy mistakes and failures of implementation. These constraints may be more serious for some types of policies compared to others. As figure 1 shows, steps 2 and 3 involve iteration: policies identified in step 2 will often need to be redesigned or revised given the problems of implementation assessed in step 3. The role of a separate analysis of governance capacity in step 3 is to ensure that policies are only adopted after a proper understanding of their governance and implementation

Figure 1.     Steps in developing a national investment
              and technology policy

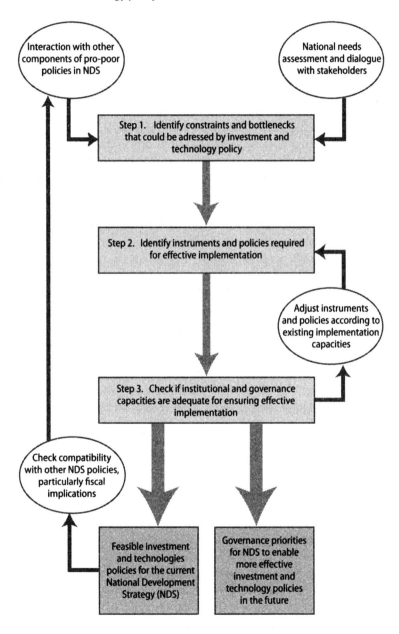

requirements, and the likelihood of success given the institutional and political capabilities of the country. This step is critical for designing and selecting instruments
and policies that are both feasible and effective.

There are two projected policy outcomes of this process. The first expected outcome is a set of feasible investment and technology policy interventions to accelerate
progress towards critical goals in the national development strategy. To be feasible,
these investment and technology policies have to be compatible with the *existing*
implementation capacities of the government. They should also be compatible and
consistent with other parts of the national development strategy. The steps suggested
in figure 1 aim to ensure that policies and instruments for investment and technology
upgrading are tailored to local capacities and objectives, that they are compatible with
other parts of the NDS (in particular, fiscal constraints), and *are implementable given
available governance and implementation capacities.* These requirements mean that a
feasible investment and technology policy will address a relatively small number of
critical constraints or bottlenecks affecting technology acquisition and investment in
specific sectors. The second expected outcome of the process is the identification of
critical governance weaknesses that need to be addressed if more effective investment
and technology policies are to be attempted in later years. Both policy outcomes
shown in figure 1 are equally important.

This Policy Note is organized in three sections:

- The **first section** explains the case for investment and technology policy by
  drawing on economic theory and the experience of successful developing
  countries. While many of the most successful developing countries used
  ambitious industrial and technology policies, they also had extensive governance capabilities to ensure effective implementation. Contemporary developing countries often have more limited implementation capacities, but they
  can use pragmatic policies to overcome specific bottlenecks and constraints
  that limit investment and technology acquisition in critical sectors.
- The **second section** goes through the three stages of the policy process shown
  in figure 1 to establish what is involved in implementing this approach in
  different developing country contexts.
- In the **final section**, this approach to investment and technology policy is
  compared and contrasted with the good governance and investment climate
  reforms that developing countries are being encouraged to adopt as a way
  of enhancing investment and its efficiency. There are areas of overlap and
  complementarity, but effective investment and technology policies require
  the development of governance capabilities that go beyond the ones identified in good governance reforms.

## The case for investment and technology policies

Countries that have achieved greater success in economic growth and poverty reduction rarely enjoyed better resources and skills than others from the outset. Their suc-

cess depended on their ability to *create* the capacity to produce. They used pragmatic policies to create incentives and compulsions for investors to invest and acquire new technologies. But success also required State capacities to enforce these policies. The capacity to enforce policies varies significantly across States, and within the same State it can vary significantly depending on economic sectors and the rules being enforced. Some States are better at enforcing some policy rules, others are better at enforcing others. It is important to remember this when devising investment and technology policies for a particular country. The strategies that worked in one country will not necessarily be easy to implement in another.

Economic theory identifies a series of market failures that explain why markets alone cannot ensure that developing countries will catch up with advanced countries. Developing countries with strong planning capacities could use an analysis of market failure to devise and prioritize their industrial and technology policy interventions. However, planning agencies in most developing countries are unlikely to have these capacities. But fortunately, it is possible to make progress by taking some pragmatic steps that could assist in moving up the technology ladder to better achieve some national development goals. The market failure analysis is important because it points out that even in sectors where there are potential gains from investment and technology upgrading this may not happen because the cost of organizing the necessary investment through the market may be too high because of market inefficiencies. Some of these market inefficiencies may be overcome through a focus on good governance and investment climate reforms. But other market inefficiencies may be difficult to overcome in the short run, and so corrective policy measures are required to achieve the investment and technology upgrading directly.

The most important market failures that can hold back investment and improvements in technology in developing countries include the following:

(i)  **Imperfections in credit markets:** The costs and risks faced by banks in identifying good borrowers may squeeze out lending to potentially profitable sectors. Lenders do not have full information about the ability and management skills of entrepreneurs who come to borrow from them. In particular, borrowers who have no intention or ability to repay the loan may be more willing to pay higher rates of interest or agree to other terms lenders may impose. Thus without spending a lot of resources investigating the quality of borrowers, and following this up with ongoing monitoring, banks who impose stringent conditions on borrowers may simply end up attracting the worst borrowers. Since banks soon find out that this is the case, in the absence of corrective interventions, they may reduce or even stop lending to important sectors like industrial investors.

(ii)  **Imperfections in equity markets:** Similarly, the costs and risks faced by small investors in identifying potentially profitable equity investments may reduce or prevent equity finance playing an important role in providing finance for development. It is not easy to set up well-working equity markets. If small shareholders are not well protected, an important source of investment in the stock market may dry up. On the other hand, if it becomes too difficult for outsiders to buy out small shareholders at a relatively low price if a company underperforms, the threat of takeover becomes less likely and it becomes easier for managers to make bad decisions at the expense of all shareholders. Stock market regulation is difficult even in advanced countries and regulatory structures are always being adjusted. But even so, most of the finance for new investments in advanced countries typically comes from other sources like retained profits or bank loans. In developing countries regulatory capacities are much weaker, as are the capacities and compulsions on companies to reveal accurate data on their performance and prospects. It is not surprising that stock markets typically play a very limited role in developing countries in driving finance to new developmental sectors.

(iii)    **Imperfections in insurance markets:** The cost of identifying the degree of risk involved in insuring against different eventualities may reduce investment in many sectors. In developing countries, where there are few firms in productive sectors, it is difficult for insurers to estimate different types of risk. This includes risks such as currency risks, or risks due to different types of accidents. In addition, developing countries are more susceptible to political uncertainties which are typically uninsurable even in advanced countries. These imperfections in insurance markets increase the exposure of entrepreneurs in these sectors and they may therefore be less likely to invest. But even in advanced countries, many of the risks involved in investing in new sectors are uninsurable, and investors have to absorb these "uncertainties". The difference is that advanced countries have many richer and risk-tolerant investors who can absorb these uncertainties in the expectation of large potential gains if their investments work out. But in developing countries, where this type of investor is much more rarely found, and where foreign investors face large political and currency risks, many potentially profitable investments may not happen without public institutions absorbing some of the risks and uncertainties.

(iv)    **Coordination failures:** Many investments are only profitable if complementary investments in other areas take place. For instance, investment in a high-end garments industry that has to respond rapidly to changing demands may only be viable if high-quality accessories and fabrics are locally available and can be quickly sourced. The costs of coordinating these complementary investment decisions through the relatively inefficient markets of a developing country may prevent or reduce many potentially profitable investments. Government assistance in coordinating backward and forward linkages can yield significant gains by bringing together investors, sharing information and creating incentives for coordinated investments.

(v)    **Externalities:** Many investments have benefits for other sectors and for broader society that may be ignored by investors in those sectors. As a result, without specific policies to encourage investments in these sectors there may be insufficient or no investment in many critical sectors. A particularly important type of externality involves investment in training labour and management. Investment in this training is beneficial for the entrepreneur but it has much wider social benefits because skilled labour and middle management can migrate from the firm to other firms or set up new businesses. The benefit to the investor is therefore less than the benefit to society and there is likely to be insufficient investment in these critically important activities.

There are also locational or "clustering" externalities when many firms providing similar services or producing similar products cluster together in particular localities. Each firm benefits from the availability of a pool of skilled labour, the shared knowledge of markets and suppliers and the rapid diffusion of technologies across firms. By the same token, firms in developing countries that often do not have these advantages face higher costs and lower productivity growth. These market failures can be addressed by government action to encourage investments in activities that have positive externalities and to encourage clustering of firms that are likely to enjoy locational externalities by developing industrial parks.

**Responses:** Successful developing countries have responded to market failures of the types discussed above with a number of types of interventions, including the provision of credit through government loan programmes, risk sharing by government through joint investments and insurance schemes, government assistance in coordination of investment in different sectors and in bargaining with external technology providers, and explicit or implicit subsidies or other interventions to encourage sectors or activities displaying positive externalities. However, apparently similar interventions have also failed to provide good results in some developing countries because appropriate governance capabilities to ensure the achievement of these desirable outcomes were missing. These governance capabilities are critically important in explaining success and failure.

Whenever governments intervene in markets, even if it is to respond to market failure, they inevitably also provide opportunities for resource capture. For instance, incentives to attract new investors can also enable inefficient investors to obtain loans, capture subsidies and free ride in other ways that can ultimately undermine the strategy unless compulsions or sanctions are available to ensure that non-performance is rapidly dealt with. Efforts at coordination, government training programmes, credit programmes or subsidies for investment in particular sectors can thus result in waste rather than more rapid development.

Governance capabilities to monitor the outcomes of interventions and to respond rapidly to correct mistakes in implementation are therefore critical for success. The ability and willingness of governments to respond can itself create strong compulsions for private sector beneficiaries of these interventions to deliver results. Equally, the absence of these governance capabilities can result in free riding as there are few or no compulsions on beneficiaries to deliver results. These failures of governance can explain why apparently well thought out investment and technology interventions have often failed in many countries.

Developing investment and technology policies therefore requires identifying a series of interventions that can address the most critical market failures as well as selecting from this list the ones that can be effectively implemented given existing or achievable governance capabilities. Few developing countries can be expected to carry out a full analysis of market failures in different sectors to identify and prioritize the most important areas of intervention. For most developing countries, the most feasible and pragmatic approach would be a less demanding one that involved identifying some of the most important constraints holding back investment and technology upgrading in already existing sectors or in sectors that are closely related. This is likely to be the most practical way of making progress with investment and technology policies in most developing countries. Policies and interventions can then be selected based on whether effective implementation capacities exist for particular strategies of investment and technology upgrading.

Most developing countries already have a few sectors where global competitiveness has been achieved, as measured by export competitiveness. A pragmatic way of identifying practical investment and technology policy interventions is to begin with sectors in which the country already has some experience and asking the following questions:

What can be done to increase output, productivity and employment in sectors where the country already has competitiveness?

- What can be done to move production in these sectors into higher value-added products?
- How can these sectors be used as lead sectors to build backward and forward linkages with new upstream and downstream sectors that can raise domestic value added beyond existing competitive sectors?
- (In some conflict or post-conflict countries there may be no activities that currently enjoy international competitiveness. In these cases the pragmatic approach will be to identify and start with activities that are closest to achieving international competitiveness).

The answers to these questions will in effect address different types of market failures in a pragmatic way by addressing issues of:

- Coordinating technology acquisition decisions across firms and sectors;
- Sharing risk and enabling the financing of investment in new technologies and sectors;
- Sharing risks in labour training and learning processes;
- Providing targeted infrastructure to critical sectors; and
- Developing regulatory capacity to maintain and enhance competitiveness.

It is best to stick to very simple criteria in making decisions about the sectors to support through investment and technology policies. It is a mistake to believe that governments in developing countries can review all possible investment options to identify the *best* ones. It is good enough to identify some *good* investment options on the basis of already existing competitive and entrepreneurial capacities. (A more ambitious process could also examine assistance for entirely new sectors but a pragmatic approach that begins with existing sectors and capacities is likely to be the best strategy for most countries.) The criterion could be that a forum of stakeholders can identify potential investments that can feasibly raise productivity, employment and/ or achieve other national development strategy goals by *achieving economic rates of return through new investments within relatively short periods of time* if feasible assistance with coordination, financing, learning and infrastructure were available. The feasibility of the assistance provided depends critically on the fiscal and administrative capacities of the State, and its capacity to monitor improvements in competitiveness achieved through these policies and take prompt corrective action if required. These issues are discussed in turn.

## Coordination of technology acquisition across firms and sectors

In Taiwan Province of China (hereafter, Taiwan PoC), from the 1950s, and the Republic of Korea, from the 1960s, Government-led institutions brought together potential investors in different sectors to coordinate their technology acquisition. The goals were to ensure the compatibility of technologies in different sectors, to ensure that critical backward and forward linkages were achieved, and to ensure that investments in high value-added products that were sensitive to complementary investments were not lost. These types of coordination can significantly enhance the incentives for investing in higher productivity sectors.

In addition, the coordination of potential domestic investors, particularly in higher technology sectors, helped to enhance the bargaining power and information available to domestic investors in their transactions with external technology providers. During the early stages of Taiwan PoC's development the Government even took the lead in identifying and licensing critical electronic technologies for domestic producers. The goal of these coordination strategies was to ensure that domestic producers had access to technologies that allowed higher productivity growth over time.

In theory, private investors should do all the coordinating themselves to maximize their potential profits. In reality, private investors face high costs of collecting the relevant information and even higher costs of negotiating and reaching agreement with other investors when there are disagreements about the package of investments they should collectively invest in. Economists call these costs transaction costs, and they are typically very high in developing and transition economies where institutions for generating information are underdeveloped and contracts are difficult to enforce. Developing country investors are likely to be particularly disadvantaged in their access to information about alternative technologies that are available in international markets. The point here is not that governments have better information about technologies, but rather that governments may have an advantage in bringing together different investors and providing a forum where options for upgrading existing sectors and technologies can be discussed.

For coordination to be successful, policymakers have to be able to follow up on shared information to develop integrated policies to assist technology acquisition in the critical areas identified. The exercise is not just about information sharing between, say, garments manufacturers, accessory manufacturers, the dyeing industry and potential investors in textiles, but also and primarily about following up on discussions with policies to assist and accelerate technology acquisition in these critical sectors.

In many developing countries, coordination efforts exist on paper, but little coordination happens in practice. Often, this is because government agencies charged with improving investment coordination are given low priority within government, and have limited access to higher level policymakers.

One way in which government agencies can play a meaningful role in effective coordination is by working as a forum through which domestic investors can collectively bargain with foreign technology providers to purchase a package of integrated technologies. If coordination enhances the information available to individual investors and their bargaining power when trying to acquire better technologies from abroad, this can provide the incentives to individual investors to take coordination efforts seriously.

A key to the success of this aspect of industrial policy in the Republic of Korea or Taiwan PoC was that coordination efforts in these countries were supported by the highest executive levels of Government, and effective incentives were provided to individual investors to participate in technology coordination exercises. In addition, despite their considerable bureaucratic capabilities, coordination efforts were limited to a few sectors at a time to avoid overstretching the available capabilities of the Government.

## Sharing risk and enabling the financing of investment in potentially profitable sectors

An important component of investment and technology policies in all high-growth developing countries has been government strategies to make finance available to critical sectors. The market failure this addresses is the inability of investors in many critical sectors to get access to finance at the market rate of interest. So even if finance is made available to critical sectors *at the market rate of interest*, this could release an important bottleneck. But in fact in many high-growth countries, government policies made finance available to critical sectors at below market rates.

Market failure happens here because investment and technology acquisition in new areas is an inherently risky activity. If credit and equity markets fail, finance is either not available, or more typically, is available but at a price or with collateral conditions that load all the risk on the investor. This can prevent investment in new areas where investors are unwilling to add to the high levels of risk they face in bringing in the new technologies by taking on finance at a high cost of capital or at high risk to themselves through mortgaging significant assets.

At the same time, governance capabilities are critical here to ensure that free riding does not reduce such strategies to failure. If credit is made available to investors who would not otherwise have had access to it, the agencies providing credit have to make sure it is not wasted. A number of strategies can be used by governments to reduce the risk of poor performance. Making finance available at market rates of interest reduces the risk that the borrower will put in suboptimal levels of effort because the borrower has to generate adequate returns to service the loan. But this does not remove the risk entirely because the borrower may have no intention of repaying a loan that has ultimately been arranged by government.

Similarly, government equity holdings in the company that is financed may improve performance by creating incentives for government to monitor and risks for the firm if performance is poor as the government could decide to sell its holdings to more aggressive investors. But again, these strategies are only likely to work in the presence of credible threats on the part of government to act in case of poor performance and the presence of a well-working stock market. These may not be present to the requisite degree in many developing countries.

The credibility of corrective government action in the face of poor performance is the key. If the government has credibility, rather simple mechanisms may be sufficient to create strong compulsions for the borrower to perform. For instance, in the Republic of Korea, lending institutions involved in financing new investments in critical sectors during its industrial takeoff set simple performance targets for borrowers, usually in the form of easy to monitor export targets. Failure to meet these targets normally resulted in growing pressure on the enterprise from banks and from the Government, and could eventually result in a transfer of the asset to new owners.

Developing countries have to think through in the context of their own institutions and political conditions how they can achieve credible sanctions for firms benefiting from industrial policy financing arrangements if they fail to perform. What they need to achieve is an effective government strategy to recover financing through a fast track process from enterprises that have failed to perform. The general effectiveness of bankruptcy laws or of stock markets as mechanisms of imposing discipline on borrowers is limited on their own in most developing countries.

Effective pressure on industrial policy borrowers may therefore depend on the creation of additional and specialized governance and recovery arrangements that create credible compulsions for industrial policy borrowers to exert high levels of effort in making their investments viable. For instance, government equity holdings in these firms could be held by specialized agencies with a clear mandate to monitor performance according to pre-arranged criteria and to terminate the relationship if necessary. Such agencies would be credible only if they had clear backing at the highest political levels.

## Sharing risk in labour training and learning processes

Market failures in organizing training and learning processes are an important impediment to technology upgrading in developing countries. The productivity gap between advanced and developing countries is typically much bigger than the wage gap, particularly in high value-added sectors. This explains why despite very low wages, developing countries find it so hard to move into high value-added sectors. The productivity gap is only partly due to poor infrastructure and the level of education of the workforce. It is primarily due to the fact that productivity growth in manufacturing often requires learning by doing, and labour productivity can typically only be raised in the workplace by operating production for a time at a loss measured in international prices. This is the main reason why financing for new technology investments is so critical. But market failures in lending and equity markets can in turn prevent the adequate availability of finance for organizing learning by doing.

Successful industrial and technology policies in countries like the Republic of Korea, Taiwan PoC and Malaysia have involved Governments sharing some of the risk and uncertainty of learning new technologies. This has taken the form of Government financing of some of the costs of learning combined with the withdrawal of support when learning fails. The latter was particularly important as success depended on the credibility of strategies of withdrawal if learning failed to take place. The credibility of withdrawal created the appropriate compulsions for firms and industries receiving support to put in the effort and achieve actual productivity increases.

In contrast, many other developing countries attempted to accelerate catching up using similar policies, but without effective State capacity to withdraw support or otherwise enforce learning. In these cases, State support for technology acquisition only resulted in infant industries that never grew up. As a result of widespread failure with these strategies, most developing countries abandoned this approach entirely. But infant industry policies failed in most developing countries because the incentives created for catching up were not combined with effective compulsions or sanctions for sectors or firms that failed to achieve satisfactory competitiveness over time.

The policy space for major interventions in this area has shrunk in most developing countries. With much greater levels of trade openness following WTO agreements in many developing countries, sharing the risk of learning requires a mix of instruments that will not violate the trade agreements. However, specific efforts to improve or accelerate learning in critical areas are not only possible but essential, if technological progress is to be assured. For this to be effective, policymakers must have the capacity not only to support learning, but also to withdraw support rapidly if competitiveness does not improve.

These instruments can be devised, and can include:

- Support for learning in the form of fiscal and other incentives for setting up in-firm training schemes;
- Assistance through targeted infrastructure for sectors involved in learning; and
- Bridging loans to finance learning.

Many incentive schemes continue to exist and operate in developing countries since WTO rules do not prohibit many forms of assistance for technological catching up. The problem is that these schemes are often not properly thought through in terms of the results expected, performance is not monitored, and no effective sanctions or systems for withdrawing support exist. Not surprisingly, the results are almost always disappointing.

The capacity to devise appropriate risk-sharing instruments is therefore a necessary capacity for overcoming technology bottlenecks in developing countries. Secondly, outcomes in most cases have been poor because of poor capacities for effectively implementing strategies. In particular, agencies involved in managing incentives for learning have to be linked to executive agencies that have the institutional and political capacity to enforce the withdrawal of support or enforce other sanctions if learning fails to show results within the expected time period. The latter remains a critical condition for success. In many developing and transition economies, developing these governance capacities is not just a matter of strengthening bureaucratic capacities, but also of creating political coalitions that will allow these policies to be effectively implemented.

## Providing targeted infrastructure to critical sectors

The importance of infrastructure for economic development is widely recognized, but, when infrastructure cannot be improved rapidly *across the board*, identifying sectors that are critical for achieving national development targets and prioritizing infrastructure to these sectors can pay high dividends. In this context, infrastructure should be broadly interpreted to include both physical and human capital; hence, it includes the ability of the State to provide resources for skills development appropriate to the needs of critical sectors.

The capacity to identify infrastructural priorities and to deliver high-quality infrastructure to these critical sectors can significantly improve the incentives for investing in high-productivity sectors, or in sectors deemed desirable according to the objectives of the national development strategy.

This capacity to deliver high quality infrastructure to critical sectors when infrastructure cannot be rapidly improved across the board is a vital capacity for accelerating investment. It can also dramatically improve the bargaining power of government in negotiating technology transfer deals with foreign investors. Foreign investors bringing in high productivity technologies sensitive to the quality of the infrastructure are more likely to invest and to negotiate with countries that can credibly offer them the required infrastructure. One reason why China continues to attract more foreign investment than any other developing country is that infrastructure can be prioritized in China to facilitate rapid investments in critical areas.

In addition, the capacity to provide targeted infrastructure can be a mechanism for providing conditional support to particular sectors and technologies for sharing the risks of learning.

However, the ability to deliver quality infrastructure, even if limited to priority sectors, assumes some minimal fiscal capacities of the State. In some developing countries, even this may not be available. In such circumstances, macroeconomic issues have to be addressed, in particular to increase tax collection and to limit spending in unproductive sectors.

## Developing regulatory capacity
## to maintain and enhance competitiveness

A crosscutting issue affecting all the questions discussed above is the capacity of government to enhance and maintain competitiveness through industrial and technology policies. Competitiveness is the capacity to produce products at a price and of a quality that can survive in open competition with the best of the rest. Competitiveness is measured by the relative unit costs of production at home compared to the international price of products of similar quality. The aim of industrial and technology policies must be to achieve competitiveness in new higher technology and higher value-added investments. These investments can then survive without further assistance, providing jobs, higher wages and other benefits for the rest of the economy. Competitiveness is not the same thing as competition. Competition is the act of buying and selling in an open market with free entry and exit for other buyers and sellers. The degree of competition in a market can be measured by the degree of freedom of entry and exit into that particular market. Under some conditions, competition can ensure the achievement and maintenance of competitiveness. But in other cases, particularly when industrial and technology policies are involved, competition may not be sufficient and other governance capabilities are necessary to ensure competitiveness.

In theory, if investors have to survive in competitive markets with free entry and exit for domestic and international firms, they can only do so by maximizing their investment in new technologies and making all efforts to sustain learning and best practices within their enterprise. As a result, competition can ensure that entrepreneurs maintain their competitiveness by innovating or by copying innovators. Since this is a hard life, from Adam Smith onwards, economists have also recognized that investors have a natural tendency to try to restrict competition in their own sectors, as this allows them to survive with lower productivity, greater inefficiency and yet achieve high profits by being able to charge consumers higher prices (Rajan and Zingales, 2003).

Not surprisingly, *competition policy* has traditionally been an important plank for ensuring competitiveness, especially in advanced countries. States in advanced countries typically have government agencies charged with investigating and punishing anti-competitive arrangements and collusion between producers, as well as regulating prices in sectors where only a few large firms can operate. However, competition policy is not always as simple as this. *It is not always the case that more competition is better than less (though that is true in most cases).* For instance, innovating firms in advanced countries have to be allowed to make extra profits to maintain the incentive to innovate. For these firms, too much competition can cut into their profits too soon, and this can be a problem. Of course, too little competition is also a problem, as it reduces the incentive to keep on improving products and technologies. Thus, in many critical innovating sectors in advanced countries, there is an optimal level of competition that is neither too much nor too little (Aghion and others, 2002). It follows that regulatory bodies have to have the capacity and personnel to make these judgements on an ongoing basis.

**Box 1.   Investment and technology policies:
justification and first steps**

Market failures in credit markets, equity markets, insurance markets, coordination failures and externalities can prevent developing countries moving up the value-added chain to create high wage employment and raise living standards. In particular, without targeted policies to enhance productivity through learning-by-doing, developing countries can get stuck in low productivity and low wage activities.

The least demanding industrial and technology policy approach in developing countries is to start with already existing competitive activities and ask:
- What can be done to increase output, productivity and employment in areas where the country already has competitiveness?
- What can be done to move production in these sectors into higher value-added products?
- How can these areas be used as lead sectors to build backward and forward linkages with new upstream and downstream sectors that can raise domestic value added beyond existing competitive sectors?

The aim is to achieve internationally competitive sectors enjoying high productivity and the potential of rapid productivity growth within relatively short time periods using industrial and technology policies of some or all of the following types:
- Coordinating technology acquisition decisions across firms and sectors;
- Sharing risk and enabling the financing of investment in new technologies and sectors;
- Sharing risks in labour training and learning processes;
- Providing targeted infrastructure to critical sectors; and
- Developing regulatory capacity to maintain and enhance competitiveness.

The mix of policies will depend on the technologies being adopted and the preexisting strengths and weaknesses of entrepreneurs, financial institutions, infrastructure and skills in the sector. The critical determinant of success is likely to be governance and regulatory capacities to maintain and enhance competitiveness through monitoring and taking tough action when required, including the early withdrawal of support if progress is unsatisfactory.

While most countries have tried variants of industrial and technology policies in the past, the main cause of their differential success has often been the efficacy with which incentives have been implemented, and the credibility with which their withdrawal has been organized in cases of poor performance.

*Sources*: Amsden, 1989; Wade, 1990; Aoki and others, 1997; Khan and Jomo, 2000.

What is true for advanced countries applies with greater force to developing countries. Regulatory bodies must have the capacity to make judgements, on an ongoing basis, about competition and competitiveness, particularly in the context of industrial and technology policies. In many sectors, high levels of competition may well be the best policy for ensuring competitiveness over time. These sectors are generally those that have already achieved international competitiveness or can achieve it very rapidly. Low technology export sectors, like the garments industry, which already have global competitiveness in many developing countries, are examples of sectors that should maintain competitiveness through competition. In other sectors that are catching up, and are being supported by industrial and technology policies, more sophisticated regulatory capacities are required.

Whenever a sector gets policy support in any of the ways described earlier for acquiring new technology and catching up, competition as a mechanism for enforcing competitiveness becomes insufficient. The sector receiving support has an advantage over others, both over other sectors within the country and, more importantly, over producers of similar goods in other countries. As a result, the sector can maintain its market share in a superficially competitive setting, even though it is not yet competitive in the sense that it would not be able to survive without the assistance. In these cases, institutions have to be set up to complement market competition in order to ensure the rapid achievement and maintenance of true international competitiveness, so that the support currently being received can be phased out.

For instance, if learning in new industries is supported through subsidies for training programmes, or access to better or cheaper infrastructure, complementary institutional measures are required to ensure that the support is for a pre-determined period, or that it is conditional on continuing improvements in performance, measured by export growth or some other easy-to-observe indicator. Without these measures, the support policy is likely to fail, and international competitiveness will probably not be achieved, because the sector will depend on the continuation of support instead of using the opportunity to catch up to achieve true competitiveness. This type of failure happened in many of the developing countries' catching-up programmes that produced infants which never grew up. Clearly, issues of coordination, financing, learning, infrastructure and competitiveness are closely related and require integrated policy responses on the part of government. Box 1 summarizes this discussion.

## Steps in developing an investment and technology policy

### Step 1.    Identifying sectors to support

The implicit market failures that have to be addressed by investment and technology policy will be different in different countries because their economic sectors have developed to different levels and they may face very specific problems. For instance, developing and transition countries have different initial conditions and levels of development of different sectors (agriculture, industry and services), different initial technical capacities and skills of entrepreneurs and workers in different sectors, the characteristics and limitations of their financial systems and infrastructure are likely to be different, and in particular, their governance capabilities may be different from other countries and vary from sector to sector within the country.

Thus, the first task is to examine the available data and evidence on investment and technology in the national economy, and to engage in a discussion with key stakeholders to identify the constraints that need to be addressed to move existing competitive sectors up the technology ladder and to establish possible backward and forward linkages with these sectors. As this is the first step in the policymaking process, not all of the priorities identified at this stage may be selected for policy attention after all steps in the process outlined in figure 1 have been completed. The ultimate aim is to select a smaller number of interventions than are feasible given the resources and governance capacities available to policymakers. However, it is desirable for the national debate and consultation to be as comprehensive as possible, and to be based on the best available sources of data and evidence on sectors where national competitiveness already exists and the constraints and bottlenecks faced by these sectors in trying to further improve productivity and gain international competitiveness in higher value-added production.

## Data requirements

The data available for assessing national performance in investment and technology are likely to vary across countries, both in extent and in quality. The more refined the available data, the better informed the identification of constraints and bottlenecks. Hence, improvements in data collection and processing by national statistical agencies are an important part of improvements in policymaking in this area. However, a start can be made with relatively crude data that should be available in almost every developing country.

Table 1 summarizes some of the data that would be useful for determining national investment and technology priorities according to the objectives identified in the national development strategy. The table *indicates* the types of data that are relevant, but not all of it will be available in every developing country. Policy progress can be achieved with much less. In some countries, other sources of data can usefully complement the information available for identifying constraints and setting priorities.

This data provides the starting point for policymakers to identify areas where investment and technology policies could make a difference to national development strategy objectives. It should also allow more informed discussions with stakeholders to identify the areas where investment and technology policies can make the biggest impact on output, productivity, employment and other development objectives.

The outcome of examining the data and the discussion with stakeholders should result in the identification of a number of priority areas where investment and technology policies can assist technology upgrading, productivity growth and the development of backward and forward linkages in sectors that already have some experience of operating at or close to international competitiveness. The next two steps will seek to narrow down the list of possible areas of assistance to a relatively small number that can be addressed given the implementation and fiscal capacities of the State. The aim in these later stages will be prioritization, to impose discipline on the policy wish list and to force policymakers and stakeholders to agree on a shorter list of feasible policy priorities. Feasibility very much depends on the limits to policy set by fiscal constraints and the implementation capacities of the State, particularly in

**Table 1.   Data required to identify goals for investment
and technology policies**

| Data/information (not all categories will be available or required in every case) | Likely source |
|---|---|
| **1.  Critical economic sectors and technologies** | |
| a.  Characteristics of broad economic activities (agriculture, industry, services) in terms of different objectives in the national development strategy (for instance, employment, value-added per person, productivity growth, exports, export growth | National income statistics, trade statistics from the balance of payments, employment surveys |
| b.  Characteristics of particular subsectors (for instance, garments manufacturing, cotton textiles, groundnut production) in terms of different objectives as above and in comparison with competitors | As above, together with censuses of economic sectors, sample surveys of particular sectors, statistics collected by industry organizations, chambers of commerce and industry, data on comparisons from World Bank and other agencies |
| **2.  Investment performance** | |
| a.  Aggregate investment (gross fixed capital formation) as share of GDP and in comparison with competitors | National income statistics, World Bank and other international agencies estimates |
| b.  Investment disaggregated by economic activities (agriculture, industry, services) | National income statistics, World Bank and other international agencies estimates |
| c.  Investment disaggregated by economic subsectors critical for the national development strategy (for instance, export sectors or high value-added sectors or employment-generating sectors) such as textiles, garments, high value-added crops, etc. | Private investment in different sectors can be estimated from a variety of sources, such as imports of capital goods of different types recorded in foreign trade statistics (to estimate investment in machines), sales of cement or other building materials to different sectors (to estimate investment in buildings). Public sector investment in different sectors can be estimated from the national budget |
| d.  Investment in infrastructure and human capital serving economic subsectors critical for the national development strategy (as above) | Spending in national budget on different types of infrastructure and education (if available) and estimates of private investment in these activities or otherwise qualitative estimates of bottlenecks |
| e.  Investment disaggregated into public and private sector investments | National income statistics, otherwise public investment can be estimated from national budget, private investment from capital goods imports and other data |

| Data/information (not all categories will be available or required in every case) | Likely source |
|---|---|
| 3. Technology and investment constraints/ bottlenecks | |
| a. Qualitative information on constraints preventing technology upgrading required for maintaining competitiveness | Dialogue with industry associations, leading entrepreneurs and technical exports, local and foreign |
| b. Qualitative information on bottlenecks and constraints limiting investments in critical sectors (for instance, inadequate infrastructure, inappropriate regulatory structure, inadequate policy support for learning, etc. | Dialogue with trade and industry associations, leading entrepreneurs, surveys of business opinion |

critical areas of governance required for successful implementation of investment and technology policies. In the medium term, improving these governance capacities to ensure effective implementation and improving fiscal possibilities to enable support to be more extensive and to cover more sectors should also be the subject of investment and technology policies.

## Data on critical economic sectors and technologies

The starting point for identifying investment and technology policy priorities is to collect and examine the most basic data about the economy: its important sectors and subsectors, its aggregate and sectoral performance in terms of growth, productivity growth, employment growth, export growth and so on, as shown in the first item in table 1. The data give us a picture of the allocation and efficiency of investment in the past. It also provides information on the characteristics of different sectors and subsectors of the economy in terms of employment, productivity, wages and so on, both relative to other subsectors in the economy, and relative to comparable competitors. Identifying critical sectors that could be prioritized by investment and technology policies can be made more tractable by identifying sectors within the country that have already achieved international competitiveness or are close to international competitiveness. (Sector in this context refers to an area of productive activity, so the ready-made garments industry, or commercial horticulture is an example of a sector in this sense.)

It is theoretically possible that there may be potential sectors that do not yet exist at all where (with the right policy push) the developing country may enjoy large gains in employment, output or productivity growth. But given the limited resources that most developing country policymakers have to carry out a full analysis of market failures that may prevent some potentially profitable sectors from emerging at all, a second-best and pragmatic approach is to start with what appears to be working and investigate how these sectors can be used as the base for investment and technology policy in the ways identified in box 1. In many developing countries, the sectors that are at or close to international competitiveness are likely to be sectors using labour-intensive technologies to produce manufactured or agricultural products for export markets. The data can help to identify these sectors, and although in many cases these sectors will already be well-known to policymakers, the data will back up the case for further investigation.

The initial data are also useful for identifying the direction in which more advanced developing countries that had similar sectoral specializations in the past have moved. Did they move into higher-value products within these sectors, into higher productivity methods of production, and what backward and forward linkages did they develop? For some sectors, this investigation may reveal that the sector does not offer many possibilities for upward mobility in terms of productivity, or linkages, compared to other sectors. This information will be very useful for prioritizing sectors for attention. For instance, if a country has international markets in ready-made garments and in producing stuffed soft toys, an examination of trajectories of more advanced developing countries could show that ready-made garments have greater potential for productivity upgrading and linkages than stuffed toys. A very precise calculation of potential growth or productivity improvement in different sectors is not necessary. But policymakers should have data and evidence at hand for stakeholder discussions that aim to identify the most likely sectors where productivity and technology upgrading is feasible on the basis of existing national competences and international evidence of possible improvements.

Discussions about national priorities are likely to be contested by potential winners and losers from particular policy positions. At this stage of the exercise, the task is simply to collate the data and information on different sectors and subsectors in the most transparent way possible.

### Data on investment and investment performance

The second item in table 1 describes data that can be used to assess the share and allocation of investment in the economy at a number of different levels: aggregate and sectoral and also in specific categories like infrastructure, human capital and investment in the private and public sectors. Long-term economic growth depends on both the magnitude of investment and the efficiency of investment. Thus, the first item of table 1 gave us data on economic growth, productivity growth and so on; the second item measures the share and allocation of investment across sectors and in the economy. The relative efficiency of investment between sectors or countries can be deduced from these two sets of data. The higher the historical rates of growth achieved for any given rate of investment, the more efficient the investment.

Data on investment, particularly at the level of sectors, is typically weak in developing countries and sometimes entirely unavailable. Nevertheless, it is useful to marshal the available data to see if some or all of the following questions can be answered. This will help in the policy discussion about directions of upgrading and sectoral priorities. First, it would be useful to know the areas of the economy in which

## Box 2. Sectoral choices in the national development strategy

For many developing countries, identifying major technological challenges for upgrading and extending their competitive sectors is a relatively simple task. What is required is data on the technologies used by other developing countries that are in similar industries but have moved further up the technology ladder. The policymaking process can look for evidence on how upgrading the value of products produced, improving productivity or product quality was achieved in more advanced countries and the results these countries achieved in areas important for the national development strategy, such as employment generation, wage growth, output growth, export growth or other indicators. This comparison of present with potential conditions in competitive sectors can suffice to identify the directions of upgrading that appropriate investment and technology policies should aim to achieve.

However, the national development strategy also needs to consider whether the existing competitive sectors and activities in the country are desirable to maintain and extend over the long term, or whether steps should be taken to develop some sectors over others. There may be many factors to consider here, many specific to particular countries. For instance, if agricultural landholdings are very fragmented and there is significant landlessness in agriculture, or if agricultural land is very poor in quality and suffers from significant ecological or environmental handicaps, it may be prudent to focus on a faster development of high value-added industry or services to create a greater proportion of non-agricultural jobs in the future.

A further consideration that could inform the choice of sectors to prioritize is the statistical observation that a faster growth of the manufacturing sector tends to result in faster growth in productivity in the manufacturing sector, adding to its competitiveness and allowing faster growth to be sustained (Kaldor, 1966). Because such a relationship between output growth and productivity growth is not in general observed in the agricultural or service sectors, many economists have argued that developing countries trying to raise social productivity on a sustained basis should put somewhat more emphasis on the manufacturing sector as an engine of growth. In addition to the possibility of virtuous cycles of productivity and output growth, it is also often easier to generate large increases in employment in manufacturing compared to agriculture or services.

Policymakers need to take these statistical observations seriously but in many developing countries some high value-added service or agricultural activities have created many relatively high-wage jobs. A good example of this is the business-outsourcing sector in India. There may be questions about the rate of employment growth in India compared to China where the manufacturing sector is growing much faster, but developing countries should not ignore high value-added subsectors in services and agriculture even though in general it is still true that manufacturing offers the most plausible source of employment growth for low-skilled workers.

significant public and private investments are taking place. Secondly, are these the areas where international competitiveness exists and needs to be further developed? Thirdly, what can we deduce about the efficiency of these investments from the output or productivity growth that has been achieved through these investments? The answers to these questions may indicate either that not enough investments are being made in critical sectors where competitiveness can be further developed, or that the investments that are being made are not achieving the output or productivity that competitors are achieving.

If national data on investment at the sectoral level is not available to answer these questions, policymakers can still proceed with second-best data on the types of investment that are taking place in sectors that are internationally competitive by looking at the types of output and export growth that the country is achieving. Is the growth in exports in sectors with international competitiveness primarily of low value-added products, or are there signs of moving up the value-added chain over a number of years, as indicated by changes in the average value of exports in these sectors? If the growth of exports is low, this is an indirect indication of insufficient investment in increasing output or keeping up with growing competitive pressures coming from other countries. If output is growing, but the unit value of exports in these sectors is moving up very slowly or not at all, this may be an indication that investments are primarily in output expansion rather than in technological upgrading.

In some countries, the absence of investment data means that policy discussions may have to proceed on the basis of indirect evidence on the scale and type of investment in critical sectors. This may be sufficient for initiating some steps in investment and technology policy, but better statistical data would be an important priority in these countries for future policy development.

## Information on constraints

The third item in table 1 describes the most important type of information required for informing a national debate on investment and technology policy. The information discussed earlier identifies critical competitive sectors, and their performance and limitations. It should also identify the types of technologies and products that are feasible next stages for upgrading in these sectors on the basis of the experience of more advanced developing countries. The critical question here is why the upgrading has not already happened. There may be important market failures that may be preventing upgrading and new investments taking place in these sectors, and preventing the development of backward and forward linkages with new competitive sectors.

The information that is available to assess the constraints that may be preventing upgrading and technological progress is typically not quantitative data, but qualitative information that can be used to answer a number of questions that follow from the discussion of market failures summarized in box 1. If investment or technical progress is slow in competitive sectors, why is that so? It could be that progress into new higher value products or higher productivity technologies involves coordination, or risks or learning costs or finance of a type or extent that is deterring investment in this sector (see box 1 for a summary of the issues). Identifying the most important constraints that are relevant for a particular sector can only be achieved through a process of qualitative assessment of what is blocking the appropriate investment in that sector based on consulting industry associations, leading entrepreneurs in that sector, and local and foreign technical experts, particularly those working in similar sectors in more advanced developing countries that have achieved technical progress, as well as other domestic stakeholders.

This largely qualitative information can help to identify the specific constraints and bottlenecks preventing the developing country from: (i) increasing investments in sectors that are internationally competitive or close to achieving international competitiveness, (ii) investing in upgrading technologies and improving productivity in these sectors and (iii) developing new backward and forward linkages to create new competitive activities.

While dialogue with investors and industry or sectoral associations is an important source of information, the procedure here cannot simply be to carry out surveys, but to go beyond surveys on the basis of the comparative data available (some of it referred to in the first two items of table 1). Comparative data are very important because investors and industry associations are, on their own, likely to give responses based on conventional wisdom that are not necessarily the most important constraints faced by a developing economy in a comparative perspective. For instance, investors in all developing countries want to see improvements in good governance and are likely to respond to general surveys by identifying the absence of good governance as the most important constraint to technology acquisition and long-term investment in the country. In the final section of this Policy Note, we will see that while these responses are perfectly understandable, they do not translate into an achievable policy goal for most developing countries.

In particular, we have seen that at early stages of development, many developing countries can begin to perform better and to converge with advanced countries even when they are not able to achieve significant improvements in good governance conditions in the short run. The evidence from successful high-growth countries is that while immediate improvements in "good governance" are hard to achieve, successful countries have governance capacities that enable them to overcome specific investment and technology constraints in an effective and pragmatic way.

It follows that surveys of investors should be designed to identify pragmatic steps to overcome specific problems that may be constraining investment in new technologies and developing new products using the expertise already existing in internationally competitive sectors. Critically, the opinion of domestic producers and entrepreneurs should be complemented with information and evidence from more advanced developing countries to identify the processes and possibilities of value and productivity enhancement in existing competitive sectors, and the possibilities of developing profitable backward and forward linkages. The types of issues that policymakers can assist with and should look for in a general sense are the ones we have already discussed and summarized in box 1.

Thus, the dialogue with stakeholders should try to identify steps that can be taken to improve the (effective) coordination of technology acquisition, improve the information available and assist with the process of bargaining with external technology providers, relax financing constraints, share some of the financial and other risks involved in learning, and provide effective targeted infrastructure to critical sectors. Policymakers also have to be concerned with improving institutional arrangements for ensuring that competitiveness is rapidly achieved through these interventions, a requirement that is absolutely necessary for the successful implementation of all the other measures referred to. The particular policy focus that could be most appropriate will be different in different contexts, depending on the characteristics of the country and the technologies being absorbed (see box 3).

## Step 2.   Identifying instruments and policies for effective implementation

The next two steps (see figure 1) involve limiting the number of potential areas of policy intervention to a manageable number of areas where it is both feasible to intervene and where the payoff, in terms of contributing to the achievement of national development goals, is likely to be large. Step 2 is simply matching a number of policy interventions to the list of possible areas of intervention identified in step 1, keeping in mind that the institutional capacities of most developing country bureaucracies are limited and a further narrowing of options may be necessary once governance capacities are specifically taken into account in the next step.

Given the very different activities and competitive sectors in different countries, different strategies may be appropriate for improving productivity and employment in each context. The general areas where theoretical market failures may be operating and where pragmatic policy interventions may be justified are summarized in box 1. These broad areas of concern (coordination, financing, learning and so on) can provide decision makers with a template for discussing various pragmatic policies.

The most appropriate way to proceed, for countries that do not already have a successful track record in investment and technology policies, is to begin with a relatively modest set of policies, observe implementation for a few years, and then move on to more ambitious programmes or to re-design existing programmes as necessary. Given that the types of interventions that are likely to be necessary or feasible will vary significantly across countries, we can only consider some examples of policies and interventions that may be appropriate in terms of the policy goals discussed and summarized in box 1.

### Coordination of technology acquisition across firms and sectors

At the practical level, coordination requires setting up agencies with the effective power to bring together industrial, trade and business associations, identify areas where coordination of investment, production or marketing can enhance competitiveness across the board, and then follow this up with pragmatic policies to achieve these outcomes. The leadership of these agencies is critical. Successful countries often relied on lateral transfers to bring in enterprising and experienced individuals, often from the private sector to lead critical agencies tasked with industrial and technological upgrading. The agency leadership will have the task of assessing the data, identifying technologies and coordination strategies that are likely to achieve

**Box 3.    Identifying possible areas where investment
and technology policies may be useful**

Identifying a list of possible areas where investment and technology policies may assist output, productivity and/or employment growth involves a number of steps. The possible list will later be narrowed down further when implementation and governance capacities are taken into account.

- Use national and international evidence to identify activities where the country already has international competitiveness or is close to achieving international competitiveness. These activities are in any case very obvious as they will be activities producing products or services that the country is already successfully exporting.
- Use national and international evidence to identify the magnitude and efficiency of investment in these areas: is output increasing over time; is productivity improving over time (measured by the maintenance of market share against competitors); is product quality (measured by unit values) improving over time; are new products being added to the portfolio of products produced by the sectors in question?
- Use primarily international evidence from more advanced developing countries to identify the extent to which these sectors can serve as critical sectors for upgrading products (to higher value products), improving productivity (to allow higher wage employment and to maintain competitiveness), and establishing backward and forward linkages (to develop other sectors of the economy and to enhance competitiveness of existing sectors). The conclusion here may be to reject some sectors as likely candidates for significant upgrading attempts and to identifiy of others as possible candidates.

**Example 1.    Poor developing country with low investment rate**

Economic sectors (not an exhaustive list) include: low productivity peasant agriculture, low productivity garments manufacturing export sector enjoying international competitiveness, and medium productivity large-scale chemical industry built under import protection that is currently far from international competitiveness.

Examples of areas where investment and technology policies could be useful:
- Absence of backward linkages in the garments industry, necessitating the import of all accessories and of finished fabrics, some of which could be domestically produced. Potential for enhancing investment and technology acquisition through coordination, financing and sharing risks in introducing new machineries to improve product quality and move up the value chain, introducing on-the-job training programmes for workers and middle management to increase supply of skilled labour and share risks and costs of financing learning-by-doing.
- Large losses in the chemical industry preclude internal investment to upgrade. Potential of enhancing investment and competitiveness through risk-sharing to bring in new investment (possibly foreign partnerships attracted with special incentives that are clearly defined over limited time periods and tied to performance outcomes), coordinating tie-ups with foreign and domestic buyers to increase markets and changing product mix to serve new markets.
- Emerging export crops in agricultural sector constrained by low bargaining power in foreign markets to attract necessary investments in quality control, refrigeration and marketing. Potential of offering selective incentives to foreign technology providers to attract new technologies, coordinating marketing of high-value products like horticulture or fisheries with foreign retailers (possibly with special incentives limited in time and tied to specific performance outcomes).

**Box 3.   Identifying possible areas where investment
            and technology policies may be useful** (*continued*)

**Example 2.   Middle income developing country
                with moderate investment rate**

Economic sectors include significant large-scale manufacturing sector suffering from low competitiveness in many subsectors; international competitiveness is achieved in a limited number of niche manufacturing and service sectors; low productivity large farms dominate agricultural sector.

Examples of areas where investment and technology policies could be useful:

- Foreign technology and investment in potentially competitive large-scale manufacturing constrained by poor infrastructure and the risk of slow progress in learning. Scope for targeted infrastructure support and assistance in financing on-the-job learning to attract high-technology multinational investment and licensing of technology.
- Absence of coordination within potentially successful clusters of manufacturing (engineering, electronics, etc.) to acquire higher productivity technologies. Potential for coordination and assistance in bargaining with foreign technology suppliers and investors.
- High value-added agricultural products constrained by lack of infrastructure and high risk in moving into high-value export crops. Scope for targeted infrastructure for some agricultural sectors.

productivity, output or employment growth (as prioritized in the national development strategy) and following that up with feasible incentives to achieve the coordination.

To be effective, the agency leadership also needs to have the support of the executive to achieve credibility for the incentives and arrangements that are available. These incentives could range from technology licensing coordinated through the agency, to fiscal or infrastructural incentives to achieve coordinated investments. External technology providers and investors are also much more likely to engage in negotiations on the types of technology transferred in investments or through licensing to domestic producers if effective government backing for agreements is visible and credible.

*Sharing risk and enabling the financing of investment*

Market failures in credit and stock markets are very likely in developing countries. The provision of targeted credit to critical sectors to finance investment in new technologies and in backward and forward linkages is likely to be an important part of effective investment and technology policies.

Loans from banks at market rates of interest may overcome critical constraints, and these loans are more likely from commercial or public sector banks if the government is closely involved in the coordination of these investments and in policing performance. Entrepreneurs may be unwilling to borrow on the relatively brief re-payment timescales required by private commercial banks backed by their personal collateral. But they may be willing to accept a longer-term contract with a credible claim on their asset that lenders may effectively exercise with government support if competitiveness is not achieved and repayment is at risk.

The government may also finance technology acquisition and productivity up-grading through equity purchases in companies. This too needs to be credibly con-structed so that entrepreneurs risk effectively losing control of their companies if performance is poor. Otherwise, there is little credible compulsion on businesses to put in effort to the fullest extent to raise productivity and achieve rapid learning after receiving government-supported financing for technology acquisition.

### Sharing risk in labour training and learning processes

The problem of low labour productivity at the initial stages of introducing new tech-nologies and processes can often deter their introduction. At the initial stages, while learning-by-doing is still going on, the individual entrepreneur financing learning will face losses. However, if learning is successful, the entrepreneur can eventually become profitable, but the skilled labour may now decide to leave the firm as other entrepreneurs copy the success of the pioneers. This external effect can in turn deter the individual investor undertaking these investments in learning.

As industrial skills are a public good, coordinated strategies for acquiring these in-firm skills are therefore justified.

A number of different types of schemes can be used to share the risks and costs of in-firm learning. The government can assist with in-firm training schemes where skilled personnel from more advanced developing countries are invited to train labour of different categories either within the firm or in training agencies that closely mimic firm environments. In the past, learning could be financed through various subsidy schemes, including protection for infant industries, but these are increasingly diffi-cult and some schemes are entirely disallowed under WTO rules. Most developing countries are coming under WTO jurisdiction and the country agreements they have signed up to need to be carefully examined in designing firm-level training support schemes to ensure that they do not inadvertently fall foul of WTO rules. As most types of labour training are allowed under free trade agreements, a careful design of training schemes such that they do not amount to a free subsidy for the firm should enable these schemes to be legally introduced.

### Providing targeted infrastructure to critical sectors

These interventions are part of any coordinated strategy to accelerate technology acquisition and upgrading in critical sectors. Fiscal constraints in developing coun-tries prevent across-the-board improvement in infrastructure at early stages of devel-opment. However, if investment and technology policy agencies are well coordinated with the relevant public works ministries and the finance ministry, the critical infrastructural bottlenecks that may be constraining investments in competitive sectors seeking to upgrade can be overcome.

This approach involves making transport networks, utilities and other infrastructure available on a prioritized basis for sectors that are also part of a coordinated strategy of investment and technological upgrading. Clearly, an effective policy of prioritizing infrastructure for some sectors requires support from the highest executive levels if it is actually to be implemented. Once again, leadership of investment and technology policy agencies and close contact and support from the executive are critical for effective implementation.

### Developing regulatory capacity to maintain and enhance competitiveness

None of the investment and technology acquisition strategies discussed above are likely to work if complementary regulatory capacities are missing to ensure that supported sectors do not free ride on the support to maintain low productivity beyond reasonable learning periods.

We have seen earlier that interventions that seek to change the level and type of investment must, by their nature, assist some investors more than others. As long as the support policies continue, market competition is not sufficient for ensuring that underlying competitiveness is increasing at the desired rate. An important compulsion for productivity growth and learning is now the credibility of government promises to withdraw support if performance is poor, or even to reclaim loans or other support offered by acquiring ownership of designated assets and either selling them, or more likely, re-allocating them to new and more efficient ownership. Once again, competent and professional regulatory agencies have to be developed to work in parallel with agencies offering support to devise appropriate performance criteria, particularly for monitoring loans and other forms of financial support.

Box 4 shows examples of some types of policies that may emerge through the consultation process in the hypothetical developing countries discussed in box 3.

## Step 3.   Are institutional and governance capacities adequate for effective implementation?

This is the last of the three steps identified in figure 1. From the list of possible policy interventions identified in step 2, it is now prudent to select only the policies that can be effectively implemented given the emerging regulatory and implementation capacities of the government. The costs associated with overstretch are more serious than the costs associated with a more modest rate of progress in introducing investment and technology policy. This is because failure associated with excessively ambitious policies can result in the demoralization of policymakers and of the enterprise sector, and indeed undermine the broader political support behind the strategy. These setbacks can therefore be serious in having lasting negative effects on the gradual enhancement of investment and technology policy capacities in developing countries.

**Box 4.   Examples of investment and technology policies in our hypothetical developing countries**

**Example 1.   Poor developing country with low investment rate**

- Create an effective coordinating body to bring together investors in garments and related industries, particularly those with strong backward linkages to garments. Constructing integrated incentives to encourage investments in backward linkage sectors. Getting expert opinion on upgrading technologies used in the garments industry, to improve styling, packaging and marketing to move up the value chain. Identifying risk factors and determining the type and extent of risk-sharing that may be warranted. If market finance is not available on terms that existing producers will accept for technology upgrading loans, consider equity or loan schemes for garment producers investing in new technologies to improve productivity or product value, backed by strong and credible withdrawal strategies if performance is poor. Set up in-firm training schemes to train workers in new technologies and improve productivity through learning-by-doing when new machinery is introduced.

- Set up a high-powered agency to consult with foreign technology providers and identify the investment required and the risks involved in upgrading the loss-making chemical industry. Investment may be required both in fixed capital, but also in changing management styles and/or changing management. Offer incentives to foreign investors bringing in designated technologies and markets to share risk. Incentives can take the form of targeted or prioritized infrastructure, tax reductions over designated periods, fast-track approvals and so on.

- For high-value agricultural products, offer selective incentives to foreign technology providers or domestic firms investing in new technologies to upgrade quality control, refrigeration and marketing. Strengthen critical regulatory functions to ensure that pre-agreed targets and competitiveness improvements are achieved.

**Example 2.   Middle-income developing country with moderate investment rate**

- Set up a high-powered agency to identify investment and technology upgrading required for converting currently uncompetitive large-scale enterprises into profitable enterprises enjoying international competitiveness. Provide incentives for foreign investors bringing in designated technologies and investments to share risks. This could include prioritized infrastructure, tax breaks, more liberal profit repatriation over designated periods and so on. Adding the credibility and weight of government can assure foreign investors that appropriate regulatory structures, fiscal incentives and infrastructural support will be available. Develop regulatory agencies to monitor progress and set time limits for support.

- Set up coordinating agency to identify and bring together investors in critical clusters of industry (engineering, electronics, etc.) to identify possibilities of technology upgrading and backward and forward linkages. Involve government in bargaining with foreign technology suppliers and investors, offering prioritized infrastructure and tax and other incentives if required.

- Provide targeted infrastructure for high value-added agricultural sectors or sectors deemed to contribute to the national development plan. Regulatory support is particularly important in preventing wastage of support in the relatively dispersed agricultural sector.

At this stage of the policymaking process, the political and executive leadership of government have to consider very carefully the bureaucratic and political requirements for the effective implementation of particular policies. The bureaucratic requirements include being able to recruit the appropriate high-powered and experienced personnel with an exposure, not just to business in that particular country, but also to countries at more advanced stages of using technologies that the developing country is aspiring to. This is a serious constraint, but is a less serious constraint than trying to reform the entire bureaucracy. A few effective people at the top, charged with carrying out a very narrow remit of policies, can achieve significant success, provided clear and effective political backing is forthcoming for these policies.

The political requirements of effective investment and technology policies are much more demanding, and vary depending on the types of interventions being attempted. This could make some types of interventions viable while others not, and it is at this stage that non-viable or non-implementable policies should be temporarily abandoned, while the requisite bureaucratic and political capacities are being developed.

The political requirements include, but are not restricted to the following:

- *First*, the political leadership should be open enough and legitimate enough to be able to engage in a national dialogue about investment and technology priorities without appearing to be engaged in a sham discourse that intends to benefit supporters of the current regime. Support for investment and technology policy can be developed on a non-partisan basis by involving, from the outset, all industry associations and stakeholders regardless of their partisan and factional affiliations.

   If the discussion is seen to be open and responsive, and if the beneficiaries of policies come from a broad range of camps, the political conditions for successful implementation can be achieved. The consultation exercise should not be treated as one that tries to "optimize" the selection of sectors that should be prioritized, since there are many grey areas and an accurate optimization would be impossible in any case. Rather, *the task of consultation should be one of selecting a number of important sectors on which to concentrate the limited fiscal and regulatory capacities of the State to accelerate national development.* This realization can allow a number of diverse sectors to be selected for upgrading to defuse tensions and limit unnecessary rent-seeking that seeks to influence government policy. But it has to be recognized that these minimal conditions do not hold in some developing countries, and in these cases progress will be more limited. In these countries, effort first has to be put into constructing a broad political support behind investment and technology policies by engaging with business and trade associations.

- A *second* political condition required for more ambitious interventions to assist learning and provide targeted infrastructure is for regulatory agencies to have the effective capacity to negotiate regulatory agreements and withdraw support or assistance from sectors that fail to achieve regulatory targets. This capacity is not just a bureaucratic or institutional capacity (although that is also required); it is primarily a political capacity because regulatory agencies have to have the ability to withdraw support if necessary even from favoured clients of the government. While rent seeking and corruption are widespread in many developing countries, the variant of corruption that involves the political protection of powerful clients has often been the main reason for the failure of investment and technology policies in developing countries (Khan, 1996, 2002 and 2006).

Developing countries that cannot ensure the separation of the regulation of investment and technology policy from the horse-trading of patron-client politics are unlikely to succeed in these strategies. Note that what is required for success is not the much more demanding task of reducing corruption and rent-seeking across the board. What is required is the much less stringent condition that only the critical regulatory agencies charged with implementing and regulating investment and technology strategies should be insulated from rent-seeking and political interference. The greater the consensus on the importance of this, the greater the chances of success. In the absence of any consensus within the main political parties, the chances of success are more limited and it may be better to limit investment and technology policies to areas where ongoing regulatory management is not required. For instance, coordination and the provision of help in bargaining with external technology providers are less onerous in terms of regulatory requirements than sharing risks in technology acquisition through the provision of finance or prioritized infrastructure provision.

The final stage of the policymaking process should take these considerations and other political constraints into account to further limit the range of policies being considered to those that can actually be implemented, given existing political and institutional realities (see figure 1). This is not necessarily a minimalist approach, since *current investment and technology policy can also identify appropriate governance reforms to address some of the political and institutional conditions that would allow more extensive investment and technology policies to be attempted in subsequent years.* We conclude with box 5, which suggests how the policies identified in box 4 for our two hypothetical countries need to be further whittled down in line with the current (hypothetical) governance capacities of the two countries. The exercise also identifies the relevant governance reforms that need to be prioritized in each country.

A final check is now required to ensure that the policies going forward as national investment and technology policies have fiscal implications consistent with the macroeconomic policy and fiscal claims of other policies.

The conclusion of the process described above should lead to two types of policy outcomes:

*First*, we should be able to identify a pragmatic and feasible set of investment and technology policies that can make a contribution to the broader goals of the national

## Box 5.   Final selection of investment and technology policies in our hypothetical developing countries

**Example 1.   Poor developing country with low investment rate**

- **Current institutional and governance capacities:** Weak bureaucracy, but has capacity to appoint competent professionals at the top of critical agencies. Political party in power enjoys broad legitimacy and is willing to concede entry to rival factions in determining industrial policy.
- **Selection of policies from box 4:** All three types of policies discussed in box 4 are potentially feasible in this case. Nevertheless, given bureaucratic limitations, it would be prudent to begin with progress on one of these sectors, say by setting up a coordinating body for upgrading the garments sector and its backward linkages. If there is observable progress, policy can be extended to other sectors in subsequent years.
- **Identification of governance priorities for strengthening investment and technology policy in the future:** Further strengthening of bureaucratic capabilities in key regulatory agencies. Building on consensus between major parties by institutionalizing joint consultations on key investment and technology issues.

**Example 2.   Middle-income developing country with moderate investment rate**

- **Current institutional and governance capacities:** Moderately competent bureaucracy; capacity to appoint competent professionals to head key agencies. But politics is intensely competitive between competing factional parties, with no agreement on national priorities or possibility of reaching agreement in the short term. Rapid turnover of parties with short-time horizons.
- **Selection of policies from box 4:** Regulatory capacities for providing targeted infrastructure or risk-sharing finance to enable upgrading of uncompetitive large-scale enterprises or the agricultural sector are unlikely to be sufficiently effective. A coordination agency for identifying technology requirements and upgrading in the major industrial clusters may be the most appropriate place to start, providing shared information and creating pressure on government for targeted infrastructure and fiscal incentives. However, even these can, at best, be modest, given the absence of regulatory capacities to ensure improvement in competitiveness.
- **Identification of governance priorities for strengthening investment and technology policy in the future:** The main priority in this case would be to attempt to construct a minimal consensus between the competing parties on national investment and technology priorities. Political skill needs to be deployed to identify joint benefits for clients of different factions to allow national strategies to be identified and implemented.

development strategy. Depending on the economic characteristics of the country and its existing governance capacities, these policies may be more or less extensive.

But *secondly*, we should also be able to identify a number of critical governance priorities that can go ahead as recommendations from policymakers involved in investment and technology policy as necessary conditions for proceeding further with national strategy. These governance priorities are inevitably going to be more limited than the broad good governance reforms that come from the conventional reform agenda. This is an advantage, because concentrating on a limited and relevant set of governance reforms that have some chance of being partially achieved can significantly improve the relevance of governance reforms and their impact on development outcomes.

## Investment and technology policy compared with good governance and investment climate reforms

Investment and technology policies often do not receive very detailed attention in many developing countries in their national policymaking process. Instead, it is often assumed that general reforms to improve *good governance* and the *investment climate* will indirectly improve the quantity and quality of investment, and help to attract better and more productive technologies. While these reforms are highly desirable in themselves, there are good reasons why the implementation of good governance reforms in developing countries is likely to be very slow, and have a very limited impact on improving investment and technology acquisition over a reasonable planning horizon. A reliance on these policies alone is therefore likely to result in lost opportunities for enhancing investment and technology acquisition in many developing countries. This section provides policymakers with some basic arguments for not relying exclusively on good governance and investment climate reforms, and instead focusing on appropriate pragmatic governance reforms that can improve the implementation of effective investment and technology policies.

In making the case for a dedicated investment and technology policy, it is important to understand the case for the good governance and investment climate approaches, their merits but also their limitations. Given the importance and appeal of many good governance reforms as goals in their own right, an evaluation of the limits of these reforms for achieving other objectives is particularly important. Figure 2 summarizes the policy priorities of the good governance and investment climate approaches and the linkages through which these reform priorities are expected to lead to increased investments and to improvements in technology.

These approaches stress "horizontal" policies in that they do not target specific investment or technology bottlenecks. Rather, they seek to improve the institutional and infrastructural *environment* in which investments and technology decisions are made. The expectation in these approaches is that if the general environment in which a market economy operates can be improved, market efficiency will improve and better investment and technology decisions will follow. In a poor economy with insufficient investment and poor technology, the expectation is that an improvement in market efficiency and in essential infrastructure will lead to increased private investment and the adoption of superior technologies.

In the *good governance* and *investment climate* approaches, the main constraint to long-term investments in developing countries is assumed to be the absence of efficient markets where investors have the confidence to invest for the long term. The critical requirement for efficient markets is that market participants should be able to contract complex exchanges at low "transaction cost", and for this we require stable property rights and a rule of law. Stable property rights and the rule of law are the critical factors that allow complex contracting at low cost. These characteristics are therefore necessary if markets are to allow high levels of investment and investments that take a long-term perspective.

However, in developing country markets, the costs of finding trading partners, making contracts and particularly of enforcing contracts are notoriously high. These high transaction costs can, in general, be attributed to insecure property rights and contracts, and these, in turn, therefore explain why private investment is low and of low quality. With insecure property rights, many investors simply do not invest. In addition, investors stay away from high technology investments with long gestation periods as these investments, in particular, require stable and complex contracts for investors taking significant risks. The good governance approach therefore focuses on a series of governance reforms that address the problem of weak property rights and contracts that, in turn, prevent markets in developing countries from operating efficiently.

This is elaborated in figure 2. Important reform priorities in this approach are to improve the rule of law and to constrain State and non-State expropriators from threatening to expropriate private property. In addition, transaction costs are also

Figure 2.   Good governance and investment climate reform priorities

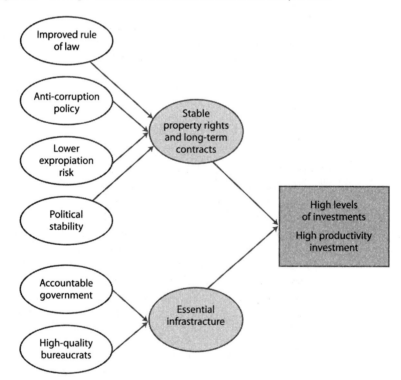

raised by rampant corruption which forces investors to work their way around a maze of restrictions and demands for bribes. Thus, anti-corruption strategies play an important role in the good governance reform agenda. Finally, political stability is required to ensure policy continuity and to reduce uncertainty about future expropriation.

These requirements define the reform priorities for good governance reforms in developing countries. Many of these reforms are desirable for their own sake, but in the good governance approach they are also necessary *means* for improving market efficiency and, thereby, increasing investment and enabling investment in more complex higher technology sectors. This is why governance is increasingly at the top of the reform agenda in many developing countries, and these reforms often also dominate the reform agenda for investment and technology policy.

The investment climate approach agrees about the importance of these governance reforms and adds that public infrastructure is often also essential to attract more and better investment. These infrastructure requirements include the efficient supply of utilities like electricity, water, telecommunications, roads, railways and ports. It is assumed that improvements in the accountability of government and improvements in the quality of bureaucrats in key service delivery areas will lead to more effective delivery of key public infrastructure. The size of the bureaucracy should therefore be reduced and the remaining bureaucrats should be selected for quality and paid properly.

Clearly, many of these reform agendas are interdependent; for instance, accountability reforms should improve political stability and reduce corruption, while anti-corruption reforms should improve the quality of public infrastructure. The quality of infrastructure has a direct effect on investment. With better infrastructure, investments become more profitable, thereby increasing both the quantity of investment and investment in high productivity areas that are more sensitive to the quality of infrastructure.

As summarized in figure 2, these theoretical considerations lead the good governance and investment climate approaches to argue that reforms in these areas will lead to more investment and better quality investment in developing countries. In support of these theoretical arguments, a large number of studies have found correlations between measures of good governance and the growth rate, the rate of investment and the rate of R&D expenditures in developing countries (Knack and Keefer, 1995 and 1997; Mauro, 1997; Kauffman and others, 1999).

While these reforms are highly desirable in themselves, as the central policy plank for achieving better investment and technology performance, the good governance and investment climate approaches are inadequate for most developing countries. It is important to understand why. We argue that *specific policies and instruments are required to tackle some of the bottlenecks in investment and technology upgrading directly,* and that such policies are more likely to yield results in the context of most developing countries.

## Limitations of good governance and investment climate reforms

The good governance and investment climate reform priorities seek to achieve governance and infrastructure goals that are desirable in themselves. But in many developing countries, *progress in achieving good governance goals and infrastructure improvements across the board is likely to be very slow, with a correspondingly limited impact on investment and technology acquisition.*

However, significant progress in achieving good governance goals—in particular the key goals of stable property rights, a satisfactory rule of law or significant reductions in corruption—requires substantial fiscal resources to finance the requisite policing and enforcement of property rights and contracts (figure 3). Achieving stable property rights is one of the most expensive public goods, as evidenced by the size of the transaction cost sector in advanced countries like the United States, which, by some estimates, absorbs close to half the country's GDP (North and Wallis, 1987).

In other words, stable property rights and low transaction costs at the point of exchange in advanced countries can only be achieved if significant expenditures of resources in legal costs, public policing, private arbitration, legalized and regulated lobbying, political processes and so on can take place.

Given the expense involved, and the intense competition for fiscal resources in developing countries, it is not surprising that developing countries that have set themselves the target of achieving good governance improvements have not, in general, achieved significant success in improving their governance indicators in the short to

**Figure 3.    Limitations of good governance and investment climate approaches**

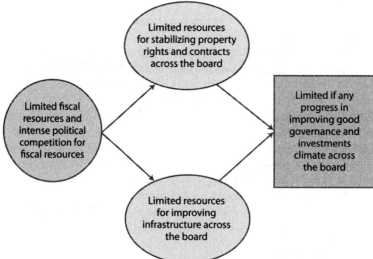

medium term. For very similar reasons, it is not easy rapidly to improve the quality of infrastructure *across the board* in developing countries, given fiscal constraints and the intense political competition for fiscal resources.

Thus, for most developing countries, achieving good governance and infrastructure improvements across the board have proved very difficult to achieve, even when the political will has been there and these goals have been identified as reform priorities. It follows that, if progress on these fronts is slow, progress in investment and in technology adoption that depends on improvements on these fronts is also likely to be very slow. This is summarized in figure 3.

Given the economic constraints preventing the achievement of stable property rights and low transaction costs across the board in poor countries, it is not surprising that the historical evidence shows that high-growth developing countries did not achieve significantly higher property right stability than low-growth developing countries. Figure 4 uses the composite property rights index (IRIS-3, 2000), constructed by Knack and Keefer at the IRIS centre at Maryland as an aggregate of indices for corruption, rule of law, bureaucratic quality, contract repudiation and expropriation risk. Figure 4 uses the 1990 values of the property rights index for all available countries, and compares their growth rates over the next 13 years for which data are available.

While there is a weak positive relationship discernible between better governance according to the good governance indicators, and the growth rate (just as the good governance policy approach asserts), *we do not observe any significant difference*

Figure 4.   Composite property rights index and growth, 1990-2003
            (using Knack-IRIS data)

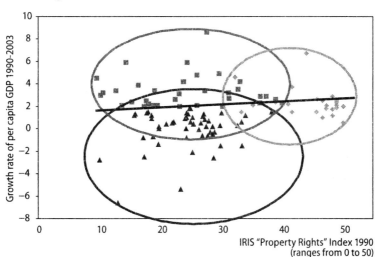

IRIS "Property Rights" Index 1990
(ranges from 0 to 50)

◆ Advanced countries
▦ Converging developing countries
▲ Diverging developing countries

*in the average score or the range of scores when we compare high- and low-growth developing countries.* In figure 4, advanced countries are shown with blue diamonds, converging developing countries (with growth rates higher than the median advanced country growth rate) are shown with green squares and diverging developing countries (with growth rates lower than the median advanced country growth rate) are shown with red triangles. The important observation is that high growth developing countries had, on average, a very similar mean score and dispersion on good governance indicators compared to low-growth developing countries (Khan, 2004; United Nations, 2006).

What this shows is that high-growth developers did not, in general, succeed because their average property right stability was significantly higher than that of low-growth developers, and they certainly did not have property right stability comparable to advanced countries. Given what we know about the cost of providing the public goods required for achieving stable property rights and effective contract enforcement systems, it would be surprising if the observation was otherwise. Similarly, while it is undoubtedly true that better infrastructure is preferable for investment, growth takeoffs in high-growth countries have not waited for across-the-board improvements in infrastructure. Rather, as growth took off, infrastructure improvements became easier to finance, and better infrastructure made further investments more profitable, thereby setting off virtuous cycles. Exactly the same is true for expenditure on property right stabilization and further improvements in the investment climate.

## Critical governance capacities required for investment and technology policy versus good governance capacities

The discussion of policy measures, through which investment and technology acquisition can be accelerated, has identified a number of critical governance capacities that States in developing countries need to have if they are to implement these types of policies and programmes successfully. For instance, for some investment and technology policies, governance capacities have to be developed to identify areas of technology coordination and to follow up coordination discussions with effective policies to overcome bottlenecks. In the case of other policies that seek to accelerate learning or to improve competitiveness, governance capacities are required to identify and deal with failing performance through the withdrawal of support and the transfer of support to other sectors and technologies (Khan, 2000). Managing exit from support strategies is one of the critical governance capacities required for the success of investment and technology policies.

This analysis clearly shifts the focus of governance reforms appropriate for investment and technology policy away from the broad good governance reforms that many developing countries are already trying to implement, often with very little success. This does not mean that the *goals* of good governance are unimportant. Good governance goals are desirable on their own terms, and developing countries should attempt to maximize their achievement of these goals at every stage of development. But it does mean that the attempt to improve these conditions to any significant extent with very limited fiscal and reform capacities is too ambitious, and the expected effects on investment and technology acquisition are likely to be low. *While good governance reforms are desirable on their own terms, developing countries should not exclusively depend on these policies to improve their investment and technology performance.*

The capacity to address critical market failures that may prevent investment and technology upgrading and the capacity to prioritize a few sectors at a time has often been wrongly characterized as a strategy of "picking winners". If investment and technology policy really depended on the foresight of policymakers to pick winners, its potential success would indeed be highly questionable. In reality, success in investment and technology policy of the type we have been describing has been based on a pragmatic identification of bottlenecks and constraints hindering progress in critical economic sectors, combined with the institutional and political capability to respond to continuing poor performance by changing policies or changing the focus of policies towards other priority sectors (see box 6).

---

**Box 6.   Investment and technology policy
              is not about "picking winners"**

"Horizontal" policies of improving the investment climate are likely to take too long to produce significant improvements across the board in most developing countries. Not surprisingly, successful developing countries have always had specific investment and technology policies to overcome the most important bottlenecks. At any particular time, these policies implicitly favour some sectors over others, though these change rapidly over time as bottlenecks are overcome. As a result, investment and technology policies have often been misleadingly described as policies of "picking winners".

In fact, bureaucrats, politicians or industry associations are likely frequently to be wrong if they were trying to pick "winning" sectors or technologies for support.

In reality, successful investment and technology policy is based on a pragmatic identification of a few bottlenecks and constraints that are preventing critical sectors from improving competitiveness and moving up the technology ladder. Rather than the ability to pick winners, successful countries have had the capacity to change policies if investment and technology performance in priority sectors turned out to be poor. The capacity to change policy or to shift focus to other sectors is a critical and necessary condition to ensure success. Ex post flexibility of response, rather than the ex ante ability to pick winners, has distinguished success from failure in investment and technology policy. Successful investment and technology policies did not "pick" winners, rather they helped to "make" winners, and if winners could not be made in some sectors, policy shifted quickly to other promising sectors.

## References

Aghion, Philippe, Nicholas Bloom, Richard Blundell, Rachel Griffith and Peter Howitt (2002). "Competition and innovation: an inverted U relationship". Working Paper No. WP02/04. London: Institute for Fiscal Studies.

Amsden, Alice (1989). *Asia's Next Giant: South Korea and Late Industrialization*. Oxford: Oxford University Press.

Aoki, Masahiko, Hyung-Ki Kim and Masahiro Okuno-Fujiwara, eds. (1997). *The Role of Government in East Asian Economic Development: Comparative Institutional Analysis*. Oxford: Clarendon Press.

Hellman, Thomas, Kevin Murdock and Joseph Stiglitz (1997). "Financial restraints: toward a new paradigm", in *The Role of Government in East Asian Economic Development: Comparative Institutional Analysis*. Masahiko Aoki, Hyung-Ki Kim and Masahiro Okuno-Fujiwara, eds. Oxford: Clarendon Press.

IRIS-3 (2000). *File of International Country Risk Guide (ICRG) Data*, Stephen Knack and the IRIS Center, eds. College Park: University of Maryland.

Kaldor, Nicholas (1966). *Causes of the Slow Rate of Growth of the United Kingdom; An Inaugural Lecture*. Cambridge: Cambridge University Press.

Kauffman, Daniel, Aart Kraay and Pablo Zoido-Lobatón (1999). "Governance matters". World Bank Policy Working Paper No. 2196. Washington, D.C.: World Bank.

Khan, Mushtaq (1996). "The efficiency implications of corruption", *Journal of International Development*, vol. 8, No. 5, pp. 683-696.

_____(2000). "Rent-seeking as process", in *Rents, Rent-Seeking and Economic Development: Theory and Evidence in Asia*, Mushtaq Khan and Jomo K. S., eds. Cambridge: Cambridge University Press.

_____(2002). "Corruption and governance in early capitalism: World Bank strategies and their limitations", in *Reinventing the World Bank*. Jonathan Pincus and Jeffrey Winters, eds. Ithaca: Cornell University Press.

_____(2004). "State failure in developing countries and strategies of institutional reform", in *Toward Pro-poor Policies: Aid Institutions and Globalization*. Bertil Tungodden, Nicholas Stern and Ivar Kolstad, eds. Proceedings of Annual World Bank Conference on Development Economics. New York: Oxford University Press for World Bank.

_____(2006). "Corruption and governance", in *The New Development Economics*, Jomo K. S. and Ben Fine, eds. London and New Delhi: Zed Press and Tulika.

Khan, Mushtaq, and Jomo K. S., eds. (2000). *Rents, Rent-seeking and Economic Development: Theory and Evidence in Asia*. Cambridge: Cambridge University Press.

Knack, Stephen, and Philip Keefer (1995). "Institutions and economic performance: cross-country tests using alternative institutional measures". *Economics and Politics*, vol. 7, No. 3, pp. 207-227.

_____(1997). "Why don't poor countries catch up? A cross-national test of an institutional explanation", *Economic Inquiry*, vol. 35, No. 3, pp. 590-602.

Mauro, Paolo (1997). "The effects of corruption on growth, investment and government expenditure: a cross-country analysis", in *Corruption and the Global Economy*. Kimberly Elliot, ed. Washington: Institute for International Economics.

North, Douglass, and John Wallis (1987). "Measuring the transaction sector in the American economy 1870-1970", in *Long-Term Factors in American Economic Growth*. S. L. Engerman and R. E. Gallman, eds. Chicago: Chicago University Press.

Rajan, Raghuram, and Luigi Zingales (2003). *Saving Capitalism from the Capitalists*. London: Random House.

Singh, Ajit (1997). "Financial liberalisation, stockmarkets and economic development", *Economic Journal*, vol. 107, No. 442, pp. 771-782.

Singh, Ajit (1999). "Should Africa promote stock market capitalism?", *Journal of International Development*, vol. 11, No. 3, pp. 343-365.

United Nations (2006). *World Economic and Social Survey 2006*. Department of Economic and Social Affairs of the United Nations, New York.

Wade, Robert (1990). *Governing the Market: Economic Theory and the Role of Government in East Asian Industrialization*. Princeton: Princeton University Press.

# Social policy

Isabel Ortiz*

## Introduction

Modern government is based on a social contract between citizens and the State in which rights and duties are agreed to by all to further the common interest. Citizens lend their support to a government through taxes and efforts to a country's good; in return, governments acquire legitimacy by protecting the people's rights and through public policies that benefit all. However, policymaking is often captured by powerful groups and elites, making government policies biased and unaccountable to the majority of citizens. With half the world's population living below the two-dollar-a-day poverty line, ineffective social policies can be the spark for State breakdown. Lack of opportunity, authoritarian rule, gross inequity, exclusion and deprivation—all increase the likelihood of a State's de-legitimization and withdrawal of its citizens' support, leading to social disintegration, conflict and violence.

Social policy is an instrument applied by governments to regulate and supplement market institutions and social structures. Social policy is often defined as social services such as education, health, employment and social security. However, social policy is also about redistribution, protection and social justice. Social policy is about bringing people into the centre of policymaking, not by providing residual welfare, but by mainstreaming their needs and voice across sectors, generating stability and social cohesion. Social policy is also instrumental in that governments use it pragmatically to secure the political support of citizens, and to promote positive economic outcomes by enhancing human capital and productive employment. Social policies can also create a virtuous circle linking human and economic development that, in the long run, will benefit everybody by boosting domestic demand and creating stable cohesive societies.

*   The author would like to thank Jomo K. S., Assistant Secretary-General for Economic Development, United Nations; Joseph Stiglitz, Professor of Economics at University of Columbia; José Antonio Ocampo, former Under-Secretary-General for Economic and Social Affairs, United Nations; Dorothy Rosenberg and Darryl McLeod, Bureau for Policy Development, UNDP; Bob Huber, Sergei Zelenev and Thomas Schindlmayr, Division for Social Policy and Development, UNDESA; Bob Deacon, Director Globalism and Social Policy Programme, UK; Katja Hujo, Yusuf Bangura, Terence Gomez, Shahra Razavi and Peter Utting, UNRISD; Harry Shutt, UK; Sylvie Cohen, Anna Falth, Sibel Selcuk and Wenyan Yang, Division for the Advancement of Women, UNDESA; and Gabriele Kohler and Enrique Delamonica, UNICEF, for their helpful comments and suggestions. Special appreciation to Khoo Khay Jin, who edited the UNDESA Policy Notes.

This Policy Note seeks to promote inclusive social policies. It highlights opportunities to enhance equity, and concentrates on selected social policies crucial to the preparation of inclusive national development strategies. The first section provides a historical perspective on the application of social policy and the arguments for investing in inclusive social development. The following sections concentrate on how to draft national social development strategies. The final part discusses selected social policy priorities on employment, education, health, social protection, culture and conflict prevention. References and essential supporting documentation are provided in the references section at the end.

## Social policy

*Background:* In the 1980s and 1990s, the scope of social policy, focused on delivery of limited services and welfare, was insufficient to achieve balanced social and economic development. Social policy was considered residual, secondary to the focus on growth as then mainstream development theory focused on "economic growth first" (box 1). As such, social policy was given lesser importance and funding, and often was centred on mitigating the unintended consequences of economic change. This residual approach was dominant for about two decades, and led to increasing social tensions and malaise.

This minimalist vision of social development was not common in earlier times in the twentieth century. On the contrary, today's high-income economies invested heavily in social development, and the populations of Europe, Japan, North America, Australia and New Zealand experienced a level of prosperity unseen in history. Following their example, many developing countries also saw the need to apply social policies as an instrument for nation building. East Asia's social policies, or the comprehensive social security systems in some Latin American countries are examples of these initiatives. These governments saw that social investments were essential not only to modernize and develop a country, but also to achieve social cohesion and political stability.

Many of these pre-1980s social initiatives were weakened as redistributive policies were sidelined by market-oriented reforms and critical attacks on State interventionism. The structural adjustment programmes launched after the 1982 debt crisis severely curtailed social expenditures, to the point that UNICEF appealed for "adjustment with a human face".[1] After having been pared to a minimum, social policies were reconsidered during the 1990s with the renewed attention of development policies to poverty reduction. Even then, social policies were treated as marginal, reduced to little more than the idea of social safety nets in times of economic crisis as in the Asian financial crisis and the extension of basic education elsewhere, often left to donor-funded social investment programmes. These were well-intentioned initiatives by committed professionals but not adequate as lasting solutions. These interventions

---

1   A critical assessment of the impacts of structural adjustment programmes in Giovanni Andrea Cornia, Richard Jolly and Frances Stewart, 1987.

did not address the structural causes of social tensions or build institutions to ensure equitable and sustainable development, decent work and social cohesion.

In the early twenty-first century, a consensus has emerged that social policy is part of the primary function of the State, and that social policy is more than a limited set of safety nets and services to cover market failure. Well-designed and implemented social policies can powerfully shape countries, foster employment and development, eradicate marginalization and overcome conflict. They are an essential part of any national development strategy to achieve growth and equitable social outcomes.

Social policy is also necessary in a globalizing world. The extreme inequality in the world distribution of income and assets seriously undermines the effectiveness of global growth in reducing poverty. The magnitude of distribution asymmetries is significant: In 2000, the richest 1 per cent of adults alone owned 40 per cent of global assets, and the richest 10 per cent of adults accounted for 85 per cent of total world

## Box 1.   Growth alone is not enough

Some argue that social policies should not be a primary policy objective for developing countries. Instead, it is said that economic growth should be the first priority, as the benefits of growth will eventually "trickle down" to the poor. The rationale of this conservative argument is that:

- Growth is a pre-requisite for poverty reduction. The benefits of growth will eventually trickle down to the rest of society.
- The rich save more; higher inequality means higher rates of savings, investment and future growth.
- Poverty keeps the labour force cheap and thus encourages investment.
- Minimal social policies and regulations make labour markets flexible, and employment more likely.
- Taxation on higher income groups should be limited to maximize the retained income available for investment.
- Later, as the country becomes richer, defenders of this view argue, governments may invest in social development.

Such views are still influential in development debates, mostly in the form of a vague "trickle down plus" approach: growth as first priority, with some basic education, health and other limited social development interventions. Such arguments serve to delay social development and other equitable policies.

However, a considerable amount of recent research shows that economic growth and social development policies must be pursued simultaneously, rather than sequentially, as:

- Poverty and inequality inhibit growth, depress domestic demand and hinder national economic development. Developing countries with high inequality tend to grow slower.
- A low-wage policy has adverse effects on productivity, encouraging countries to compete on the basis of cheap labour, in a "race to the bottom", further depressing real wage levels.

**Box 1.    Growth alone is not enough** (*continued*)

- While sustained high rapid growth may lift people out of poverty, growing inequality may undermine its impact on poverty reduction, as in China recently. For the vast majority of developing countries, more modest growth and growing inequality have limited, even no, poverty reduction impact.
- The greater the inequality, the less the "trickle down" effect.
- Only 4.2 per cent of the world's growth reaches the poorer half of the world's population.
- Poverty and inequality are an obstacle to social progress, and can lead to social conflict and political instability.
- Historically, social development accompanied industrialization and economic development in most countries. In much of Europe and elsewhere, popular struggles led social development. In East Asia's "late industrializers", social investment was an integral part of modernization processes, nation building and productive development.

There is now a consensus on the urgency to promote robust social and economic policies in parallel, in a complementary and mutually reinforcing manner. Economic growth permits sustained investments in social development; and human development raises the capacities of people to contribute to growth. Sustainable growth and poverty reduction require socially inclusive national development strategies.

*Sources:* Birdsall, 2005; Ocampo, 2006; Ranis and Stewart, 2005; United Nations, 2005; UNRISD, 2005; Woodward and Simms, 2006; World Bank, 2005.

assets; in contrast, the bottom half of the world adult population owned barely 1 per cent of global wealth.[2] This urgent need to reduce poverty, exclusion and conflict has brought social policy to the forefront of the development agenda.

**Justification:** Social policies are necessary because the benefits of economic growth do not automatically reach all. Inadequate social policies ultimately limit growth in the medium and long term. Social policies are justified not only from a humanitarian viewpoint; they are an economic and political need for future growth and political stability, minimally to maintain citizen support for their governments. Specifically, the arguments for equitable development policies are:

- Investing in people enhances the quality and productivity of the labour force, thus improving the investment climate and, hence, growth.
- Raising the incomes of the poor increases domestic demand and, in turn, encourages growth; greater consumption ratios among lower-income groups contribute to expanding the domestic market.
- Highly unequal societies are associated with lower rates of growth.
- Among children, poverty and malnutrition damage health, reduce body weight and intelligence, resulting in lower productivity in adulthood; a high tax for a country to pay.

---

2    See UNU-WIDER, 2006; Jomo and Baudot, 2007.

- Investing in girls and women has numerous positive multiplier effects for social and economic development.
- Unequal societies are not only unjust but also cannot guarantee social and political stability in the long term, which is a barrier to economic growth.
- Gross inequities and their associated intense social tensions are more likely to result in violent conflict, ultimately destabilizing governments and regions, and may make people more susceptible to terrorist appeals and acts.
- Not least, inequality is inconsistent with the United Nations Charter, the Millennium Declaration and the Universal Declaration of Human Rights according to which everybody is entitled to minimum standards of living (food, clothing, housing, education, medical care, social security and others).

For these reasons, economic and social policies need to be promoted in parallel, in a mutually reinforcing way, from an early development stage, as part of the country's national development strategy and the social contract between government and citizens.

*Importance of political commitment:* At the World Summit for Social Development (1995), world leaders discussed how residual approaches to social policies had led to adverse consequences, and highlighted the need for comprehensive universal social policies to ensure a "society for all", in which economic and social development are mutually reinforcing. Their concerns and recommendations were incorporated into

---

**Box 2. Redistribution is critical to reduce poverty and sustain growth**

Sustained poverty reduction is a twin function of the rate of growth and of changes in income distribution. Redistribution has faster impacts on reducing poverty than growth, but economic growth is necessary to sustain the process over time. An exclusive focus on distribution leads to inflation and stagnation, leaving populations worse off—the fate of some "populist" governments. An exclusive focus on growth leads to large inequalities, as many countries experienced in the 1980s and 1990s. Redistribution is not antagonistic to growth; it stimulates consumption, raises productivity and is important to sustain growth itself. What is needed is to find combinations of instruments and policies that will deliver both growth and equity (Kanbur and Lustig, 2000).

World Bank Chief Economist F. Bourguignon stresses that income distribution matters as much as growth for poverty reduction. Redistribution is a legitimate goal of public policy, to balance the tendency of the market to concentrate resources. Redistribution may be achieved through domestic taxation, increased development aid and new proposed international sources such as taxes on short-term speculative financial transactions, on arms trade, pollution and others. Jeffrey Sachs, Director of the UN Millennium Project, notes that poverty could be eradicated with only 1 per cent of the combined GDP of OECD countries. Without equitable policies, poverty will not be eradicated.

*Source*: Bourguignon, 2004; Daddeviern, Van der Hoeven and Weeks, 2001; Kanbur and Lustig, 1999; Sachs/UN Millennium Project, 2005.

the Millennium Declaration, which restates international commitments to core values of freedom, equality, solidarity and peace. Adopted in 2000 by a vote of 189 member nations of the United Nations, it serves as the basis for the Millennium Development Goals (MDGs), a set of quantifiable and time-bound targets that measure progress in achieving public goods essential to the welfare and cohesion of a society. These were reaffirmed at the 2005 World Summit, with governments' pledging more ambitious national development strategies, backed by increased international support.

To achieve the MDGs, political commitment is necessary, particularly at a time when governments have a reduced national "policy space" (a constriction of domestic policymaking capacity in an open economy), less autonomy in public sector interventions and reduced fiscal capacity.

- To be sustainable, social policies also require the creation of supportive political coalitions, and need to be designed with an eye to constituting such coalitions, while resisting policy capture by elite or vested interests.
- In an era of constricted policy options for national administrations, creativity is needed to enhance capacity for development; governments and development agencies are rethinking State-market relations, abandoning minimalist government approaches and proposing ways to expand a country's policy space through different macroeconomic and sector policies.
- Successful social policies require the political commitment of a country's leadership, and cannot be imposed by donor-driven conditionalities. There is no "one-size-fits-all" policy. Choices ultimately depend on country context, domestic needs, internal political agreements/alliances, fiscal space and government motivation. A State's underlying motives for social policy may include nation building, fostering domestic development, social cohesion and political stability.

## Social policy in national development strategies

Governments launch national development strategies to build countries that are socially inclusive, employment generating, economically robust and politically stable. Figure 1 presents a flow chart of the process; details are provided in later sections. National development strategies are an opportunity to rethink a country's social contract. Technocratic sectoral approaches alone are insufficient. To be effective, national strategies have to be articulated in an integrated manner and supported by a coalition of social and political forces, or social pacts, involving State, business and organized civil society (see box 16). This shared vision is the critical factor to sustain development processes. Ultimately, it is the willingness of different social groups to pursue a common interest that allows development to succeed.

National development strategies entail:

1. A diagnosis of social and economic issues, identifying national socio-economic objectives to promote equity, growth and political stability;
2. A review of the effectiveness of current policies to address them;

## Figure 1.  National development strategies

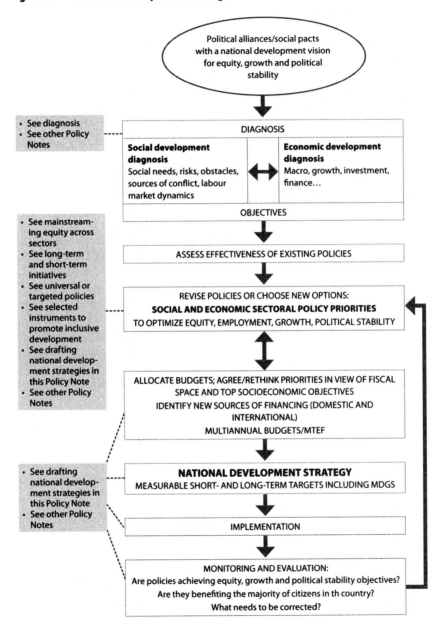

3. A proposed set of short-, medium- and long-term policies to optimize developmental impacts;
4. Choosing options in view of a country's fiscal space and national socio-economic priorities;
5. Drafting a national development strategy and action plan, with the agreed priority policies in the short, medium and long term to achieve national development targets, including the MDGs;
6. Adequate budgetary allocations to support priority policies, preferably in an MTEF (Medium-term expenditure framework) linking programmes to a multi-annual budget;
7. Effective implementation arrangements; and
8. Monitoring and evaluation mechanisms, to assess effectiveness and to allow for adjustments and improvements when the national development strategy is revised (normally every 3-5 years).

## Box 3.   Common problems of national development strategies

### Lack of information:

- Diagnosis is done without adequate statistical information and analysis, e.g., generalizations about "the poor", or failure to consider some social group in a country, or ignoring sources of conflict.

### Lack of coherence between diagnosis, priorities and budgets:

- Diagnosis is correct, but strategies and action plans do not follow from it; national priorities are not based on the diagnosis.
- Strategies and action plans say the correct things but do not have targets or deadlines.
- Diagnosis, strategies and action plans are fine, but priorities are not backed by adequate budgetary allocations, which tend to perpetuate earlier expenditure patterns. Many strategies and plans, including some PRSPs, are not properly translated into public investment pipelines.

### Lack of participation:

- Diagnosis, strategies, plans and/or budgets done with very limited or non-representative public consultation, resulting in poor policy design or later rejection.
- Sector plans are technically good but lose perspective on the reality facing people; it is necessary to develop participatory national action plans for the elderly, youth or indigenous populations, to ensure they are served adequately by all sectors.

### Lack of understanding of the interaction between economic and social policies:

- Linkages between economic and social policies not clear to many, e.g., education does not result in employment, education raises productivity, but employment is mostly a result of adequate macroeconomic policies.
- Poverty reduction does not happen only because of targeted micro-interventions at the local level, but mainly because of equitable policies at the macro and sector levels.

A recommended approach to national development strategies includes:

- Optimizing interactions between economic and social development, focusing on social policies that improve well-being and promote growth, and economic policies that lead simultaneously to growth and social progress; for instance, the set of distribution-sensitive macroeconomic policies presented in the UN Macroeconomic and Growth Policy Note.
- With respect to social policy, abandoning residual approaches and investing solidly in the two main aspects of social policy, redistribution/protection (supporting people's needs and buffering risks) and production (building human capital and promoting employment);
- Combining quantitative and qualitative analyses to understand social, economic and political dynamics;
- Using participatory institutions and processes involving development partners to draw on their expertise and to ensure alignment with national priorities.

## Social diagnosis

Designing good social policies requires understanding the needs of a country's population from different perspectives. The objectives of social policy are to enhance the well-being of all citizens, build human capital, support employment and enhance social cohesion. Thus, the needs and risks of populations, as well as labour market dynamics and sources of conflict, have to be identified in order to determine the priority objectives of social development.

*Identifying needs:* As agreed by international declarations, conventions and national legislation, and simply by the social contract between the State and citizens, all the population groups of a country have a right to a decent life (food, clothing, education, health services, employment standards, social security, accessible housing, etc). Whether starting from the rights of people or from a simpler basic needs approach, the gaps between the reality of citizens and their potential well-being need to be mapped with a drive towards finding solutions.

- What are the gaps? Who is excluded from a decent life and basic needs, and why? Which social group(s) should be targeted with the highest priority? What social policies are needed?
- Provide quantitative and qualitative data with a view to prioritizing needs of the different social groups in the country:
- *Life cycle and gender differentials*:
    - Children (boys and girls);
    - Youth (males and females);
    - Male and female adults of working age;
    - Old-age males and females.
- Income groups:
    - Groups of people above and below the national poverty line(s);

- Head count ratios: always use the national poverty line, the $2/day (international poverty line) as well as the $1/day (extreme poverty line);
- Middle classes are important for development (often a small group in low-income countries) and should be differentiated;
- Whenever possible, disaggregate the findings by region, age, ethnicity, gender and minority status.
- People in the formal/informal sector:
  - Men and women working in the formal and informal sectors;
  - Main employment categories/livelihoods of people should be considered, as well as differences between urban and rural populations.
- Special population groups:
  - Discriminated groups (because of caste, sex, ethnic origin, etc.);
  - Men and women with disabilities;
  - Indigenous peoples;
  - Migrant men and women;
  - Refugees, internally displaced persons (IDPs).

*Identifying obstacles:* In order to build a good strategy, it is essential to identify the barriers and structural reasons that impede social development. What are the reasons for lack of opportunity and access?

- *Political:* The most common obstacles are usually related to elites and vested interests insistent on holding on to their privileges. There are no easy solutions to this problem. They must be tackled in the context of public policies that promote public information, transparency, civil society engagement and other activities that strengthen the social contract. Public expenditure reviews are useful tools for public discussion. Well-designed universal policies may help break the deadlock.
- *Economic:* Most developing countries lack sufficient economic investments and activity fully to employ labour and finance social development (policy priorities can be found in the section on employment); sometimes existing resources (e.g., land, water) are in short supply, even when evenly distributed.
- *Social:* Traditional social norms may perpetuate inequality and discriminate against the excluded, for instance by preventing them from entering certain professions, or using public services, etc. There may be racial, caste or religious exclusion; choice to maintain ethnic traditions; or confining women to the home, and depriving them of access to certain occupations, autonomous sources of income, legal assistance and means of redress in cases of discrimination and exploitation. These must be tackled in the context of sectoral policies.
- *Institutional:* Requirements and procedures that hinder the excluded from benefiting from services; these barriers to access tend to be easy to correct.
- *Environmental and geographical:* Lack of accessible infrastructure is an obstacle for persons with disabilities; geographical isolation and some physi-

cal environments (e.g., desert) are obstacles for many communities to benefit from development processes.

- *Psychological:* Prejudice and negative attitudes towards some groups. Distrust and apathy work against inclusive development. Prejudice, values and behaviour may be changed by adequate social policies, as illustrated in the tackling prejudice section.

*Identifying risks:* Poverty and deprivation are not static conditions. Populations, households and individuals may be in a good condition at one point, but may face various risks that can plunge them into poverty over time. Societies have to take steps to reduce their vulnerability and to cope with shocks when they occur. Vulnerability and risk profiles are good tools for this dynamic approach.

- Vulnerability indicates exposure to hazards and the likelihood that the welfare of an individual or a household falls below minimum consumption levels and/or living standards.
- Risks may include natural disasters, financial crises, harvest failure, war and serious illness, among others.
- Communities have traditional mechanisms to cope with risks, which should not be disturbed unless replaced by more effective options. However, community and family arrangements should not be the centre of social policies, as they fail to provide one of the most important functions of social policy: ensuring the equitable distribution of the benefits of growth at a national scale.

*Identifying labour market dynamics:* Work is the main source of income for the majority of citizens and particularly the poor. A labour market strategy is critical to reduce poverty, develop human capital, address gender discrimination and enhance welfare and productivity. Labour market assessments require a coordinated effort among different ministries and a good understanding of the linkages between economic and social policies. The assessment of the labour-absorbing development pattern of the country is based on an analysis of the composition of economic growth and the relative labour intensities, the leading sectors and subsectors of the economy, the size of the informal sector, domestic and foreign investment prospects, and growth and population projections in the medium and long term. The links with macroeconomic policies are critical. This provides the basis for evaluating options to overcome the mismatch between supply and demand for labour, and to determine which growth, investment and labour market policies may best promote employment with good working conditions.

- What are the characteristics of growth, employment and poverty? Has the poverty rate been reduced at the same speed as the rate of growth? Has growth been "pro-poor", or trickled down? Has growth generated sufficient and remunerative employment?
- Which are the most dynamic sectors of the economy? Are they labour intensive? What is their contribution to public revenue (e.g., taxes)? What can

be done to promote them and generate more revenue that can be directed towards social development?

- What is the percentage of the population below 18 years of age? Will the economy be able to absorb all new entrants into the labour market? Which policies should be prioritized to ensure youth employment? What policies can ensure equal opportunities for women or people of excluded ethnic groups?
- What can be done to accelerate employment-generating growth? Which macroeconomic policies and sector interventions should be promoted in the short/medium term to secure employment and prosperity for all citizens? What specific active and passive labour market interventions should be prioritized to promote labour demand and good working conditions? Options are provided in the section on employment.

*Identifying sources of conflict:* Conflicts of interest among different groups are intrinsic to societies, but problems emerge when there are no mechanisms to deal with them or when these are ineffective. Unattended conflicts leading to violence, whether at the micro or macro level (war), carry high human and economic costs. Economists and development specialists tend to design national strategies assuming peace and stability, without taking into account on-going or potential conflict. By ignoring internal tensions, conflicts often escalate.

- *Early warning is essential:* Most conflicts are ignited by grievances in respect of economic disparities (unequal distribution of resources, unemployment), cultural differences (ethnic, religious), or militarization and human rights abuses. Listening to people's grievances and identifying effective solutions, including mechanisms to deal with dissent, are essential for conflict prevention. National development strategies can be mechanisms to start dialogue, build trust and achieve social cohesion.
- *Conflict prevention analysis* is a useful tool to identify sources of conflict and priorities to deal with them; this is explained later in this Policy Note (see section on beyond traditional social policy).

*Gender inequality issues:* It should never be assumed that policies benefit men and women equally. Women comprise more than 50 per cent of the population and are among the most excluded groups in all too many societies, particularly when poor, informal, disabled, indigenous, etc. Gender status is generally a predictor of relative exclusion (discrimination, violation of equal rights, lower access to education and paid employment, and lack of agency). However, women are found in equal numbers in each income decile, rich and poor. Combining gender data with age, caste, ethnicity, religion, language or geographical location produces a much stronger predictor of vulnerability. Furthermore, women's critical role as social protection providers is often invisible and unpaid: they are involved in unpaid care and called upon as care providers in times of economic crisis.

*Listening to people:* "Nothing about us without us" is a major motto of organizations of people with disabilities. National development strategies are often designed by economists and specialists with inadequate attention to people's perceptions and claims. Listening to people's voice is not only essential for good governance, but also to understand people's grievances and prevent conflict.

*Disaggregated quantification is essential*: It is important to identify indicators that distinguish conditions and outcomes for different categories of people. This includes disaggregating as much as possible by income, sex, age, and other social categories (e.g., persons with disabilities, refugees, caste or ethnic origin), formal/informal sector, rural and urban areas, geographical regions. Identifying the different social groups may appear obvious but, unfortunately, many development policies overlook differences among population groups or the intensity/depth of their problems. No matter how technically solid national development strategies may appear, social development priorities are often inappropriate or misdirected because they are based on insufficient or overly aggregated information (box 4). Baseline indicators should be established for each population group, allowing monitoring of measurable improvement.

### Box 4.  Avoiding generalizations about the poor

There are many differences among the poor, particularly in developing countries where the poor represent a large percentage of the population. Differences should be established to ensure adequate policy choices:
- Different causes of vulnerability/risk and needs of populations living below the poverty line are crucial starting points: some may be nomad pastoralists, others may be farm labourers; some may live in catastrophe-prone areas, others may live in urban shanty towns; some may be refugees and others persons with disabilities. These different categories require different policies.
- The moderately poor, the extremely poor and destitute require different strategies, starting with urgent action to overcome food insecurity.
- Poverty and social exclusion are different concepts, e.g., in Kyrgyzstan, the majority of the population is poor but not excluded; in Bolivia, the majority could be categorized as being both poor and excluded.
- Social policy is not only about reducing poverty; identifying multiple factor exclusion (age, sex, ethnicity, religion, geographical location) is useful to focus a social diagnosis.

### Box 5.  Data issues: the politics of information

- The definition and measurement of poverty and inequality are highly politicized. Poverty tends to be understated as it implies public policy failures. Poverty measurements are most accurate in OECD and Latin American countries.
- National poverty lines use different methodologies and are often not comparable. They are usually based on the per capita expenditure needed to attain 2,000-2,500 calories per day, plus a small allowance for non-food consumption, often inadequate to cover basic needs—clothing, drinking water, housing, access to basic education and health, among others. If these elementary needs were fully accounted, the number of people living in poverty would soar.

**Box 5.   Data issues: the politics of information** (*continued*)

- This is why international organizations started using the one- and two-dollar-a-day poverty lines; but this too has obvious flaws. There are criticisms on how these money-metric poverty lines are developed, particularly on the limited meaning of PPP adjustments for the poor.
- In countries where the poor represent a large percentage of the population, poverty lines (headcount ratios) tend to be very sensitive. A few cents more or less per day make a huge difference in the millions of people to be considered poor, as shown in the following example.

**Indonesia 1996: sensitivity of the poverty line**

| Poverty line | | | Headcount poverty (% population below poverty line) | Millions of people below poverty line |
|---|---|---|---|---|
| US$ per person/ day, PPP adjusted | PPP equivalent US$ per person/ month | Equivalent Rupiah per person/month | | |
| 0.56 | 16.91 | 28 516 | 9.75 | 19.2 |
| 0.59 | 17.76 | 29 942 | 12.01 | 23.7 |
| 0.62 | 18.60 | 31 358 | 14.39 | 28.3 |
| 0.65 | 19.45 | 32 793 | 16.93 | 33.4 |
| 0.70 | 21.14 | 35 645 | 22.06 | 43.5 |

*Source*: SMERU and World Bank, 2000, based on 1996 SUSENAS data. For reference, a dollar equivalent has been added, adjusting the official exchange rate (2,342 Rupiah per dollar) by a PPP conversion factor (0.3889 per dollar).

- Inequality estimates show the distribution of income, consumption or any other indicator. Benefit incidence analysis is a common tool to show the distribution of expenditures/benefits by (i) income group from the richest to the poorest, (ii) social groups and (iii) geographical area/region. These analyses are not systematically developed in all countries.
- The World Bank conducts Living Standards Measurement Surveys in many countries. They are a good data source, as they often provide disaggregated data on social variables. However, the most vulnerable groups are not included as homeless people or people in institutionalized care are not in households. Intra-household disparities may also not be reflected.
- UNDP has consolidated different social indicators at the national and often regional level, and created a composite Human Development Index (HDI), a useful poverty proxy.
- Researchers are exploring measures of well-being in terms of "capabilities" covering domains such as income, health, education, empowerment and human rights. Social scientists, e.g., Bennett in Nepal, are also developing other indices to measure empowerment and inclusion.
- Understanding the limitations of data is very important; existing data must be critically evaluated and complemented with studies to fill gaps in knowledge and

interpretation. Topics for which no documentation exists should be identified for future research.
- There is an urgent need to harmonize and strengthen social statistics across the world.

*Source*: Bennett, 2005; Pogge and Ready, 2005; Ravaillon, 2003; UNDP, *Human Development Reports*.

## Drafting development strategies and action plans

In order to ensure more equitable and inclusive societies, governments develop national and sector strategies accompanied by action plans with specific targets and deadlines, normally within a three-to-five year time frame. Strategies and action plans start from an impartial diagnosis of problems, leading to determining national priorities. The process of evaluating options is discussed in the context of the available fiscal space. In subsequent sections, financing, implementation, monitoring and participation issues are presented. The rest of this Policy Note discusses selected issues (universal versus targeted policies, distribution and equity issues across sectors, short-term initiatives, priorities to generate decent employment, education, health, social protection and social cohesion).

*Determining national objectives:* The diagnosis should have established the major social priorities in terms of needs of population groups, the risks they face, the obstacles for social development as well as the sources of conflict. This is likely to be a long, detailed list, and it is important to keep it in mind when elaborating the national development strategy. The objectives should summarize goals to address these pressing social priorities. Determining objectives is important because it gives the relative priority of sectoral policies. For instance, a typical first objective is to generate decent employment, given this is the most effective tool to reduce poverty and raise living standards in a country.

*Reviewing the effectiveness of existing policies:* The ranking of national objectives should provide direction on national priorities. The next step consists of:
- Listing the existing social programmes in a country.
- Assessing the gaps: Do social policies address the priorities identified in the diagnosis? Who benefits? Which groups/areas are not covered?
- If existing programmes were scaled up, would they redress the social problems? Are they the right programmes? How effectively do they contribute to achieving the MDGs and national development goals?
- Are there more cost-effective options to meet the social needs identified in the diagnosis?

In general, all countries have some social policies in place. However, perhaps with the exception of basic education, the effectiveness of existing programmes is often limited due to:
- *Limited coverage:* Most social programmes tend to serve only a part of the formal sector, the wealthier segments of society, instead of the neediest

## Box 6. Typical social objectives of national development strategies

| Objective | Main policies |
|---|---|
| 1. Generate decent employment for all to reduce poverty and raise living standards | A combination of macroeconomic policies and decent work agenda |
| 2. Address urgent social needs | Short-term high-impact multi-sector initiatives |
| 3. Reduce vulnerability and promote equity | Adequate social protection policies; mainstreaming equity across sectors |
| 4. Improve health status of population | Expanding health coverage and programmes |
| 5. Raise education level of population | Increasing enrolments, retention, investing in all levels of education |
| 6. Reduce internal conflict | Interventions targeted to source of conflict |
| 7. Promote social cohesion among social groups | Fostering multicultural societies and tackling prejudice against excluded groups Addressing lack of opportunity and access through sector interventions National action plans for elderly, youth, etc. |

that remain in the informal sector in rural areas and not covered by social services.

- *Inadequate policy design:* Often programmes were designed long ago and require significant improvements in equity and efficiency (e.g., avoiding regressive impacts, overlaps with other programmes, cost savings). Many sectoral policies designed in the 1980s-1990s are inadequate to generate decent employment, equity and social cohesion, or maximize synergies with economic development (e.g., residual social policies, labour market flexibilization, fees-for-services); they require re-thinking. A discussion by sector and options is presented in later sections of this Policy Note.
- *Insufficient funds:* Developing country governments traditionally have invested little in social sectors, especially during the 1980s and 1990s.
  - *Under-funded recurrent expenditures:* Although recurrent expenditures like salaries absorb most of the social budget in developing countries, they remain under-funded. Salaries of qualified staff should be a priority; social development happens because of human care (a teacher does not need a school to teach, and many countries correctly started by expanding low-cost medical staff, e.g., China's "barefoot doctors"). If resources are increased, they need to cover recurrent expenditures, such as medical supplies or textbooks, better, as they are critical to programme success.

- *Limited capital investments:* Capital expenditures (and even expenditures for rehabilitation of existing facilities) tend to be limited in developing countries, often financed by donors. Capital investments are necessary, particularly in rural areas; but new construction should be carefully evaluated to assess the social cost-benefit, in the context of the overall budget, as infrastructure is expensive and creates new recurrent costs.

- *Funds incorrectly distributed among programmes:* Often, most funds go to high-cost low-impact programmes that benefit a few, e.g., highly specialized hospitals in the capital, instead of being invested in high-impact programmes that benefit the majority, such as more and better funded and staffed village health programmes.
- *Lack of intersectoral linkages,* wasting development potential. For instance, providing wheelchairs for people who need them can help to promote mobility, but unless accessible urban infrastructure and transport exist, people in wheelchairs cannot have independent living. Similarly, spending heavily in education without parallel macroeconomic policies that generate employment.

*Prioritizing options:* Social needs are many, but resources are limited. Often, countries have limited fiscal space, insufficient to cover all required investments. The key to any strategy is prioritizing, so limited resources are directed to interventions that have larger impacts and are cost-effective.

Making policy choices is difficult. It requires an evaluation of the trade-offs within and across sectors, having a clear vision of the contributions of different programmes to development, and their cost-effectiveness, governance and sustainability (box 7).

Given that most developing countries have limited fiscal space and implementation capacity, the timing and phasing of policies is important. Most countries expanded coverage of social programmes progressively (see the sections on universal policies and options for the expansion of coverage); given the urgent imperative to reduce poverty, committing to an ambitious timing is essential for an equitable national development strategy.

*Ensuring budgetary allocations:* With the exception of education (and pensions in some countries), social development policies suffer from a "second class" stigma and few funds are allocated, particularly to the Ministries of Health, Labour, Culture and Social Affairs. It is normally necessary to negotiate with the Ministry of Finance, planning agencies and relevant authorities for a larger share of the budget, providing the economic and political arguments. An additional strategy is to identify some high-cost low-impact investment (inside or outside social sectors, e.g., dams, military procurement, etc.) and debate the opportunity costs of such investments compared to other proposed low-cost high-impact social initiatives. Engaging civil society organizations, donors and the media in public discussion of budgetary allocations for social spending is often beneficial.

National administrations are usually not opposed to the social development of their citizens, but find themselves in situations in which powerful ministries or groups fight for a significant share of the budget, collapsing expenditures for social development. Resistance may come from international organizations, whose experts may push for sectoral approaches ignoring wider social needs. Very often, both in developed and developing countries, the debate is manipulated by vested interests and/ or ideological posturing —for instance arguing that social expenditures are causing unmanageable deficits while not mentioning military or other non-productive expenditures that are much larger. In this case, public expenditure reviews and, if available, thematic budgets (budgets showing the distributional impacts on gender or other social groups), are useful tools to bring transparency and rationality to decision-making.

## Financing and implementing social policies

The design of any social programme is directly linked to the analysis of how it can best financed and delivered.

*Financing:* The variety of social policies may be financed through various means:

- *Public budgetary support* is the most common financing method, normally through general tax revenues. Sometimes a specific tax can be raised for social purposes, e.g., a health tax on alcohol and tobacco, securing funds to medical services.

- *Fees and income-related contributions* were expanded in the 1980s-1990s. However, most programmes, particularly those targeted to the poor, require either public support or cross-subsidization from upper- to lower-income groups. Unless nominal, user charges often result in sharp reductions in the use of services among low-income groups and are not recommended for basic services.

- *Charitable donations* tend to be discontinuous and therefore do not allow sustainable social programmes. Such financing can only help fill the gaps on a temporary basis.

Financial commitments under a programme, including its future contingent liabilities, must be evaluated to be sure that they can be met. Many comprehensive social policy programmes failed in the past because governments initiated them without fiscally responsible financing. Successful social outcomes tend to result from progressive tax regimes; governments often undermine the capacity for social development by reducing taxes on the rich. If existing revenue should be inadequate to meet commitments and the policy is judged sufficiently important, then ways of raising revenue have to be considered, including new progressive taxes; or else, cuts have to be made in other less socially important areas, e.g., military expenditure.

External financing is an option, provided debt does not jeopardize macroeconomic stability. For the poorest countries, grants, concessional assistance and debt relief are preferred options, particularly if they come as general budget support (GBS) and sector-wide approaches (SWAps), presented in the final section of this Policy Note. A discussion of the impacts of external financing on the exchange rate is presented in the Policy Note on macroeconomic and growth.

*Affordability:* Many argue that social policies are not affordable in developing countries because (i) of a loss in potential investment/GDP due to a supposed equity/efficiency trade-off, and (ii) large social needs will likely create unmanageable fiscal deficits. As discussed earlier in this Policy Note:

- Social development is also an important investment. Investing in people enhances their productivity and thus growth; the most productive world economies committed to social spending in the early stages of their development, while in OECD nations, productivity is much higher in those countries with higher social expenditure per capita.[3]
- Raising the incomes of the poor encourages domestic demand, thus growth.

---

**Box 7.  Assessing social policies and programmes**

**Social impacts:**
- Population covered by a programme/policy, including the distributional impacts on the different population groups of a country.
- The adequacy of benefits to serve the identified needs/risks of people.
- Tips: Generally it is advisable to:
  - choose programmes that serve the critical needs of the majority of citizens (e.g., generating employment, universal services).
  - choose programmes that address the intensity and depth of urgent problems (e.g., famine) and obstacles to development, including conflict prevention.

**Cost-effectiveness:** Evaluating the cost-effectiveness of a programme/policy requires impartial assessment of the following:
- Programme coverage (beneficiaries and benefits).
- The cost of the programme/policy (as a percentage of gross domestic product and total public expenditure), including contingent liabilities, as a result of possible government guarantees to the programmes (e.g., pensions), compared to other programmes.
- Administrative costs, as a percentage of total costs, and how the costs compare with other programmes (e.g., means-testing targeting tends to be expensive).
- Long-term social benefits and positive externalities on development.
- The opportunity cost of the policy/programme and its alternatives.
- Tips: Results vary depending on programme design and implementation, but some generic low-cost high-impact interventions (e.g., nutrition programmes) are presented later in this Policy Note.

---

3   M. Cichon, et al., 2006, based on OECD data.

> **Box 7.   Assessing social policies and programmes** (*continued*)
>
> **Governance issues:**
> - Implementation capacity to deliver programmes (e.g., complex targeted programmes should be avoided where local government capacity is low).
> - Governance concerns: staff absenteeism; evidence that resources may be siphoned off.
> - Participation and responsiveness to citizens.
> - Tips:
>   - Resist pressures from vested interests to deliver services (e.g., water or insurance companies, ministries wanting a larger share of the budget) or pressures to prioritize programmes with low social returns (e.g., serving only the elite).
>   - Be inclusive from the outset, providing attention to all groups, not only those with strong voices—sometimes, a group may be well organized and monopolize the development debate; policymakers need to make fair decisions based on the magnitude of the problems identified in the diagnosis, and also support programmes for those who may be voiceless and have few opportunities.
>
> **Sustainability and affordability:** Is there sufficient fiscal space to maintain the programme over time? This requires:
> - An estimation of projected costs and a country's revenues.
> - The government's medium-term sectoral plans and expected changes in allocations as a result of development priorities. The existence of an MTEF is very helpful here.
> - If there is a financing gap, evaluate possible internal sources of funding, starting by use of non-productive expenditures (e.g., military, representational) or expenditures with low social returns (e.g., benefiting only upper-income groups).
> - The role of international transfers through GBS and SWAps is increasingly important for financing social development and is discussed at the end of this Policy Note.

- A significant proportion of national budgets is spent on non-productive activities, such as the military, or activities with very low returns; social investments do not need to displace highly productive economic investments.
- In developing countries, social policies have to grow with the fiscal space made available by increasing GDP or aid.

Ultimately, affordability depends on a society's willingness to finance social policies through taxes and contributions. Affordability is at the core of the social contract between governments and citizens: how much a society is willing to redistribute, and how. Countries at the same level of economic development differ significantly in their social spending—OECD countries spend between 15 and 35 per cent of their GDP.

There are no comparable worldwide estimates for labour and social protection expenditures. However, aid agencies estimate that even the most redistributive social

**Table 1.  Public expenditures in education and health by region** (*percentage of GDP*)

| Region | Education | Health |
|---|---|---|
| OECD countries | 5.6 | 6.7 |
| East Asia and Pacific | 3.2 | 1.9 |
| East Europe and Central Asia | 4.1 | 4.5 |
| Latin America | 4.3 | 3.3 |
| Middle East and North Africa | n.a | 2.7 |
| South Asia | 2.4 | 1.1 |
| Sub-Saharan Africa | n.a | 2.4 |

*Source*: World Bank, *World Development Indicators 2006*. Legend: n.a. = not available.

policies, such as non-contributory unconditional cash transfers (or social pensions), can be affordable:

- UNDESA (2007) simulations on a hundred countries show that the cost of universal social pensions to keep older persons out of poverty averages between 0.2 and 1 per cent of GDP.
- ILO estimates that a combined package of non-contributory public universal pensions (old age and disability) and child benefits is affordable in most countries, at about 1-5 per cent of GDP; these schemes can reduce poverty by 35 to 40 per cent.
- The cost of providing a more simple targeted social transfer equivalent to $0.50 a day to the poorest 10 per cent of households ranges from 0.1 to 0.7 per cent of GDP of Africa's poorest countries; the proportion is greatly reduced for countries with higher GDP.
- This must be compared to the costs of other social sector programmes with lower social returns, e.g., private contributory pension schemes, reaching as much as 7.3 per cent of GDP in Brazil.

*Redistribution:* Redistribution is a primary legitimate objective of social policies. Equity enhancing policies are needed to balance the unequal distribution of the benefits from economic growth resulting from unregulated market forces. Public policies can mitigate or exacerbate social differences; the design of any social policy should carefully evaluate its distributive impacts to (i) ensure coverage to excluded groups such as the poor, and (ii) above all, avoid regressive redistribution, e.g., building systems with public resources that mostly benefit upper-income groups. Financing social policies implies some transfer of resources, either from taxed citizens to those outside the formal sector, or, as in the case of social insurance, from the working population to the unemployed and older people.

*Implementation arrangements:* When thinking about new social programmes or expanding existing ones, it is important to define who will implement them and provide sufficient human resources to ensure success. Often, social policies have failed because they only exist nominally (e.g., Ministries of Labour with a small pool of labour inspectors to monitor standards countrywide).

- Is the relevant ministry capable (in terms of number of staff, staff skills/ capacity, equipment, transport, procedures) to implement the programme adequately? What is needed? Are needs adequately budgeted?
- Are there existing institutions to support operation of a new programme? If not, can they be set up quickly? What type of alternative institutional delivery mechanism could be used?
- Do citizens, particularly poor and excluded groups, face any constraints in accessing the benefits of the programmes (high transport costs, language barriers, social stigma, lack of documentation and information)?
- Are systems adequate for participation, to listen to people's voices? Have beneficiaries participated in the design? Are there ombudsmen and/or citizen complaints offices? Are they effective and easily accessible?

There are four main social service delivery mechanisms:

- *Public sector-based*, through central line ministries and local governments, normally best to achieve expansion of coverage and to reduce poverty and social exclusion nationwide;
- *Market-based*, normally good for efficient delivery of services to higher-income groups;
- *NGOs and charitable institutions*, normally good for working with communities; and
- *A mix of the above:* Given the scarcity of resources for social policies in developing countries, the best solution may be a mixed delivery system.

Each mechanism has its limitations. Despite the need for efficiency gains in public service delivery, the many shortcomings and failures experienced in the private provision of public services during the 1980s and 1990s should be noted. In some areas, public institutions have been privatized only to be put to some other use, representing a net loss in social capital. Stories abound of companies entering into monopolistic contracts for service delivery and then holding local (and central) governments "hostage" with demands for user fee increases and subsidies. Additionally, the commercialization of social services has reinforced gender inequalities, increasing women's workload, as they had to assume more care for their families when services became unaffordable. This means that if public-private partnerships are to be established, they must be carefully designed and regulated, and potential market failures identified.

Government intervention is especially needed where natural or quasi-natural monopolies exist (e.g., water, electricity), where private provision is insufficient or not forthcoming (e.g., transport services to remote and scarcely populated areas) or where large capital requirements may create an entry barrier to new companies. Market-based schemes have often found servicing low-income communities unattractive, as compared to the higher returns from servicing higher-income groups. The private sector is often not interested in lower-income groups and/or remote areas because the associated transaction costs are high and returns low. In countries where the poor represent a significant proportion of the population, public universal provision is generally recommended for primary/secondary education and health, and basic social protection.

NGOs tend to work flexibly with excluded groups, and may deal better with the most difficult aspects of development—changing behaviour and empowering people. In developing countries, local NGOs often are also providers of social programmes, despite being not ideal service providers: local NGOs tend to be uncoordinated nationally with an uneven presence, normally not broad enough to ensure equitable expansion of coverage in a country, their funding tends to be sporadic and discontinuous, and they generally have inconsistent evaluation, monitoring, audits or accountability systems. Local NGOs may be encouraged to continue working on empowerment aspects, but governments may want to take over social services, developing universal systems.

*Monitoring:* Monitoring allows governments to assess progress in implementing national development strategies, and have an early indication of results.

- A set of monitoring indicators refers to programme implementation (activities, disbursements, etc.).
- Equally important is the monitoring of results, the impact of a national development strategy on:
  - Achieving the MDGs.
  - Population groups: A "reality check": What programmes are reaching which social groups? How much has their quality of life improved?
  - Early identification of bottlenecks permits corrective action and revision of a national development strategy to ensure it delivers its proposed objectives.

Monitoring of the situation of population groups is facilitated through elaboration of action plans that evaluate the status of people, for instance, national action plans for youth, older persons or indigenous communities, with specific milestones and timeframes. These act as "watchdogs" over the different ministries in a country, to ensure that the needs of each population group are mainstreamed across sectors. Normally, a department or government office is responsible for reporting and monitoring, liaising with sectoral ministries. Adequate participatory techniques to hear beneficiaries' perceptions and claims are critical to monitor and have a good understanding of what happens from a citizens' perspective. Engagement with other government offices has to be as early as possible, and reporting achievements should be tangible and measurable.

## Ensuring participation and political sustainability

All stages of policymaking are amenable of being participatory:

- Drafting plans.
- Elaborating budgets.
- Executing programmes.
- Monitoring and evaluation, including expenditure tracking and beneficiary assessments.

Bringing participation to these different stages is a good practice that helps to improve accountability and transparency in public administration. It is a mechanism to involve all relevant players in decision-making, to engage them in the development process, to resolve sources of conflict and to ensure more equitable distribution of resources. Participation is essential for building political alliances for national development and to sustain redistributive commitments over time.

Participation ranges from the superficial to the "well-built", from the passive exchange of information to full engagement (box 9). Transparency and validation of proposals through consultation are very important, but it is not until people feel that they have influence over decisions and resources that affect their lives, until accountability mechanisms extend to them, that citizens develop a sense of ownership and develop trust in governments. The critical issue is who is consulted, and how much.

Participation normally starts with a coalition of social and political groups, or social pacts, involving State, business and organized civil society, and with the legitimate democratic institutions in a country (parliaments, political parties); but efforts should be made to move beyond that to a broader range of stakeholders, who may well be the key stakeholders. All too often, key stakeholders are not consulted, or insufficiently consulted, over public policies, resulting in policy mismatch, avoidable

---

**Box 8.   Participatory budgeting in Brazil**

Porto Alegre was an indebted, de-industrialized city. In 1989, the Workers Party won the local elections and decided to break the tradition of elaborating municipal budgets behind closed doors by consulting citizens on how to spend scarce municipal resources. Public consultations led to spectacular local development. From 1989 to 1996, among other achievements:

- Households with access to water increased from 80 per cent to 98 per cent.
- Households with sewerage system rose from 46 per cent to 85 per cent.
- School enrollments doubled.
- Local tax collection increased 50 per cent, reflecting citizens' satisfaction with public services.

Participatory budgeting tools have been widely applied by left-leaning local governments in Latin America and Europe and are now spreading to Asia and Africa.

*See*: Wagle and Shah, 2003, Porto Allegre—participatory approaches in budgeting and public expenditure management, The World Bank.

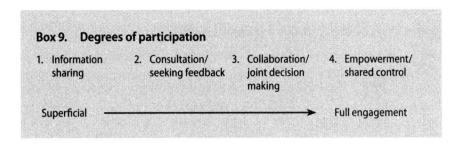

**Box 9.  Degrees of participation**

| 1. Information sharing | 2. Consultation/ seeking feedback | 3. Collaboration/ joint decision making | 4. Empowerment/ shared control |

Superficial ————————————————————➤ Full engagement

tensions and conflicts, loss of trust in government and, ultimately, policy failure. The winners and losers of policy change must be taken into account. Policies that may encounter greater resistance need more intense participatory approaches and more extensive consultations with the relevant stakeholders.

Participation is successful when people are empowered to make informed decisions. Participatory processes need to adhere to the principles of transparency and fairness. If participation is manipulated—presenting very partial information, not allowing primary stakeholders sufficient opportunity to speak, etc.—the result will be uninformed decisions and undesirable developmental outcomes. The success of participatory budgets appears to be due to the fact that local governments clearly showed the social consequences of public investments to the public.

Participation is costly in terms of time and resources. Many development initiatives have spent a lot on ad hoc consultations—sometimes resulting in very poor outcomes due to inadequate procedures. A good way to ensure adequate participation in a cost-effective manner is by institutionalizing permanent consultative mechanisms that are able to follow up matters, like the national economic and social councils.

National Economic and Social Councils (ESCs) are a good example of institutionalized participation of representative stakeholders in a society. Reporting to the higher authorities of a country (Parliament, Presidency, etc), the ESCs are advisory bodies that systematically assess the social impacts of public policies and provide alternative proposals for employment-generating economic growth and social justice. The ESCs are a respected "civil society voice" with an impact in policy-making in several countries of the European Union and Latin America. The ECSs function under the social partnership principle to develop social consensus for policy advice, and are formed by elected representatives from major socio-economic groups, like business associations, labour unions, social movements and NGOs. In Spain and Nicaragua, consumer associations are also included; in the Netherlands and Mexico, university professors and think tanks; in Costa Rica, indigenous representatives are also part of the national ESCs.

For very specific or local issues, the most standard mechanism is consulting directly with the affected people to identify best solutions.

Social development would not have happened in history without the struggle of civil society. Organizing civil society, forging consensus and uniting voices is essential. Unions are the best example of organized civil society; since the nineteenth cen-

**Box 10.    The Irish Economic and Social Council**

Established in 1973, the Irish Economic and Social Council is an independent body formed by a partnership between:
- Major political parties;
- Employer associations;
- Trade unions;
- Farmer organizations;
- Community and voluntary sector (women groups, groups of older persons and persons with disabilities, youth councils, antipoverty networks); and
- Central and local government.

The function of the Council is to analyse and report to the Prime Minister on strategic issues relating to economic and social policymaking, and to provide alternatives for improved social outcomes. The Irish ESC has been very successful in promoting social cohesion. In 1986, the Council formulated an agreed strategy to escape from Ireland's vicious circle of stagnation and unemployment, which led to a national recovery programme accompanied by area-based approaches to fight poverty and social exclusion. Since then, the Irish ESC has been cited as a highly successful example.

See: http://www.nesc.ie/; Wagle and Shah, 2003. "Ireland", *Participation in Macroeconomic Policy Making and Reform*.

tury, unions have managed to elect leaders democratically, to collect contributions, to mobilize members for common causes and to unite into national and international federations. Sometimes, strategic alliances with different groups must be forged to get messages across, no matter if they are not exactly the same. Often in the late twentieth century, civil society lost ground by being too fragmented.

## Mainstreaming equity across sectors

Social policies rely traditionally on education, health, social security/social protection and labour measures explained in later sections. If adequately designed and financed, they can be major instruments for promoting equity. Building equitable societies, however, requires more. It requires ensuring equity in all domains, from finance to transport. It requires making public services accountable to all citizens, particularly to those that may be excluded. This implies re-engineering public administrations and their sector ministries to have them address the needs of the poor, women, informal sector workers, persons with disabilities and other socially excluded, marginalized or disadvantaged groups.

Mainstreaming equity across sectors, whether housing or energy, requires sectoral strategies that:
- Identify the sector-related needs of different population groups. Are needs being addressed? How well?
- Assess distributive deficiencies in current sector policy.

**Box 11. Mainstreaming equity across sectors**

| Area | Typical interventions with equitable/progressive outcomes | Typical interventions with inequitable/regressive outcomes | Good guidance source | Comments |
|---|---|---|---|---|
| Culture | Antidiscrimination public campaigns, multicultural events that foster social cohesion | Subsidies to elitist events/exclusive art | UNESCO, UNFPA, UN Policy Notes | Culture has been out of the donors' domain and needs to be strengthened |
| Education | Universal primary and secondary education; programmes to ensure access and retention of students | User fees in primary and secondary education; commercialization of education | World Bank's PRSP Sourcebook, UNICEF, UNESCO | |
| Energy and mining | Rural electrification; life-line tariffs (subsidized basic consumption for low-income households) | Large power plants, untaxed oil/mineral extraction | World Bank's PRSP Sourcebook, DFID | Issues such as (re)negotiating contracts with foreign companies are absent |
| Finance | Regional rural banks, microfinance; managing finance (current accounts, capital flight...) | Reform/rescue of banking system (transfers to large banks); subsidies to large private enterprises | UN Policy Notes, CGAP | |
| Health | Universal primary and secondary health services, nutrition programmes | User fees, commercialization of health, tertiary highly specialized clinics (e.g., cardiology centres) | WHO, World Bank's PRSP Sourcebook, UNRISD, UN Policy Notes | Health financing issues require attention from equity standpoint |

**Box 11.   Mainstreaming equity across sectors** *(continued)*

| Area | Typical interventions with equitable/ progressive outcomes | Typical interventions with inequitable/regressive outcomes | Good guidance source | Comments |
|---|---|---|---|---|
| Housing | Subsidized housing finance, upgrading of substandard housing | Public housing finance for upper-income groups | IDS, UN-HABITAT | The sector needs stronger equity approaches |
| Industry | Technology policy to support competitive, employment-generating domestic industries, SMEs | Deregulation | UN Policy Notes | |
| Labour | Active and passive labour programmes | Labour flexibilization | ILO, UN Policy Notes | |
| Macroeconomics | Employment-sensitive monetary and fiscal policies, counter-cyclical policies, direct taxation | Cyclical policies, indirect taxation (VAT) | UN Policy Notes, UNDP, UNRISD | |
| Public expenditures | Pro-poor expenditures; fiscal decentralization with adequate equalization transfers | Military spending | World Bank's PRSP Sourcebook | |
| Rural development | Secure access to land, water, markets, livestock, credit for smallholders | Large investments such as irrigation systems that benefit landowners, rather than poor labourers | World Bank's PRSP Sourcebook | Issues such as land reform should be expanded |

| Social protection | Non-contributory pensions, cash transfers, social services, etc.; almost all SP are aimed at redistribution | Private funded pension systems | ILO, DFID, World Bank's PRSP Sourcebook, UNRISD, UN Policy Notes | Address exclusion, and equity, particularly in WB's pension reform |
|---|---|---|---|---|
| Tourism | Small-scale local companies | Poorly taxed luxury hotel chains | DFID, Overseas Development Institute | Tourism is quite a new topic and needs to be strengthened |
| Trade | Linking employment-generating local companies with export markets | Most bilateral free trade agreements | UN Policy Notes | |
| Transport and Infrastructure | Rural roads, affordable public transport, non-motorized transport for households (bicycles, buffalos ...) | Large (and costly) infrastructure investments that the poor do not use | World Bank's PRSP Sourcebook, DFID | |
| Urban development | Slum upgrading, accessible universal design | Large urban infrastructure projects in wealthy areas | World Bank's PRSP Sourcebook, DFID | |
| Water and sanitation | Rural water supply and sanitation | Poorly negotiated privatizations | World Bank's PRSP Sourcebook | |

- Assess institutional weaknesses/obstacles and plan measures to overcome them.
- Prioritize sectoral inventions that benefit the majority of citizens and specific population groups in the short term.
- Assess adequacy of budgetary allocations and calculate necessary expenditures for prioritized interventions.
- Consult beneficiaries as part of social accountability. Is there transparency in planning, decision-making and budget elaboration? Do government agencies facilitate access to information? Are communities making informed investment decisions? Are they fully aware of the implications of their options and choices?
- Design monitoring and evaluation systems to ensure equity targets are being met.

A malpractice to be avoided at all costs is designing policies/programmes based on sector specific issues, and then indicating they are equitable because eventually, in the long term, they have some beneficial impacts on the poor/excluded groups— when benefits in the short term go to the wealthy. This has been particularly common in large infrastructure projects and financial/enterprise restructuring programmes. When looking at distribution issues, it is important to distinguish between:

- Short and long term.
- The intensity of distributional impacts of different policy options.

Whenever addressing equity issues in a sector intervention, vague references to social benefits are to be avoided. The analysis/assessment should consider the needs and potential developmental role of different population groups, and try to accommodate high-impact low-cost interventions that will benefit them most.

This requires conducting *ex ante* analysis to assess the distributional impacts (income and non-income) from the outset, and study different policy options to maximize positive social outcomes. Examples of *ex ante* distributional analysis can be found in the poverty and social impact assessments (PSIA) done by development agencies. This line of work needs to be improved and expanded, given that so far is only done under a piecemeal approach (e.g., in the IMF only when dealing with utilities, IMF not studying the distributional impacts of macroeconomic options). For this, governments need policy space to evaluate different alternatives in an open manner. Governments can win the political support of citizens by being accountable through a public debate on the social consequences of policy options.

## Universal or targeted policies?

The debate over universal versus targeted policies is not new. Most developing countries initiated universal policies from the outset. The "late industrializers", in their goal to foster domestic development, nation-building and social standards, realized that targeting was unnecessary and administratively costly: universal policies achieved social objectives faster, and provided buy-in and political support for government policies (box 12).

However, the experience was not as positive in most developing countries, where universal services did not accomplish their purpose: coverage was low, often serving a portion of the formal sector and the wealthiest segments of society who captured benefits, while the poor and excluded groups remained unserved.

In the 1990s, with the renewed attention to poverty reduction, most development agencies strongly recommended targeting services to the poor. Since this came after the 1980s ideological shift in which the welfare State was attacked and commercialization and user fees for social services were introduced, many developing countries were left with a segmented system, a public system for the poor, and a private system for the upper and middle classes. This generated growing dissent from the latter and severely undermined the political coalitions and social pacts legitimizing governments behind universalistic policies. Additionally, "structural adjustment programmes and PRSPs, driven by a 'targeting' rationale, begin by dismantling the exclusive rights of formal labour on the grounds that this will lead to greater labour market flexibility and 'pro-poor' policies" (Mkandawire, 2005). This policy mix did not work well and appears an incorrect policy choice. The combination of targeting to the poor and commercialization of services for the middle/upper classes, plus flexibilization of labour markets, did not encourage the necessary political alliances for economic development and nation-building, weakening governments, development processes and social cohesion. Universalism, as utilized by the "late industrializers", appears a far better political economy choice.

There are major problems associated with targeting:
- It is costly; means testing absorbs an average 15 per cent of total programme costs.

## Box 12.  Models of welfare

There are three main types of welfare regimes:
- Liberal regimes tend to have residual welfare, safety nets targeted to those individuals in dire need; this is the dominant model in English-speaking countries. It can be traced as far back as the English Poor Law (1598) and it remains highly influential within international financial institutions.
- Social democratic regimes tend to favor universalism, based on the principle of solidarity, in which benefits/services reach everyone on the same terms, such as in modern Sweden and the Netherlands.
- Corporatist regimes tend to universalism, linking first benefits to people's contribution to national development, and expanding them over time though subsidies. In most "late industrializers", such as Germany and Japan, welfare entitlements were first directed to groups whose cooperation in economic modernization and nation-building was deemed indispensable by the government, the "productive" working and middle classes; universalism took place gradually, over time new beneficiaries were added by specification of new eligibility criteria.

*Source*: Esping-Andersen, 1990; Mkandawire, 2005.

- It is administratively complex, requiring significant civil service capacity, and leading to large under-coverage (people not being served) making targeted programmes ineffective; the world's most successful targeted programmes have large under-coverage rates (e.g., Brazil's Bolsa Escola, 73 per cent of the poor are not reached; U.S. Food Stamps, 50 per cent of the poor are not reached).
- It generates incentive distortions and moral hazard.
- It creates two-tier services, one for upper-income groups and another for low-income groups—and services for the poor tend to be poor services.
- In some countries, targeting has dismantled provision for the middle classes and weakened the politics of solidarity, contributing to a residual welfare approach. Targeting can backfire politically as middle-income groups may not wish to see their taxes go to the poor while they have to pay for expensive private services.
- Targeting can be effective if the poor are a small percentage of the population; when poverty is widespread, the administrative cost, and problems associated with identification, monitoring and delivery of programmes tend to outweigh benefits.

### Box 13.  Targeting methods

- *Categorical or group targeting:* Benefits are provided to a specific group, such as mothers, persons with disabilities, children, older persons or communities in a specific geographic area. This is the easiest and cheapest targeting method. Although leakage to the non-poor is normally large, categorical/group targeting increases political support and programme sustainability.
- *Means testing:* Means-tested targeted programmes provide benefits to individuals or households under certain criteria (e.g., single mothers, households below the poverty line). Means testing is more accurate in targeting poverty, but it has high transaction costs, tends to create social stigma, and normally excludes large numbers of qualified beneficiaries due to complex administrative procedures.
- *Proxy means testing:* This is a subset of means testing, in which targeting is done through other (easy to collect) indicators or proxies of the level of income/poverty of beneficiaries, e.g., give discretion to local governments or community groups since they know who is in need. Proxy means testing is cheaper but less accurate than means testing. It has been used to empower communities, but caution is needed because popular values often discriminate against the most excluded members of society, e.g., single mothers for being "impure" or "dirty", defeating the purpose of many social policies. Additionally, it creates stigma, and it may be easily captured by local politicians to reward supporters.
- *Self-selection:* Self-selection avoids moral hazard by imposing disincentives on programme participants, either because the benefits are too low, or because there is some social stigma associated with them, e.g., public works, as normally only those truly in need would accept them.

There is a strong rationale for adopting universal policies in developing countries, particularly if a large number of poor and excluded groups exists. A number of development organizations, including UNDESA, UNDP, ILO, WHO, UNRISD, UNFPA, UNESCO and the World Bank in selected instances, are currently recommending universal public provisioning.

Nevertheless, targeting can be useful to complement universal policies:

- To ensure quick expansion of coverage (e.g., establishing non-contributory targeted benefits or services for poor and excluded groups, fast-tracking universal coverage).

- To address the special needs of minorities and specific population groups (e.g., the visually impaired).

## Speed matters: long-term policies and short-term high impact initiatives

When a government intends to develop equitable social policies, it may want to consider two different sets:

- *Medium- and long-term policies* include most important initiatives such as expanding coverage of education services, health and social security, improved labour standards, adequate wage and employment policies, multicultural programmes to enhance social cohesion, or other equitable policies such as rural income generation, land reform, among others.

- *Short-term high-impact initiatives:* While government efforts must concentrate on building long-term structural policies, these take time to develop. Often governments with a commitment to equity need faster results, to address urgent social needs and meet the expectations of people who elected them. A set of fast high-impact initiatives can assist governments address basic needs among the neediest segments of the population. These programmes may contain components such as:
  - food stamps, free school meal programmes, nutrition supplements for mothers and children,
  - emergency employment programmes,
  - upgrading programmes for substandard housing (water, sanitation, energy-efficiency, household repairs),
  - free access to basic health and essential drugs,
  - literacy campaigns, free basic education for all,
  - conditional cash transfers to ensure student retention in schools and child vaccination, and
  - unconditional cash transfers such as pensions for the elderly poor or persons with disabilities.

Programmes like Fome Zero (Zero Hunger) in Brazil have been essential for rapid poverty reduction and to securing support for President Lula da Silva's Gov-

**Box 14.    Brazil and Argentina: short-term high-impact initiatives**

|  | Brazil: Zero Hunger (2003) and associated programmes | Argentina: Urgent Hunger (2003) and associated programmes |
|---|---|---|
| Priority population/ generic targeting criteria | Households in poor areas with:<br>• Children below 5 years of age<br>• Persons with disabilities<br>• Malnourished<br>• Pregnant women<br>• Older persons | Households below the poverty line with:<br>• Unemployed head of household<br>• At least 1 child/young person under 18 years<br>• Family member ill or with disabilities<br>• Pregnant mother<br>• Adults older than 60 not receiving a pension |
| Formulation | NGO Instituto Ciudadanía | NGO Poder Ciudadano y Red Solidaria, other |
| Coordination | Presidency | National Council for the Coordination of Social Policies (with the Ministries of: Social Development, Health, Education, Science and Technology Economy and Production, Labour Employment and Social Security, Federal Planning and Public Investment) |
| Execution | • Ministry of Food Security<br>• Other line ministries<br>• Private sector and NGOs | • National level: Ministries of Social Development and Health<br>• Regional and municipal governments<br>• NGOs |
| Financing | • Public<br>• Private (companies "adopt" cities financing them), donations | • Public<br>• Accept private donations |
| Food and nutrition component | • Food card (US$ 17 monthly per household) conditional transfer<br>• Incentives for family farming<br>• Food stamps | • Household card permits withdrawal of US$ 50 from bank cashiers |

| Component | | |
|---|---|---|
| | • Creation of food bank with products from supermarkets/retailers<br>• Distribution of food baskets in poor urban areas (not in rural areas)<br>• Subsidized community soup kitchens | • Incentives to food production and distribution (low-cost eateries, community centres, kindergartens, schools and others)<br>• Incentives for family farming |
| Education component | • Bolsa Família: Transfer programme (US$ 6-19 per month) conditional on children attending 85 per cent classes, immunization, mother and child visits to clinics<br>• Literacy programmes<br>• School lunch programmes | • Meals in schools |
| Water/housing component | • Programme Cisternas: grants for water and sanitation | • Housing assistance |
| Employment Component | • First employment programme for young people<br>• Support to family agriculture in rural areas—technical assistance, credit, etc. | • Microenterprise promotion<br>• Cooperatives<br>• Capacity building<br>• Promoting associations for local development and social change leaders<br>• Special projects for persons with disabilities |
| Health Component | • Bolsa Família: transfer programme (US$ 6-19 per month) conditional to children attending 85 per cent classes, immunization, mother and child visits to clinics | • Health and social train—programme targeted to poor areas, free access to primary health<br>• Assistance for drugs and pharmaceuticals<br>• Community centres (integrating health and social development at the local level) |
| Non-contributory social pensions | • Rural pensions<br>• Urban pensions for the old-age below minimum wage<br>• Disability pensions | • Pensions for adults above 70 years old<br>• Disability pensions<br>• Pensions for mother with more than 7 children |
| Website | http://www.fomezero.gov.br/ | http://www.desarrollosocial.gov.ar/ |

ernment, enabling it to establish longer-term structural policies. If well designed, these high-impact programmes are very low cost (Fome Zero costs only 0.2 per cent of GDP). This has been associated with other low-cost high-impact social transfers, like the Brazilian non-contributory pension programme (costing 1 per cent of GDP), presented in box 14.

These programmes involve multisector interventions, and can be additionally used as an instrument to start mainstreaming equity across sectors. If an inter-ministerial commission is formed, directed by a high authority of a country like the President, this sign of political commitment can persuade ministries to modify traditional approaches and demonstrate accountability in serving the needs of the poor and excluded groups.

## Selected instruments to promote inclusive societies

This section presents selected instruments and policy options to fast-track equitable and inclusive social development in the areas of employment, education, health, social protection, culture and conflict prevention.

The selection of inclusive instruments is based on:

- Generating decent employment as a first priority to reduce poverty and raise living standards;
- Addressing urgent social needs through adequate social protection and multisectoral programmes;
- For *social services*, it is generally suggested:
  - On the **supply** side:
    - To increase budgetary allocations for social programmes to expand coverage, aiming at universal provision.
    - To eliminate barriers to access for poor and excluded groups such as:
      ◊ Fees for services and hidden fees such as school uniforms, extracurricular activities, under-the-table payments, etc.,
      ◊ Complicated or restrictive administrative procedures, and
      ◊ Services provided in languages not spoken by the population;
    - To address the differing needs of women and men, for instance addressing women's double work burden and ensuring access to adequate infrastructure in water, sanitation, transport and child care;
    - To target inaccessible remote areas;
    - To include minorities and special population groups, designing targeted programmes if necessary; and
    - To improve the quality of services from a user-perspective.

  On the **demand** side:
    - To raise awareness and promote behavioural changes; and

- To support demand for services (e.g., ensuring that people have knowledge of them, using conditional cash transfers, if necessary).

## Employment and labour

*Generating decent employment* must be a primary development objective. It is estimated that 430 million jobs are needed to provide employment in the next decade, but the pattern of job creation in recent years has been the opposite: increased labour insecurity, "jobless growth" and segmented labour markets with large wage differentials.

Labour market policies were widely used after the Second World War until the mid-1970s, coinciding with significant real wage and employment growth. Historically, countries with successful developmental experiences intervened in their labour markets; governments progressively formalized the labour force as a way to expand the tax base, build social protection systems, raise social standards and develop their domestic markets. However, during the 1980s and 1990s, "the United States deregulated labour market and residualist welfare state became widely acknowledged as the model for good employment performance ... lower wages, less job security, and reduced income support" (Howell, 2005). Wage and income inequality increased in most countries including the United States, fostered by labour market reforms. In 1965, CEOs were paid 51 times as much as a minimum wage earner in the United States; in 2005, this had risen to about 821 times; in most developing countries, particularly in Africa, the number of "working poor" has increased. Labour flexibilization reforms did not lead to increased employment; according to the ILO, world averages show that both unemployment rates and employment-to-population ratios have remained constant between 1995-2005. Instead, labour reforms led to increased informalization of the labour force, predominantly in Latin America, Eastern Europe and the former Soviet Union. This increased precariousness of work not only had negative impacts on people selling their labour, it also reduced the national tax base, limited financing for social policies, contracted domestic markets and induced migration.[4]

National development strategies should promote labour-absorbing development patterns. This requires coordinated action of all development-related ministries and an appreciation of the inter-linkages between economic and social policies. Different policies and different sectoral patterns of growth affect poverty reduction; poverty reduction is stronger when growth is labour intensive. In the 1980s-1990s economic policies were detached from social objectives such as generating employment and protecting people's incomes. Economic policies were left with a narrow focus on containing inflation, budget deficits, liberalizing product/factor markets and trade, and were a major reason why inequality increased worldwide. Ultimately, full employ-

---

4   Economic Policy Institute, 2006, *The State of Working America*, ILR Press, Cornell University; ILO, 2006, *Global Employment Report (trends brief)*. Geneva: International Labour Organization.

---

**Box 15.   How to generate decent employment**

Decent jobs are a result of adequate macroeconomic and labour policies:

(i)   Employment-sensitive macroeconomic and sector policies:
   • Monetary and fiscal policies that boost aggregate demand; a tight monetary policy focussed on containing inflation does not generate jobs.
   • Adequate exchange rate policy combined with technology policy to stimulate output growth; gradual and sequential trade opening to support it.

(ii)   Labour policies: Decent employment is not only about generating jobs, most poor people work long hours but they cannot bring their families out of poverty; it is also about adequate salary and working conditions.
   • Social pacts/dialogue
   • Active and passive labour market policies, including labour standards and fair income.

---

ment only occurs if a country's economic growth and activities absorb labour. For this, governments need employment-sensitive macroeconomic policies, as presented in other UNDESA Policy Notes. In contrast to conventional wisdom in macroeconomic theory, the effects of monetary and fiscal policy on aggregate demand are important for employment.

Employment generation is a necessary but not sufficient condition for poverty reduction; many people in developing countries work long hours for insufficient pay, under bad working conditions and are not able to bring their households out of poverty. This is why the ILO introduced the "decent work agenda" in 1999. It involves (i) fair income, (ii) standards in the workplace, (iii) social protection for all, (iv) skills development for enhanced productivity and (v) social dialogue.

*Labour market policies and programmes* are important to reduce poverty, facilitate human capital development, address discrimination, enhance working conditions, allocate human resources to their most productive uses, and encourage growth and development. The following programmes and policies may be considered:

### Active labour market programmes
   • Direct employment generation (promoting small and medium enterprises, cooperatives, wage subsidies, public works, guaranteed job schemes).
   • Labour exchanges or employment services (job brokerage, counselling offices).
   • Skills development programmes (training and retraining of labour to enhance employability and productivity).
   • Special programmes for youth and persons with disabilities.

### Passive labour market policies
   • Unemployment insurance.
   • Income support policies.
   • Labour regulations and standards such as adequate wage policies (minimum salaries, wage indexation, equal pay for work of equal value), job security

provisions (recruitment/dismissal of employees), working conditions (minimum age, maximum working hours and overtime, leave provisions, occupational health and safety), industrial relations, special protection for mothers, and antidiscrimination provisions to protect women and minorities.

*Labour administration issues* are very important, particularly the capacity of labour ministries adequately to inspect working conditions in order to ensure enforcement and compliance.

- A labour department needs to have sufficient staff at national and local levels.

- There are two types of inspections: (i) routine contract and payroll reporting from firms and (ii) on-site inspections.

- Dispute settlement mechanisms need to exist: oversight commissions, labour courts. These must include complaint and appeal processes for both employers and employees.

### Critical policy issues

### (1)  Starting the decent work agenda: social pacts for employment-generating policies

National development strategies are best to articulate labour market policies with positive synergies between economic and social development. National development strategies, through their social pacts, are well suited to arrive at optimal solutions in macroeconomic policy, the need for productivity, job and income security and support for employment-generating enterprises. The level of protection, benefits and flexibility will vary from country to country; the key is identifying a balance to ensure sustained economic activity and positive social outcomes, where employers can win on productivity gains and workers from job and income security.

Adequate coordination of economic and social policies is critical for success. Social dialogue on labour and competitiveness matters is not enough; tight, employment-constraining, highly contractionary macroeconomic policies have adverse effects on employment. There needs to be coherence between labour and competitiveness policies, and monetary and fiscal policies. Recent success stories include Denmark, Ireland, the Netherlands and Sweden; these countries balanced macroeconomic policies, social protection and labour standards for workers, and competitive policies for employers. Some of these countries outperformed the United States experience in terms of employment generation, without embarking on labour flexibilization programmes.

Transparency of information and social dialogue are the best instruments to promote consensus among all parties involved and to reach optimal solutions. For this, certain conditions are necessary:

- A good understanding of the links between economic and social policies.

**Box 16.   Spain: the Moncloa social pacts**

In 1975, Spain entered a transition to democracy after decades of authoritarian regime. Labour unrest grew with the deterioration of the economy, no collective bargaining schemes in place and political instability. In October 1977, the newly elected Government called for a national political agreement to make the transition successful. Major political parties, economic and labour groups set aside their differences. Meeting at the Moncloa Government palace, they agreed on a new development consensus for the country. This included a recommended 20 per cent wage increase, a reduction of enterprise controls and restrictions, fiscal reforms, better governance and a redefinition of the role of the State, the army and the police, as well as freedom of speech and association. The Moncloa Pacts is regarded as one of the most successful social pacts of recent times.

*See*: Maravall, 1986. "Political change in Spain and the prospects for democracy", in O'Donnell, Schmitter and Whitehead,eds., *Transitions from Authoritarian Rule.*

- Successful collective bargaining tends to happen when negotiations are centralized (not at the factory level), when unions have large numbers of members and are well coordinated.
- Promoting freedom of association may require providing workers with protection and security, as violations of their right to associate persist in different forms, including murder, violence and refusal to allow organizations the legal right to exist and function.
- Unions can be a positive force for development, but, if too confrontational, may damage development. Ideally unions, companies and government work together to adequately time employment-generating macroeconomic policies, achieve productivity increases to enhance enterprise competitiveness, and maintain labour security and social protection. Additionally, unions can work together with governments to improve corporate governance, helping to eliminate malpractice and abuse among entrepreneurs.
- The costs of not engaging in social dialogue include productivity losses due to labour disputes, conflict and potential collapse of the necessary social pacts for national development.

## (2)   Labour standards and fair income

Countries must aim for an appropriate legislative framework that strikes a balance between economic efficiency and labour protection, including provisions on issues such as minimum age, occupational health and safety, minimum salary, maximum hours and overtime, job benefits, or antidiscrimination provisions to protect women, persons with disabilities, and minorities.

Most countries have ratified international conventions on the matter, and have national legal provisions.

*Core labour standards:* No explicit ratification is needed for them to be part of the legislative framework of a country; by virtue of their membership in the ILO, all countries are held to promote the fundamental core labour standards consisting of: (i) freedom of association and the effective recognition of the right to collective bargaining, (ii) abolition of all forms of forced or compulsory labour, (iii) elimination of discrimination in respect of employment and occupation and (iv) elimination of child labour.

Normally, labour standards are implemented progressively, starting with key aspects or sectors, for instance, time-bound programmes to combat child labour that start, in a first phase, by avoiding children's work in hazardous activities (prostitution, mines, explosives, etc.)

---

### Box 17.  Arguments for the decent work agenda

In the 1980s and 1990s, the conventional free-market argument was that a flexible labour market with limited regulation was better for development as it reduced costs and made firms more competitive, expanded entrepreneurial activities and thus enabled firms to create more employment. However, recent evidence points out that:

- *Employment:* Labour flexibility has not been accompanied by increased employment in economies where the demand for labour is low, a situation common to most countries. Instead, it leads to informalization and job precariousness. Many European countries (e.g., Denmark, Ireland, the Netherlands, Spain and Sweden) substantially reduced unemployment without labour market reforms and while maintaining generous unemployment schemes (Howell, 2005). Employment is not related to labour market flexibility, but to macroeconomic policies that are effectively coordinated with social policies. The strong welfare States of Northern Europe (Denmark, the Netherlands, Norway and Sweden), with employment rates as high as the United States and the United Kingdom, demonstrate that employment is fully compatible with "rigid" labour markets, high social protection and collective bargaining.
- *Productivity:* It is fully demonstrated that decent work raises productivity; it improves workers' health, skills and motivation, reducing wasteful labour turnover.
- *Labour costs:* There is more controversy regarding its effects on labour costs. Raising standards correlate with increasing labour costs; but there is also evidence that:
  - Higher labour standards, unless very high, do not reduce FDI (OECD, 2000); in developing countries, FDI shows more concern for non-labour issues such as accessing domestic markets, corruption or quality of infrastructure.
  - Higher labour standards impact local labour-intensive firms using unskilled labour at very low wages with no protection; however, the competitiveness a country may have by exploiting cheap labour is short lived, pushes a country into a "race-to-the-bottom" and does not contribute to the development of a domestic market.
  - Both investor and consumer activism in developed countries demand higher standards and exporting local firms can build on it (DFID, 2004).
- *Poverty reduction:* Impacts on poverty reduction are large. Work-related injuries can plunge families into poverty, avoidable with adequate occupational health

**Box 17.   Arguments for the decent work agenda** (*continued*)

and safety and social protection. Better earnings reduce poverty, and have positive impact on reducing child labour, and increasing the chances that a child will be educated.

- *Domestic demand:* By raising incomes, the decent work agenda contributes to boosting domestic demand and expanding national markets.

- *Equality:* Labour standards address discrimination in employment and are key to supporting inclusive policies for women, or ethnic and minority groups. Freedom of association may allow even informal workers to negotiate better prices for their work.

- *Political stability:* Social dialogue may form national coalitions for development; citizens living with more dignity and income tend to support their governments.

All governments committed to support "full employment and decent work for all ... as a central objective of our ... national development strategies" at the 2005 World Summit. The decent work agenda is officially supported by UN agencies and by major financiers like the EU.

*Sources:* DFID, 2004, "Labour standards and poverty reduction"; EU Commission, 2006, "Promoting decent work for all: the EU contribution to the implementation of the decent work agenda in the world"; Howell, 2005, "fighting unemployment: why labour market reforms are not the answer"; OECD, 2000, "International trade and core labour standards"; United Nations, 2005, *World Summit Outcome.*

*Legislation on recruitment* includes affirmative action to promote certain groups (e.g., women, persons from a low caste or excluded ethnic group, persons with disabilities; see box 18); a variety of countries have developed affirmative action policies to empower excluded social groups; the policy is opposed by those supporting meritocracy and by arguments of group capture of benefits.

*Legislation on termination:* Normally, employers are required to give a legal period of notice before firing employees, meet minimum severance conditions, negotiate large-scale retrenchments with unions, help displaced workers to recover outstanding legal entitlements such as wage arrears.

- *Issues:* Minimal or no legislation on termination gives firms all the power, particularly when allowing them to fire employees without notice or compensation, and has negative impacts on productivity, as job insecurity discourages workers from improving performance for the company. Advance termination notice, fair compensation and redeployment policies are necessary from a social development point of view. On the other hand, excessive labour regulations/rigidity are disincentives for entrepreneurial activities; in particular, practices like life-tenure are strongly discouraged. The optimal solution is again somewhere in between, balancing job security and support for employment-generating enterprises.

- *Implementation:* Adequate labour law on job recruitment and dismissals. Dispute settlement mechanisms need to be in place.

**Box 18.   Malaysia's affirmative action**

Introduced in 1970, Malaysia's New Economic Policy from 1970 enacted pro-Bumiputra policies in response to the racial riots of 1969. Aimed at "restructuring society" to reduce interethnic disparities, it used quotas (university and college admissions, public scholarships,
positions in Government and business ownership) as a strategy to provide opportunities
to the ethnic Malay population, at the time, an economically and socially excluded group
of mainly poor farmers, while the local business sector was controlled by ethnic Chinese.
After more than 30 years of affirmative action for the Malay majority, the system is no longer
justified and is being phased out and replaced by a more meritocratic system. However, once
introduced, such programmes are difficult to phase out.

See: Jomo K. S., 2004, *The New Economic Policy and Interethnic Relations in Malaysia.*

*Wage policies* are important from a human rights perspective. During recession, crisis or in conditions of large excess labour supply as in most developing
countries, employers find themselves in a very strong bargaining position. Employers can obtain labour at salaries as low as the value of a daily meal, even if productivity criteria allow for higher wages, because the only alternative for workers may
be starvation. Properly enforced minimum wage legislation can and should prevent
such abuses.

During the 1980s-1990s, wage policies were discouraged in developing countries as ineffective given the large number of people in the informal sector, enforcement difficulties and companies' search for low labour costs. However, recent empirical research shows a positive relationship between minimum wage and poverty
reduction (Lustig and McLeod, 1997). The relationship is found across different
poverty measures (headcount ratio for extreme and moderate poverty lines, poverty
gap, calorie intake) and population groups (rural and urban). Additionally, there is
strong evidence that increased wages lead to productivity gains and boost domestic
demand; this has led large companies to pay workers above national standards at
times, e.g., automobile manufacturers such as Ford (United States) and Fiat (Italy).

- *Identifying an adequate minimum wage increase:*
  - Minimum wages vary from country to country, even region to region.
    In principle, they should allow for an average family to meet its mini-
    mum basic, not just food, needs.
  - Minimum wages may be a good tool to reduce poverty, but they should
    not be raised uncritically. The costs to the public and private sectors
    (and their links to pensions and other social benefits which tend to be
    indexed to minimum wages) should be carefully evaluated to ensure
    that the policy is affordable and that there is an optimal balance that
    contributes to both development and poverty reduction. The adequate
    wage level should be determined through balancing social contribu-
    tions/benefits, taxes and employers' profit share.

- *Implementation of minimum wage:*
  - By ordinance or law, ideally universal, applicable to any worker in the country;
  - Enactment of laws does not guarantee enforcement; this normally depends on labour inspectors and unions holding companies accountable and compliant. Dispute settlement mechanisms need to be in place.

Other wage determination mechanisms are *indexation of wages to inflation.* A great worker concern worldwide is to maintain the real value of wages. Employers (concerned about labour costs), and governments (about inflation), often find themselves sharing the same position when it comes to wage increases in tripartite negotiations, and indexation tends to be lower than inflation.

- *Identifying an adequate wage increase:* Some European and Asian countries have instituted national wage councils for tripartite negotiations to ensure optimal solutions and maintain good levels of productivity and international competitiveness. In Singapore, additional to wage increases through the national wage council, profit-sharing in the form of bonuses has been encouraged as a productivity incentive and a way to share interest in enterprise development by unions; in 2006, as part of the "Progress Package", a programme to enhance redistribution of growth profits among Singaporeans, the "Workfare Bonus Scheme" was introduced by the Government to support low-wage workers (ranging US$ 75-375 monthly, to be paid 90 per cent as a cash transfer and 10 per cent as a contribution to the "Medisafe" medical scheme).
- *Implementation:* By ordinance/law, or as a government recommendation.

## (3)   Skills development for enhanced productivity

*Skills development* includes a variety of pre-employment training programmes for young people, and retraining and skills upgrading for workers. Training may include workers from skilled operators (drivers, machine operators) to technicians and para-professionals (electronics, para-medical, nurses, etc.). Skills development programmes are delivered by both public agencies (Ministries of Labour or Education) and private companies. What is essential is an adequate linkage with labour market demand and employer requests; this may be best achieved when combined with internships in companies.

Often, short-term training to upgrade skills is also provided at *labour exchanges or employment services.* These are job brokerage and counselling offices. The main objective is to link supply of labour with demand, matching people searching for employment with job vacancies, assisting job-searchers to improve their CVs or biodata, doing first interviews, and helping workers improve productivity and find better jobs (e.g., typing, telephone skills, etc.). Labour exchanges or employment services are relatively inexpensive and should be promoted as they are important elements for facilitating a dynamic labour market; however it is important to recognize their limits in countries where the demand for labour is low.

## (4)   Productive and freely chosen employment

These include direct employment-generation interventions to promote public works, self-employment, youth employment programmes, guaranteed job schemes, wage subsidies to companies, support to cooperatives or small and medium enterprises. They are the most heavily funded employment programmes in OECD countries. These interventions can positively create employment and support disadvantaged or at-risk workers, but substitution, deadweight and displacement effects can dissipate their potential benefits. Good programme design, implementation and most particularly careful monitoring are essential, requiring that benefited companies disclose information transparently.

*Wage and employment subsidies:* Often, companies receive tax breaks, grants, secured government contracts, subsidized credits and other financial incentives; the logic of this public strategy is to attract investment. Employment generation can be added as a criterion for receiving public support. Cooperatives, small and medium enterprises and large enterprises can be subsidized according to the number of jobs they create. By supporting companies, governments may encourage longer-term job creation and economic development. Determination of the duration and degree of a wage subsidy varies country to country; under the United States Targeted Job Tax Credit, companies are paid a 50 per cent wage subsidy for up to two years. Special benefits to companies can be added if firms employ people with fewer opportunities such as young people or persons with disabilities; e.g., "Jobstart" programme for youth in Australia and the United Kingdom.

*Public works programmes* are widely used as a short-term employment measure. Public works do not reduce long-term unemployment; the objectives are: (i) providing emergency jobs (e.g., antipoverty measure, during economic crisis) and (ii) keep-

---

**Box 19.   The Indian Rural Employment Guarantee Act**

Inspired by Maharashtra's State Employment Guarantee Act in 1976, a national programme was enacted in September 2005. The programme is a major strategy to fight poverty in rural India, promising wage employment at least 100 days to every rural household in which adult members volunteer to do unskilled manual work. Any adult who applies for work under the Act is entitled to be employed on public works within 15 days—thus, the Employment Guarantee Act provides a universal and enforceable legal right to basic employment. The programme is starting in 200 districts, to be expanded to all 600 districts of India in five years. State governments and Panchayat Raj institutions as well as NGOs are involved in implementation. It is expected that the programme will cost 2 per cent of GDP and have a significant positive impact protecting rural households from poverty and hunger, reducing rural-urban migration and fostering a more equitable social order in rural areas.

*See:* http://rural.nic.in/rajaswa.pdf ; J. Ghosh, 2006, *India: Right to Work as Social Policy.*

ing workers in contact with the labour market, reducing the chance that they become stigmatized by being unemployed for too long. Normally the targeting method is self-selection (box 19).

### (5)   Social protection for all

This is part of the decent work agenda but in this Policy Note is addressed in the section on social protection policies.

## Education

Education is closely linked to virtually all dimensions of development— human, economic and social. An educated, technically skilled workforce is critical for long-term economic growth. Expanding girls' education has positive effects on fertility, infant mortality, nutrition and enrolment rates of the next generation. Education is also a key factor in improving governance, as education empowers people, allowing them to develop critical thinking and life skills. Education comprises:

- **Early child development** (ECD) to ensure the balanced psychomotive development of the child through basic nutrition, preventive health and educational programmes
- **Primary education**
- **Secondary education**
- **Higher education**
- **Vocational and technical education and training** (TVET)
- **Non-formal education and adult programmes**
- **Special education** for persons with intellectual or psycho-social disabilities.

### *Critical policy issues*

### (1)   Eliminating fees and promoting universal free primary education

Achieving the MDGs has translated into school enrolment ratios rising significantly in recent years. Part of this progress is a result of the elimination of school fees. This includes eliminating hidden fees such as school uniforms, extracurricular activities, under-the-table payments, etc. Fees were introduced during the 1980s-1990s as part of cost-recovery mechanisms to promote sector efficiency and to cope with the severe budget cuts resulting from adjustment programmes; it had remarkably negative social impacts. Uganda was one of the first countries to move away from fees, introducing a policy of free universal primary education in 1996 that managed successfully to reduce first the gap in schooling for the poor and later the gender gap in enrolments. Experience in other countries (e.g., Cameroon, Kenya, Malawi and the United Republic of Tanzania) strongly supports the argument that fees curtail student enrolment, and currently there is worldwide agreement on the need to eliminate fees for primary and basic education.

Eliminating fees in schools is not sufficient to ensure educated populations; education requires keeping children in school. Inequality in retention and completion rates remains high for many, particularly girls, given the pressing needs of poor households (household care economy that pulls girls out of school, opportunity costs of children in school instead of working, deficient nutrition, etc.). Conditional cash transfers like PROGRESA/Oportunidades in Mexico (box 20), conditional on school attendance, are good practices to ensure that girls attend class, to deter using child labour as a risk coping strategy, to promote demand for services and to provide opportunities for children in poor/excluded households. Other retention policies may include school feeding programmes, scholarships, school fee waivers and special safety measures for girls (transport, separate latrines, increased number of female teachers).

## (2)   Importance of secondary, VTET and tertiary education

The priority given to achieving the MDGs has put a lot of emphasis on basic education and often the importance of other essential education services is overlooked, damaging development efforts. Secondary, VTET and tertiary education are essential for developing professional skills and critical thinking in a country. Countries at all stages of development require trained experts such as medical graduates and teachers, and management skills essential for sound public administration and economic activities. This may appear obvious, but the emphasis given to basic education has often come at the cost of higher education, ignoring the positive externalities of universities. Technical and vocational education is particularly important because it provides people with market relevant skills that improve employment prospects.

---

### Box 20.   Mexico's PROGRESA/Oportunidades programme

The programme started in 1997 and currently covers 20 per cent of Mexcio's population: low income rural and urban households. The programme consists of conditional cash transfers to mothers, specifically:

- Education: Up to $58 (boys) and $66 (girls) if children attend 85 per cent of classes.
- Health: Free basic health care for all members of the family; a number of check ups and training on health and nutrition grants access to nutrition cash transfers.
- Nutrition: $15 per family for improved food as well as vitamins/micronutrients for children and pregnant/lactating mothers.

The programme has been very successful. Providing cash to poor households reduced the number of people below poverty by 10 per cent in a few years. By promoting the use of education and health services, PROGRESA/Oportunidades had positive impacts on family health and student retention, particularly of girls, as well as people's satisfaction with public services. Cash transfers also had a very positive effect in monetizing rural areas. The programme was so successful the Fox Administration expanded it, adding savings plans for young people's studies and other components.

See: http://www.progresa.gob.mx/ and Coady and Skoufias, 2000, "The education, health and nutrition program of Mexico (PROGRESA)".

This is particularly true when curricula are properly designed to respond to local productive activities. When linked with employment support programmes like "first employment" for young people, it can have major positive social impacts. A critical issue is funding. Historically, many OECD countries in the nineteenth century, including the United States, provided free secondary and tertiary education as part of their development strategies, but the financing realities of many developing countries have not made this possible. In most places, secondary, VTET and tertiary education receive public support but require fees from students. The UN Convention on the Rights of the Child supports free primary education and, where appropriate, free secondary education to expand access.

### (3) Quality and relevance of education

Education systems need to ensure that children and young people acquire critical thinking, problem-solving skills and knowledge needed to be successful in today's world. Curriculum reform, including improved curricula that meet local needs (particularly in rural areas, linking with local economic activities), teacher training, school accreditation and strengthened national educational standards are essential for education to be a catalyst for growth and poverty reduction.

### (4) Other programmes for education for all

Education for all requires bringing the benefits of education to every member of society in all countries, having special attention to girls, indigenous communities and children with disabilities. Ensuring enrolment and retention of children at risk, combined with multicultural and special education, can redress inequities in education. The prevalence of high adult illiteracy is a strong sign of inequity and exclusion in a country. Non-formal basic education and literacy programmes for adults and out-of-school youth are important for increased equality and productivity in a country. Additionally, educating women of childbearing age has large positive impacts in households.

## Health

Progress in health and social security (or social protection) has been much less positive than in education, to say the least. According to the ILO, only 20 per cent of the world's population has some type of health and social security coverage—and in Sub-Saharan Africa and South Asia, only 10 per cent have some form of rudimentary coverage. This is, 80 per cent of the world's population have no coverage at all.

The availability of health-care services and access to them are critical for the well-being of individuals and communities, and have a direct impact on their productivity and economic performance. Many people think of health as a personal consumption issue, not realizing that improvements in health provide substantial economic payoffs. In low-income countries, as much as 95 per cent of private financing for health comes from individual out-of-pocket expenditures, while this figure is only 37 per cent in high-income countries. Developing countries should consider ways and means to provide public funding. The arguments for public support of health services are strong: improved health increases worker productivity and reduces the number of days off because of illness; in children, malnutrition reduces intelligence, body weight and returns on educational investment. Public health interventions are vital to the health of a society as a whole, and are the only effective means of preventing widespread transmission of communicable diseases such as malaria, HIV/AIDS, tuberculosis, cholera and polio.

- *Primary health care* comprises essential levels of health care provided equally to everyone, such as emergency care; basic curative care, including minor surgery and drug management; dental and oral health; maternal and reproductive health; and preventive services (health promotion, health education, vector control, immunization and vaccinations). As primary and secondary care have the most important impacts on the general health of a population, public and free (or at a nominal rate) services are encouraged.
- *Secondary health care* includes ambulatory medical services and commonplace hospital care (outpatient and inpatient services) via referral from primary health-care services.
- *Tertiary health care* includes specialized medical services (i.e., cardiology) and are generally only available in the capital, at the national level.

There are multiple issues regarding health financing. Generally, three main options exist:

- Fully public health systems, funded from tax revenues, to which any citizen has access for free or at a nominal fee; if well managed and financed, this has the best impact on national health.
- Fully private health systems, financed by individuals; from an equity stand point this is not an advised option, particularly in developing countries. Fee waivers for low-income groups are an option.
- Social insurance schemes by which individuals pool risks, so households covered by the scheme do not pay the full cost to service providers when they use services. This is a most common practice as there is significant private provision of health services. Governments start by an insurance scheme for formal sector workers, and expand progressively to other groups as a supplementary scheme, normally though cross-subsidization and/or support from general tax revenues. Some options for the expansion of coverage are provided below. The key is who is covered and what is covered; the latter requires careful analysis as governments may not want to see the health budget wiped out by expensive curative treatments.

## Critical policy issues

### (1)  Extending coverage of health care

In order to raise the health status of populations, the main priority is expanding the coverage of affordable health services. This requires some degree of public support. Historically, many countries pursued redistributive health care based on universalist objectives, either by subsidizing social insurance or providing tax-based public health services. This was the case in most OECD countries (except the United States), and some low- and middle-income countries, such as Costa Rica, Taiwan Province of China and the Republic of Korea. Many African States in their early post-independence period attempted to expand rapidly public provision of health services to their populations, but the effort was truncated. Additionally, all socialist States such as China, Cuba, Sri Lanka and the former Soviet Union before the 1980s built public health services.

In the 1980s, the push for market-based reforms and a residualist approach to social policy resulted in a trend to commercialize health services in middle- and low-income countries. Development agencies encouraged a "private-public mix"; liberalization of private clinical provision, insurance and pharmaceutical sales; moving away from tax-based systems to encourage local resource mobilization, including user charges for government-provided services, drugs and supplies. This represented a retreat of the State from provision of health services. Governments were advised to maintain a minimalist regulatory role, with the responsibility to address market failures and provide basic health services for the poor when the private sector failed to deliver.

The renewed attention to poverty reduction at the end of the 1990s led to a questioning of this model, as evidence emerged that it had increased inequalities and caused greater poverty:

- Fees and cost-recovery mechanisms are regressive; people who cannot pay are excluded, while catastrophic health costs are a key cause of impoverishment where health care is paid from people's pockets. According to UNICEF and WHO, user fees generally provide a very small portion of health budgets, rarely more than 5 per cent; however, they have highly negative impacts on poor people as health services may not be affordable to them.

- Given very limited public resources, health services for the poor did not expand sufficiently and, when they did, quality was very low, so most people in the world remain without access.

- Pro-poor health services that excluded the better off and the healthy did not allow for cross-subsidization and risk pooling, the essence of public health systems in most developed countries.

- Private health care is expensive and has many failures and perverse incentives (providers may over-treat patients and costs escalate). In the United States, health inequities are significant and the residual public system for low-income/uncovered citizens actually absorbs a significant amount of public funds, particularly for older persons. Well-managed public systems can be cost-effective.

- Paradoxically, developed countries have almost universally established progressive social insurance or government-based health-care systems (only the United States and Singapore have private shares over 50 per cent), while most low- and middle-income developing countries, with the largest number of poor people who cannot afford payment for services and drugs, have regressive private health-care systems. This includes India and China, whose populations suffer severely from this barrier to health-care access.

- Statistically, countries with longer life expectancy, lesser morbidity and higher productivity have redistributive health-care systems and higher public health expenditures.

Currently, UN agencies and sections of the development banks are focusing health policy on expanding coverage and reconstructing public sector capacity. Addressing barriers to health starts by investing in comprehensive health-care services, with adequate service provision at the local level, including access to emergency obstetric care. Fees for basic health services and essential drugs are discouraged (unless nominal).

The main options for expanding health coverage are:

- *Option 1: Extending progressively an existing social insurance scheme, making it universal by targeting poor/excluded groups.* Starting by covering people in the formal sector and expanding towards inclusion of the self-employed. Universalization requires significant subsidies to those outside the formal sector, whose irregular forms of employment do not permit standard insurance arrangements. A recent good example is the Republic of Korea; remarkably, the Government managed to achieve full health coverage in only 12 years. If this option is followed, a critical issue is timing.

- *Option 2: Introducing universal benefits/services at once,* financed from general taxes/State revenues. In Thailand, Prime Minister Thaksin Shinawatra declared in 2001 that health care would be available to all Thais immediately through a universal health-care system for a nominal fee (the so-called *30-baht insurance scheme*) equivalent to US$ 0.75 co-payment per visit. For this option, the critical issue is resources; the boldness of such a political commitment may help ensure they are made available.

- *Option 3: Encouraging contributory micro-insurance schemes for the informal sector* and waiting until they expand, in the expectation that eventually the coverage gap between the formal and informal sectors may disappear—as in Bangladesh and India. Several important issues emerge with this option. First is the sustainability of some micro-insurance schemes; while there are extremely successful examples, including Grameen Kalyan in Bangladesh and SEWA in India, a myriad of other smaller schemes present problems of sustainability and adequacy of benefits, given the modest contributions the poor can afford; better linkage to microfinance and reinsurance schemes must be encouraged. Second, progress is very slow; voluntary schemes will likely take decades, if ever, to cover everybody in the informal sector. If this were to happen, then a third issue would be harmonizing and merging schemes. Mutual and self-help schemes should not be discouraged, given that they are assisting as many as 40 million poor and excluded people; however, they are no panacea and should not be taken as a substitute of a universal national social security system.

## Box 21.  SEWA micro-insurance scheme, India

The Self-Employed Women's Association (SEWA) is a registered trade union working mainly with women in the informal sector. Since 1972, its struggle has been to ensure that the minimum wage is obtained, to provide legal recourse where necessary and to ensure democratic representation at every level of the organization. The trade union has almost 250,000 members. They are mostly hawkers and vendors, home-based workers, and labourers. The scheme covers health insurance (including a small maternity benefit component), life insurance (death and disability) and asset insurance (loss or damage to housing unit or work equipment). SEWA members can choose to become members of the insurance scheme (at present, only 14 per cent of all SEWA members are insured). The asset and health components come as a package, and life insurance is an option. The total premium is approximately $1.5 (Rs60) per annum for the combined asset and health insurance package and an additional Rs15 provides life insurance as well. Premiums and benefits are presently being restructured. Membership and claims processing are done through the SEWA Bank, along with a considerable field presence. Mobile services are also available for premium collection (normally associated with microfinance deposits and loan repayment collections).

*See:* http://www.sewainsurance.org/; Ortiz, 2001, *Social Protection in Asia and the Pacific.*

From a variety of points of view, option 1 appears most feasible. In most low-income countries (sub-Saharan Africa, South Asia), the predominant form of primary care comes from small-scale private providers treating individuals for fees, particularly in rural areas. This may be complemented by better public health services under a social insurance scheme. In most middle-income countries public and private health systems coexist, and their services could also be combined under a social insurance scheme. Starting by covering the formal sector (middle and working classes), universalism can be fast-tracked through non-contributory targeted benefits for poor/excluded groups, financed from general budget revenues. For instance, providing low-income households with a health card allowing people to use health services for free or for a nominal fee quickly reduces the gap between the poor and non-poor—a similar policy was developed in Colombia in 1993 with very successful results: in only four years access to medical services expanded from 10 per cent to 50 per cent of the poorest quintile of the population.

## (2)  Maternal and reproductive health

These services include curative and preventative health services for women of reproductive age. The challenges of reproductive health are large, and free public services are advised, given their positive impacts on (i) women's health, (ii) infant and toddler health and (iii) fertility regulation. Approximately one woman dies every minute from complications of pregnancy and childbirth; but reproductive health is not only about mortality/morbidity, it is about the recognition of women's rights to control their fertility and sexuality, and empowering women to avoid sexual violence, rape, genital mutilation and honour killings, to mention a few.

### (3)  Combating HIV/AIDS and malaria

This is a global priority and part of the MDG commitments. In developing countries, combating the spread of HIV/AIDS and malaria requires significant international assistance, as their fiscal space is limited and treatment expensive. In the United Republic of Tanzania, direct budget support from donors is supporting 50 per cent of health expenditures. Global funds are also essential, e.g., for fighting malaria.

### (4)  Other programmes to promote health for all

- Nutrition programmes are low cost and have high impacts on the poor. They have been highlighted in several places in this Policy Note and are a very cost-effective priority for governments to consider.

- Health education is additionally very important for households—issues such as healthy lifestyles, adequate use of water, nutrition, prevention of transmittable diseases including HIV/AIDS, occupational health and safety at work, and awareness of health problems in the community can be taught and have major impacts on the well-being of populations.

- Immunization programmes also belong to this category of low-cost high-impact interventions

- Often the availability of health services is not sufficient to ensure their use: demand has to be promoted—conditional cash transfers as described for Argentina, Brazil and Mexico in box 14 and box 20 are good instruments to foster demand, explained in detail later in this Policy Note.

- Remote communities can be served by mobile services, like Bolivia's "Health Brigades" who deliver periodic check-ups and emergency services to indigenous communities in the Andes.

- Persons with disabilities require special services that must be built-in such as orthopaedics and rehabilitation.

- Avoiding exclusion in indigenous communities requires their consent, medical staff speaking native languages and integrating traditional practices in a complementary (but never substituting) manner.

## Social protection

Social protection or social security provide a set of instruments to bridge the gap between vulnerable groups and the non-vulnerable by diminishing people's exposure to risks and enhancing their capacity to protect themselves against hazards/loss of income. Because of the strong redistributive character of most social protection policies, they were not favoured by conventional approaches during the 1980s-1990s (except pension reform projects); in extreme cases like Bolivia, the Ministry of Social Security was closed down. However, social protection is necessary in any society because the benefits of growth do not reach all, and people do not have the same capacity to overcome risks. Given the urgency to eradicate poverty, social protection is currently at the forefront of the social development agenda.

Social protection programmes include:

- *Social insurance* to cushion the risks associated with unemployment, poor health, disability, work injury and old age.
- *Social assistance* for groups with no other means of adequate support, such as:
    - Social services, institutionalized or community-based, to vulnerable sections of the population, such as severe cases of disability, orphans, street children, battered women, substance abusers, migrant workers, refugees.
    - Conditional or unconditional transfers of cash or goods.
    - Temporary subsidies, such as energy life-line tariffs, housing subsidies or price-support mechanisms (e.g., supporting the price of staple food in a crisis).
- *Other schemes to assist communities and the informal sector* include agricultural insurance, food insecurity programmes, social funds and disaster prevention and management.

The adequate mix of social protection policies will vary country to country, depending on the specific risks and vulnerabilities identified in the diagnosis of the national development strategy. The extensive variety of social protection instruments cannot be described in detail in this Policy Note; for this, references are provided in the bibliography. A discussion on selected priority policies is presented below: pensions and social transfers, and other complementary programmes for the informal sector, women and children.

### Critical policy issues

### (1) Expanding pension coverage

In the 1990s many pension reform programmes were fostered in developing countries, particularly in Latin America and Eastern Europe. The idea was to avert an old age crisis in which social expenditures would swamp government spending, promote individual contributions to ease workers' mobility, avoid government mismanagement of pension funds and have positive externalities for the financial sector as people's savings are invested in capital markets.

The general model used for reforms is a multi-pillar system. Pillar I involves contributory and non-contributory pensions, normally with a defined benefit, funded through a Pay-As-You-Go (PAYGO) public system (current working generation paying retirees through tax contributions), the most common pension scheme worldwide. Pillar II consists of defined contributions (instead of a secure defined benefit) invested in financial instruments normally through private insurance/pension funds. Pillar III consists of voluntary additional pensions for upper-income groups. Most radical reforms involved a complete abandonment of PAYGO (Pillar I) to develop fully funded (Pillar II) pension systems.

As presented earlier, social insurance is important because it allows for equitable cross-subsidization—e.g., in health insurance, the healthy pay for the sick; in publicly provided pensions, the younger generation is custodian for the older generation. This equitable intergenerational social contract was broken in many countries when privately funded systems were introduced; however, the critical need to reduce poverty and achieve the MDGs has led many people to question this approach in developing countries. The arguments are:

- Reforms did not have any impact on improving coverage given that the poor do not have any capacity to contribute to expensive private insurance systems, nor do private pension fund companies have an interest to serve the poor.
- The transition from a public to a funded private system is costly, difficult to afford for most countries, as the current generation has to pay for the retirees under the old system (through taxation) and pay their own private contributions. Many developing countries, starved of resources for basic social investments, reformed their pension systems and now are paying the high fiscal costs of transition.
- The administrative costs of insurance/pension fund companies tend to be very high, making returns lower.
- The risk of financial market fluctuations is left to pensioners, who risk losing all their life savings if financial markets collapse. In many cases, the State (the taxpayer) acts as a guarantor of last resort, having to bail out private companies and provide safety nets for citizens in case of financial downturns.
- The positive effect of funded private systems on capital markets did generally occur, making them more liquid and mature; however, the objective of a pension system is not to develop capital markets, but to provide effective old-age income support.
- Additionally, investing savings in financial instruments other than national bonds meant a loss of resources for governments, as pension savings have been crucial in financing public investments in many of the "late industrializers" (e.g., electrification in Finland, housing in Singapore, etc.).

There are a variety of options when reforming a pension system, and they should be carefully evaluated, avoiding pressures from insurance companies and other vested interests. Recent experience shows that public pension systems (PAYGO/Pillar I) under good governance remain best from an equity point of view in developing countries; these may be accompanied by private pension schemes for upper-income groups.

Countries like Argentina, Bolivia, Brazil, Namibia or South Africa, have introduced universal non-contributory pension schemes as an instrument to fight poverty (box 22). This has taken a variety of forms, from the universal Bono Solidario

> ### Box 22. Namibia's social pensions
>
> After independence from South African colonial rule in 1990, the Namibian Government had to deal with large social disparities and extremely vulnerable population groups due the impacts of HIV/AIDS and the exclusionary effects of apartheid—Namibia has one of the highest income disparities in the world. The Government reformed the inherited social security system, expanding coverage through non-contributory social pensions to deal with these vulnerabilities. It provides a flat-rate means-tested unconditional cash transfer to (i) all Namibians above 60 years old (US$ 30 per month, in 2001 coverage had reached 92 per cent of the targeted population), (ii) persons with disabilities (US$ 25 per month), (iii) child support benefits (approximately US$ 15 per child/month), and (iv) additional grants for foster parents (US$ 15 per child/month, to encourage adoption of HIV/AIDS orphans). Total costs are 2.6 per cent of GDP, currently the Namibian Government is studying how to further target the programmes and provide higher benefits to the poor, excluding the non-poor.
>
> *See:* Schlegerger, 2002, "Namibia's universal pension scheme", ILO.

(BONOSOL) in Bolivia (US$ 225 per year to any old person on or above 65) to Brazil's pensions for rural population on or above 60 (men) and 55 (women) with a monthly benefit equivalent to the national minimum wage (approximately US$ 87 per month). While benefits provided are modest, the impacts on poverty reduction have been large. ILO points out that social pensions and transfers have reduced South Africa's poverty gap by 47 per cent. In countries like Senegal and the United Republic of Tanzania, ILO estimates that poverty could be reduced by 35 to 40 per cent. For rural poor households, having an older person has become an asset, a source of income to sustain basic needs for the whole family. Additionally, transfers serve as cash injections to rural economies, having a positive impact on local development. The United Nations, DESA and ILO estimated that these basic non-contributory pensions may be affordable for most countries, at around 0.2 to 1 per cent of GDP on average, at least much more affordable than contributory private funded schemes. In Brazil, contributory pensions cost 7.3 per cent of GDP, while the poverty-reducing non-contributory rural pension programme is estimated to cost only 1 per cent of GDP.

In low-income countries, transfers, whether conditional or unconditional, are fast redistributive mechanisms that are increasingly used to (i) reduce poverty and food insecurity in low-income households, (ii) expand coverage of pensions in countries where social security is not well developed, (iii) promote use/demand for social services and (iv) monetize rural economies. Box 23 describes the mechanisms.

## (2) Addressing urgent community needs

Other social protection instruments for the informal sector include:
- Multisector short-term high-impact programmes, described earlier.
- *Food security programmes* should be a top government priority, and must start with early warning systems mapping food-insecure households (by

degree of inadequate food consumption and under-nutrition), and combating the causes of food vulnerability with medium-term policy options such as small-scale agriculture and cash transfers. Except in extreme emergency or exceptional circumstances, distribution of food is inadvisable, as it hinders development efforts; in particular, distributing food brought in from the outside has a negative impact on local farmers, who may then be unable to sell their products, causing more poverty. It is preferable to

## Box 23.   Social transfers—how they work

**Types of social transfers:** There are two types:

(*a*)   Social pensions or unconditional cash transfers (e.g., disability or old-age pensions, child benefits, given to anybody who is disabled, in old-age, has children) (see examples in boxes 14 and 22).

(*b*)   Conditional cash transfers (released on accomplishment of pre-set conditionalities, for instance, child attendance at 85 per cent of school classes and getting immunization vaccines) (boxes 14 and 20). It is important to understand that conditional transfers can only be developed where education/health services exist and where government has significant administrative capacity. Unconditional cash transfers are much easier to implement and more effective to reduce poverty rapidly.

**Scope:** Conditional transfers normally start in selected areas, and expand progressively depending on outcomes; social pensions tend to have nationwide coverage.

**Targeted or universal benefits?** Conditional transfers tend to be targeted (e.g., PROGRESA/Oportunidades and Bolsa Familia in boxes 13 and 14 are targeted to households below the poverty line); unconditional transfers may be universal, given to the whole population of a country (e.g., universal child benefits), or group targeted (e.g., anybody who has a disability, is chronically ill or is in old age).

**Financing:** Public, normally low cost. Basic social pensions tend to cost between 0.2 and 1 per cent of GDP; conditional transfers cost 0.1 per cent to 0.7 per cent of GDP depending on scope and benefits.

**Typical implementation arrangements:**

- *Disbursements*—To be effective, social transfers must be regular and predictable. Two main aspects are important: periodicity of disbursements and method. Where developed financial systems exist, beneficiaries should be given transfers on a monthly basis, as this is best to ensure a stable income for basic needs. Where systems are less developed, or administrative costs larger, governments may opt for a yearly payment (e.g., Bolivia's BONOSOL) or semi-yearly (e.g., pensions in India). With regards to the disbursements methods, different alternatives exist:
  - Banking system: in Brazil and Argentina, beneficiaries use electronic cards; as positive externalities, cards serve as a credit instruments in local shops. If no electronic banking system exists, rural banks or microfinance institutions can de used; it can be a way to expand banking services to communities.
  - Postal services, as in the case of pensions in India.
  - Schools or health centres for remote locations (teacher or nurse collects funds from district bank and delivers to families; this system has been successful in Kalomo, Zambia).

**Box 23.   Social transfers—how they work** (*continued*)

 – NGOs can also deliver transfers, as in Mozambique.
 – Armed convoys—where insecurity is high, e.g., Namibia, armed vehicles have been used.
• Monitoring of compliance (for conditional transfers): Done by professional/technical staff; in the case of child class attendance, teachers fill out a form; in the case of mother and child attendance at health clinics, getting vaccinations, etc., nurses fill out specific forms. It is important to notice that these administrative procedures are complex and thus slow down the expansion of conditional cash transfers; these conditional programmes tend to have large under-coverage rates.

*Source*: DFID, 2005, "Social transfers and chronic poverty"; HelpAge, IDS, Save the Children, 2005, "Making cash count"; Cichon, et al., 2006, "Changing the paradigm in social security: from fiscal burden to investing in people", ILO.

monitor food insecurity with early warning systems, and provide poor households with food stamps, cash transfers and agricultural inputs, stimulating local economic activities.

• *Community-based social funds* are typically managed at the local level, empowering communities, NGOs and local governments. They provide finance for small-scale projects, such as livelihood programmes and infrastructure, using local labour, encouraging skills development and contributing to a community's social capital.

• *Disaster preparedness and management* are essential to assist communities at risk to cope and mitigate impacts. Developing countries are where most people are killed, injured, affected and left homeless as a result of disasters, due to low construction standards and the vulnerability of people. There has been a recent trend towards increased disaster relief aid programmes. However, the huge economic and human losses caused by disasters point to the critical need to invest in disaster preparedness. Relief efforts are notorious for their bad governance; the World Bank estimates that as much as 50 per cent of funds/goods have disappeared in corruption in some cases. In any case, relief does not reduce vulnerability. Investing in better construction standards and housing programmes, disaster management centres for hazard assessment, risk reduction and monitoring programmes, emergency response and assistance systems, and strengthening community-based preparedness are better mechanisms to reduce loss of human life and the scale of damage.

## (3)   Supporting women and the unpaid care economy

Both in developing and developed countries, the bedrock of social protection is women's unpaid family care. Societies would not survive if women (and girls) did not perform many tasks, including housework, cooking, childcare, care for the elderly and sick family members, and generally holding the social fabric together.

This unpaid work covers shortfalls in formal social protection, but carries important costs borne by women (and girls), resulting in the tendency for them to fall far behind men in educational and remunerative economic attainment. Worse, this unpaid work is usually not even socially dignifying. It often results in humiliation, restriction of freedom, even slavery. Women's development requires increased social protection. In developed countries, birth grants, child benefits, extended maternity leave, kindergartens, home care and free or low-cost access to medical services, were central to women's emancipation, integration into the paid labour force and had the positive externality of population regulation.

### (4)   Child protection

Children and youth constitute about half of the world's population. Thus, investing in them is critical for raising labour force productivity and a country's international competitive advantage. Lack of adequate protection and under-nourishment result in stunting, poor health and low intellectual capacity which have high costs to societies. Additionally, as agreed in the UN Convention on the Rights of the Child, children should be protected from all forms of abuse and exploitation, such as child labour, child prostitution or the adversities faced by the girl child. ECD, nutrition and school feeding programmes, child allowances, initiatives to help street children, programmes to empower the young to avoid marginalization, criminality, sexually transmitted diseases, early pregnancies and drug addiction are some important social protection instruments.

## Beyond traditional social policy: tackling prejudice, changing behaviour, building social trust and cohesion

The 1995 Copenhagen Social Summit, held just after genocidal massacres in Yugoslavia and Rwanda, emphasized the need to disseminate values of tolerance, peace, democracy and social integration.

This refers to value formation. Value transmission is particularly intense during childhood, as children internalize attitudes, rules and expectations of parents and teachers. But values are permanently redeveloped and keep changing during adulthood through peer groups, media, arts, culture, religion, experiences and personal thinking. While the transmission of values (between or among generations) generates some continuity and cohesion, value content matters tremendously. Value orientations that promote tolerance, non-violence, diversity and solidarity, build much more cohesive societies. Social scientists have long developed theories on the importance of norms, beliefs and values as the cement of society. Yet the topic remains largely off the radar screen of the development community, probably because of its intangibility; aid agencies have concentrated on hard-core investments like infrastructure and seldom entered such topics.

Values can be built and promoted. Tolerance, respect for diversity, non-violence, solidarity, trust in society and contribution to the community are beliefs and behaviours that can be taught. Attitude and behaviour changes are also essential to transform stereotypes and relations that discriminate and inhibit women to enjoy substantive equality. This requires that programme designers:

- Understand the existing cultural values.
- Have clear objectives on the values that need to be altered for social progress.
- Gain support from the local structures including religious leaders; a technique is providing solid scientific evidence of the benefits from other countries, putting aside emotions and value judgements.
- Support allies and "drivers of change"; encourage local-level groups and organizations in dialogue.
- Design adequate programmes. The following options may be considered:
  - *Educational curricula:* Multicultural education is best to ensure equity and respect for cultural diversity in countries where more than one language/ethnic group exists, giving students the opportunity to understand and respect other cultures, instead of imposing a dominant language and excluding a culture. It also makes children respectful of and curious about other cultures internationally.
  - *Media programmes:* Media can play an essential role in changing attitudes and tackling discrimination and exclusion. Journalists are key for informing and equipping the public to understand and participate in development debates. Alternative approaches include mixing entertainment with educational approaches on developmental issues; BBC, UNESCO, UNDP and other agencies and NGOs have good practice experiences in promoting values and behavioural change through well-researched mass-audience entertainment/educational radio and television programmes like soap operas (box 24).
  - *Public education and information campaigns* have long been used for sensitization and educational purposes. They use marketing techniques for snappy, clear and well-targeted content messages (e.g., TV and radio

---

**Box 24.    Afghanistan's "new home, new life"—transmitting values through media**

In 1994 during the Taliban regime, the BBC World Service Pashto service for Afghanistan, launched an educational radio soap opera, "New Home, New Life", designed by BBC staff and donor agencies to meet educational needs of both refugees and those in Afghanistan. The story line presented the lives of fictional villagers in Afghanistan and delivered important social messages related to reintegration of war returnees, women, mine awareness, health, hygiene and sanitation, tolerance and conflict resolution. The soap opera remains highly popular even today, as many Afghanis identify with the characters.

*See:* UNESCO http://www.unescobkk.org/index.php?id=1647.

spots). Educational campaigns have been very successful in promoting healthy lifestyles, anti-discrimination and other issues. They can be utilized to inform people of their rights, deal with all forms of discrimination, stigma or non-compliance with labour standards.

- *Investing in culture:* Educating people in their heritage and the heritage of other cultures promotes understanding, tolerance and respect for diversity—if bias and myth creation are avoided. Investing in tangible and intangible heritage also has positive externalities for tourism. Heritage must be accompanied by cultural activities supporting: (i) the arts, promoting creativity of new artists to keep culture alive, and (ii) popular collective events that everybody can enjoy, such as street activities/parties, in a spirit of recreation, fun and informal "intercultural get-together", an important way to promote social cohesion.
- *Supporting drivers of change:* Community and national leaders who promote equitable arguments and inclusive alternatives are natural allies for progressive value change.
- *Empowering people and promoting associations:* Excluded people tend to internalize inferiority and repress their voice. Lack of voice and inability to dialogue creates social risks, as it may lead to violence. When people associate and share their problems, the result is often increased encouragement, capacity for self-advocacy and the ability to organize and to create positive change for themselves and their communities. Associations help communities to defend their interests, and can be linked to microfinance, cooperatives and other local development programmes. As people's associations sometimes stand up against powerful local interest groups, it is necessary to protect them from extortion and intimidation.
- *Making governments accountable:* Distrust and apathy are a result of people being isolated and de-linked from decisions that have impacts on their lives, and may lead to alienation, marginalization and violence. Ultimately, citizens trust governments that respond to their problems and expectations, are reliable, avoid large inequities, work towards building stable societies that benefit people and deliver social justice. Maintaining the social contract between government and citizens is essential to promote social trust.

## Conflict prevention

Conflict prevention has attracted significantly more attention than social cohesion/integration, despite the two being intrinsically linked. According to a recent World Bank document, the key characteristics of a society resilient to violent conflict include:

- • Political and social institutions which are largely inclusive, equitable and accountable.

**Box 25.   Burundi: conflict prevention strategies**

Since independence in 1962, Burundi has experienced recurrent genocide mass killings (1965-1969, 1972, 1988, 1991, 1993) with an approximate toll of 350,000 dead and 1.3 million refugees and IDPs. The risk that ethnic violence between Hutu and Tutsi will resume is high. After a period of limited donor assistance "doing no harm", in 2004 the Permanent Secretariat for Economic and Social Reforms of Burundi and donors engaged in a conflict prevention analysis to address the structural causes of conflict, in order to ensure that development aid would effectively contribute to prevent a recurrence of violence. It was found that the main cause of conflict was inequity in a context of extreme poverty; to address disparities, programmes to support employment, land distribution, rural development, social protection and human development were identified for excluded groups. It was also found that the conflict is essentially elite-driven and manipulated; therefore, media projects and public information campaigns were proposed to promote social cohesion and end a culture of myth-making and prejudice. The analysis also showed that conflict was caused by a culture of impunity towards violence in the context of militarization and of small arms proliferation; to address this, the following measures were identified: support to national judicial and security systems, truth and reconciliation processes, and demobilization and reintegration programmes.

*Source*: Brachet and Wolpe, 2005, "Conflict sensitive development assistance—the case of Burundi", The World Bank.

- Economic, social and ethnic diversity rather than polarization and dominance.
- Growth and development that provide equitable benefits across society.
- Culture of dialogue rather than violence.

However, in practice, conflict prevention remains a specialized issue, dealt with by conflict prevention specialists. Most national and sector strategies, done by economists and sector specialists blind to conflict matters, are designed ignoring internal frictions and sources of tension as it is perceived as "political", thus beyond the development domain. Yet social contestation has often shaped countries and driven social reform in history; if ignored or suppressed, it may lead to further violence. It is essential that national development strategies recognize sources of conflict and address them, before tensions escalate.

*Early warning:* The sources of conflict vary from country to country but generally involve severe grievances due to vertical inequalities (e.g., class conflict and struggle) or horizontal inequalities (e.g., differences among ethnic or religious groups). Risk screening indicators include: (i) history of earlier conflicts, (ii) high prevalence of poverty and inequality, (iii) political instability and non-responsive governments, (iv) denial of political and civil rights, (v) militarization, (vi) proliferation of small arms, (vii) ethnic dominance, (viii) conflicts in neighbouring States, (ix) high male youth unemployment and (x) culture of violence, myth-making, public perceptions.

*Tackling potential causes of conflict:* National development strategies are the perfect setting to prioritize interventions to deal with the internal sources of tension identified, before conflict takes violent forms, e.g., reforms aimed at equity and youth employment programmes. This includes supporting participatory processes where people can voice their grievances, and institutions for effective dispute resolution.

Beyond developing equitable and tolerant values and preventing conflict, social cohesion is also about the other intangible aspects of citizens' well-being, their right to live in dignity, to use freely their mother tongue, to enjoy time with their community, to laugh, to have fun, to be creative, all essential aspects of mankind and signs of healthy societies. This is not only a result of material well-being, but of living in societies with no fear, with no exclusion.

## International redistribution and social justice

The global system that emerged in the late twentieth century has generated much resistance. Inequality has increased between and within countries. The richest 10 per cent of the world's adult population receive 85 per cent of total world wealth; the poorest 90 per cent gets only 15 per cent of it. If power is the ability of groups to protect and advance their interests, 90 per cent of the world's population is disempowered. Global rules reflect global power, the interests of the world's elite top 10 per cent who enjoy almost all the income generated by mankind. The huge gap between the rich and the poor has become more worrying since the world is facing the threat of organized terrorism from groups based in some of the world's poorest countries.

While the economic benefits of globalization go to a few countries, companies and individuals, social policies and their costs must be dealt with at the national and local levels, with fewer resources, within a diminishing policy space.

The justification for international redistribution, through increased and improved development aid, cannot be stronger. For globalization to be accepted, it will have to be a globalization that benefits the majority, a globalization for all, instead of a few.

Accepting global responsibility for social development may be done by:
- Having global accountability for the MDGs and promoting international standards to halt the "race to the bottom".
- Building global and regional social policies.
- Supporting committed governments in developing countries with equitable national development strategies with increased aid, aligned and harmonized, particularly with budgetary support.

### Global and regional social policies

Cross-border problems such as health pandemics or illegal migration have highlighted the need to manage global public goods. Many social issues are beyond national boundaries and governments may want to consider coordinating global and regional social policies such as:

- Health (e.g., transmittable diseases such as SARS or avian flu).
- Social redistribution mechanisms like global/regional social funds to target depressed areas or to redress inequalities.
- Economies of scale in social investments, e.g., not all countries can develop high-quality universities/research centres or pharmaceutical industries to produce cheaper generic drugs, but these can be developed regionally.
- Labour regulations (e.g., migration agreements, labour standards) to combat "the race to the bottom".
- Cooperation on regulation of public and private delivery of social services (water, electricity); regional formations in principle are in a stronger position than isolated governments to negotiate with private providers to ensure access, affordability and quality standards in commercial services and utilities.
- Social charts, human rights councils; the European Union's European Court of Justice or the Council of Europe's Court of Human Rights could serve as useful models of mechanisms by which citizens can be empowered to challenge the perceived failures of national governments to fulfil their rights.
- Cooperation to promote employment-generating local investment and allow more progressive tax systems (e.g., through coordinated measures to control capital flight, tax havens and tax competition).
- Risk pooling mechanisms such as international agricultural insurance against crop or livestock risks; most agricultural insurance experiences have failed across the world because of their small size, collapsing when a major catastrophe occurred. However, by pooling risks internationally, and by adequate reinsurance, schemes can work.

Beyond specific topics, there is an urgent need for a framework of global governance to construct a safer and fairer world, an international consensus to make globalization work for all—a global social contract.

## New instruments of development aid

The instruments of aid have been progressively evolving from projects to transfers from developed to developing countries, either in the form of GBS (general budget support to a government) or SWAps (sector wide approaches, budget support to a specific sector like health), supporting governments with good governance, multi-annual budgets/MTEFs (medium-term expenditure frameworks) and minimized fiduciary risks.

How can governments ensure that the new instruments of aid work to support social development and, ultimately, people? How can GBS and SWAps be best used to support equitable national development strategies?

- It is essential that SWAps and GBS be used as instruments of redistribution and social justice, this is, that they reach people, and are not utilized to sustain institutions (e.g., a ministry) or development processes (e.g., completion of an MTEF), or are simply used as fast disbursing mechanisms of donors aid.

- Some GBS donors like the European Union believe in linking disbursements to outcomes—this could include attainments in respect of effective impacts on excluded groups.
- Social transfers become particularly attractive from the point of view of direct and quick impacts on low-income households; governments can finance social transfers through both GBS and SWAps.
- GBS has allowed citizens to contribute to policy and distribution debates around the budget. In some countries, GBS has supported participatory budget processes and gender responsive budgets; governments could also promote other thematic budgets (e.g., showing distribution impacts on other excluded groups).
- In practical terms, this means moving aid away from donor projects and small grassroots activities to support structural change and governments building equitable social systems. Ultimately, GBS supports governments as the legitimate institutions with a social contract to supervise a country's economic and social development to benefit its citizens.
- Civil society activities at the national and local levels must be expanded, funded through special funds.

Increased aid could support equitable national development strategies in which social policies go hand in hand with economic development under good governance. In that way, developed and developing countries would better share responsibility on achieving global prosperity and the Millennium Development Goals.

## Conclusion

Effective policies to redress poverty, inequality and lack of opportunity are an urgent imperative. Social policy, as an integral part of public policies, provides a set of instruments to regulate and supplement market institutions and social structures, ensuring redistribution, protection, cohesion and social justice. Social policies complement and reinforce economic development by enhancing human capital and productive employment.

Governments launch national development strategies to build countries that are socially inclusive, employment generating, economically robust and politically stable. National development strategies are not only a technocratic exercise; they are an opportunity to rethink a country's social contract. This requires the creation of supportive political coalitions, while resisting policy capture by elite or vested interests.

This Policy Note presents the steps necessary in drafting inclusive national development strategies: diagnosis of social priorities, selection of policy options, financing, implementation, monitoring, participation and political sustainability.

A set of critical issues are discussed: the need to mainstream equity across sectors, from energy to transport; the need for universal policies, with attention to the poor and excluded groups; and the need for short-term initiatives complementing long-term policies, to ensure that urgent social issues are addressed rapidly, and political support for governments remains stable.

Selected social policy instruments to fast-track equitable and inclusive social development are presented in the areas of employment, education, health, social protection, culture and conflict prevention. These selected policy options are accompanied by implementation issues. There are no best solutions or "one-size-fits-all" formulas. Each country has different social needs, development objectives and fiscal capacity to achieve them, and will choose a different set of policies.

Finally, this Policy Note closes with some remarks on the need for better global governance to reduce global poverty and social inequities. The challenge of our generation is to shape globalization, to manage it equitably and sustainably. This may be done by means of international and regional social policies, accompanied by increased development aid, aligned and harmonized, supporting equitable national development strategies. The responsibility to build a better twenty-first century for all is now in our hands.

## References

Birdsall, Nancy (2005). "Why inequality matters in a globalizing world". World Institute for Development Economics Research Annual Lecture, Helsinki.

Booth, David, and Zaza Curran (2005). "Aid instruments and exclusion". Report for the UK Department for International Development. London: Overseas Development Institute.

Bourguignon, Francois (2004). "The poverty-growth-inequality triangle". Washington D.C.: World Bank.

Cichon, Michael, Krzysztof Hagemejer and John Woodall (2006). "Changing the paradigm in social security: from fiscal burden to investing in people". Geneva: International Labour Office.

Conceiçao, Pedro, Pedro Ferreira and J. K. Galbraith (1999). "Inequality and unemployment in Europe: the American cure". UTIP Working Paper 11. Austin: University of Texas.

Cornia, Giovanni, Richard Jolly and Frances Stewart, eds. (1987). *Adjustment with a Human Face: Protecting the Vulnerable and Promoting Growth.* Oxford: Clarendon Press.

Deacon, Bob (2007). *Global Social Policy and Governance.* London: Sage.

Deacon, Bob, Isabel Ortiz and Sergei Zelenev (2007). "Regional social policy". UNDESA Working Papers No. 38. New York: United Nations Department for Economic and Social Affairs.

De Haan, Arjan (2006). "Reclaiming social policy: globalization, social exclusion and new poverty reduction strategies". Processed. Ontario: University of Guelph.

Devereux, Stephen and Rachel Sabates-Wheeler (2004). "Transformative social protection". IDS Working Paper No. 232. Sussex: Institute of Development Studies.

DFID (2004). "Labour standards and poverty reduction". London: Department for International Development.

_____ (2005). "Reducing poverty by tackling social exclusion: a DFID policy paper". London: Department for International Development.

_____ (2005). "Social transfers and chronic poverty: emerging evidence and the challenge ahead". London: Department for International Development.

Esping-Andersen, Gøsta (1990). *Three Worlds of Welfare Capitalism*. London: Blackwell.

HelpAge (2004). "Age and security: how social pensions can deliver effective aid to poor older people and their families". London: HelpAge.

Holzmann, Robert and Steen Jorgensen (1999). "Social protection as social risk management". Washington, D.C.: The World Bank

Howell, David (2005). "Fighting unemployment: why labor market reforms are not the answer". CEPA Working Papers. New York: Schwartz Center for Economic Policy Analysis.

ILO (1999). *Decent Work. Report of the Secretary General 87th International Labour Conference*. Geneva: International Labour Office.

_____ (2004). *A Fair Globalization: Creating Opportunities for All. Report of the World Commission on the Social Consequences of Globalization*. Geneva: International Labour Office.

_____ (2005). *Decent Work and Poverty Reduction Strategies*. Geneva: International Labour Office.

Jomo, K. S., and Ben Fine, eds. (2005). *The New Development Economics*. London: Zed Books.

Jomo, K. S., and Jacques Baudot, eds. (2007). *Flat World, Big Gaps: Economic Liberalization, Globalization and Inequality*. London: Zed Books.

Kanbur, Ravi, and Nora Lustig (1999). "Why is inequality back on the agenda". Paper presented at Annual Bank Conference on Development Economics. Washington D.C.: The World Bank.

Lustig, Nora, and Darryl McLeod (1997). "Minimum wages and poverty in developing countries: some empirical evidence", in *Labor Markets in Latin America*, Sebastian Edwards and Nora Lustig, eds. Washington D.C.: Brookings Institute.

Mackintosh, Mary, and Meri Koivusalo, eds. (2005). *Commercialization of Health Care: Global and Local Dynamics and Policy Responses*. Basingstoke: Palgrave.

Mesa-Lago, Carmelo (2002). "Reassessing pension reform in Chile and other countries in Latin America". Paper presented at Social Protection for the Poor Conference. Manila: Asian Development Bank.

Mkandawire, Thandika (2005). "Targeting and universalism in poverty reduction". Social Policy and Development Program paper No. 23. Geneva: United Nations Research Institute for Social Development.

Mkandawire, Thandika, ed. (2006). *Social Policy in a Development Context*. Basingtoke: Palgrave Macmillan.

Norton, Andy, and Diane Elson (2002). "What's behind the budget? Politics, rights and accountability in the budget process". London: Overseas Development Institute.

Ocampo, J. A. (2006). "Market, social cohesion, and democracy". DESA Working Papers No. 9. New York: United Nations Department for Economic and Social Affairs.

Ocampo, J. A., Jomo K. S. and Sarbuland Khan, eds. (2006). *Policy Matters: Economic and Social Policies to Sustain Equitable Development*. London: Zed Books.

Ortiz, Isabel, ed. (2001). *Social Protection in Asia and the Pacific*. Manila: Asian Development Bank.

Ortiz, Isabel, et al. (2001). *Handbook for Poverty and Social Analysis*. Manila: Asian Development Bank.

Pal, Karuna, et al. (2005). "Can low-income countries afford basic social protection? First results of a modeling exercise". Issues in Social Protection Discussion Paper No. 13. Geneva: International Labour Office.

Ranis, Gustav, and Frances Stewart (2005). "Dynamic links between the economy and human development". UNDESA Working Paper No. 8. New York: United Nations Department for Economic and Social Affairs.

Ravallion, Martin (1998). "Poverty lines in theory and practice. Living standards measurement study". Working Paper 133. Washington D.C.: World Bank.

Reddy, Sanjay, and Thomas Pogge (2005). *How Not to Count the Poor*. New York: Columbia University.

Sachs, Jeffrey (2005). *Investing in Development: A Practical Plan to Achieve the MDGs*. UN Millennium Project. New York: United Nations.

Stiglitz, Joseph (2000). *Economics of the Public Sector (Third edition)*. New York: W. W. Norton.

United Nations (1995). *Report of the World Summit for Social Development. Copenhaguen, 6-12 March 1995*. A/CONF/166/9.

_____(2005). *The Inequality Predicament: Report on the World Social Situation 2005*. New York: United Nations, Department of Economic and Social Affairs.

_____(2005). *World Summit Outcome. New York, 14-16 September 2005*. A/RES/60/1.

_____(2007). *Development in an Ageing World: World Economic and Social Survey 2007*. New York: United Nations, Department of Economic and Social Affairs.

United Nations Millennium Project (2005). *Preparing National Development Strategies to Achieve the Millennium Development Goals: A Handbook*. New York: United Nations.

UNDP (2005). *Human Rights: A Practice Note*. New York: United Nations Development Programme.

UNFPA (2004). *Tips for Culturally Sensitive Programming*. New York: United Nations Population Fund.

_____(2005). *Adding it Up: The Benefits of Investing In Sexual and Reproductive Health Care*. New York: United Nations Population Fund.

UNIFEM (2006). *Budgeting for Women's Rights: Monitoring Government Budgets for Compliance with CEDAW*. New York: United Nations Development Fund for Women.

UNRISD (2001). *Visible Hands: Taking Responsibility for Social Development*. Geneva: United Nations Research Institute for Social Development.

_____(2005). *Gender Equality: Striving for Justice in an Unequal World*. Geneva: United Nations Research Institute for Social Development.

UNU-WIDER (2006). *The World Distribution of Household Wealth*. United Nations University-World Institute for Development Economics Research, Helsinki.

Van der Hoeven, Rolph, Hulya Dagdeviren and John Weeks (2001). *Redistribution Matters: Growth for Poverty Reduction*. Geneva: International Labour Office.

Van Ginneken, Wouter (2003). "Extending social security—policies for developing countries". Extension of Social Security Paper No. 13. Geneva: International Labour Office.

WHO (2004). *Reaching Universal Coverage via Social Health Insurance*. Geneva: World Health Organization.

Wiman, Ron, Timo Voipio and Matti Ylonen (2007). *Comprehensive Social Policies for Development in a Globalizing World*. Helsinki: STAKES.

Woodward, David, and Andrew Simms (2006). "Growth is failing the poor. The unbalanced distribution of the benefits and costs of global economic growth". DESA Working Paper No. 20. New York: United Nations Department for Economic and Social Affairs.

World Bank (2002). *PRSP Sourcebook*. Washington, D.C.: The World Bank.

_____ (2003). *A User's Guide to Poverty and Social Impact Analysis*. Washington, D.C.: The World Bank.

_____ (2003). *Preparing Public Expenditure Reviews for Human Development*. Washington, D.C.: The World Bank.

_____ (2005a). *Conflict Analysis Framework*. Processed. Washington, D.C.: The World Bank.

_____ (2005b). *World Development Report 2006: Equity and Development*. Washington, D.C.: The World Bank.

# Trade policy

## Murray Gibbs

## Aims and objectives

This Policy Note addresses (*a*) how governments can provide a specific pro-poor and pro-development focus to their trade policies in a manner that is supportive of MDG achievement, and suggests (*b*) how they can pursue these goals in international trade negotiations.

## Background concepts, past and current debates

Trade policy can constitute a key tool for the achievement of the MDGs. Using trade policy as an instrument of industrial diversification and the creation of value added remains key. Moreover, exports of goods and services can provide increased incomes for poor people, government revenue and opportunities for employment, including high paid jobs abroad, particularly for women and young job-seekers. Exports can thus contribute to the achievement of MDGs, by lifting people out of poverty (MDG1) and empowering women (MDG3), while supporting MDG8, whose target 12 aims at a trading system in which developing countries can extract greater benefit from the international trading system.

However, the gains from exports may accrue to the richer segments of the population, and export industries can damage the environment and otherwise undermine the livelihoods of poor people. Imports of goods and services can crowd out domestic producers, undermine livelihoods, exacerbate inequalities and push people into poverty. At the same time, trade liberalization can bring vital capital and technology, as well as essential inputs for improving infrastructures and increasing productivity, including that of poor people.

All WTO members are taking part in the Doha Round of multilateral trade negotiations, and most are actively engaged in the negotiation of free trade agreements

* Special thanks go to Kamal Malhotra for his inputs and constant support, and particularly his contributions to the section on tariffs and industrial policy and the section on exports and poverty. The author is also particularly grateful to Joseph Stiglitz for his valuable comments which have been incorporated to the extent possible. Furthermore, thanks go to Lamin Manneh, Sebastian Matthew, Yilmaz Akyuz, Carlos Correa and the UNDP Geneva Trade and Human Development Unit staff for their comments on an earlier draft. The author also wishes to thank Margherita Musollino for the research assistance provided.

(FTAs). In designing and pursuing a trade policy to achieve the MDGs, developing countries face the constraints posed by the trade agreements that they have accepted. The WTO Multilateral Trade Agreements (MTAs) are both extensive, i.e., they discipline a wide range of policy areas central to development strategies, and intrusive, i.e., they impose a detailed legal framework on national economic and social policies. In addition, many developing countries have entered into regional and bilateral, often extra-regional, FTAs which go beyond the WTO ("WTO plus") in terms of their scope and intrusiveness.

This new international trading system thus has the disadvantage of constricting the policy space available for countries to pursue a development-oriented national trade policy. Nevertheless, this presents the opportunity for developing countries to press for international trade rules and seek commitments on the part of their trading partners that are supportive of their development goals—which is precisely what MDG8 is intended to achieve. However, this requires that developing countries are able (*a*) to define such goals in their national policies, and (*b*) effectively pursue these goals in international trade negotiations.

## The case and options for widening the policy space

Trade negotiations are aimed at achieving the mutual reduction of tariffs and other barriers to trade in goods among the participants. However, they also deal with measures affecting trade in services (e.g., communications, finance, transportation, energy, immigration, even health and education and sanitation), the flow of investment and the enforcement of intellectual property rights. The prevailing underlying view is that this will lead to improved access to markets and a more efficient allocation of resources, stimulating economic growth and development.

Trade policy should be focused on achieving specific development goals such as the elimination of poverty and the achievement of the MDGs. It should aim at (*a*) enabling poorer people to compete in a globalized world market, by increasing their productivity. It should also (*b*) ensure the most equitable sharing of benefits of trade, so that poor people, women and other disadvantaged groups can draw benefits from exports and equality within the country and between social groups, regions and genders can be promoted. Such policies should (*c*) shield vulnerable groups from the impact of trade liberalization when this threatens their livelihoods and (*d*) ensure that the liberalization of goods and services effectively contributes to these objectives. It should be noted that some MDGs, such as access to energy, water and health services, are now the subject of international trade negotiations.

Governments must ensure that the international commitments they enter are supportive of these goals. International trade negotiations must aim at providing free access to markets for the goods and services of developing countries, while committing stronger trading partners to measures supportive of these goals. The overall outcomes of such initiatives will be central to the achievement of MDG8, the Global Partnership for Development.

## Effective design and implementation

Government's ability to define such strategies and to defend and pursue them in international trade negotiations is enhanced by more active participation of civil society and other stakeholders, who stand to be affected either positively or negatively by trade agreements. This process should assist in identifying the pro-poor and pro-development elements of trade policy which should be incorporated in legislation and defended in trade negotiations. At the same time, the actions of other countries that could frustrate these objectives should also be identified, and pursued in trade negotiations both by seeking systemic improvements or specific concession by trading partners. A further essential element is to anticipate the actions of other countries and seek a national consensus on an appropriate reaction.

## Coverage

This Policy Note is intended for policymakers seeking to pursue a development strategy through the application of trade policy. It addresses many of the questions which every trade policy "practitioner" will inevitably face over the next few years, and provides background facts and a set of tools available for the pursuit of the MDGs and the development objectives mentioned above. It contains the following sections, in addition to this one and appropriate sectoral annexes:

Policy space for future national development strategies
Tariffs and industrial policy
Exports and poverty
Agriculture and food security
Trade in services and development strategies
Investment, jobs for youth and access to technologies
Movement of natural persons—access to the world employment market
Intellectual property rights for the poor
The FTA option.

# Policy space for future national development strategies

## Theoretical context

The purpose of this Policy Note is not to discuss or focus on trade theory. Nevertheless, some theoretical context is nevertheless useful to anchor the policy discussion elaborated in this paper. A brief theoretical context is, therefore, summarized below.[1]

---

1  See UNDP, et al., 2003, *Making Global Trade Work for People*, London and Sterling, Virginia: Earthscan (www.earthscan.co.uk), p. 25.

Few branches of the literature on economics are richer or more controversial than that on international trade. There has been little consensus on the relationship between trade and short- to medium-term economic growth—and even less on its role in long-term economic development.

The principle of comparative advantage, first described by David Ricardo, forms the theoretical basis for traditional trade theory and provides the rationale for free trade. The principle states that even if a country produced all goods more cheaply than other countries, it would benefit by specializing in the export of its relatively cheapest good (or the good in which it has a comparative advantage).

Some classical economists believed that comparative advantage was driven by differences in production techniques. Later theoretical developments identified differences in factor endowments as the principal basis for comparative advantage. Traditional trade analysis acknowledged the argument for policy intervention (protectionism) if market failures created a need for temporary protection of infant industries—though direct subsidies were still considered preferable. Intervention was also justifiable, though still discouraged, if it could improve a nation's terms of trade by deploying market power. But these were exceptions to the general principle that free trade is best.

Traditional trade theory has been challenged because it often cannot explain actual trade patterns. Careful empirical investigations show that many of the theory's basic assumptions–perfect competition, full employment, perfect factor mobility within countries, immobile factors between countries—are unrealistic and do not conform to theoretical predictions. When these assumptions are relaxed, welfare and other outcomes are less clear. Moreover, the introduction of assumptions on differential learning effects, positive externalities and technical changes associated with different economic activities creates the theoretical possibility of weak (if any) gains from trade for countries that specialize in low value-added, labour-intensive products.

Several analysts have tried to modify, expand or reject some of the conclusions of traditional trade theory. New trade theorists cite the role of scale economies and imperfectly competitive markets in determining intra-industry trade patterns among industrial countries. This view led strategic trade theorists to argue for subsidizing certain industries, to give them strategic advantage in oligopolistic international markets. The recent literature on trade and growth also emphasizes that, in dynamic terms, comparative advantage can be created based on human capital, learning, technology and productivity. It can also change over time based on economic policy.

Other responses come from theorists who question the validity of the comparative advantage principle, arguing that absolute or competitive advantage is a more reliable determinant of trade outcomes. One such response is a macro-level analysis that looks at trade in the context of low aggregate demand, structural unemployment and inflexible wage adjustments. Another argues that international industrial competitiveness is determined by the technology gaps between nations.

The common thread in these different theories is that trade can contribute to growth by expanding markets, facilitating competition and disseminating knowledge. Controversy continues to surround the efficacy of growth-promoting policy intervention. And the trade literature says little about how trade and trade policy relate to human development over time.

## The expanded reach of international trade obligations

In addition to this theoretical context, national trade policies are formulated and implemented within the constraints of international trade commitments that cover a wide range of policy areas, many central to development strategies. As such, what is possible through national trade policy is being continuously redefined by the ongoing trade negotiating process. In parallel to their participation in the Doha Development Round, most WTO members are also actively engaged in the negotiation of free trade agreements (FTAs) with both regional and extraregional partners. What is the scope for the application of pro-poor and pro-development trade policies in this context? How can developing countries ensure that the outcome of such negotiations is consistent with their development strategies and the pursuit of the MDGs?

International trade obligations at multilateral, regional and bilateral levels have become increasingly more extensive and intrusive. Multilateral obligations were accepted as part of a package that was supposed to have given freer and more secure market access to developing countries by bringing the textiles and clothing and agriculture sectors under multilateral disciplines. It was also expected to provide a dispute settlement mechanism that would strengthen the rights of smaller countries. The WTO "single undertaking",[2] agreed by founding WTO members, intensified

---

### Box 1. Terms of accession[a]

Countries that have acceded to the WTO have been obliged to accept WTO-plus obligations and commitments as part of their terms of accession. These have included across-the-board tariff bindings often at low rates; extensive commitments on trade in services, going far beyond those made by developing countries in the Uruguay Round; lack of recourse to permitted TRIMs (e.g., on transfer of technology); abolition of export taxes; little or no recourse to special safeguards inn agriculture; additional commitments on energy prices in excess of the normal WTO disciplines on subsidies; no access to export subsidies even when their GDP is less than $1,000. Furthermore, some acceding countries have been denied full WTO rights based on the argument that they are still in the category of "non-market economies". Acceding countries have more recently obtained recognition that the extensive commitments contained in their terms of accession should be taken into account in multilateral trade negotiations.

---

a See, for example, UNCTAD, 2001, WTO Accessions and Development Policies, New York and Geneva. An acceding country is in a much weaker position under the WTO than it was previously under GATT, where the possibility of invoking the non-application clause was excluded once bilateral negotiations had been engaged.

---

2 For a complete assessment of the outcome of the Uruguay Round and insight into the adoption of the "single undertaking", see UNCTAD, 1994, *Trade and Development Report 1994*, UNCTAD/TDR/14 and Supp.1, Geneva.

existing multilateral rules relating to tariffs and subsidies, bringing developing countries under disciplines from which they had previously been exempt. It also extended trade obligations into new areas such as national policies on services (e.g., finance, communications, energy, environment, culture, immigration, transportation, health and education) and intellectual property rights. Those countries which acceded to the WTO after its establishment find themselves subject to even greater constraints, as the major trading countries have followed a policy of seeking maximum, "WTO plus", concessions in their terms of accession.

This has constricted the policy space available to developing countries to pursue development strategies.[3] The WTO Doha Development Round aims at continuing the process of liberalization with tighter disciplines. However, it also provides the opportunity for developing countries to address difficulties encountered in the implementation of the Uruguay Round results.

## Some FTAs are more constraining

All developing countries have been caught up in the proliferation of FTAs, both with other developing countries (South-South) and between developed and developing countries (North-South). Some of these manifest a more ambitious approach by

---

**Box 2.   Frontiers of the trading system**

Considerations of policy space should bear in mind that there has been a recent tendency for multilateral and bilateral trade agreements to overstep the "frontiers" of the trading system. As a result, governments find that their trade commitments may conflict with other instruments and commitments based on consensus, established in other international forums, which they have accepted. These include the Convention on Biodiversity, the FAO Treaty on Plant Genetic Material, the UN Convention on the Protection of Cultural Contents and Artistic Expression, the Johannesburg Sustainable Development Plan of Action, the Rome Declaration on Food Security and the Global Strategy on Health for All.

To carry the analogy further, WIPO accepted that the whole set of intellectual property instruments would be incorporated into the WTO TRIPS Agreement as this gave them more "teeth" under the WTO dispute settlement mechanism. On the other hand, there has been considerable resistance from WHO and UNESCO to subjecting what are seen as fundamental rights to health, education and cultural identity to trade disciplines. The FAO, on the other hand, is actively preparing technical papers on issues related to its central goals, such as food security. The "frontiers" between the WTO rules and the Multilateral Environmental Agreements (MEAs) are currently being defined under the Doha mandate.[a] The inclusion of labour standards was not accepted.

---

a   See WTO, 2001, Matrix on trade measures pursuant to selected MEAs, WT/CTE/W/160/rev.1, 14 July 2001 (www.wto.org).

---

3   UNDP, et al., 2003, *Making Global Trade Work for People*, London and Sterling, Virginia: Earthscan (www.earthscan.co.uk).

developing countries to the pursuit of the traditional objective of regional integration. Others, however, are extraregional, reflecting strategies of individual countries to seek privileged market access conditions which they consider cannot be achieved in multilateral negotiations. For certain developed countries, the negotiation of bilateral FTAs with developing countries has a highly political motivation. It also manifests a strategy on their part of imposing tighter and more extensive disciplines on their trading partner than can be achieved, at least in the near future, in the WTO, or to consolidate positions they are pursuing multilaterally vis-à-vis other major players in the WTO. Major trading countries are also involved in the pursuit of geopolitical objectives through some bilateral and regional trade negotiations, while smaller countries struggle to ensure that their vital sectoral interests are protected.[4] The implications of such FTAs for development are discussed in the section on the FTA option.

## Development strategies and trade negotiations

This new emerging trading system imposes rules on the exercise of trade policies (in the broadest sense) both through general obligations, which apply to all WTO members, and specific commitments that individual countries have accepted. All developing countries are being subject to intense pressures to enter into additional binding commitments, at multilateral, regional, subregional and bilateral levels, to liberalize trade and investment and accept intrusive disciplines over an ever widening scope of development policy areas. Governments in developing countries will need to make major decisions on the extent they are willing to constrict policy options in order to gain trade benefits. The dilemma they face is on how to preserve development strategies in the context of multiple negotiations with regional and extraregional, developed and developing partners.

A prerequisite to participating in trade negotiations should be a clear definition of a pro-poor national trade and development policy. Such a policy should be aimed at ensuring that the poor do not bear the burden of adjustment inordinately, but maximize the benefits from trade liberalization and trade disciplines. The pursuit of three complementary and mutually supportive goals, on (*a*) an industrial policy based on tariffs, investment and services, (*b*) a proactive attack on barriers to exports supported by measures that ensure that the benefits of export growth are shared equitably and (*c*) the protection of food security and rural livelihoods, should set in play a virtuous spiral of growth, poverty reduction and human development. The objective of trade negotiations should be the preservation of national policy space needed for development and achievement of the MDGs, while obtaining commitments from trading partners supportive of these development objectives.

---

4   See Murray Gibbs and Swarnim Wagle, with Pedro Ortega, 2005, *The Great Maze: Regional and Bilateral Free Trade Agreements in Asia*, UNDP Asia Pacific Trade and Investment Initiative, Colombo (http://www.undprcc.lk/Publications/Publications/Great_Maze_-_FTA_-_completed.pdf).

## Preparing a strategy

A first step would be to review trade policies (i.e., trade in the broad sense of covering all matters subject to "trade" concessions) to target those most conducive to pro-poor and pro-development outcomes and the achievement of the MDGs. These can be divided into those where the maintenance of domestic policy space would seem crucial, and those where the objective would be to obtain action on the part of other countries, with the support of policy measures at the national level. Policy measures at the national and international levels would focus on (*a*) preventing the poor from bearing the burden of trade disciplines and liberalization and (*b*) equipping poorer people to derive maximum benefit from trade and globalization. In both cases, the achievement of the MDGs would be a central objective.

Governments which have not clearly defined their interests and goals inevitably find themselves on the defensive in trade negotiations. A pro-development trade policy not solidly based on a broad national consensus will not be defensible for long in negotiations, as it will come under pressure from foreign trade negotiators, multilateral financial institutions and special interest groups within the country. A solid consensus-building exercise should, therefore, be seen as a prerequisite for effective participation in trade negotiations. This is to pre-empt the risk of "elite capture", where special interests are successful in distorting priorities to serve their own interests at the expense of other segments of society. This can result in undermining development strategies and give rise to political conflict. An intensive consensus-building process involving all stakeholders can greatly strengthen the ability of governments to achieve a pro-development, pro-poor outcome in trade negotiations. A consensus should be reached on a list of priorities to be pursued in trade negotiations, whether at the multilateral, regional or bilateral level.

This strategy would incorporate pro-poor and pro-development objectives into national trade legislation and regulation, and anticipate the requests of trading partners so as to prepare to protect existing pro-MDG programmes and preserve policy space for future initiatives. A bottom-up pro-poor and pro-development trade strategy could be devised so as to attain the following goals in domestic policy and trade negotiations:

*Goal A*: To protect the most vulnerable segments of the population and to ensure greater equality within national societies, notably by providing universal access to basic services, health, education, water and sanitation and energy, and to protect poor farmers from disruptive surges of imports that could threaten their livelihoods.

> *Negotiating strategy:* To defend national policies and regulations in negotiations on trade in services and investment ("Trade in services and development strategies" and "Investment, jobs for youth and access to technologies") and flexibilities in agricultural trade regimes ("Agriculture and food security"), and of ensuring access to medicines ("Intellectual property rights for the poor").

*Goal B*: To empower people to become productive members of their national societies and compete in the world economy.

*Negotiating strategy:* To retain the flexibility to implement a coherent industrial policy, and export strategy setting off the virtuous upward spiral ("Tariffs and industrial policy" and "Exports and poverty"), obtaining advanced capital and technology ("Agriculture and food security", "Trade in services and development strategies", "Investment, jobs for youth and access to technologies" and "MNP—access to the world employment market") while building upon traditional knowledge and community achievements ("Intellectual property rights for the poor").

*Goal C*: To establish a set of objectives which should be pursued as a *demandeur* in trade negotiations, seeking commitments from other trading partners either in terms of specific concessions on their part or acceptance of trade rules that will serve to make the international trading environment more supportive of the national development strategy.[5]

*Negotiating strategy:* To pursue the elimination of tariffs and tighter disciplines over the application of restrictive trade measures in negotiations at the multilateral, regional, plurilateral and bilateral levels ("Policy space for future national development strategies", "Tariffs and industrial policy" and "The FTA option").

## The WTO multilateral negotiations and the MDGs

The goals of the Doha Declaration are consistent with the objectives outlined in this Policy Note. In this context, developing countries have been insisting that commitments be made to deal with measures most inimical to their exports (e.g., agricultural subsidies in developed countries) as a prerequisite to liberalization on their part. All WTO members are participating in the Doha Round whose final package was more clearly defined at the sixth WTO Ministerial Conference in Hong Kong Special Administrative Region in December 2005.[6]

While the Doha Declaration sets out objectives aimed at further liberalization, it also recognizes development objectives and the need to revisit certain obligations from a development perspective. Certain actions have already been taken, such as the Declaration on TRIPS and Public Health and some measures deriving from it (e.g., paragraph 6). Some of the new "Singapore" issues opposed by developing countries have also been withdrawn from the agenda as a result of the Cancun Ministerial Conference. What can be achieved in the multilateral trade negotiations that could

---

5  See UNCTAD, 2000, *A Positive Agenda for Future Trade Negotiations*, UNCTAD/ITCD/TSB/10, New York and Geneva, which sets out the spectrum of developing country goals in multilateral trade negotiations (http://www.unctad.org/en/docs/itcdtsb10_en.pdf).

6  See Hong Kong Ministerial Declaration, WT/MIN(05)/Dec, and other relevant documents on www.wto.org.

---

**Box 3. Doha Round suspension**

On 27 July 2006, the WTO General Council took note of the statements that had been made by delegations and the Director General to suspend the Doha Round of multilateral trade negotiations. The talks broke down due to the inability to reach trade-offs between the liberalization of industrial tariffs and the reduction of domestic subsidies and tariffs on agriculture.[a] In particular, the United States did not consider that it was in a position to accept a commitment to reduce its total trade distorting domestic support below $23 billion. Such breakdowns in multilateral negotiations are not new (e.g., Brussels 1990),[b] and in January 2007 the WTO Director General announced the full resumption of the negotiations.

  a  See analysis by B. L. Das in SUNS, 2 August 2006, www.sunsonline.org.
  b  See comparison to breakdown of 1990 Brussels GATT Ministerial Meeting by Chakravarthi Raghavan in SUNS, 28 July 2006, www.sunsonline.org.

---

be supportive of development strategies and is it possible to foresee the main elements of the Doha outcome that will set the multilateral framework within which trade policies will be formulated and pursued.[7]

*Policy space objectives*

Some action will require multilateral agreement, and thus must be pursued in concert with other interested countries, such as flexibilities to protect poor farmers (SP

---

**Box 4. Trade policy space rationale**

The question arises: why protect "space" for trade policy?

It can be argued that before 1995, developing countries largely "enjoyed" a free hand in the area of trade policy, and for the most part, with the exceptions that will be noted in the text, did not take advantage of this policy space to develop their economies.

The contraction of policy space which resulted through trade negotiations in GATT, but most dramatically after the entry into force of the WTO on an almost universal basis, was aimed to provide greater security of access for traders and investors, while the more stringent rule of law in the trade field was seen to be beneficial to developing countries as weaker partners in the international trading system.

Acceptance of the more intrusive and extensive trade disciplines described above is also seen as providing governments with an effective defence against protectionist pressures at home. For developing countries, such disciplines were viewed as needed to "lock in" the trade regimes imposed under temporary structural adjustment programmes imposed by the Bretton Woods institutions, which were considered as inherently beneficial for developing countries. These binding disciplines would provide the base for further trade liberalization and the further extension of the "frontiers" of the trading system to submit an ever

---

7  See Bhagirath Lal Das, 2005, *The Current Negotiations in the WTO, Options, Opportunities and Risks for Developing Countries,* London: Zed Books, www.zedbooks.co.uk.

widening range of policy measures to enforcement through the threat of trade sanctions. This was assumed to lead to ever increasing trade and accelerated economic growth.

However, this logic overlooked three important factors.

First, the process of development followed by successful countries, both those now considered highly developed and those which have more recently industrialized (e.g., Asian Tigers), has not followed the Bretton Woods model. These countries have applied a set of "tools" to protect infant industries, obtain advanced technologies and penetrate world markets that had been available under the more flexible GATT. These are now severely constrained under WTO. Some of these countries were never GATT contracting parties and only recently acceded to WTO. The intensified disciplines under WTO have reduced the policy space available to other countries and precluded the possibility of their emulating some of the strategies which had proven successful earlier.

Second, the pursuit of ever more stringent trade disciplines did not take into account the potential conflict with other development objectives, particularly those aimed at improving the living conditions of poorer people in developing countries as set out in the MDGs. In one dramatic case, the Declaration on TRIPS and Public Health had to be introduced in Doha literally to save people's lives. Beginning most dramatically at the 1999 Seattle WTO Ministerial Conference, some governments and civil society groups have challenged the goals of the ongoing negotiating process, drawing attention to a serious conflict between the goals of ever more intrusive and extensive trade disciplines and the need for policy space to pursue pro-poor policies such as food and livelihood security (agriculture), universal access to basic services, access to technology (services) and traditional community interests (TRIPS). There has been a growing democratization of trade policy formulation in both developed and developing countries. A wider range of stakeholders have demanded that their vital interests be protected and have rejected a secretive negotiation process. They have also observed that with the establishment of the WTO, the multilateral trading system has also extended its "frontiers" into policy areas where international consensus had been reached in other organizations such as the FAO, UNESCO and WHO.

Third, the commitment of the major trading countries to the multilateral trading system has declined, as they have pursued the negotiation of reciprocal FTAs with developing countries that had previously enjoyed unilateral preferential access to their markets. Furthermore, the return to bilateralism has also reflected a resurgence of political considerations in trade relations, precisely what the post-war GATT system had been set up to avoid.[a] FTAs exacerbate the difficulties described above, as they often totally eliminate any policy space that developing countries may have succeeded in defending in the WTO. They represent a negotiating process that is more political, less transparent and less likely to be based on national consensus than the multilateral trade regime.

The most important decisions relating to policy space to be faced by policymakers in the WTO multilateral trade negotiations relate to (a) measures to protect food security, (b) preservation of flexibility in industrial tariff negotiations and (c) response to formula approaches for commitments on trade in services. However, by far the greatest overall challenge lies in devising a response to the proliferation of FTAs, which cover all issues addressed in this Policy Note.

---

a   Craig VanGrasstek, 2003, "U.S. policy towards free trade agreements: strategic perspectives and extrinsic objectives", UNDP Asia Trade Initiative on Trade and Human Development, Phase 1, technical support document, Hanoi (available at www.undprcc.lk/Publications/Publications.asp?C=4).

and SSM), maintenance or exclusion of plant varieties from patenting, more effective rules to prevent bio-piracy, more flexibility to raise bound tariff rates and resistance to excessive liberalization through formulas in tariffs and services. Others will involve defence of policy measures in direct negotiations with trade partners in response to requests for liberalization commitments on tariffs and services.

## Market access objectives

- Elimination of agricultural export subsidies and meaningful reduction of production subsidies, including with respect to all "boxes", a significant increase in TRQs maintained by developed countries or the elimination of over-quota tariff rates;
- Bound, duty- and quota-free access to developed country markets for all (not just 97 per cent) exports of LDCs, i.e., including textiles and clothing; and duty-free access to developed country markets in other sectors of key export interest to developing countries;
- Tighter multilateral rules on resort to contingency trade measures affecting exports (e.g., to introduce more stringent disciplines in resort to anti-dumping duties against developing country exports, and measures to reduce the impact of such duties when applied);
- Improved access under Mode 4 of GATS for movement of service suppliers in occupations of export interest to developing countries, and the protection of traditional knowledge and prevention of bio-piracy for exported products (e.g., GIs).

---

### Box 5.  Trade negotiations and human development

The UNDP Asia Pacific Initiative on Trade, Human Development and Economic Governance took on the task, in 2002, of assessing the impact of various potential outcomes of trade negotiations on human development. The conduct of such analysis required at least a working definition of human development as applied to trade. The Asia Trade Initiative examined the literature on human development and identified four central components against which trade outcomes could be assessed, focusing on selected areas of trade negotiations for which the outcome could be expected to impact a large number of people, particularly poor people (agriculture, fisheries, MNP, energy services, environmental services, investment, TRIPs and textiles and clothing as well as the WTO plus provisions of FTAs ). Each trade measure proposed in the negotiations was assessed against whether it (a) would enhance the empowerment of poor people, i.e., would they gain more ability to shape the processes and events that affect their lives, (b) would permit poorer people to increase their productivity so as to enable them to compete in a globalized world economy, including through open and secure access for their exports, (c) would contribute to equity through increasing opportunities for those disadvantaged segments of the population (e.g., isolated regions, women, minority and ethnic groups), including through their access to vital services, and (d) would be sustainable, in the sense the measures could be implemented without entailing welfare losses for poorer groups of the population or future generation.

# Tariffs and industrial policy

With the general elimination of quantitative restrictions, tariffs remain the main measure available for the protection of domestic industries. Tariffs are also a major source of revenue for the governments of many developing countries, particularly LDCs and small island developing States (SIDS). Tariffs are, therefore, an essential tool for industrial policy for both reasons. How can such policy be oriented to achieving the MDGs? What is the role of tariffs in industrial policy and how should governments react to requests for further tariff liberalization commitments?

## Industrial policy and trade negotiations

Industrial policy requires a coordinated approach to most of the spectrum of trade policies subject to international disciplines which are currently the subject of trade negotiations. These include tariff policy, subsidies, policies to develop an efficient services infrastructure and producer service sector (e.g., telecommunications, financial services, transportation services, other producer services, policies with respect to movement of persons), investment policy and intellectual property rights. The execution of a coherent industrial policy thus calls for a coordinated negotiating strategy covering all aspects of trade negotiations. The effectiveness of tariffs as a

---

**Box 6.   Components of trade-related industrial policy**

In addition to formal trade measures, such as import and export tariffs and quantitative restrictions, other trade measures, which are currently the subject of trade agreements or negotiations, are also essential components of a coherent trade and industrial policy. These include:

Export promotion policies, which provide employment, higher incomes and foreign exchange to finance industrialization;

Agricultural policies, which reduce dependence on imports of essential food products and provide support for agro-industrial export income where possible;

Policies aimed at establishing an efficient services infrastructure, obtaining advanced producer services and associated technology, and access to distribution channels, as well as access to low cost energy;

Investment policies that maximize the contribution of FDI to industrial development through access to capital and technology in key sectors;

Intellectual property policies aimed at facilitating access to technology and low cost generic drug production;

Provisions to promote industrial cooperation in FTAs;

MNP can also be an important component of industrial policy, providing export income and upgrading the skills of industrial workers.[a]

---

[a]   See Vu Quoc Huy, et al., 2003, "Trade in services, movement of natural persons and human development: country case study—Viet Nam", UNDP Asia Trade Initiative on Trade and Human Development, Phase 1, technical support document, Hanoi (available at www.undprcc.lk/Publications/Publications.asp?C=4).

tool for industrialization is also linked to the monetary policy framework within which it operates. When the capital account is liberalized, control over exchange rates may be lost and the appreciation of exchange rates can obviously undermine export competitiveness and the impact of tariff protection.

## Public-private partnerships

Industrial policy is likely to work best if it is based on a strategic partnership between the public and private sectors and if government policy is successful in eliciting relevant information from the private sector—on the most binding constraints and externalities which the private sector faces—and is able to deal with them effectively. This is most likely to stimulate the entrepreneurial spirits of the private sector which are a crucial ingredient of successful industrial policy. Nevertheless, while the government should be close to the private sector's concerns, it must avoid being captured by special private sector interest groups if this policy is to serve the broader national interest. Strong State institutions and a clear government vision will be crucial to achieving this.

## Tariff liberalization and bindings

Tariffs are only one crucial ingredient of industrial policy, albeit an important one. Over the past twenty years developing countries have phased out quantitative restrictions and many have reduced tariffs, in some cases dramatically. The tariff reductions have usually been implemented as conditions for World Bank/IMF structural adjustment loans and programmes, which are by nature temporary. However, there has been strong pressure on developing countries to bind these low tariffs in the WTO, so as to "lock in" economic reforms, as an element in their Uruguay Round "package" of concessions. The pressure to do this has increased for countries newly acceding to the WTO or within the framework of FTAs. At present, developing countries are under pressure to further reduce, and bind, industrial tariffs in the Doha Round in line with a tariff cutting and harmonization formula being worked out in the NAMA (non-agricultural market access) group.[8]

Tariffs reductions can impact the achievement of the MDGs in at least three ways.

- They may lead to a surge in imports forcing domestic competitors out of business and causing increased unemployment in developing countries. Those so losing their jobs as a result are unlikely to find any alternative employment and many will sink below the poverty line.
- Tariff cuts can result in a reduction of government revenue, leaving the government with fewer resources for fighting poverty and for other social programmes.

---

8   The Third World Network had drawn up a table showing the tariff cuts that would result from the application of the "Swiss" tariff cutting formula using different coefficients. See www.twnside.org.sg.

- Tariff reductions may undermine industrialization policies in developing countries ("nip industrialization in the bud") by exposing industries to competition before they are strong enough to compete in the world.

Over 77 per cent of MFN tariffs in developing countries, and 44 per cent in LDCs, are bound[9] in the WTO, although many at relatively high rates, greatly exceeding current applied rates and allowing a considerable degree of flexibility. The use of tariffs as a tool of industrial policy is obviously a function of the flexibility that individual countries retain in their tariff schedules. Many developing countries have avoided across the board tariff bindings. For a number of relatively advanced developing countries in Asia, for example, the level of bindings on industrial products is around 60 per cent of tariff lines. In Africa there is no set pattern. Almost one third of African countries have bound less than 10 per cent of their industrial tariff schedules, while another third have bound over 90 per cent. Over 85 per cent of Latin American countries have bound over 90 per cent.[10] Flexibility is also provided by the levels of tariffs, as many countries have bound their tariff at relatively high rates and maintain an applied tariff at much lower levels. These high tariff bindings generally cover all industrial products, without much variation among sectors. Tariff policy is also restrained by FTAs that eliminate tariff flexibility among partners, and can drastically affect the scope for industrial tariff policy.

---

### Box 7.  The fiscal implications of trade liberalization

Trade liberalization over the past 20 years has indeed primarily taken the form of reductions in tariffs levied on imports in the context of bi- or multilateral agreements. Yet, customs duties continue to represent a significant share of fiscal revenue in most developing regions—and in particular in the least developed countries and small island countries, where reliance on trade taxes may exceed 25 per cent. The net revenue impact of trade liberalization, which has received much attention in the literature,[*] depends on assumptions that make it theoretically ambiguous. It has been argued that in addition to the marginal (assumed to be positive) effect of trade liberalization on growth, the introduction of consumption-based taxes—and of a Value Added Tax more specifically—would offset the short-term negative impacts on government revenues.

Yet, empirical results suggest that such has not been the case, in particular for countries that rely most on trade taxes: for every dollar lost in tariffs, poor and middle-income countries have at best been able to recover 30 cents from other sources.[a] Even more troubling is the fact that these countries are those where government revenues as a share of GDP are already among the lowest for a variety of structural reasons—urbanization rates, population density, dependency ratio- and economic reasons, and where public investments

---

**9**  See Santiago Fernández de Córdoba, 2005, *Coping with Trade Reforms, Implications of the WTO Industrial Tariff Negotiations for Developing Countries*, UNCTAD, Geneva.

**10**  See Marc Bacchetta and Bijit Bora, 2003, *Industrial Tariffs and the Doha Development Agenda*, WTO discussion paper, Geneva, http://www.wto.org/English/res_e/booksp_e/discussion_papers_e.pdf .

Box 7.    The fiscal implications of trade liberalization (*continued*)

are much needed to reduce poverty and achieve the MDGs. Explanations for the inability of poorer countries to make up for the loss in tariffs revenues include the institutional and administrative challenges posed by the introduction of VAT in economies where a sizeable share of transactions occurs in the informal sector, and where central and local tax authorities lack the technical capacities required to collect taxes, prevent leakages and tax evasion and implement necessary controls. Further, it has been argued[b] that a revenue-neutral reform of tariffs and VAT rates could be welfare-reducing in the context of highly informal economies where the increased reliance on VAT will exacerbate the distortions between the formal and informal sectors. It is clear, therefore, that trade liberalization has far-reaching fiscal and institutional implications and calls for the design of comprehensive technical assistance and capacity building programs that should be a priority of aid-for-trade initiatives.

* *Sources*: David Dollar and Aart Kraay, 2001, "Trade, growth and poverty", World Bank Working Paper 2615; David Greenaway, Wyn Morgan and Peter Wright, 2002, "Trade liberalization and growth in developing countries", *Journal of Development Economics*, vol. 67; and Francisco Rodríguez and Dani Rodrik, 1999, "Trade policy and economic growth: a skeptic's guide to the cross national evidence", NBER Working Paper 7081.
a   Thomas Baunsgaard and Michael Keen, 2005, "Tax revenue and (or?) trade liberalization", IMF Working Paper WP/05/112, June 2005.
b   Joseph Stiglitz and M. Shahe Emran, 2004, "Price neutral tax reform with an informal economy", *Econometric Society*, 2004 North American Summer Meetings 493.

## Tariff policy and industrialization strategy

A successful industrialization policy is one which allows a country to draw benefits from the globalization process by moving from static to dynamic comparative advantage. In this context, an appropriate balance in industrial policy design needs to be struck between the need for countries to take advantage of external effects that lead to the emergence of dynamic competitive advantage over time while at the same time recognizing that different countries will be better at producing different goods.

Within this framework, the starting point is typically resource-based and labour-intensive manufactures, often, but not always, the development of a textile and clothing industry (see annex A). The industrialization process starting from this initial type of industry should lead to the production of medium technology consumer goods and then up the ladder to high technology consumer and capital goods production. The success of some developing countries in world trade (e.g., Republic of Korea) has, to a significant effect, been a function of their ability to manufacture and export increasingly higher technology manufactured goods.

The need for tariff protection changes as countries move up this ladder. At the first stage, tariffs are required to develop domestic labour-intensive consumer goods industries. At a subsequent stage, it is the relatively more advanced technology production that requires tariff protection to encourage investors to enter into technologically more complex activities. At this stage, the protection for the lower-stage

**Box 8.   Social sustainability threshold**

In the absence of the "virtual upward spiral" mentioned above there would be a risk of a downward spiral that could drop below the "social sustainability threshold", i.e., the absolute limit of negative effects of policies or economic reform measures (such as trade liberalization), in terms of the deterioration of the situation or their economic prospects and opportunities, which a social group or society in general is willing to support without revolting in one way or another. Below this threshold, a country enters a turbulent area of social disturbance, economic breakdown and overall instability where economic laws no longer hold (preventing anticipated future positive effects of reform from materializing).[a]

---

[a]   See Ivan Martin, in "Search of development along the Southern border: the economic models underlying the Euro-Mediterranean partnership and the European neighbourhood". Policy paper presented to Seminar on Free Trade Agreements in the Arab Region, 9-11 December 2006.

industries can be phased out. Such an approach can help attain the MDGs by ensuring that new, higher value added more advanced industries are established to provide better quality employment opportunities for those in the more labour intensive industries before the latter are exposed to international competition. This should also provide more decent and productive work for youth in higher technology industries (MDG8, Target 17) by stimulating a virtuous spiral of growth, poverty reduction and human development.[11]

Such tariff policy should ensure that industries clearly perceive that high tariff protection will not be maintained indefinitely and industries that do not become competitive will be allowed to disappear. Moreover, it is important to assess whether tariffs are really forward looking and for genuine infant industry protection or whether they are actually for the protection of dying industries or those which have no chance of becoming viable and internationally competitive. They should be favoured for forward-looking industries and purposes, not for dying or unviable industries.

Despite these caveats, however, developing countries should ensure that they retain the ability to shift tariff protection from low to intermediate to high technology sectors as they move up the technology ladder, through a system of "cascading" tariffs. This could be achieved by not binding tariffs, or binding them at very high levels, or seeking exceptions for strategic sectors in the application of any tariff reduction formula. Ways should be sought to introduce more flexibility to tariff bindings accepted by countries at lower levels of industrialization, for example, a streamlined and more liberal interpretation of GATT Article XVIII:C which permits developing

---

11   See also Kamal Malhotra, "National trade and development strategies: suggested policy directions", 2006. Background paper for UNDP Asia-Pacific Human Development Report, *Trade on Human Terms: Transforming Trade for Human Development in Asia and the Pacific*, UNDP, June 2006. See also Yilmaz Akyuz, 2005, *The WTO Negotiations on Industrial Tariffs, What is at Stake for Developing Countries*, Geneva.

countries to deviate from their multilateral commitments, if necessary for the "establishment of a particular industry".[12] While it is true that some countries, especially LDCs, may not have all the necessary prerequisites to use tariff policy effectively in the manner described because of a small internal market or no clearly identifiable dynamic manufacturing industry, they should retain the policy space to pursue such strategies in the future in case either of their circumstances change, or they are able to enter regional integration agreements with other developing countries which make such policies and industries viable.

Successful countries have used tariff treatment in tandem with other trade measures (quantitative restrictions, subsidies) and investment regulations (performance and ownership requirements, incentives) to achieve this upward spiral. As WTO has reduced the scope to apply many of these measures (e.g., export subsidies, local

---

**Box 9.   The experience of the Republic of Korea**

The Republic of Korea moved up the virtuous spiral, graduating in two decades from a largely agricultural country exporting cheap labour-intensive products, such as textiles and clothing, to a fully industrialized country where manufactures represent 88 per cent of exports and 37 per cent of GDP. GDP in 1960 was a mere US$ 82, lower than most LDCs today, while its per-capita GDP in 2005 was US$ 16,291 and is fast approaching US$ 20,000. It also has a very high HDI. The Republic of Korea prioritized export promotion as the means of financing higher value added industries on its way up the technological ladder. Its strategy was to use a range of "tools" including tariffs and quantitative restrictions (QRs), local content, transfer of technology and export performance requirements to increase bargaining power with foreign investors, favouring those willing to transfer technology or with more effective export distribution channels.[a] The formation of large conglomerates was actively promoted. Building on the success in the production and export of light industry products, the Republic of Korea established heavy industries such as steel, petrochemicals, shipbuilding, industrial machinery, non-ferrous metal refining and electrical industries. It has now prioritized high technology industries such as semi-conductors. There has been substantial development and transformation in the Republic of Korea in the past 45 years. The major industries during the 1960s were labour-intensive industries such as wigs, artificial eyelashes, clothes and plywood while in 2005 the major industries were shipbuilding, automobiles, semiconductors and steel. The top three export items in the 1970s were textiles, plywood and wigs while in 2005 these were semiconductors, automobiles and wireless telecom.[b]

---

a   See Jang-Sup Shin and Jang-Sup Chang, 2004, "Foreign investment policy and human development country study: Republic of Korea", in Seih Mei Ling, ed., *Investment, Energy and Environmental Services: Promoting Human Development in WTO Negotiations*, University of Malaya, UNDP and Malaysian Institute of Economic Research (Kuala Lumpur, March 2004) http://www.um.edu.my. See also Kim DoHoon, 2006, Presentation on trade promotion and economic development in Korea, Korea Institute for Industrial Economics and Trade, 29 May 2006, in file with author.
b   See Kim DoHoon, op. cit.

---

12   This possibility was highlighted in the Decision on Implementation Issues and Concerns, annexed to the Doha Ministerial Declaration.

content requirements, QRs), tariff policy has become relatively more important as a tool for industrialization in developing countries.

In the example given above, the Republic of Korea relied on QRs to protect infant industries and as a "carrot" for investors. These were covered by the balance-of-payments provisions of Article XVIII:B of GATT. It lost the use of this instrument during the Uruguay Round. Countries unable otherwise to justify QRs (under balance-of-payments provisions) are not permitted to impose local content or trade balancing requirements which are prohibited under the TRIMs Agreement.

Tariff policy also has to address the question of the impact of tariffs on the cost of inputs for export industries. For example, should industries producing inputs be given tariff protection to foster backward linkages, or should all protection on inputs be eliminated to reduce costs for the processing industry? Tariffs can be an impediment to good export performance because they could raise the cost of inputs and make the final products uncompetitive. For example, in the case of Pakistan, protection against man-made fibre imports to shelter the cotton industry led to a decline in competitiveness for exports of made up articles and clothing.[13] Tariff draw back schemes can also be a solution, but they are often difficult to administer.

Export duties can also be an element of an industrialization strategy, by ensuring supplies of lower-cost raw material inputs for domestic industry.[14]

---

**Box 10.    Mongolia—removal of export restrictions and taxes**

Mongolia was obliged to eliminate its export restrictions and phase out its export duties on raw cashmere under its terms of accession to the WTO. As a result, raw cashmere is now exported to China and the cashmere processing sector has all but disappeared.[a] It is estimated that if all raw cashmere produced in Mongolia were fully processed into finished knitted and woven products before export, such exports would generate $206 million in reserve, more than all T&C exports. Moreover, employment in the processing industry would more than double.[b] On the other hand, the poor herders were able to obtain higher prices for their raw cashmere from Chinese buyers who required the longer Mongolian fibres to improve the quality of their fabric.

---

   a  See Damedin Tsogtbaatar, *Mongolia's WTO Accession: Expectations and Realities of WTO Membership* (www.wto.org/English/res_e/booksp_e/casestudies_e/case29_e.htm).

   b  See Ratnakar Adhikari and Yumito Yamamamoto, 2006, "Sewing thoughts, how to realize human development gains in the post-quota world", UNDP Asia Pacific Trade and Investment Initiative, April 2006 (www.undprcc.lk/Publications/Publications/TC_Tracking_Report_April_2006.pdf).

---

13  See Zubair Khan, 2003, *The Impact of the post-ATC Environment on Pakistan's Textiles Trade*, UNDP Asia Trade Initiative on Trade and Human Development, Phase 1, technical support document, Hanoi (www.undprcc.lk/Publications/Publications.asp?C=4).

14  Under WTO export duties have the same status as import duties, they are limited only to the extent that they have been bound in multilateral trade negotiations.

## Services and industrial policy

The services sector should also be seen as relevant to industrial policy. For some countries, it will simply make little sense, at least in the short term, to develop a manufacturing sector. In such cases, priority should be given to the development of a dynamic non-manufacturing sector (e.g., tourism).

Energy services will also be central to industrial policy, especially the ability to provide energy domestically at rates less than those prevailing on the world market. The Doha Round is the first time that energy policy has been seriously addressed in multilateral trade negotiations, covering subsidies, export restrictions and taxes, energy services, trade and environment and domestic excise taxes.[15] Concessions on energy policy have been made by countries acceding to the WTO.

However, a wide range of TRIMs are still permitted including transfer of technology and export performance requirements (see section on investment, jobs for youth and access to technologies). Moreover, performance requirements are encouraged for developing countries as a means of acquiring technology or access to information networks and distribution channels in the services sector (see section on trade in services and development strategies), even though some acceding countries have agreed to eliminate certain TRIMs and performance requirements that would otherwise have been permitted by WTO.

## Subsidies

Developing countries are permitted to apply production subsidies unless these are shown to cause serious prejudice to the interests of other countries. Any subsidy that is not specific, in that it is generally available to all enterprises is "non actionable" under the WTO Agreement on Subsidies and Countervailing Measures. For example, the provision of energy at costs lower than those prevailing on the world market (dual price system) is not considered to constitute an actionable subsidy, so long as the cheaper access is generally available throughout the economy.[16] Export subsidies, i.e., subsidies contingent upon export performance, are prohibited to all WTO members, except LDCs and a group of lower-income countries which will enjoy this freedom until they reach $1,000 per capita GNP.[17]

---

15  See Murray Gibbs, 2004, *Energy in the WTO: What is at stake?*, in Sieh Mei Ling, ed., *Investment, Energy and Environmental Services: Promoting Human Development in WTO Negotiations,* University of Malaya, UNDP and Malaysian Institute of Economic Research, Kuala Lumpur, March 2004 (www.um.edu.my).

16  See UNCTAD, 2005, *Energy and Environmental Services, Negotiating Objectives and Development Priorities,* Simonetta Zarrilli, ed., UNCTAD/DITC/TNCD/2003/3, Geneva, July 2005.

17  WTO Agreement on Subsides and Countervailing Measures, Annex VII.

# Exports and poverty

Can developing countries "export their way out of poverty", can they export their way to achievement of the MDGs? How can the poor in developing countries achieve productivity and the means to compete in the world market? How can governments ensure that the benefits of exports are widely shared and that they reduce inequalities? How can it be assured that export industries are sustainable, that adequate working conditions are maintained, that environmental impacts do not undermine the livelihoods of people in other sectors. What are the constraints faced by governments in promoting exports? What contribution can "aid for trade" programmes make to addressing "supply side" constraints which inhibit a country's ability to export?

## Export growth and the MDGs

Increased exports of goods and services can provide increased incomes for poor people, government revenue and new opportunities for employment, including high paid jobs abroad, particularly for women and young jobseekers. Exports can contribute to the achievement of MDGs by lifting people out of poverty (MDG1) and empowering women (MDG3), and by contributing to the achievement of MDG8. MDG8 aims at a trading system in which developing countries can extract greater benefits from the international trading system.

Trade policies should be aimed at enabling poorer people to compete in the world market and derive benefits from globalization. The *simple orthodoxy* would suggest that trade liberalization will allow resources to be redeployed from low productivity to high productivity export sectors. However, it ignores the basic fact that there are already high levels of unemployment in developing countries. Human resources are available for the export sector, they do not have to be "liberated" by creating unemployment in other sectors.[18] Import and export policy should be twin elements of an overall industrialization strategy, targeting the import of essential food, fuels, raw materials, inputs, capital equipment, machinery, spare parts and intermediate inputs goods, supporting export growth and earning the foreign exchange necessary to finance such imports. Priority should be given to the expansion of those export sectors that will provide opportunities for achieving the MDGs and other development goals.

One problem is that many poorer developing countries have suffered a decline in their share in world exports, even when benefiting from tariff preferences which they now find eroding. Other countries have been able rapidly to increase exports in response to certain trade policy measures which have worked in their favour, but are finding themselves unable to compete when faced with a more open, competitive situation. One example is textiles and clothing, where many poorer countries have developed a successful export industry within the framework of the discriminatory structure of the Multi Fibre Agreement (MFA) and are now faced with the challenge

---

18   See Joseph Stiglitz and Andrew Charlton, op. cit., pp. 25-26.

## Box 11.   Aid-for-trade

The need for scaling up aid-for-trade resources to LDCs and other low-income countries was widely recognized by the international community in 2005, culminating with the inclusion in the December 2005 WTO Hong Kong Ministerial Declaration of key paragraphs on both an enhanced Integrated Framework for Trade Related Technical Assistance for the LDCs (IF) and broader aid-for-trade. Ministers in Hong Kong Special Administrative Region agreed to establish a new Aid-For-Trade Task Force with the mandate to provide recommendations on how to operationalize aid-for-trade components beyond an enhanced IF, so that it can most effectively contribute to the development dimension of the Doha Round. Following wide-ranging consultations with WTO member States, international agencies and other stake-holders, the Task Force submitted its report to the WTO General Council on 27 July 2006. The report, which was finalized after the suspension of the Doha negotiations, makes clear that aid-for-trade is a complement to the Doha Round and not conditional upon its success.

The main thrust of the Task Force's recommendations is that existing arrangements and commitments should be built upon in financing aid-for-trade needs, guided by the Paris Declaration on Aid Effectiveness. In this context, the WTO Director General is urged to "seek confirmation from donors and agencies that funds are readily available for the implementation of the aid-for-trade initiative ...".

As for the scope of aid-for-trade, this should be broad enough to cover the diverse needs of developing countries, and clear enough to differentiate aid-for-trade from other development assistance (of which it is a part). Trade-related development priorities included in the recipients' national development strategies should be considered as falling under the aid-for-trade umbrella.

Specifically, aid-for-trade is expected to encompass trade policy and regulations; trade development; trade-related infrastructure; building productive capacity; and trade-related adjustment.

This is a broad enough definition to cover the wide array of supply-side constraints affecting developing countries' competitiveness on world markets, including investments in projects addressing cross-country and regional impediments to trade development, such as regional transport corridors, standards, disease or pest issues—areas that have traditionally been neglected and require a much higher priority than they have received so far.

Another important area that is, quite innovatively, covered, even though there is no consensus on its inclusion, are short-term adjustment needs (i.e., fiscal loss of government revenue as a result of MFN tariff reduction, changes in terms of trade for net food importers, preference erosion through MFN or FTA tariff reductions, or the elimination of special preferential arrangements). The costs of adaptation to the elimination of the quota system on textiles and clothing (see annex A) and the implementation costs of trade agreements are also included in many definitions.

The Task Force's report also makes provision for AFT reporting requirements—either as donor or recipient—in periodic trade policy reviews of WTO member States. A global periodic aid-for-trade review is also recommended. This is to be convened by a monitoring body to be set up within the WTO. The Director-General is expected to establish an ad hoc consultative group to take forward the practical follow up of the Task Force's recommendations.

*Source*: UNDP, Concept Note on Aid for Trade, January 2006 (http://www.undp.org/poverty/) and WTO document, "Recommendations of the Task Force on Aid For Trade", WT/AFT/1, 27 July 2006 (www.wto.org).

of a more competitive environment as described in annex A. Another example is the sugar sector where the erosion of EU preferences will cause inevitable adjustment costs to poor producers.

## Increase productivity

Exports should, directly or indirectly, provide employment for poor people and women. The challenge is to provide them with the means to compete and to increase their **productivity**. This requires an understanding of factors contributing to competitiveness in the sector, and policy measures to enhance them. Some countries have achieved high export growth but with low value added since such exports have not emerged from the industrialization strategy described in "Tariffs and industrial policy". The move from static to dynamic comparative advantage is manifested in the continuous upgrading of the technological content of exports, which is the expected result of moving up the virtuous spiral described in "Tariffs and industrial policy". Success in exporting is a function of the capacity to produce products domestically that are "dynamic in world trade".[19]

---

### Box 12.   China's industrialization

China has followed an approach to industrialization which is similar, in important respects, to that which was adopted by the Republic of Korea. Both have high technological content and value added in the domestic economy. Tariff and quota protection and TRIMs were used as "carrots and sticks" to oblige firms to move up the technological ladder. China's impressive export performance has been a result of its ability to produce "dynamic" export products of ever increasing technological content. China's pattern of production and exports were not left to be determined by traditional forces of comparative advantage. Government policies have nurtured domestic capabilities in consumer electronics and other advanced technology products.[a]

a   See Dani Rodrik, 2006, *What is so Special about China's Exports?*, London: Centre for Economic Policy Research, February 2006 (www.cepr.org).

---

## Promote equity

In most cases, even when they have occurred, the benefits of impressive export gains have not always been widely shared. In certain circumstances, exports have even undermined the livelihoods of poor people. Policies to increase exports should be mindful of equity concerns, ensuring that benefits of exports do not accrue mainly to richer segments of the population. Additional measures are necessary to ensure that poorer segments of the population derive direct gains from export expansion, rather than rely only on trickle-down benefits. Evidence shows that

---

**19**  For a list of dynamic products in world trade and an analysis of their contribution to export performance, see UNCTAD, *World Investment Report 2002* (www.unctad.org).

> **Box 13.   Equity issues in fisheries sector**
>
> The fisheries sector is a good example where a successful export industry can actually undermine the livelihoods of poorer producers, unless a strict policy framework is imposed to protect the latter, as described in annex B to this paper. The main exporters are large fishing fleets which deplete the coastal water and thus reduce availability to small fishers. Similarly the great success of aquaculture exports has resulted in the saline pollution of agricultural lands.

export growth built on an inequitable distribution of income can simply exacerbate existing inequalities.[20]

## Ensure sustainability

Export policies should also ensure that exports are sustainable in the sense that current gains do not prevent subsequent generations from improving their own welfare. The concept of sustainability encompasses environmental concerns, as well as human capabilities such as health and education. Export industries may damage the environment, exhausting resources and otherwise serving to undermine the livelihoods of people employed in other sectors. Employment opportunities may entail unhealthy and dangerous working conditions, resulting in workers not being able to sustain more than a few years of employment in the export industries. Hence, export orientation should be part of a comprehensive development strategy that incorporates measures to ensure that these human development objectives are attained.

## Elements of a comprehensive pro-poor export strategy

These should comprise the following:
* Improving the infrastructure supporting export activities of small and poor producers, including access to credit and to land;
* Providing them with access to training and technology to improve skills;
* Assisting them in raising the quality of the goods and services they produce, to meet SPS, TBT and buyer preferences;
* Ensuring adequate working conditions, health and safety standards;
* Obtaining freer and more secure access to markets for their products,
* Liberalization of trade in services should be targeted to sectors where investment supports the competitiveness of the export sectors, and should be subject to conditions that enhance this positive contribution;

---

20  See UNDP, 2005, "International cooperation at a crossroads: aid, trade and security in an unequal world", *Human Development Report 2005*, chapter 4, New York, 2005 (http://hdr.undp.org/reports/global/2005/).

- Strengthening community participation in export benefits through such techniques as the protection and application of traditional knowledge and the encouragement and protection of geographical indications;
- Strengthening positive linkages with other sectors of the economy, and dealing with negative externalities, e.g., working conditions, environmental degradation;
- Facilitating the temporary movement of persons abroad to gain skills and foreign exchange.

---

**Box 14.  Export policies and WTO and other trade agreements**

The Agreement on Subsidies and Countervailing Measures (Article 27.2(a)) exempts LDCs from the prohibition on export subsidies. The same exemption is also provided to a list of countries as long as their per capita GDP remains below $1,000. Note that some acceding countries have forsaken this right in their terms of accession to WTO. The Agreement on Agriculture permits countries to subsidize exports up to the level of their negotiated commitments. Very few developing countries have negotiated such commitments, and thus cannot subsidize.

The TRIMs Agreement prohibits trade balancing requirements, i.e., that investing firms must export to the extent they import. However, it does permit export performance and transfer of technology requirements. The GATS Agreement permits performance requirements for developing countries in order to help strengthen services in developing countries and it has no effective disciplines on export subsidies.

However, many countries have given up the right to these and other performance requirements in their terms of accession or in bilateral agreements (BITs and FTAs).

---

## Access to export markets

Export-led development strategies obviously require the most free and secure access to world markets possible. For several decades developing countries have enjoyed preferential access to developed countries' markets under the Generalized System of Preferences negotiated in UNCTAD. These had the advantage of being non-reciprocal, but the serious disadvantages of not being bound and thus insecure, and of containing many exceptions, precisely in sectors (e.g., textiles and clothing and agriculture) where developing countries possess a comparative advantage. Some poorer developing countries, notably those in the ACP group, benefited from contractual preferences in the EU. Most developed countries (excluding the United States) have complied with their commitment to extend duty free treatment to LDCs. Other developing countries are granted autonomous preferences to assist them in dealing with specific problems, such as dependence on exports of illicit drugs.

Many developing countries are seeking to negotiate FTAs with major developed countries as a means of ensuring conditions of access equal to those of their competitors. Negotiations have already begun to convert ACP preferences into reciprocal FTAs ("Economic Partnership Agreements").

However, barriers and distortions to world trade, particularly subsidized agricultural production and exports in the industrialized countries, have heavily penalized many developing countries. Contingent measures such as anti-dumping duties have served to "nip in the bud" export expansion in developing countries, while stricter sanitary and technical regulations have also had a disproportionate impact on poor people, excluding them from export income. Stringent rules of origin have resulted in many exports not benefiting from available tariff preferences. Poorer people are much more adversely affected by insecure access to markets, as sudden disruptions to their exports can provoke immediate unemployment in export industries and bankrupt small independent producers.

---

**Box 15.  Catfish, globalization and the poor**

Many poor communities have invested in aquaculture production in the Mekong Delta of Viet Nam. Exports of catfish were having impressive success in the United States market and became a model of how globalization can benefit the poor. However, protectionist groups in the United States launched a policy of trade harassment against Vietnamese catfish, first by attempting to portray the catfish as being produced in unsanitary conditions, a claim which was debunked by the U.S. Department of Agriculture, then by obtaining legislation requiring the Viet Namese product to be sold as "basa" and "tra" rather than "catfish". When this measure had little effect on imports, anti-dumping action was taken, facilitated by Viet Nam's "non-market economy" status in United States law, and the fact that, as a non-member of WTO at that time, Viet Nam had no multilateral rights and no access to dispute settlement mechanisms.[a]

---

a   See Lam Quoc Tuan, 2003, "Trade in fisheries and human development—country case study—Viet Nam", UNDP Asia Trade Initiative on Trade and Human Development, Phase 1, technical support document, Hanoi (available at www.undprcc.lk/Publications/Publications. asp?C=4).

---

## Agriculture and food security

### Agriculture and the MDGs

The large majority of people living in extreme poverty live in rural areas of developing countries. Most of them are engaged in the subsistence agricultural sector. In some poor countries, agriculture constitutes up to 80 per cent of the labour force. Thus, the achievement of MDG1, MDG3 (e.g., in some countries women do over 60 per cent of cultivation work) and others in most developing countries will depend on the success of reforms aimed at providing higher standards of living in the agricultural sector. Trade policy is an essential component of any such reforms. These millions of poor people are extremely vulnerable; their livelihoods can be suddenly undermined by surges in imports of cheap agricultural products. Trade can provide opportunities for the poor, if their products are able to penetrate lucrative export markets. Success in policies to raise poor farmers' incomes at the national

level will be directly linked to the direction taken in the ongoing process of reform
of the international trade regime governing agricultural trade. Developing countries
are actively participating in the current WTO negotiations with the objective of
designing an international regime more coincident with development objectives. At
the same time many are further liberalizing trade in agricultural products within
the framework of FTAs.

## Complex multilateral regime

Trade in the agricultural sector is subject to a multilateral regime of extreme com-
plexity. The process of "tariffication" conducted in the Uruguay Round under which
non-tariff measures (e.g., quantitative restrictions) and variable levies were converted
into equivalent tariff rates (and all tariff rates were bound) resulted in very high
MFN tariffs in most major importing countries.[21] Market access (at least 5 per cent
of domestic consumption) was provided by a system of tariff rate quotas (TRQs),[22] at
lower, but usually positive, rates, often allocated to individual suppliers. As the out of
quota tariffs are usually prohibitively high, imports of a large number of agricultural
products into developed countries are in fact subject to de facto quantitative limits.
This protective regime is supplemented by a Special Safeguard Mechanism (SSM),
which permits additional import charges to be applied when imports of "tariffied"
products exceed trigger prices or trigger volumes.

Thus, the new regime retained, in a somewhat different form, the quantitative restrictions (de facto) and variable levies that were central to the EU protective
regime. It also established a framework for "micro-negotiation" for the granting of
bilateral quotas reminiscent of the MFA. Within such a structure, analysis based on
average tariff rates provides little useful guidance for policymakers.[23]

The WTO Agriculture Agreement also imposed some discipline on agricultural
subsides. Export subsidies are subject to sectoral commitments (volume and payments). Domestic production subsidies designed to have a distorting effect (e.g., price
supports) are also subject to overall negotiated ceilings (based on AMS-aggregate
measure of support) with a *de minimis* exception (5 per cent for developed, 10 per
cent for developing countries). Two other categories of subsidies are not subject to
limitations: (i) direct payments to producers when linked to supply reduction ("blue"
box) and (ii) those determined to have minimal trade impact ("green" box). This
structure has not served to limit agricultural subsidization, which has increased to

---

21  An exception to the prohibition of QRs on agricultural products is contained in annex 5
to the Agreement on Agriculture. Section B in that annex enables developing countries to
maintain QRs on "a primary agricultural product that is the predominant staple in the traditional diet of a developing country". Only the Republic of Korea, the Philippines and Israel
make use of this provision.

22  In practice not all countries have met the 5 per cent access commitment and the TRQs have
been significantly under utilized.

23  Stiglitz and Charlton, op. cit., pp. 217-234.

almost $300 billion annually. Subsidy programmes have simply been directed to those "boxes" where no limits are applied.[24]

Bound limits of domestic production subsidies (AMS) total $64 billion. However actual subsidization does not reach these limits. The utilization rate was 88 per cent in the United States, 62 per cent in the EU and 17 per cent in Japan.[25] Twenty nine WTO members have made AMS commitments. They are phrased in terms of overall payments, e.g., the European Community's commitment is EUR 67 billion, that of the United States $19 billion.

---

### Box 16.  Legal and political initiatives—the example of cotton

Trade negotiations are not the only way of addressing the export interests of the poor in international trade. The WTO dispute settlement mechanism enables developing countries to challenge measures that are inconsistent with multilateral obligations. One example is the successful case launched by Brazil, with the support of numerous developing countries, against many elements of the United States subsidy schemes on cotton. The United States was found to have subsidized exports of cotton at a level exceeding its WTO commitments and in breach of other provisions of the Agreements on Agriculture and on Subsidies and Countervailing Measures (such as favouring the use of domestic over imported cotton).[a]

In parallel to this case, four poor African countries—Benin, Burkina Faso, Chad and Mali, introduced a "sectoral initiative in favour of cotton"[b] which described the damage caused to their poor cotton producers by the lavish subsidies offered to rich cotton producers in developed countries. The objective was to shame the major trading countries into taking action to eliminate these subsidies.

The initiative by Brazil was instrumental in dealing with United States export subsidies. As LDCs, these four countries should benefit from duty-free treatment into all developed markets, however, the major issue of achieving the accelerated reduction of domestic production subsidies on cotton is still being pursued in the resumed Doha Round. Disputes against subsidies in the agricultural sector will likely proliferate with the expiry of the "peace clause".[c]

---

a   See "United States—upland cotton", WTO Dispute DS267, Appellate Body Report, circulated 3 March 2005 http://www.wto.org/english/tratop_e/dispu_e/cases_e/ds267_e.htm.
b   See WTO document, Committee on Agriculture—Special Session—WTO Negotiations on Agriculture, "Poverty reduction: sectoral initiative in favour of cotton"—Joint Proposal Benin, Burkina Faso, Chad and Mali, TN/AG/GEN/4, 16 May 2003, www.wto.org.
c   Article 13 of the WTO Agreement on Agriculture. For an up-to-date analysis of current issues in the multilateral negotiations on agriculture at the time of their suspension see David Blandford and Tim Josling, 2006, "Options for the WTO modalities for agriculture", International Food and Agricultural Trade Policy Council, May 2006, http://www.agritrade.org/Publications/DiscussionPapers/WTO%20Modalities.pdf.

---

24   There is a concise description of the subsidy boxes on the WTO website at http://www.wto.org/english/tratop_e/agric_e/agboxes_e.htm.
25   See presentation by Ralf Peters, UNCTAD at UNECA Ad Hoc Meeting on Agriculture, Tunis, November 2004, http://www.uneca.og/eca_programes/trade.

## Further agricultural liberalization

The logic of the Uruguay Round was to ensure minimum access to markets, while placing ceilings on protection and subsidization, as a starting point for further agricultural liberalization in future multilateral rounds. For developing countries, however, this process served to "lock in" World Bank structural adjustment programmes, resulting in an asymmetrical system that penalized developing countries, as they were not permitted to increase their existing levels of subsidies and tariff protection. Countries acceding to WTO found themselves obliged to accept even more stringent conditions. Developing countries found themselves in a situation in which their markets became relatively open to imports (all agricultural tariffs were bound), even when such imports benefited from export subsidies in OECD countries, while their exports were restricted by restrictive tariff quotas and met subsidized competition from developed country competitors in third country markets. Overall, developing countries, once net exporters of agricultural products, have become net importers with a deficit of $11 billion in 2001. The major subsidizing developed countries, the EU and the United States, have gained at the expense of most developing countries with a few notable exceptions, such as India and the most competitive southern hemisphere exporters (e.g., Argentina and Brazil).[26] For the net food-importing developing countries (NFIDCs), taken as a group, imports represent 35 per cent of calorie intake. Paradoxically, those countries most dependent on agricultural exports witness higher levels of malnutrition.[27]

National trade policies must be designed to reflect the complexities of the agricultural sector in most developing countries. Some countries have been very successful in the export of widely traded agricultural commodities. However, in many cases small-scale farmers have not benefited, production of export crops has resulted in the displacement of small-scale farmers and exacerbated their plight by contributing to environmental degradation posing an overall threat to food security. Large segments of the population are small-scale farmers whose livelihood can be suddenly eroded by imports of cheap, often subsidized imports. Countries have adopted both "offensive" and "defensive" strategies. On the one hand, they have pursued improved access to markets, and, on the other hand, have sought to ensure protection of vulnerable segments of their populations.[28]

Developing counties are seeking an international regime that reflects these complexities, as well as the varying, often conflicting, interests of different developing countries. They are seeking better market access and the reduction of subsidization by the developed countries, for example through the elimination of export sub-

---

26  See Stiglitz and Charlton, op. cit., pp. 217-234, notably table AI.3.

27  Pal, op. cit.

28  See for example Abdul Aziz Rahman, 2003, "Trade in agriculture, food security and human development: country case study for Malaysia", UNDP Asia Trade Initiative on Trade and Human Development, Phase 1, technical support document (Hanoi: 2003) (available at www.undprcc.lk/Publications/Publications.asp?C=4).

sidies, the drastic reduction of amber box commitments, capping and phasing out "blue box" limits, and imposing some meaningful disciplines on "green box" subsidies. Many argue that the reduction of agricultural support in OECD countries would be the most significant pro-poor result of the Doha Round. The refusal of the United States to accept limits on its total trade distorting subsidization (amber plus blue box plus *de minimis*), which are lower than its actual levels of subsidization, has been given as the main reason behind the suspension of the multilateral negotiations in July 2006.[29] The resumed negotiations are aimed at achieving a breakthrough on subsidies combined with liberalization of tariffs and tariff quotas and agreement on Special Products and a Special Safeguard Mechanism (see below).

Other areas of the international trade regime, which can affect the interests of small farmers, include notably sanitary and phytosanitary (SPS) regulations, liberalization of distribution services (see section on trade in services and development strategies) and intellectual property rights (see section on MNP—access to the world employment market).

## Liberalization and food security

A key coalition of developing countries, the G33[30] are seeking to make any further liberalization in agricultural trade conditional upon the preservation of their policy space to intervene to protect livelihoods, and ensure food security. This approach has been manifested in the Special Products[31] and Special Safeguards proposals currently before the WTO. While it is recognized that such measures could increase import prices of foodstuffs for urban consumers, on balance rural producers are the poorest members of society in developing countries, far poorer than those segments of the population who purchase imported food.[32]

A **Special Safeguard Mechanism** (SSM) would provide developing countries with a facility comparable to those already available to "tariffied" products to deal with sudden surges. Additional duties could be imposed on imports "triggered" by

---

29  See the statement by the EC Agriculture Commissioner, Mariann Fisher Boel, following the suspension of the WTO Doha Round negotiations: http://ec.europa.eu/commission_barroso/ fischer-boel/doha/index_en.htm#2407. The United States, on the other hand, claims that the proposals of the G33 on SP would effectively block meaningful access to their markets for U.S. agricultural exports.

30  G33 members are: Antigua and Barbuda, Barbados, Belize, Botswana, China, Congo, Côte d'Ivoire, Cuba, Dominican Republic, Grenada, Guyana, Haiti, Honduras, India, Indonesia, Jamaica, Kenya, Mauritius, Madagascar, Mongolia, Mozambique, Nicaragua, Nigeria, Pakistan, Panama, Peru, Philippines, Republic of Korea, St. Kitts and Nevis, St. Lucia, St. Vincent and the Grenadines, Senegal, Suriname, Trinidad and Tobago, Turkey, Uganda, United Republic of Tanzania, Venezuela, Zambia and Zimbabwe.

31  According to the terminology used in the WTO, "sensitive" products are those for which developed countries are seeking less than formula liberalization.

32  See Stiglitz and Charlton, op. cit., p. 230

increased import volumes or declining import prices.[33] It should be noted that the agricultural tariff profiles of the proponents of SSM vary considerably. The bound tariff rates of some members of G33 well exceed 100 per cent, which provides adequate margin at present to deal with import surges.[34]

---

### Box 17.   Identifying special products

Criteria: The Special Products (SP) proposal aims at ensuring that future commitments on market access for agriculture will permit a special degree of flexibility for products central to the objectives of (*a*) food security (all people have physical and economic access to sufficient safe and nutritious food to meet their dietary needs for an active and healthy life), (*b*) livelihood security (adequate and sustainable access to resources or assets by household and individuals to realize a minimum standard of living, recognizing that poor farmers have very low risk thresholds) and (*c*) rural development (the potential of an agricultural product to improve the living standards of the rural population including both directly and through its forward linkages to non-farm rural activities).[a]

The question of the criteria to be used in determining which products are "special" is the subject of current debate in the WTO and is also relevant to developing countries in their national agricultural trade policies. Basic indicators that should be examined include:

- **Food security**: the share of consumption of the product in total agricultural consumption, and the share of its domestic production in domestic consumption. These could be used as indicators of the importance of the product for food security. A certain percentage of domestic consumption of the basic food basket should be met by domestic production, since dependence on imports create high vulnerability for products for which world trade volume is relatively small compared to world demand;
- **Livelihood security**: the share of employment as a result of production of the product in the total agricultural labour force; if the majority of farmers producing a particular product are low income and resource poor, any disruption caused by imports can cause deprivation and even starvation;
- **Rural development**: the share of production of the product in total agricultural production. This could serve as an indicator of the contribution of the product to rural development.[b]

Different products emerge at the top of the potential SP list when the criteria are applied in different countries, e.g., maize in Ethiopia, yams in Côte d'Ivoire, cassava in Nigeria and rice in Bangladesh.[c]

These "macro" indicators should be supplemented by the additional factors listed below to address the needs of the main target group, the rural poor, including women and small farmers.

---

[33] See the G33 Proposal on SSM for developing countries, JOB(06)64, 23 March 2006, available at: http://www.agtradepolicy.org/output/resource/G33_revised_proposal_SSM_23Mar06.pdf.

[34] For an analysis of the bound tariff rates of G33 countries and their ability to respond to import surges, see Mario Jales, 2005, "Tariff reduction, Special Products and Special Safeguards: an analysis of the agricultural tariff structures of G33 countries", ICTSD Geneva, June 2005, http://www.ictsd.org/dlogue/2005-06-16/Jales.pdf.

**Box 17.   Identifying special products** (*continued*)

- **Geographical concentration** of production and employment within the country (for example, it has been possible to draw a food insecurity map of India[d]), with a focus on particularly disadvantaged regions. This should also be examined.[e]
- **Household incomes and production capacity** of small farmers.
- The potential that locally produced products could be displaced by substitute products, not produced in the country concerned.
- **Caloric intake**: share of product at national or regional levels.
- **Expenditures**: Share of income spent on a particular product at the national or regional levels.

External factors should also be considered, including:

- Import penetration of identified products and directly competing products;
- Financial capacity of the country to finance food security programmes;
- Subsidization, the extent to which a product benefits from export or production subsidies in supplying countries.

---

a  See Proposal of G33 on the modalities for the designation and treatment of any agricultural product as a Special Product (SP) by any developing country member, JOB(05)304, 22 November 2005 http://www.agtradepolicy.org/output/resource/G33_proposal_SPs_22Nov05.pdf.
b  FAO Support to the WTO Negotiations (2003), www.fao.org.docrep/005.
c  Ibid.
d  See Parthapratim Pal, 2006, "The ongoing negotiations on agriculture: some observations", presentation at the Workshop on WTO related issues for Government Officials in the SAARC Region, The Energy and Resources Institute (TERI), 1-3 May 2006, New Delhi, India http://www.teriin.org/events/docs/wtopresent/partha4.ppt.
e  This discussion draws heavily from the paper by Luisa Bernal, 2005, "Methodology for the identification of special products and products for eligibility under special safeguard mechanism by developing countries", ITCSD (Geneva, October 2005) http://www.ictsd.org/dlogue/2005-10-14/Luisa%20Bernal%20Methodlogy%20paper.pdf.

Defining the indicators for these special protective measures is a crucial element both in national trade policies and in the ongoing multilateral trade negotiations, as well as in FTAs. The SP criteria and SSG mechanisms should be incorporated into national regulations so as to provide the basis for their inclusion in the WTO agreement and any FTAs.

SPS regulations present a serious barrier to exports of agricultural products, particularly those of small-scale farmers. Improvement in the implementation of the WTO SPS regime is being sought in the Doha Round. The aim is both giving more time to developing countries to adjust to new regulations, and seeking a commitment on the part of the importing country to provide the technical and financial assistance necessary to permit the developing country to meet the standards. This should also be a priority in any aid-for-trade programme.

Agricultural products have proven to be a complex issue in the negotiation of FTAs. In some cases, North-South FTAs have excluded major export products of interest to the developing partner (rice, sugar), while failing to impose any dis-

---

### Box 18.  Applying Special Safeguards

Article 5 of the WTO Agreement in agriculture institutes a system of Special Safeguards (SSG) under which countries can apply additional charges to imports based on trigger volumes or trigger prices. This facility is available only for items which have been "tariffied" and have been designated for SSG by the country concerned. While some 21 developing countries have been able to make use of this facility, it has been used overwhelmingly by developed countries.

Agricultural markets are by nature cyclical and are affected by natural factors such as weather. To this is added the man-made factors of subsidization and the behaviour of trading firms. The food price index has actually become more volatile since the WTO's establishment.[a] As a consequence of massive subsidization in the United States and the European Union, export prices of key food commodities are below the costs of production, for example wheat (by 43 per cent), rice (by 35 per cent) and maize (by 13 per cent).[b]

The further reduction of bound tariff rates on agricultural imports could expose vulnerable producers in developing countries to severe external shocks that could drastically affect their livelihoods.[c] It was confirmed at the sixth WTO Ministerial Conference that developing countries should have access to a Special Safeguard Mechanism (SSM) which would be used to shield vulnerable producers from surges of low priced imports. The SSM would be activated by trigger volumes and prices. The G33 proposed that the trigger price would be the average monthly price of that product, and the trigger volume would equal the average annual volume, for the most recent three-year period. The SSM would apply to all products and all trade including that under FTAs. The specifics of the proposal are yet to be agreed.

---

a  Pal, op. cit., and Julio Paz, 2005, "Identificación de productos especiales y mecanismos de salvaguardia especial en el Perú", ICTSD, Geneva.
b  IATP.
c  See Dale Hathaway, 2002, "A special agricultural safeguard: buttressing the market access reforms of developing countries", comments in FAO Papers on Selected Issues Relating to the WTO Negotiations on Agriculture, FAO, Rome (http://www.fao.org/docrep/005/Y3733E/y3733e05.htm).

---

ciplines on the subsidization provided by the developed partner (although agreements not to apply export subsidies to mutual trade have been included in some FTAs). FTAs often preclude the possibility of excluding Special Products. While some FTAs include safeguard measures on agricultural imports, these are often to be removed at the end of the phase-in period of the FTA. Paradoxically, some FTAs among developing countries target selected agricultural products for an "early harvest", while other agricultural products have been placed on sensitive or excluded lists. The various considerations involved in the "FTA option" are examined in "The FTA option".

## Gender and agricultural trade

The gender aspects of agricultural production are particularly complex, and therefore the effects of various agreements on the employment of women in the agricultural sector are also complex. Men and women in developing countries have different roles: the majority of women are engaged in subsistence agriculture and are responsible for food security in the household, while men are concentrated in the sector producing export crops. The liberalization of imports of agricultural products tends to disadvantage women producing subsistence food.[35]

In summary, pro-poor policy positions in negotiations on trade in agriculture should, at a minimum, include:

- Acceleration of agreed elimination of export subsidies,
- Substantial reduction in trade distorting subsidies (amber and blue boxes),
- Reduction in tariffs and increase in TRQs in markets of developed countries,
- Right to SP for developing countries,
- Rights to SSM for developing countries, and
- Technical and financial assistance to meet SPS regulations.

## Trade in services and development strategies

Trade in services, as defined in the GATS, covers a wide range of policy areas, including investment, communications, transportation, finance, energy, environment, health, immigration and many others. Government policies to develop the services sector are essential to the attainment of the MDGs. Governments are now faced with the challenge of formulating domestic policies in the services sector which provide universal access for key social services, while faced with pressures to accept bound liberalization commitments in trade agreements. The services sector should simultaneously support efficiency and growth, and increase developing country participation in the world market for services.

### Services and the MDGs

The provision of universal access to key services such as health, water and sanitation, energy and education is central to the achievement of the MDGs. Ill health, poor education and lack of access to electricity lock millions of people in a poverty trap. Access to these services enables poor people to become productive members of the economy and society and reduces rural/urban and gender disparities. The strengthening of national services sectors and the creation of an efficient services infrastructure contributes to the productivity of other sectors and to international competitiveness. Trade in services can assist in the attainment of the MDGs by providing new and better employment opportunities, particularly for new job seekers, including women, by contributing to the productivity of poorer people, in both the agricultural and manufacturing sectors, and by facilitating access of domestic service providers

---

35  See UNCTAD, "Trade and gender: opportunities, challenges and the policy dimension", UNCTAD/TD/392, 2004, para. 25 (http://www.unctad.org/en/docs/edm20042_en.pdf).

to more lucrative world markets. The main objectives of a national services policy are thus (*a*) to provide universal coverage for basic services such as health, water, sanitation, education and energy, (*b*) to strengthen the services infrastructure of the country to improve the competitiveness of the national economy, and (*c*) to penetrate international markets for trade in services.

## Universal access to services

Many social and infrastructural services in developing countries have traditionally been under public ownership. A priority development objective has been to ensure universal access to key services, notably health, water and sanitation, education and energy. For various reasons, including lack of ability to pay, geographical isolation or ethnic and gender factors, poor people have been excluded from access to the most basic services necessary to maintain their health, and to enable them to be productive members of the national economy. Governments have attempted to make basic services affordable to poor people by subsidizing free medical and education services, cross-subsidized prices for electricity, and investment incentives for sanitation and energy production in isolated areas. In some cases, the pressing need for capital and technology to increase supply has led governments to open up public services to private ownership, including the participation of foreign suppliers. This has brought these service sectors within the scope of trade negotiations.[36] The entry of foreign suppliers in the domestic market for key social services can often exacerbate inequalities and undermine policies aimed at ensuring universal access, for example, by draining off professionals (doctors, nurses, teachers) from the public system and exacerbating urban/rural disparities.

## Services and competitiveness

Services policies empower and enhance the productivity of poor people (*a*) through the provision of advanced services as inputs into the productive process at all levels and (*b*) by facilitating the export of services. Despite the heterogeneity of the service sector, governments should aim at devising an overall services development strategy that provides policy measures applicable to all services sectors. Such a strategy must address imports under "Mode 3", i.e., the conditions imposed on foreign investment in service sectors. Priority should be given to ensuring access to those key producer services that contribute to the competitiveness of other services, or of the manufacturing sector. The annexes to this section illustrate some of the considerations facing developing countries in negotiations on trade in selected service sectors where developing countries are faced with requests for liberalization commitments.

---

36  The implications of GATS negotiations in traditional public service sectors are discussed in Rolf Adlung, 2005, *Public Services and the GATS,* WTO Working Paper, ERSD-2005-03, Geneva, July 2005, http://www.wto.org/English/res_e/reser_e/ersd200503_e.htm.

In services liberalization, priority should be given to services that serve as inputs into the productive process and enhance productivity. Service strategies should ensure that imports do not exacerbate inequalities by reducing access to essential services, crowding out small suppliers or giving control of key sectors to large TNCs. Liberalization of services with no productive role, but with a possible negative impact on social programmes, national sovereignty or cultural integrity should be avoided as far as possible.

## Exports of services

On the other hand, developing countries are major exporters of certain services, notably in areas where they possess a labour cost advantage (comparable to textiles and clothing). Such exports usually involve the movement of persons as (*a*) consumers, e.g., tourism (Mode 2), and (*b*) suppliers, movement of workers abroad (Mode 4). More recently some developing countries are exporting labour-intensive services electronically (Mode 1), a process which has been termed "outsourcing". Often, however, developing countries' exports of such services, where they can expect to have a comparative advantage (e.g., construction), are frustrated by lack of access to capital and constraints on the short-term movement of semi-skilled labour. Also, restrictive business practices, such as those prevalent in the tourism sector, can greatly reduce the actual benefit of exports to the exporting developing country. Success in these areas requires a coherent strategy on the part of the developing countries, as well as secure access to markets accompanied where relevant by sector-specific provisions to deal with anti-competitive practices.

## Negotiations on trade in services

The WTO GATS Agreement established a framework for the negotiation of multilateral commitments relating to trade in services, which were defined as covering four Modes of Supply (Mode 1—cross-border movement, Mode 2—movement of consumers, Mode 3—commercial presence, i.e., investment, and Mode 4—temporary movement of persons to supply services). GATS members accept the principle of progressive liberalization, but also that commitments should aim at strengthening the service sectors of developing countries through access to technology and to distribution channels and information networks as well as the liberalization of services of export interest to them. The GATS itself does not impose access commitments and these are to be negotiated in successive "rounds". However, the current GATS negotiations seem aimed at reaching agreement on a formula approach, requiring a certain degree of commitment from all participating countries. Developing countries have all made commitments in their WTO Service Schedules, and are in the process of negotiating further "progressive liberalization" in the Doha Round. FTAs include much more extensive commitments in services, often according to a structure and based on definitions that depart from GATS.

## A strong regulatory framework is required

Trade in services is normally subject to detailed regulation. Some of the "tools" for such regulation are the subject of negotiation in GATS (as set out in GATS Article XVI), and include limitations on the number of suppliers, or service operations, or the numbers of persons employed in the supply of services, or on the value of service assets or transactions, usually enforced by economic need tests, as well as measures which require specific types of legal entities or limit the participation of foreign capital. In most sectors, the focus of negotiations is on investment measures. In particular, there is no obligation under the GATS Agreement to grant national treatment to foreign suppliers. Rather, the national treatment of foreign firms is a subject for negotiations on a sectoral basis. It does not constitute a "right" for foreign firms. Governments are free to regulate services so long as these regulations do not constitute "unnecessary barriers to trade" in services. Regulations that apply equally to domestic and foreign suppliers would be in conformity with national treatment commitments. On the other hand, where commitments are made on commercial presence, and the cross-border movement of capital is an essential part of the service itself, members are committed to allow such movement of capital.[37]

Performance requirements aimed at strengthening the service sectors in developing countries by acquiring access to technology or to distribution channels and information networks are specifically permitted by GATS. In their negotiations for the further liberalization of services, developing countries should focus on the extent to which imports of services effectively contribute to development. Liberalization of trade in services can have a positive impact on the development of the national services sector so long as there is a strong prior regulatory framework in place that supports national policy objectives. It is thus essential that the domestic regulations for the use of such imports be in place before engaging in negotiations on trade in services.

In addition, other measures that affect trade in services such as qualification requirements and procedures, technical standards and licensing requirements are subject to the general provision that such requirements should not constitute unnecessary barriers to trade in services. WTO members should be encouraged to enter into mutual recognition arrangements to overcome problems of this nature.

## Investment policy is central to trade negotiations on services

In essence, the main thrust of the GATS negotiations is investment, with the developed countries as *demandeurs*. Thus, this section should be read in juxtaposition with "Investment, jobs for youth and access to technologies". GATS provides a structure in which an optimum middle way can be negotiated in which foreign investors are granted access to markets subject to development-related conditions which are inscribed in the GATS schedules. Neither the liberalization of export markets, nor liberalization of trade and investment in services, will necessarily improve the

---

**37**   See footnote 2 to GATS Article XVI.

situation of the poor in developing countries without supportive policy measures by governments.

Requests to developing countries for liberalization of trade in services usually focus on Mode 3 commercial presence/investment. The challenge facing developing countries is to negotiate the optimum conditions of access for such investment. The situation in several selected sectors is described in relevant annexes.

The process of the proliferation of FTAs has covered trade in services and subjected services to more stringent disciplines at the bilateral or sub-regional levels. In some cases, definitions have departed from those used in GATS. The use of negative lists and the inclusion of GATS Mode 3 measures in "Investment" chapters covering both goods and services are more than mere questions of form and can have an adverse developmental impact, as they can eliminate the possibility of conditioning access on the acceptance of development-oriented performance requirements or social obligations.

## Investment, jobs for youth and access to technologies

Developing countries are actively seeking FDI as a means of acquiring capital and technology and providing employment and export opportunities. Many governments wish to maintain an investment regime which, while attractive to investors, protects the national interest against potential adverse effects, such as crowding out of domestic producers and exacerbating inequalities. Such a regime should also channel investment toward development objectives. Investment measures, including incentives and performance requirements, are used to integrate FDI into development strategies, for example by assuring a transfer of technology and higher-level employment for nationals, particularly young people (consistent with MDG targets 16 and 18). However, developing countries are increasingly faced with requests to accept commitments in trade agreements that would further reduce the scope for investment policy.

### International commitments on investment policy

The efforts of some developed countries to include the negotiation of a Multilateral Framework for Investment in the Doha Round were unsuccessful.[38] However, the ongoing GATS negotiations are primarily aimed at reducing conditions on FDI. These "Mode 3" negotiations are currently underway as discussed in "Trade in services and development strategies" and their objective is to agree on further limitations on investment policy in services. GATS occupies a large part of the overall territory of investment measures and the services sector absorbs some two thirds of FDI flows. Moreover, the bulk of investment entry restrictions are in the services sector.[39]

---

**38**  As were similar efforts in the OECD.

**39**  See Murray Gibbs, 2004, "Statement on investment policy and human development", in Sieh Mei Ling, ed., *Investment, Energy and Environmental Services: Promoting Human De-*

GATS negotiations focus on limiting the tools for investment policy, both entry and establishment regulations (Article XVI), including limitations on foreign capital, restrictions on the type of legal entity or joint venture, limitations on the number of service suppliers or on the value or quantity of transactions, including through the application of economic needs tests, as well as the extent to which the principle of national treatment is applied, including with respect to access to subsidies (Article XVII). It should be noted that when making a market access commitment on a sector or subsector, a member is also committed to enable free movement of capital related to the provision of that service.[40] In drawing up their overall investment strategies, developing countries should therefore decide to what extent these various "tools" are essential to the accomplishment of their development objectives. If they are, they should be defended in trade negotiations.

## Investment performance requirements: a tool for development

The use of performance requirements are not restricted under GATS and are actually encouraged, as a means of strengthening the service sectors in developing countries, through access to technology, or information channels or distribution networks. In the area of trade in goods, however, two important investment performance requirements are prohibited by the TRIMs Agreement: (*a*) local content requirements, and (*b*) trade balancing requirement under which, for example, imports by investors are conditional upon foreign exchange earnings or export volumes. Hence, the WTO permits a wide range of investment performance requirements, including export performance (those conditional on export volumes and earnings), and transfer of technology requirements, both of which have been used effectively by countries which have demonstrated rapid growth rates.[41] Given the failure of initiatives to establish general disciplines on investment policy in the WTO, capital-exporting countries are pursuing the objective of eliminating performance requirements, as well as the gamut of other investment measures being negotiated in GATS, through FTAs and other bilateral agreements.

Transfer of technology performance requirements are aimed at increasing productivity by enhancing human potentials to compete in the world market. Export performance requirements orient production toward world markets and oblige firms to prepare people to compete more effectively in a world of globalized production and to seek new export opportunities. Performance requirements can also aim at

---

*velopment in WTO Negotiations*, Kuala Lumpur: UNDP, Malaysian Institute of Economic Research and University of Malaya, March 2004 (www.um.edu.my).

40 See footnote to GATS Article XVI:1.

41 See case studies of the Republic of Korea, China and Viet Nam in Seih Mei Ling, ed., *Investment Energy and Environmental Services: Promoting Human Development in WTO Negotiations*, Kuala Lumpur: UNDP, Malaysian Institute of Economic Research and University of Malaya, March 2004 (www.um.edu.my).

improving equity, by channelling investment to poorer regions or disadvantaged segments of the population, or by ensuring universal provision of key services, such as electricity, water and sanitation. Sustainability can be promoted by giving priority to environmentally friendly technologies.

Universal access to energy and environmental services, essential to the achievement of MDGs, will require huge amounts of investment over the next few decades. The terms under which this investment will take place are being defined in the current GATS negotiations, as described in annexes C and D.

The same goals can be pursued through investment incentives of a fiscal and financial nature. However, such incentives may result in a loss of precious revenue for the government of the host country and provoke competition among host countries to attract investors, leading to a race to the bottom, which can undermine human development goals (e.g., suspension of labour rights in FTZs). Fiscal incentives may also be inconsistent with WTO rules (e.g., the prohibition on export subsidies). Incentives can be used in parallel and as a complement to performance requirements. However, fiscal incentives can lead to a race to the bottom scenario. It is estimated that developing countries lose $35 billion annually due to competitive pressures to reduce corporate tax rates combined with the transfer of profits out of developing countries to low tax regimes.[42]

Among the different approaches to the use of investment measures, the example of the Republic of Korea has been cited as the most successful. Its strategy was first to encourage investment in labour intensive export industries, following the logic that export earnings should finance industrialization. The Government of the Republic of Korea mobilized an arsenal of tools, including investment measures such as national ownership and export and transfer of technology requirements, combined with trade measures such as subsides, quantitative restrictions and tariffs (see "Tariffs and industrial policy"), with the sole purpose of increasing its bargaining power with foreign firms. The objective was to move up the technological ladder, the virtuous spiral described in "Tariffs and industrial policy".[43] China has followed similar goals, using some of the same techniques, moving rapidly up the technological ladder in export production.[44] Different countries have achieved considerable success following different approaches, the common factor being that overly successful countries have adopted selective and strategic, rather than ideological, approaches that either

42  See Stiglitz and Charlton, 2003, op. cit., pp. 266-267, drawing from Andrew Charlton, "Incentive bidding wars for mobile investment; economic consequences and potential responses", OECD Development Centre technical paper 203, OECD, Paris (http://www.oecd.org/dataoecd/39/63/2492289.pdf). See also OXFAM, 2000, *Tax Havens, Releasing the Hidden Billions for Poverty Eradication*, Oxford (http://www.oxfam.org.uk/what_we_do/issues/debt_aid/tax_havens.htm).

43  See Jang-Sup Shin and Ha-Joon Chang, 2004, "Foreign investment policy and human development country study: Republic of Korea", in Seih Mei Ling, op. cit.

44  See Dani Rodrik, 2006, "What's so special about China's exports?" CEPR Discussion Paper No. 5484, London: Centre for Economic Policy Research, February 2006 (www.nber.org/papers/w11947).

uncritically welcome or overly restrict foreign investment.[45] Such investment measures have also been a component of a broader industrial strategy that incorporated trade measures (e.g., tariffs and QRs) as well as subsidies (see "Tariffs and industrial policy").

## A "new generation" of bilateral investment treaties

There are now over 2000 Bilateral Investment Treaties (BITs) in force.[46] Traditionally used as instruments for the protection of investments, BITs are acquiring different characteristics. Some developed countries are pursuing a "new generation" of BITs which incorporate trade provisions, notably obligations on entry and establishment, and prohibitions on performance requirements. These usually apply to both goods and services and thus undermine the commitments included in the GATS services schedules. They also employ a wider definition of investment, including portfolio investment and cover a wide range of domestic regulation that can be challenged by the foreign investor. They also identify dispute settlement and arbitration mechanisms that allow foreign investors to bypass the national judicial system to a larger extent than was previously possible. Sometimes lack of coordination between the government ministry responsible for trade policy and that responsible for investment policy can lead to less than optimal results.

FTAs are being used to impose more stringent disciplines over the scope of investment polices. As will be discussed in "MNP—access to the world employment market", many FTAs make national treatment a general obligation for both goods and services, reducing or eliminating the various policy tools listed in GATS Article XVI. Often this is accomplished through the technique of dissecting the Services Chapter of such FTAs, and bringing all investment policy, on both goods and services, under the scope of an Investment Chapter. FTAs can also include mechanisms for promoting investment among the concerned parties. In fact, many developing countries believe that FTAs with major trading partners will attract FDI. However, evidence shows that, with few exceptions, BITs and FTAs generally have little impact on attracting FDI.[47]

## MNP—access to the world employment market

Movement of national persons (MNP) across frontiers to supply services provides a major source of potential employment and export income for many developing countries. However, it can also have negative social and economic impacts. What are the elements of a coherent strategy to maximize the contribution of MNP to development and the achievement of the MDGs?

---

45  See Shin and Chang, op. cit.
46  UNCTAD, *World Investment Report 2002*.
47  See Stiglitz and Charlton, op. cit., pp. 149-152.

## MNP and the MDGs

The movement of persons across frontiers to supply services is a major potential source of employment for poor people and an opportunity to increase their earnings dramatically.[48] MNP provides a means for developing countries to draw upon their competitive advantage of lower wage costs in trade in services as they have traditionally done in trade in goods. Labour remittances are a major source of foreign exchange for many developing countries. These can help reduce the vulnerability of poor communities from the impact of domestic economic crises, finance small local businesses and support extended family safety nets. MNP can also increase equity since labour remittances often provide income to particularly disadvantaged regions of developing countries. Work abroad can provide women with opportunities for wage income that do not exist at the national level. MNP can thus lift persons out of poverty, empower women, and provide job opportunities for youth, i.e., MDGs 1, 3 and 8 (target 16). On the other hand, the permanent emigration of professionals can detract from efforts to establish universal, quality services in key public service sectors such as health and education and, if not properly managed through an intergovernmental bilateral or multilateral agreement, can contribute to "brain drain" rather than "brain circulation" or "brain gain".

## Impact of MNP

Economic models suggest that expansion of MNP could generate impressive welfare gains for the exporting countries.[49] Even though this includes more than MNP, remittances by workers abroad to developing countries reached $167 billion in 2005 and this figure may be considerably higher since many transactions are realized through informal channels.[50] For a number of developing countries, such remittances account for over 10 per cent of GNP.[51]

Short-term movement of people is often essential for developing country enterprises to participate effectively in international trade in services. It is a necessary component of a services package offered by a service exporter, with payments being made to employees in the exporting country. MNP can also lead to an upgrading of skills; unskilled rural persons can become more productive by acquiring the capacity to perform as industrial workers and thus, upon their return, improve their

---

**48**  We use the GATS acronym "MNP" rather than "labour movement" (which would suggest unskilled workers) or "movement of persons" (which could imply permanent migration ) so as to cover the whole range of the provision of services that involves suppliers moving temporarily from one country to another from unskilled agricultural workers to highly skilled medical, engineering and IT professionals.

**49**  See discussion in Stiglitz and Charlton, op. cit., pp. 247-252.

**50**  See statement of UNCTAD Secretary-General to ECOSOC Round Table on Globalization and Labour Migration, 6 July 2006, United Nations, New York (www.unctad.org).

**51**  Lesotho, Vanuatu, Jordan, Bosnia and Herzegovina, Albania, Nicaragua, Yemen, Moldova, El Salvador and Jamaica. For more info visit www.migrationinformation.org.

home country's industrial competitiveness and attract investment to the manufacturing sector.

Restrictions on MNP can result in prohibitive barriers to developing countries' exports in a variety of services exports, in sectors such as software, energy services and construction.

However, workers abroad can be subject to exploitative and degrading working conditions. While MNP can empower women by giving them a unique source of income, women are too often victims of harassment and sexual exploitation.[52] Foreign workers may be forced to work at lower salaries despite advanced levels of skills. Separation of family members can lead to neglect of children and other social problems. Labour earnings can be squandered on imported consumer goods without any investment in the communities. MNP is also vulnerable to political factors which can suddenly cut off access to markets.

## Access for service suppliers

The inclusion of Mode 4 short-term cross-border movement of natural persons in the GATS framework enables developing countries to acquire secure access for their service workers as part of the overall balance of multilateral trade rights and obligations. The main barriers to MNP are economic needs tests that permit the entry of foreign persons only when locals are not available to provide the services required. MNP is the subject of bilateral agreements (MOUs) and is now being included in FTAs. MNP is thus clearly an element of trade policy and trade negotiations, although it has been neglected in the GATS schedules of commitments.[53]

Skilled workers generally have better access to foreign markets, creating a shortage of skilled workers in the "exporting" country which may perpetuate since skilled workers are much more likely to remain in the "importing" country. MNP can in some cases increase inequalities, if only persons with skills and higher incomes are given access to foreign markets. This unequal treatment is reflected in the structure of GATS commitments where bound access is normally provided to high-level employees and managers of TNCs, or for essential professionals and skilled workers, such as medical staff. However, it is unlikely that GATS commitments would exacerbate the flow of permanent emigration of skilled professionals in short supply in economically advanced countries. Contrary to such movement which often exacerbates "brain drain", MNP commitments may actually reduce "brain drain" as, given the security of access, individuals may see less need to seek permanent residence in the

---

52  See Tereso S. Tullao and Michael Angelo Cortez, *MNP and Human Development in Asia* and Sanath Jayanetti, *Movement of Natural Persons and its Human Development Implications (Housemaids and Unskilled Migrant Workers)*, as well as other studies on MNP UNDP Asia Trade Initiative on Trade and Human Development, Phase 1, technical support document (Hanoi: 2003) (available at www.undprcc.lk/Publications/Publications.asp?C=4).

53  It should be noted that most of the GCC countries, which are major importers of labour, only became WTO members at the end of the Uruguay Round, or subsequently, by accession.

importing country. The idea of a "GATS visa" has been suggested as a means of facilitating entry of service suppliers covered under GATS commitments, while ensuring
the temporary nature of their stay.

## A strategy for MNP

MNP, if appropriately designed at the intergovernmental level, can support the attainment of the MDGs. However, this requires a clear strategy on the part of governments to maximize the benefits and deal with the adverse factors mentioned above.
MNP exports should not be viewed as a manifestation of failure of national economic
policy but rather as a means of drawing benefits from globalization. Governments
should formulate clear, comprehensive strategies with regard to MNP and incorporate these into national development strategies and trade policies. Governments
should view MNP from a competitive standpoint. Workers can be trained in skills
deemed to be in demand on the world market, and niche markets can be targeted.

Arrangements can be entered into with importing countries to upgrade skills
to fit needs. Such policies should include measures to encourage the return of skilled
migrants and incentives to discourage the emigration of people in occupations in
short supply in developing countries.

Mode 1 service exports, often termed "outsourcing", have been a way for developing countries to export labour-intensive services, without confronting the barriers
to MNP. However, studies have shown that successful outsourcing operations are
significantly dependent on the ability of technical staff to travel to their overseas
market countries.[54]

Labour remittances could have a greater development impact if transferred
through specialized financial services and financial instruments which lower the level
of transaction costs. Microcredit and micro-enterprise support can channel savings
into investment in productive facilities in the worker's communities.

Bilateral labour agreements can be pursued in certain circumstances. However,
bound commitments in GATS or FTAs would provide greater security of access and
stronger negotiating leverage for the exporting country. Specific commitments for
access of clearly defined occupations can be negotiated in the framework of GATS
or in FTAs. These can include the elimination of economic needs tests and the
facilitation of visas, quotas for entry of workers in specific sectors or occupations.[55]
Mutual Recognition Agreements or "occupational certificates"[56] can facilitate ex-

---

54  See Rupa Chanda, 2006, "Intermodal linkages to services trade", OECD Trade Policy
    Working Paper No. 30, 2006.
55  See suggestions in Jolita Butkeviciene, "Movement of natural persons under GATS", in *A
    Positive Agenda*, UNCTAD, op. cit. See also UNCTAD, "Report of Expert Meeting on
    Market Access Issues under Mode 4", document TD/B/COM.1/64, 27 November 2003.
56  See various papers presented at the Joint WTO/World Bank Symposium on Movement of
    Natural Persons (Mode 4) under GATT, Geneva, 11-12 April 2002 (available at www.wto.
    org/english/tratop_e/serv_e/symp_mov_natur_perso_april02_e.htm).

port of skilled and professional services, and ensure that remuneration is commensurate with qualifications. Similarly, trade agreements should contain obligations to protect the rights of foreign workers and shield them, particularly women, from exploitation.

# Intellectual property rights for the poor

The WTO TRIPS Agreement has probably been the most onerous and intrusive of all WTO commitments for developing countries. It dramatically increased the scope of multilateral trade obligations by bringing the whole set of intellectual property instruments negotiated in WIPO into the WTO, where they are enforced through the possibility of trade sanctions. The TRIPS Agreement establishes minimum standards, but provides governments with considerable flexibility as to the mechanisms through which they meet their obligations. It is precisely with a view to reducing this flexibility that bilateral pressures have been exercised on developing countries to adopt "TRIPS plus" legislation. The provisions of the TRIPS Agreement that relate to the exclusion of plants and animals and biological processes for their production are open for review and possible amendment. Against this background, governments are faced with the challenge of making IPRs useful for poor people and supportive of the MDGs, by ensuring their access to medicines, protecting against bio-piracy and protecting and consolidating community ownership of traditional knowledge.

## TRIPS and MDGs

The implications of the TRIPS Agreement (and of subsequent bilateral pressures on developing countries to tighten its provisions further) for the attainment of the MDGs—notably MDG6, have already been recognized by the international community. The Declaration on TRIPS and Public Health was agreed by the international community to ensure that the TRIPS Agreement prioritized public health concerns. Developing countries must also draw up IPR legislation that ensures that the attainment of the MDGs will not be frustrated, while protecting the right of poor people to use their traditional knowledge and genetic resources.

Developing countries are faced with policy decisions at three levels, first to ensure that the results of the current multilateral review of the TRIPS regime and related initiatives in WIPO[57] are supportive of their pursuit of the MDGs; second, to draw up national legislation and regulations aimed at achieving these goals and targets within the framework of their international obligations; and third to thwart effectively pressures to accept "TRIPS plus" commitments at the bilateral level. The

---

57  Negotiations of a Substantive Patent Law Treaty have been initiated in WIPO. For an analysis of the development implications, see Carlos Correa, 2006, *An Agenda for Patent Reform and Harmonization for Developing Countries*, paper presented to Open Forum, 1 March 2006, available at www.wipo.int/meetings/2006/sep_of_ge_06/presentations. See also GRAIN, 2003, "One global patent system? WIPO's Substantive Patent Law Treaty", GRAIN briefings 2003 (http://www.grain.org/briefings/?id=159).

manner in which developing countries adapt to the TRIPS regime and pressures from developed countries is crucial to their attainment not only of the MDGs directly related to health (e.g., MDG to combat HIV/AIDS, malaria and other diseases, MDG8 provision of access to affordable essential drugs in developing countries), but given the relevance to the agricultural sector, that of eradicating poverty and hunger (MDG1) as well.

One of the key elements of FTAs has been the inclusion of "TRIPS" plus provisions dealing with (*a*) restrictions on the use of compulsory licences, (*b*) restrictions on parallel imports, (*c*) greater protection of undisclosed data through market exclusivity, (*d*) broadening of the spectrum of patentability, (*e*) extension of the duration of patents and (*f*) links between patents and health registration (see "The FTA option").

## Health

There had been concern that the TRIPS Agreement will have a negative impact on human development by resulting in higher prices for essential medicines in poor countries. It was a result of concerted action by private firms and some countries to pressure developing countries into giving up certain crucial rights under the TRIPS Agreement that provoked the negotiation of the Doha Declaration on TRIPS and Public Health. The Declaration was agreed at the Doha Ministerial Conference to confirm the right of governments to impose compulsory licenses when faced with national public health issues. However, one aspect, that of permitting countries having no domestic capacity to produce medicines to issue compulsory licenses to producers in other countries for import into the affected country, required an amendment to the TRIPS Agreement. This was finally accomplished in December 2005 after a period of protracted negotiations.[58]

It is now incumbent on developing countries to ratify this Amendment, and to draw up legislation to govern compulsory licensing. Such legislation may also require provisions to ensure the admissibility of parallel imports. However, such legislation is only part of the comprehensive approach required to ensure that public health objectives can be met within the framework of TRIPS.[59]

## Competition

The need for the acceptance of parallel imports and the use of compulsory licensing are not confined to the health sector, although this is where they are most urgently needed. Both mechanisms can be used to ensure that patents are not abused for anticompetitive purposes. Under the principle of the "exhaustion" of IPRs, once a patent holder has placed patented goods on the market or allowed a licensee to market, the

---

58  WTO document, Amendment of the TRIPS Agreement, Decision of 6 December 2005 (WT/L/641).

59  See Carlos Correa, 2000, *Integrating Public Health Concerns into Patent Legislation in Developing Countries,* South Centre, Geneva (www.southcentre.org).

patent holder has no right to control the resale of such goods, i.e., "parallel" imports are permitted.[60] The TRIPS Agreement, however, leaves WTO members to decide whether or not to incorporate this provision into their legislation. Developing country governments should draw up legislation confirming the admissibility of parallel imports. This will avoid patent holders imposing high prices on the domestic markets for essential goods that are available, under the same patent, at lower prices in other countries. At the same time, compulsory licensing legislation should be drawn up to ensure that patents are not used to block further innovation by competitors. A desire to acquire control over the patents of competitors has been one of the motives behind the dramatic increase of mergers and acquisitions resulting in a high level of concentration in many developing country markets.

## Genetic resources, agriculture and bio-piracy

The TRIPS Agreement permits members to exclude plants and animals other than "micro-organisms" from patentability. Plant varieties must be protected, but members are free to accomplish this by effective *sui generis* systems.[61] These provisions are currently under review by the WTO TRIPS Council.[62]

One major concern is that the patenting of plants and plant varieties can lead to situations where farmers become dependent on industrial suppliers for vital inputs such as seeds.[63] This has prompted a number of developing countries to pass legislation to exclude the patenting of all genetic materials. These countries have met their obligation to protect plant varieties through *sui generis* legislation, usually based on a "breeder's rights" system which allows farmers the possibility of saving and replanting seeds, and the right to use a protected variety as a source for further research and breeding (the prevalent practice in developing countries).[64] They should incorporate the concept of Farmers' Rights as embodied in the International Treaty on Plant Genetic Resources, and draw on the experiences of those developing countries which have drawn up legislation on these matters.

Another concern is the possible conflict between the TRIPS Agreement and the Convention on Biodiversity (CPD), which stresses the sovereignty of States over their genetic resources, and respect for the innovations, knowledge and practices of indig-

---

60  See Carlos Correa, 2000, *Intellectual Property Rights, the WTO and Developing Countries*, New York: Zed Books.

61  See "Beyond UPOV—Examples of countries preparing non-UPOV sui generis plant variety protection systems for compliance with TRIPS", GRAIN briefings 1999 (http://www.grain. org/briefings/?id=127).

62  As provided in TRIPS Article 27:3(b).

63  See Vandana Shiva and Radha Hola-Bhar, *Piracy by Patent; the case of the Neem Tree*, quoted in Correa, op. cit.

64  For detailed suggestions as to how IPR legislation can make use of the flexibilities in the TRIPS Agreement in pursuit of the MDGs and development friendly outcomes see Carlos M. Correa, 2000, *Intellectual Property Rights, the WTO and Developing Countries: The TRIPS Agreement and Policy Options*, London/New York: Zed Books (www.zedbooks.co.uk).

enous and local communities. The focus has been on the need to prevent bio-piracy, defined by the CPD as "unauthorized access to use of biological resources or traditional knowledge of the indigenous peoples by third parties without compensation and without necessary authorization". In addition, patents derived from such genetic material may not involve significant innovation or novelty. National laws should be drawn up to prevent bio-piracy containing obligations such as declaring the country of origin, and demonstrating its prior consent, or of a particular indigenous community if applicable, and to compensate such communities for the development of new varieties, based on material that they have supplied.[65] Such laws should also raise the threshold of plant variety protection so that protection is limited to significant innovations or inventive steps deemed socially beneficial.[66] Many documented cases of bio-piracy have been submitted by developing countries in support of their proposal[67] aiming at the inclusion in the TRIPS Agreement of an obligation to require the disclosure of the origin of genetic resources and/or associated traditional knowledge,[68] which they consider necessary for the effective application of such laws.

## GIs and traditional knowledge

Developing countries are using a variety of legal mechanisms to protect traditional knowledge. Geographical indications (GIs) may provide one effective means to this end.[69] Unlike patents and trade marks GIs are community owned, cannot be sold and do not expire. They empower indigenous communities by providing recognition and commercial value to their traditional knowledge and production techniques.[70] GIs have been associated with luxury products (e.g., champagne), but the fact is that these producers became wealthy because of the GI system.[71] For example, some

---

65  See Carlos Correa, "Reviewing the TRIPS Agreement", in *A Positive Agenda for Future Trade Negotiations*, op. cit.

66  See recommendation by the Commission on Intellectual Property Rights, 2002, "Integrating Intellectual Property Rights and Development Policy", London: (www.iprcommission. org/graphic/documents/final_report.htm).

67  See submission from Brazil, Cuba, Ecuador, India, Peru, Thailand and Venezuela, IP/C/W/420 on www.wto.org.

68  For example, the case of camu-camu recently submitted by Peru in WTO document IP/C/W458 describes in detail how a traditional product native to Peru's Amazon region had served as a basis for patents in developing countries without the knowledge or consent of Peru (www.wto.org).

69  The TRIPS Agreement (Article 22:1) defines GIs as "indications which identify a good as originating in the territory of a member, or a region or locality in that territory, where a given quality, reputation or other characteristic of the good is essentially attributable to its geographical origin".

70  See Swarnim Wagle, 2003, "Geographical indications TRIPS and promoting human development in Asia, and the development dimensions of the Sri Lankan geographical indication of camellia sinensis" (Ceylon Tea), UNDP Asia Trade Initiative, Hanoi.

71  See Dwijien Rangnekar, "The socio-economics of geographical indications", at www.iprs online.org/unctadictsd/docs.

developing countries have viewed GIs as one way to mitigate low commodity prices in the coffee sector. Partly in reaction to the theft of geographical expressions (e.g., Ceylon tea, basmati rice, Phu Quoc fish sauce) many developing countries are supporting the objective of extending the more stringent GI protection of wines and spirits to all products, in order to reduce the difficulties and costs of enforcing GIs in foreign jurisdictions which limit the effectiveness of GIs in protecting traditional knowledge. The outcome of these negotiations will become an important element of the Doha package in this area.

However, effective use of GIs requires government actions at the national level to (a) pass legislation to protect GIs and (b) adopt measures to identify and promote GIs, as public investment is required to establish the reputation of little known GIs in developing countries.

While the development of GIs at the national level and participation in a multilateral register as has been proposed in the WTO will inevitably involve significant costs, these should be viewed against the long-term perspective of the losses that will occur if such products are appropriated by TNCs. In addition, there will be costs associated with monitoring and challenging IPRs issued around the world.[72] Moreover, if geographical expression becomes an accepted generic term, it will become freely useable by all.

---

**Box 19.    Thailand's "One Tambon, One Product"**

Thailand's "One Tambon, One Product" programme, launched in 2003, stands out. The Government has set out to select 60 community products and has upgraded and certified their quality with the intention of expanding, first, their domestic market, followed by exports. Trade fairs organized to generate incomes and develop local products at the grassroots in all the country's 76 provinces have led to the identification of distinctive fabrics, artistic creations, processed food and fruit, utensils, wickerwork and fermented liquor that the Government now seeks to promote. It has already begun pro-actively to showcase its famous produce of Hom Mali rice in big regional markets.[a] This Thai example offers a rural development example for bottom-up engineering of awareness and action on promoting traditional community products. The irony, however, is that this rural development programme has not been overtly linked with the idea of GIs because of insufficient inter-ministry coordination. This missing link is noteworthy because GIs are the only form of modern IP that grassroots communities are likely to own. The risk of driving GI awareness with a top-down legislative decree, possibly triggered only by external treaty obligations, or supply-driven foreign aid programmes is that it may not command enough national ownership for effective enforcement.

a   Visit www.boi.go.th/thai/focus/prd_03jan13.html#2. The Commerce Minister led a
    delegation in December 2002 to promote the sale of Thai Hom Mali rice to China where, in
    2001, 240,000 tons of Jasmine rice was exported, compared with 200,000 tons to the U.S.
    Another small example of conscious Thai promotion is gifts of GIs such as 20g boxes of
    Longan fruits from Lamphun province on Thai Airways flights during 2003.

---

72   Commission on Intellectual Property, op. cit.

## The FTA option

While continuing to participate in the Doha Round of multilateral trade negotiations, virtually all developing countries have been caught up in the proliferation of FTAs. Many countries are actively engaged in subregional and regional integration, and at the same time involved in bilateral FTAs with extraregional partners, including the major trading countries. Involvement in multiple trade negotiations at different levels gives rise to a series of implications for development strategies. Developing countries are faced with major policy choices: whether to enter into FTAs, if so with which partners, as well the challenge of undertaking an analysis of costs and benefits of each potential agreement.

### FTAs and the MDGs

FTAs, by definition, reduce policy space to a much greater extent than multilateral obligations and would seem, at first glance, to be in conflict with MDG8 target 12, which calls for a non-discriminatory trading system. FTAs are high risk in the sense that their potential negative impact for the attainment of MDGs can be exacerbated through the further contraction of policy space. This is likely to be particularly true for North-South FTAs, where political considerations are often paramount. On the other hand, FTAs (especially those involving South-South cooperation between countries at roughly similar stages of development) can provide innovative, pro-development provisions that would be difficult to apply at the multilateral level. The outcome of FTAs depends largely on the power relationships between the parties and the extent to which all stakeholders can exert an influence on the negotiating process.

### The proliferation of FTAs

Over recent years developing countries have been involved in an ever intensifying process involving the negotiation of Free Trade Agreements (FTAs), with a multitude of partners (only one WTO member has not entered into an FTA). These have included:

- A more positive and ambitious approach to traditional efforts at subregional and regional integration between developing countries,
- Extraregional FTAs with major developed countries (North-South FTAs,)
- Extraregional FTAs with other developing countries.

Each of these involves different policy considerations, both economic and political. Access to Northern markets, once extended on an autonomous, preferential and non-reciprocal basis, is now increasingly subject to reciprocal concessions by developing countries within the framework of FTAs. This has created a chain reaction based on the "fear of exclusion", which has been exacerbated by the real or anticipated fear of the withdrawal of existing non-contractual preferences, even though a large percentage of exports often enter MFN duty free.[73] The exclusion of key products, such as clothing, from certain GSP schemes has also contributed to this pressure.[74] The negotiation of an FTA between one developing country and a major trading country creates pressure on competing developing countries to seek to enter into similar agreements for fear of losing out to competitors in terms of exports and incoming FDI.[75]

Developing countries are making broad concessions in a variety of areas, often adversely affecting human development prospects, in order to obtain the elimination of tariff rates that should be obtainable in the multilateral negotiations at much less cost in terms of reciprocal concessions. FTA negotiations are less transparent and more political than WTO multilateral rounds. They are thus more vulnerable to "capture" by those vitally interested sectors that can gain immediate benefits from concessions granted in return for broader reciprocal concessions which can adversely affect a wide range of less informed stakeholders and seriously restrict development policy options. This creates a bias towards inequitable results. FTA negotiations should, therefore, be subject to at least the same degree of transparency as WTO negotiating proposals and should be accessible and subject to public discussion.

## Development implications of FTAs

It is difficult for developing countries to achieve symmetry in North-South FTAs. They start from a situation where many of their industrial goods exports enter duty free under the GSP, albeit unbound. Bound MFN tariff rates in the OECD countries are quite low, and have been eliminated in many sectors of interest to developing countries, although tariff peaks remain in key sectors such as T&C and agriculture. Bound MFN rates in developing countries are often considerably higher. Thus, the burden of tariff liberalization in North-South RTAs weighs asymmetrically on developing countries. While it is estimated that trade among RTA and FTA partners makes up nearly 40 per cent of world trade, a much smaller amount of this trade actually benefits from preferential tariff margins as much of the trade among these countries is in items where the MFN rate is zero.[76] On the other hand, FTAs among developing countries may result in meaningful tariff reductions and substantial margins of preference.[77]

---

73  For example, the expiry of the USA Andean Trade Preference Scheme on 31 December 2006 has placed the beneficiary countries under considerable pressure to conclude FTAs with the United States.

74  See discussion in annex A.

75  See UNDP Asia Trade and Investment Initiative, *The Great Maze, Regional and Bilateral Free Trade Agreements in Asia,* Colombo, December 2005, www.undpprcc.lk.

76  See World Bank, 2005, *Global Economic Prospects*, p. 41.

77  For example only 1 per cent of India's tariff lines had MFN rates of zero, ibid., p. 41.

## More than spaghetti!

There is a need to assess the potential concrete gains from FTAs before entering into their negotiation, examining such aspects as the real improvement in access that can be achieved, the likelihood that comparable results can be obtained from multilateral negotiations and the extent to which the real access problems require a multilateral solution.[78] There is also the need to examine the objectives of the trading partner. These may have a strong political content, or may reflect positions they have taken and strategies they are pursuing at the global level. Far from being the confused "spaghetti bowl" described by some observers, FTAs are the manifestation of coherent geopolitical strategies on the part of the major trading countries.

Developed countries are using FTAs as a means of furthering their multilateral agendas by locking in developing partners to commitments that reflect their positions in the WTO negotiations. One example is the treatment of GIs, where the EU FTAs impose a TRIPS plus protection, while United States FTAs impose TRIPS minus (eliminating the possibility of *sui generis* GI systems and replacing them with regular trademark systems of protection).[79]

Sectoral interests in developing countries may gain from the elimination of duties on products not covered by preferences where MFN tariff rates present a significant barrier to trade, such as in textiles or agriculture. However, duty free entry of textiles and clothing is often subject to complicated rules of origin, while sensitive agricultural products may be excluded. Furthermore, most FTAs do not establish disciplines on agricultural subsidies in the major developed countries, thus exposing farmers in the developing partner to unfair competition, even though some involve bilateral disciplines on export subsidies.[80] Furthermore, agriculture safeguard mechanisms may only be applied over the implementation period.[81] Developing countries generally do not have the competitive strengths to take advantage of services liberalization in these agreements, particularly as many new opportunities are not provided for the short-term movement of persons (GATS Mode 4).

---

78  The FTAA negotiations have not succeeded largely because the MERCOSUR countries perceived that the main barriers facing their access to the U.S. market (agricultural subsidies and anti-dumping measures) could not be effectively addressed at the regional level.

79  See David Vivas and Christophe Spennemann, 2006, "Diálogo regional sobre propiedad intelectual, innovación y desarrollo sostenible", UNCTAD/ICTSD Project on Intellectual Property and Sustainable Development, Costa Rica, May 2006 (www.ictsd.org).

80  Some attempt has been made to deal with agricultural export subsidies in the Chile/USA FTA, however.

81  Cristophe Bellmann, "Latin American countries in bilateral and multilateral agricultural negotiations", presentation to the Andean Development Corporation (www.caf.com/attach/11/default/Lat_am_Ag.pdf).

## FTAs with the North

From the perspective of national development strategy, the advantages and disadvantages of FTAs differ considerably according to the choice of partners. In FTA negotiations with developed countries, developing countries often find themselves confronted with requests for commitments that may undermine their WTO rights and/or include commitments in areas which developing countries have not accepted as part of the WTO agenda. Thus, where the main objective of developing countries in FTAs is to obtain free access for their key export products, and avoid or pre-empt negative margins of tariff preferences in favour of their competitors, they find themselves subject to commitments of an even wider scope and deeper intrusiveness than those in WTO agreements. Some developed countries appear to be pursuing a parallel trade agenda in their FTAs, aimed at achieving commitments from their FTA partners that they have been unable to achieve in the multilateral context. In some cases, the developed partner follows a set "template" which it seeks to apply in each FTA it negotiates.[82]

## ...and the South

The expanding FTAs among developing countries generally adopt a different format. They may contain an "early harvest" of items to be liberalized immediately, with many issues left to be negotiated in subsequent stages. In some cases, this early harvest includes textiles and horticultural products normally considered as sensitive in

---

**Box 20.   The new or "Singapore" issues**

At the Marrakech Conference which concluded the Uruguay Round and established the WTO, the concluding remarks of the chairman set out the elements of a possible work programme for the new organization.[a] In addition to trade and labour standards strongly advocated by the United States, the list included a wide range of items such as the relationship between immigration policies and international trade, international trade and company law, the establishment of a compensation mechanism for the erosion of trade preferences and the link between trade, development, political stability and the alleviation of poverty. Only two of these, trade and investment and trade and competition policy were retained at the first WTO Ministerial Conference in Singapore in 1996 to which were added transparency in government procurement and trade facilitation (i.e., the Singapore issues). All but trade facilitation were dropped at the Cancun Conference in 2003.[b] Nevertheless, the developed country proponents of the Singapore issues have continued to pursue the missing three in FTAs with developing countries.

---

a   See document MTN.TNC/Min(94)/6 (www.wto.org).
b   For an insight into the events leading to this decision, see M. Supperamaniam, Epilogue, in Sieh Mei Ling, op. cit.

---

82   See www.ustr.gov/TradeAgreements/bilateral (USA FTAs) and www.ecdpm.org (EU FTAs) and www.bilaterals.org for overview of all FTA negotiations and links to many sources.

North-South FTAs. Commitments on services follow the GATS positive list format, adding regional and bilateral commitments to the multilateral schedules.[83] The proliferation of bilateral FTAs with regional trading partners is often conducted under a broad framework agreement intended to lead eventually to extensive regional integration. Individual countries and groupings of developing countries are entering into FTAs with extraregional developing partners. These usually contain considerable flexibility and are aimed at gaining a foothold in new and growing markets.

## Policy space within FTAs

While it should be expected that a FTA will result in the elimination of tariff protection for "substantially all" of the mutual trade between its members (i.e., in conformity with Article XXIV of GATT), many FTAs involve additional commitments that can severely reduce or eliminate "policy space" permitted by WTO agreements. Such commitments negatively affect the ability of developing countries to pursue development objectives. Attention should be given to policy space in such areas as:

(a) Intellectual property. Particular attention should be given to provisions of FTAs which may impose commitments which eliminate flexibilities provided by the TRIPS Agreement by seriously constraining the scope to impose compulsory licensing, even those applied to pharmaceuticals for health purposes.[84] Such provisions undermine both the spirit and the intent of the Doha Declaration on TRIPS and Public Health, in addition to permitting patent holders to block parallel imports.[85] FTAs in this area may also require the patenting of plants and/or animals or even all life forms and undermine measures intended to prevent bio-piracy.[86] Trademarks may be given precedence so as to pre-empt the use of GIs by communities, while patent and copyright protection may be extended beyond the limits established in TRIPS. Data exclusivity provisions effectively extend patent protection for periods in excess of the TRIPS limits.

(b) Investment provisions may prohibit performance requirements permitted by the WTO TRIMs Agreement, e.g., transfer of technology, export performance, or those on investment in services which are actually encouraged by the WTO GATS Agreement as a means of strengthening the service sector of developing countries. Investment chapters usually provide for across the board national treatment

---

**83** See Mario Marconini, 2003, *Acordos Regionais e o Comercio de Servicos: normativa internacional e interesse brasiliero*, Sao Paulo: Aduanieras.

**84** See Sanya Reid Smith, "TRIPs provisions in US free trade agreements that effect medicine prices", paper presented to regional meeting of civil society organizations on FTAs in the Arab region, Cairo, 9-11 December 2006.

**85** Recent United States legislation discourages the inclusion of provisions restricting parallel importation in future FTAs, Sec. 631 of Science, State, Justice and Commerce and Related Appropriations Act 2006, Public Law 109-108.

**86** See Silvia Rodríguez Cervantes, *FTAs: Trading Away Traditional Knowledge*, GRAIN briefings 2006 (http://www.grain.org/briefings_files/fta-tk-03-2006-en.pdf).

and right of establishment undermining the commitments that have been carefully negotiated in GATS. This is most significant when "Investment" chapters provide for the "absolute right to transfer funds", thus undermining the prudential provisions built into financial service commitments in GATS. "Expropriation" may be interpreted in such a way that private investors can challenge States and obtain compensation for opportunities lost due to action by governments at different levels to protect the environment or attain other social goals. Dispute settlement provisions may permit investors to seek settlement outside of the State's domestic courts through alternative dispute resolution mechanisms, in particular but not limited to binding international arbitration.

(*c*) The cumulative effect of FTA chapters on "Investment", "Trade in Services" and "Electronic Commerce" may undermine government measures to promote social and cultural goals (e.g., universal coverage, cultural integrity, etc.). Negative lists for trade in services leave no policy space to deal with new technologically advanced services when they emerge. Particular attention should be given to the cultural sector where the combination of negative lists for services and provisions aimed at the free movement of electronic commerce (including digital products) can result in undermining reservations made in GATS schedules to preserve the "cultural exception".[87]

(*d*) Safeguards on agricultural trade can be subject to a phase out period after which total liberalization applies. Liberalization can take the form of a staged increase of TRQs to a point where no limits apply. This is often combined with a phase out of the over quota tariff rate.[88] Attention should be given to incorporating such safeguards into FTAs using the same criteria as used in the WTO, in order to protect food security, livelihoods and promote rural development. Legislation for safeguard measures (SSM), e.g., trigger mechanisms, should be in place before entering into FTA negotiations. The issue of whether an agreement in the WTO on an SSM and SP would prevail over existing FTAs has not been resolved.

(*e*) Tariff protection on sensitive products may not be permitted indefinitely, but should be subject to a longer phase out period.

(*f*) Obligations on government procurement are included. These can have the same structure as the WTO plurilateral agreement, but are applied on a discriminatory basis and cover both goods and services.

(*g*) Commitments on subsidies may prohibit dual price systems for energy, which are permitted under the WTO.

FTAs may also fall short of their objectives in terms of market access for developing countries: key export products (e.g., rice, sugar, beef) or services (e.g., MNP) may be excluded, or subject to minimal liberalization.

---

87  See Ivan Bernier, 2004, *Recent FTAs of the United States as Illustrations of their New Strategy Regarding the Audio-Visual Sector* (www.mcc.gouv.qc.ca/international/diversite-culteiurelle/eng/pdf/conf_seoul_ang_2004.pdf).

88  In the Peru USA Agreement, for example, safeguards in the form of a "snap back" to MFN tariffs are triggered by imports exceeding the TRQ by a certain percentage.

(*h*)   Rules of origin requirements may be difficult to meet and, thus, many exports may not benefit from duty-free treatment. Attention should be given to ensuring that stringent rules of origin do not undermine the competitiveness of industries, and that cumulative origin provisions are included. "Yarn forward" type rules of origin may undermine the competitive position of the beneficiary exporting country to the extent that the preferential tariff margin is not sufficient to offset competition from non-preferential suppliers.

(*i*)   Non-tariff barriers (e.g., SPS) may still impede exports.

(*j*)   Some measures distorting mutual trade may not lend themselves to bilateral or regional solutions (e.g., agricultural subsidies, anti-dumping measures). Yet, they could nullify the expected benefits of the FTA provision aimed at eliminating export subsidies which has been included in some agreements.[89]

Conversely, on the positive side of the balance sheet, FTAs may provide an opportunity to deal with issues not easily amenable to multilateral solutions, including:

(*k*)   MNP commitments, such as access for MNP at an occupational level. Measures for protection of foreign workers may be easier to negotiate at a bilateral level.[90]

(*l*)   Negotiations of Mutual Recognition Agreements, with respect to testing facilities (e.g., SPS) as well as the certification of service professionals are often better facilitated in a subregional or bilateral context.[91]

(*m*)   Assistance for net-food importing countries.[92]

(*n*)   Cooperation measures in areas such as cultural services and transportation can be worked out in FTAs.

(*o*)   SPS and TBT. Within the framework of FTAs, developing countries can obtain provisions for financial and technical assistance to overcome barriers, information exchange, guidelines for verification, certification and import checks that can provide greater security for exporters.[93] FTAs can also include provisions for

---

**89**   Some attempts have been made, e.g., Canada/Chile prohibits anti-dumping duties on mutual trade, Chile/USA and Peru/USA provide for the elimination of export subsidies in mutual trade, so long as action is taken to confront export subsidies from third countries, see www.ustr.gov/Trade_Agreements/bilateral/Peru_TPA and www.ustr.gov/Trade_Agreements/bilateral/Chile_TPA.

**90**   The last issue to be resolved in the negotiations of a Philippine-Japan FTA was the quota for the entry of nurses and respect for their professional qualifications. For a description of the issues involved see Tereso S. Tullao and M. A. Cortez, 2003, *Movement of Natural Persons between the Philippines and Japan: Issues and Prospects,* presentation at De La Salle University, Manila, September 2003 (available at http://pascn.pids.gov.ph/jpepa/docs/tullao-revised_sept%209.PDF).

**91**   See for example the approach of Singapore, www.fta.gov.sq.

**92**   See draft Economic Partnership Agreement between the EU and the COMESA countries, 4th draft EPA/8th RNF/24-8-2006 (available at www.bilaterals.org).

**93**   See B. Rudloff and J. Simon, 2004, "Comparing EU FTAs, sanitary and phytosanitary regulations", ECDPM in Brief, Maastricht (www.ecdpm.org).

technical and financial assistance in a wide range of sectors, such as energy, fisheries, protection of traditional knowledge, commodity diversification as well as infrastructural development.[94]

(*p*)  Measures to promote trade and investment (incentives, trade fairs) and address problems of competition (e.g., tourism). Also some FTAs contain programmes under which assistance is provided to upgrade the competitiveness of enterprises in the partner country.[95]

(*q*)  Rules of origin tailored to the needs of the developing partners.

# Annexes

## Annex A.  Textiles and clothing: still the first step to industrialization?

The textiles and clothing (T&C) sector has provided the first step to industrialization for a large number of countries, including those which are now highly developed. It currently provides a major source of employment and foreign exchange for a large number of poor countries. However, these governments are faced with the question of devising a strategy for enabling their T&C sectors to continue this role in the more competitive world market that emerged after the full phase-out of quotas with the implementation of the Agreement on Textiles and Clothing on 1 January 2005.

### T&C and the MDGs

The T&C sector has provided an impetus for economic growth and industrialization in a large number of countries, including those now highly developed. It provides crucial export earnings and world exports exceeded $453 billion in 2004.[96] T&C was among the top two most dynamic sectors in world trade over the past two decades despite being subject to high tariffs and quotas in the main importing countries. The growth in the world market for clothing in particular can be expected to be maintained, providing continuing opportunities of all efficient producers. Most importantly, the T&C sector is a major employer of over 40 million people, particularly women, providing them with otherwise unavailable employment opportunities. In many developing countries the achievement of the MDGs is closely linked to the future of the T&C sector.

---

**94**  See draft Economic Partnership Agreement between the EU and the COMESA countries, op. cit.

**95**  An example is the "Mise à Niveau" programme financed by the EU in its Mediterranean partners. See Faycal Lakhoua, 1998, "The Tunisian experience of 'Mise à Niveau': conceptual issues and policy orientations", Marrakech, September 1998 (http://www.worldbank.org/mdf/mdf2/papers/benefit/finance/lakhoua.pdf).

**96**  See www.wto.org.

For many developing countries, the opportunities for export-oriented growth and employment were a result of the artificial regime (the MFA and it predecessors) that governed world trade in this sector for a half century. The full implementation of the WTO Agreement on Textiles and Clothing (ATC) on 1 January 2005, which "integrated" this sector within the normal multilateral rules, has placed in question the ability of many developing countries, particularly LDCs, to compete against larger and more efficient suppliers. Developing countries, both current and potential exporters of textiles and clothing, are faced with the need for a policy response to a more competitive trading environment.

Potential new suppliers must assess whether the T&C sector, and especially the clothing subsector, still provides opportunities for growth and employment and warrants priority in development strategies. These strategies have involved (*a*) the pursuit of improved access conditions to major markets, (*b*) national strategies to enhance productivity and competitiveness, (*c*) actions to ensure that the benefits of exports are widely shared and (*d*) improvement of working conditions.[97]

### Market access

Even after the abolition of the quota system, exporting countries face difficult conditions of access to the major markets. A number of exporting countries are partners with the United States or the European Union in FTAs or otherwise benefit from preferential tariff treatment. Most major countries have complied with their obligation (MDG8) to provide duty-free access to all imports from LDCs. However, the United States appears unwilling to extend such treatment to T&C. Other developing countries benefit from GSP treatment in the T&C sector, again except in the United States. Tariff protection thus remains high in this sector.[98]

However, exporting countries are obviously extremely concerned that they should receive the most favourable access conditions possible to meet international competition. They can pursue multilateral initiatives to secure duty-free treatment in the context of the GSP, or special duty-free regimes for LDCs. LDCs are pressing for this treatment to be bound, i.e., that it would constitute a "right"' in the WTO and become defensible under the dispute settlement mechanism. However this has not yet been accepted. LDCs suffered a setback at the Hong Kong Ministerial Conference when it was agreed that developed countries could exempt 3 per cent of their imports from LDCs from the duty-free obligation after the deadline of 2008! LDCs should continue to pursue 100 per cent duty-free, quota-free access which coincides

---

97  The section draws heavily from UNDP Asia Pacific Trade and Investment Initiative, *International Trade in Textiles and Clothing and Development Policy Options: After the Full Implementation of the WTO Agreement on Textiles and Clothing (ATC) on 1 January 2005*, policy paper, Colombo: 2005 (www.undprcc.lk/Publications/Publications/T&CPolicyPaper.pdf). See also publications of the International Textiles and Clothing Bureau at www.itcb.org.

98  See chapter 4 of the UNDP *Human Development Report 2005*, "International cooperation at a crossroads: aid, trade and security in an unequal world", New York, 2005 (http://hdr.undp.org/reports/global/2005/).

with MDG8 Target 13 as the best means of ensuring preferential access to major world markets.

The Doha Round NAMA negotiating group has also considered the zero-zero option (i.e., sectoral free trade) in T&C. The most likely outcome would seem to be a tariff harmonizing formula.

The remaining tariff barriers to T&C imports have led to pressures from the industries in exporting developing countries to negotiate FTAs with major importing countries, particularly the United States, which does not accord GSP treatment in this sector. Duty-free access for textiles and clothing is usually subject to complex rules of origin which accord different treatment to different preferential trading partners. These rules of origin usually are intended to ensure a "captive market" for yarn and fabric exporters of the "importing" country. FTAs usually require important reciprocal concessions on the part of the exporting developing country. The FTA option entails the risk that T&C exporters will have excessive influence on the FTA negotiation, leading to apparent gains for T&C exporters being "purchased" at the expense of excessive reciprocal concessions in other sectors which could undermine development efforts by the exporting developing country. In negotiating FTAs, rules of origin which maximize the scope for sourcing of inputs, and contain reasonable value added criteria are crucial, if real benefits are to be derived by the developing T&C exporting country. The various considerations involved in following the FTA option are set out in "The FTA option".

T&C has been included in FTAs among developing countries, and, in some cases, given priority in an "early harvest list". Some countries such as Thailand have made use of regional agreements between developing countries to diversify their export markets.[99]

### Rules of origin

Preferential tariff treatment inevitably involves rules of origin. The U.S. FTAs, for example, impose "yarn forward" rules of origin, under which duty-free treatment is granted only to those T&C exports made from yarns and fabrics originating in either the United States or the exporting county. FTAs with different partners contain variations of the "yarn forward" rules, some more liberal than others. The EU preferences include a double transformation criterion. Stringent and complicated rules of origin may result in either (*a*) the non-compliance of exports do not comply with the criteria, thereby disqualifying them from preferential treatment. They are thus, dutiable at MFN rates, (*b*) the compliance of exports with the rules which allow them to enter duty free. However, they are so burdened by the criteria that they cannot compete, even with the benefit of preferential tariff margins. It is obvious that rules of origin

---

**99** See Ratnakar Adhikari and Yumiko Yamamoto, 2006, *Sewing Thoughts, How to realize Human Development gains in the post-Quota World, Tracking Report*, Colombo: UNDP Asia Pacific Trade and Investment Initiative, April 2006 (www.undprcc.lk/Publications/Publications/TC_Tracking_Report_April_2006.pdf).

permitting inputs from the cheapest and highest quality sources would be preferable. The extent to which the exporting country produces input (i.e., textiles and fabrics) determines the impact of such rules. Nevertheless, even major producers of raw materials have found it necessary to use imported inputs to remain competitive.

Experience has shown that rules of origin are a major determining factor in access to T&C markets. When Canada relaxed its rules of origin for clothing imports from LDCs, eliminating double transformation and reducing value added to 25 per cent, imports from LDCs increased exponentially! Stringent rules of origin may explain why preferential exporters are losing their share of markets despite tariff margins.[100] Cumulation provisions can facilitate conformity with rules of origin and promote trade among developing countries.

The post-ATC trade flows (for 2005) indicate that most preferential suppliers are losing their market shares, particularly in the United States market to China and a few other Asian countries (e.g., India, Pakistan, Bangladesh, Indonesia and Cambodia), which have held their own in the post-ATC scenario. In the absence of quotas, preferential tariff margins generally do not provide an adequate cost advantage over more competitive suppliers, particularly when handicapped by "yarn forward" types of rules of origin. In other smaller countries, where textile and clothing industries were established almost exclusively to escape quotas, the industries have already collapsed (e.g., Lesotho, Maldives and Nepal).[101]

## Increasing productivity and competitiveness

In the short run, governments can improve competitiveness by reducing direct input costs (such as labour and fabric) through (*a*) removal of tariff, fiscal and other impediments on imports of yarns or fabrics, (*b*) improvements in labour productivity, through training programmes. Higher levels of education and skills of workers can facilitate successful specialization in niche markets of more complicated clothing, such as the case of Sri Lanka in women's garments.[102]

---

100  The submission by the relevant sectoral advisory committee (ITAC-5) on the USA Bahrain FTA is quite eloquent on the impact of the yarn forward rule. A survey of major apparel retailers conducted by the National Retail Federation confirms the deficiencies of the yarn forward rules of origin. It was the unanimous view of survey respondents that a yarn forward rule is not cost-effective and results in a net increase in the cost of apparel production, even when the savings from the elimination of tariffs and quota charges are factored in. All retailers participating in the survey further reported that yarn forward rules of origin have affected their sourcing operations by accelerating the shift in apparel trade away from preferential trading partner countries, such as Mexico, that are subject to this rule to certain large Asian suppliers, notably China. Although segments of the U.S. textile industry have strongly advocated a yarn forward rule of origin in FTAs as necessary to protect domestic yarn and fabric production from Chinese competition, experience has shown that such a rule has the opposite effect and has resulted in an accelerated shift of apparel sourcing to China.

101  Ibid.

102  See Ratnakar Adhikari and Yumiko Yamamoto, 2005, *Flying Colours, Broken Threads: One Year of Evidence from Asia after the Phase-out of Textiles and Clothing Quotas, Tracking*

A series of other indirect costs can be reduced through programmes to improve infrastructure and logistics, streamline bureaucratic procedures, provide facilities for specialized education and develop human resources in design. Other factors being comparable, buyers will give priority to suppliers who can deliver new styles quickly and replenish inventory rapidly. Reduction of these indirect costs is crucial to meeting buyers' needs. With the elimination of the quota regime, buyers will inevitably reduce their number of suppliers and deal with factories that can meet their requirements. On the other hand, they will want to spread their country risk and seek competitive suppliers in several countries.

National policy measures to strengthen competitiveness and export performance, through trade facilitation, export credit facilities, particularly for SMEs, will also be important. Over the longer run, governments can encourage the creation of brands and nurture reputations. The stakes are very high because the development of an export capacity in the textiles and garment sector was the first step in the industrialization process for many countries. Given this historical context, the premature disappearance of this sector before new industries can be developed could severely constrict possibilities of creating the virtuous spiral described in "Tariffs and industrial policy" and "Exports and poverty".

## Equity: sharing of benefits

T&C exporters must also deal with the legacy of poor working conditions and abuse which have plagued the sector. The T&C sector has been associated with "sweatshop" working conditions and abuse of workers, especially women, which has raised international concern. In some cases, working conditions are unsustainable. It has been claimed that women working in the garment industry in Bangladesh are obliged to leave their jobs after five years due to deteriorating health caused by the working conditions. Such treatment is counterproductive as poor working conditions reduce productivity. Successful countries have been those which have invested in upgrading skills of workers.

Increased competition may result in reduced employment and a further deterioration in working conditions. Measures such as new legislation are needed to ensure that ILO Conventions are respected. Buyers have also become sensitive to social issues, and wish to be assured that their suppliers cannot be accused of not meeting minimum labour standards. For example, Cambodia's efforts to respect labour standards seem to have been appreciated by buyers.[103]

*Report*, Colombo: UNDP Asia Pacific Trade and Investment Initiative, December 2005 (www.undprcc.lk).

103 Ibid.

## Annex B.   Fisheries, putting the products of the poor
##            on world markets

The fisheries sector is a source of nutrition and employment to millions of poor people and has provided them with opportunities to access lucrative export markets. However, exports of fishery products give rise to a series of challenges relating to environmental protection and distribution of benefits. Developing countries are faced with the challenge of maximizing the contribution of this sector to the achievement of the MDGs. While the fisheries sector is unique in many aspects, other export industries in developing countries encounter similar challenges of distribution of benefits and environmental impact.

### Fisheries and MDGs

Fishermen are among the poorest segments of the population, small-scale fishing contributes to a more equitable distribution of resources while being a source of food and employment.[104] This is particularly true of those who have no access to agricultural land, credit and capital equipment. According to the FAO, 38 million people were directly involved in marine fisheries and aquaculture in the year 2002, of whom 20 per cent may be in the small-scale subsector earning less than US$ 1 a day. Another 17 million income-poor, including a high proportion of women, are employed in boatbuilding, net making, marketing and processing. Fisher folk are often in the lowest segments of the population in terms of human development indicators such as literacy and maternal mortality. The fisheries sector is vulnerable to weather conditions and natural disasters; the December 2004 Indian Ocean tsunami destroyed the livelihoods of millions of poor fish workers. Thus, development of the fisheries sector can play an important role in helping coastal communities reach the United Nations Millennium Development Goals (MDGs), especially Goal 1, eradicating extreme poverty and hunger.

Fisheries and aquaculture exports have been growing rapidly. Globally, fish has become a highly traded commodity, with about 37 per cent of total fisheries production (live weight equivalent) entering international trade in various forms. Net seafood export trade from developing countries has increased from US$ 10 billion in 1990 to US$ 18 billion in 2002. Total production (capture and aquaculture) rose from 118 million tons in 1997 to 132 million in 2003, although capture fish production remained stable at around 84 million tons. The small-scale fisheries subsector accounts for nearly 50 per cent of global capture fisheries. Wherever poor people have been been provided opportunities to participate in the higher value market of export species, they have increased their income substantially.

---

**104** See publications and reports of International Collective in Support of Fishworkers at www.icsf.net and www.icsf.org. See also Carolyn Deere, 2000, *Net Gains: Linking Fisheries Management, International Trade and Sustainable Development*, IUCN, The World Conservation Union (www.users.ox.ac.uk).

However, in the absence of effective fisheries management measures, exports may have a tremendous adverse impact on fisheries resources in developing countries. High prices for fish exports has led to overcapacity—excessive fishing effort, investment in modern, destructive fishing gear, and over fishing in several commercially important fisheries. In many countries this has led to a rapid depletion in coastal fisheries with a serious adverse impact on small-scale fisheries. Foreign fleets from developed countries, often benefiting from subsidies and imbalanced bilateral agreements, are also contributing to the depletion of national fishing zones, often illegally.[105] Overall, in 12 of the 16 fishing regions identified by FAO, fish stocks are either fully exploited or depleted.

Aquaculture has caused environmental degradation, for example by causing increased salinity of rice farms, and its expansion has been severely limited in many developing countries. Poor fishermen have not been able to acquire the capital to participate in aquaculture. Thus increased exports of fish and fish products have not benefited the majority of fisher folk and in many cases have actually led to increased poverty among fishermen.[106]

## Barriers to exports of fish products

Tariffs on fresh, frozen or chilled fish, or primary fish products, are low in most developed country export markets with the exception of the EC. Seafood is covered by the Generalised System of Preferences (GSP) of the major developed trading countries. Tariff escalation presents the main barrier as tariffs on processed fish and fish products can rise to 20 per cent, and there are greater in-quota and off-quota variations. Processing industries provide employment opportunities for women and supplement household income of fisher families. Additional trade barriers are being erected against developing country fisheries exports (e.g., anti-dumping duties are proliferating). Sanitary and phyto-sanitary measures, such as food safety standards, environmental measures, such as eco-labelling and certification programmes, and compliance requirements with MEAs, present serious barriers to the participation of small fishermen in export markets.

It is recognized that subsidies have contributed to an artificial increase in fishing fleets and fishing capacity which has contributed to the depletion of stocks. It is estimated that such subsidies account for up to 20 per cent of dock side revenues. A consensus seems to be emerging in the Doha Round Rules negotiations that such subsidies should be drastically reduced. However, there is also recognition of the need for public support to small-scale fisheries.[107]

---

**105** See chapter 4 of the UNDP *Human Development Report 2005*, op. cit.

**106** The section draws heavily from Ruangrai Tokrishna, 2003, "The fisheries sector in Asian countries, sustainable fisheries, human development and trade liberalization", UNDP Asia Trade Initiative on Trade and Human Development, Phase 1, technical support document, Hanoi (available at www.undprcc.lk/Publications/Publications.asp?C=4).

**107** See, for example, recent proposals by Brazil TN/RL/GEN/79/Rev.4 and the United States TN/RL/GEN/145 on www.wto.org.

*Food safety standards and small-scale fisheries*

SPS regulations have become more stringent, excluding many producers, particularly poorer fishermen, from export markets. Hazard Analysis and Critical Control Point (HACCP)—based systems and scientifically based risk assessment methods have been adopted by the United States, EC and Japan that together account for 75 to 80 per cent in value of seafood imports (FAO, 2004). The international regulatory framework for fish safety and quality is embodied in two agreements (SPS and TBT) of the WTO, and the standards, guidelines and recommendations developed by the relevant committees of the *Codex Alimentarius*. These safety and quality concepts are also enshrined in the Code of Conduct for Responsible Fisheries, particularly Articles 6 and 11 (FAO, 2004). Environmental regulations (e.g., shrimp/turtle issue) are also serious barriers for small fishermen. Voluntary eco-labeling schemes, designed to promote sustainable fisheries, can also be a barrier as small-scale fishermen are usually unable to organize so as to qualify.

While tariff escalation is a significant barrier, sanitary and environmental regulations pose the greatest barrier facing the entry of small fishermen in the world market as non-tariff barriers. These can be addressed at the multilateral level through negotiated improvements in the WTO SPS Agreement relating to equivalence of standards and rules governing the use of eco-labeling. However, action is required at the bilateral level to provide financial and technical assistance and facilities to enable poor fishermen to meet national regulations of the importing country.

A number of Multilateral Environmental Agreements are aimed at preventing the depletion of fishery resources, particularly of migratory species. Some of these have trade provisions. It is important to ensure that the provisions of the WTO or FTAs cannot be used to frustrate the effective implementation of these MEAs.

---

### Box 21.   Examples of how SPS can penalize the poor

From a small-scale fisheries' perspective, in addition to the cost aspects, one of the main problems in adopting a HACCP plan would be the difficulty in implementing such a plan at the level of fish catch, especially for beach landing fishing units like kattumaram and canoes, for example, in India. According to EU and US standards, fish need to be stored in ice or to be kept in frozen storage as soon as they are harvested. Storage of fish in iceboxes would be difficult on board traditional fishing craft like kattumaram, which are made of lashed logs. Yet, many kattumaram using long lining and bottom set gillnets are used for catching fish for the export market. Strict implementation of HACCP plans could result in small producers which use such fishing craft being excluded from the export market.

On reaching the fishing harbour or landing centre, traditional fishers are expected to handle fish for export markets without exposing them to the beach-sand as a result of the fish handling standards of import markets. Many of the fishing villages that harvest fish, shrimp and cephalopods for the export market have only the beach for landing their catch and it would be difficult for them to comply with a HACCP plan unless they invest in iceboxes and maintain them in a hygienic manner.

Developing countries are legislating to protect the interests of small fishermen, particularly by reducing capture of fish in EEZ waters and reserving portions of territorial waters for small fishermen.[108] Credit facilities to assist poor people to construct aquaculture facilities and export to world markets also provide strong support to poor fishermen. Measures to support the processing of fish products before export can also increase incomes and provide additional employment opportunities in this sector.

## Annex C.   Environmental services

The provision of environmental services is crucial to the achievement of MDG7 which includes targets to halve the proportion of people without sustainable access to safe water and basic sanitation and to improve significantly the lives of at least 100 million slum dwellers by 2015. Governments are faced with the challenge of obtaining investment to upgrade and modernize water and sanitation services, while ensuring access to the poorer segments of the population.

It is estimated that 1.1 billion people lack access to safe drinking water, while 2.6 billion people lack adequate sanitation.[109] Almost half the people in the developing world have one or more diseases or infections associated with inadequate water supply and sanitation, of which 1.8 million die every year from diarrhoeal diseases. Inadequate water supply and sanitation are the main cause of child mortality, which MDG4 aims at reducing by two-thirds. MDG4 Targets 10 and 11 aim at reducing by half the number of people without sustainable access to safe drinking water, and to achieve significant improvement in the lives of 100 million slum dwellers.

Huge amounts of investment are required to achieve this goal. The investment requirements to meet the world's water needs are estimated at up to $180 billion annually and it is widely believed that such resources, and associated technology, are available mainly from the private sector. Given the large investments required in water projects and the long period of return on such investment, investors give priority to effective control. This can be facilitated by trade commitments on environmental services under GATS and other trade agreements. The WTO Doha Declaration singled out environmental goods and services as priorities for liberalization. Plurilateral requests have sought full commercial presence for waste water and other environmental services (water for human consumption is not covered by these requests).

The privatization of infrastructure services, however, has taken place in the context of a tense debate about the appropriate roles for the private sector in this area, and has led to major conflicts, especially around large-scale projects involving multinational companies. As an alternative to full-fledged privatization, several countries have opted for Public-Private Partnerships (PPPs), where private partners are to differing extents involved in the design and construction of infrastructure and/or in the

---

**108** See Sebastian Mathew, 2003, *Trade in Fisheries and Human Development in India*, UNDP Asia Trade Initiative on Trade and Human Development, Phase 1, technical support document, Hanoi (available at www.undprcc.lk/Publications/Publications.asp?C=4).

**109** World Water Council at www.worldwatercouncil.org.

---

**Box 22.  The 4th World Water Forum**

The Ministerial Declaration of the 4th World Water Forum held in Mexico City in March 2006 reaffirmed that "governments have the primary role in promoting improved access to safe drinking water, basic sanitation, sustainable and secure tenure, and adequate shelter, through improved governance at all levels, and appropriate enabling environment and regulatory frameworks, adapting a pro-poor approach with the active involvement of all stakeholders" (see www.world waterforum4.org.mx).

---

management, operation and/or the financing of assets. The privatization of the collection, purification and distribution of water is often met with opposition, particularly from those who stand to pay increasing costs to finance the improvements in water supply. In addition, there is concern that the benefits of these improvements flow to more affluent segments of the population. Transnational water companies operating in developing countries have shown a tendency to cherry pick—concentrating on supplying large cities and those consumers who can pay market prices, while rural areas, small and medium cities and poor neighbourhoods have been disregarded.[110] In addition, liberalization in the waste management subsector of the environmental services market presents high risks of employment displacement, since excessive mechanization and modernization target the livelihoods of some of the poorest people.[111] Governments in developing countries are thus faced with a dilemma: how to obtain the necessary investment and related technology while ensuring that benefits are shared by all.

**Environmental services are big business.** The global market for environmental services sector exceeded $365 billion, in 2002, 80 per cent accounted for by water, sewage and solid waste management. The industry has a dual structure, with a small number of large firms accounting for about 50 per cent of output in individual market segments (the three largest water operators account for more than 50 per cent of the global market)[112] while a large number of smaller firms account for the remainder. In developing countries, the emphasis has been on sewage treatment and water delivery. Private investment projects have targeted high- and middle-income countries: LDCs have hardly been touched. For instance, less than 0.2 per cent of all private sector investments in the water and sanitation sector of developing countries went to sub-Saharan Africa. Only 3 per cent of the developing country population is provided with drinking water through private operators.

---

110  OECD, "Public-Private Partnerships in the urban water sector", 2003, Policy Brief, Paris: April 2003 (www.oecd.org/dataoecd/31/50/2510696.pdf).

111  UNDP, 2005, *International Trade in Environmental and Energy Services and Human Development*, Discussion Paper, Asia-Pacific Trade and Investment Initiative, Colombo, p. 22 (www.undprcc.lk/Publications/Publications/International_trade-completed.pdf).

112  John Hilary, 2003, *GATS and Water: The threat of services negotiations at the WTO*, London: Save the Children UK, p. 16.

**Box 23.    Buenos Aires water supply privatization**

Questions remain about the assumption that market liberalization automatically produces improvements in the efficiency of water utilities and in the connection of new customers. In 1993, following the advice of the IMF, the water supply system of Buenos Aires was privatized and placed in the hands of a consortium led by the giant French firm Suez. Although there were initially impressive gains in the extension of water infrastructure, the majority of the concessions' negative impacts have been most deeply felt in the poorest sections of Buenos Aires.[a] Many poor households fell into serious arrears and were disconnected from the network, especially prior to 1998. Environmentally, those living in the poorest areas of the city have also been faced the negative effects of rising groundwater and the health risks associated with nitrate-contaminated aquifers. These municipalities have some of the lowest average incomes in the greater Buenos Aires area and yet a large part of the financial burden for extending the network has fallen on these households.[b] In March 2006, the Government of Argentina cancelled the contract with Suez.

a   See www.cbc.ca/fourth/deadinthewater/argentia2.
b   A. L. Loftus and D. A. McDonald, 2001, "Of liquid dreams: a political ecology of water privatization in Buenos Aires", *Environment&Urbanization*, vol. 13, No. 2, October 2001 (www. queensu.ca/msp/pages/Project_Publications/Journals/Loftus.pdf). See also John Hilary, GATS and Water, op. cit.

The UN Millennium Project Task Force on Water and Sanitation requested countries to elaborate coherent water resources development and management plans to support the achievement of these goals. These plans should constitute a prerequisite to the negotiation of commitments in the environmental services sector.

## Annex D.    Energy services

Attainment of the MDGs will require that modern energy be made available to a large proportion of the nearly two billion people who currently are reliant on traditional energy sources. Lack of access to energy not only undermines the productivity of an estimated one third of the world's people but causes insecurity and hardship and threatens their health and future well being.[113] It constitutes a particular burden for women, and provokes reduced life expectancy and higher rates of child mortality. Again, developing countries are faced with the need to obtain capital and technology while ensuring universal access and control over this strategic sector.

### Enormous investment required to meet world demand

The World Energy Council estimates that enormous investments—about $100 billion annually—will be required to maintain adequate supplies of energy, and this

---

113  See Sieh Mei Ling, ed., 2004, Investment, Energy and Environmental Services: Promoting Human Development in WTO Negotiations, Kuala Lumpur: University of Malaya, UNDP and Malaysian Institute of Economic Research, March 2004 (www.um.edu.my).

alone will not ensure delivery to the poor.[114] Energy services constitute the value added in the chain from the location of the potential energy source to its distribution to the final consumer. The dynamism of trade in the energy services sector is accelerating due to the increasing demand for energy, the liberalization of energy markets, increased investment in the energy sector and the introduction of new technologies.

Many developing countries are engaged in structural reforms of the energy sector meant to cut costs and improve the economic performance and efficiency of the energy sector by imposing free-market disciplines and commercial criteria.[115] These can include deregulation (covering both the removal of regulations and the reassessment of regulatory methods), corporatization (placing public energy utilities under commercial discipline), unbundling (i.e., breaking up vertically integrated State monopolies), increased private sector participation and outright privatization. Efforts to ensure competition require provisions to ensure access (third party access—TPA) to networks (grids, pipelines).

The dismantling of State monopolies has provided lucrative possibilities for the private sector and led to considerable interest in obtaining bound commitments on trade in energy services, which are the subject of requests in GATS and covered in FTAs. Such requests are aimed at gaining a share of dynamic "downstream" energy, particularly electricity trading markets, while seeking to gain control of "upstream" services to improve security of supply. The energy services market is estimated at $100 billion, but it implies control over the $3 billion global trade in energy.[116]

### How to ensure universal access?

Governments of developing countries are seeking private sector participation to obtain the necessary capital and technology. The dilemma often faced by governments is how to obtain foreign investment to increase capacity and efficiency, while simultaneously keeping the price of electricity, in particular, at levels accessible to the poor. In the energy sector, conditions for entry and performance requirements are essential tools for ensuring that liberalization attains the ultimate objective of universal coverage. Such conditions may include price undertakings (as liberalization tends to result in increased prices if not controlled), universal service obligations and transfer of technology requirements. On the other hand, governments may need to subsidize investors in isolated regions, particularly those involved in renewable energy production (e.g., solar or wind energy). Fair and transparent rules governing TPA and cross subsidization can also encourage investors. The energy sector can be a source of employment for youth, providing higher paying jobs, both at home and abroad, through MNP.

---

114 In 2002 1.6 billion people did not have access to electricity. According to the International Energy Agency's estimates, 1.4 billion people will still lack access to electricity in 2030.

115 UNCTAD, 2003, "Managing 'request-offer' negotiations under the GATS: the case of energy services", UNCTAD/DITC/TNCD/2003/5, Geneva.

116 See UNDP, *International Trade in Environmental and Energy Services and Human Development*, op. cit.

In addition, it may be necessary to retain energy subsidies, but with more focus on the poor. Such requirements should be stipulated in GATS commitments or in FTA "reservations".

The scope of WTO negotiations on energy extends beyond the services sector. Energy-importing countries are seeking to expand the rules on subsidies to restrict "dual pricing" practices under which energy-producing countries maintain prices for domestic consumers at levels below those prevailing on the world market. There are also initiatives to eliminate exports taxes, as a policy tool frequently used in the energy sector.

---

**Box 24.   Energy services liberalization in Latin America**

Country case studies carried out in Latin America in 2001 show that energy market liberalization has, on balance, been beneficial to countries that have implemented it. Both energy availability and the quality of the service have been enhanced, mostly through (too broad in its sweep) rapid transfer of technology and systems, and more efficient modern management. However, energy accessibility and affordability, although better overall, has not improved for marginal populations. In general, market liberalization has tended to reduce employment in the sector as public monopoly enterprises tended to be over-staffed. Reductions in personnel in privatized companies have been accompanied, however, by increases in the number of jobs in contracting companies as a result of the increasing outsourcing of many activities.[a] Within the context of heavy reliance on services companies, there is still a great variety in the degree to which energy companies vertically integrate backwards or outsource services to external providers.

a   World Energy Council, 2001, *Energy Markets in Transition: The Latin American and Caribbean Experience*, London.

---

**Box 25.   Strategies for strengthening energy services competitiveness—the case of Venezuela**

Some energy-producing developing countries have adopted successful policies aimed at developing a strong domestic upstream energy service sector (exploration, extraction, drilling and other construction services) as a stimulus to development. For example, in 1980 PDVSA—the Venezuelan State oil company—established a policy aimed at the development of Venezuelan engineering, procurement and construction (EPC) companies. Foreign EPC companies had to establish partnerships or joint ventures with local companies to be invited as bidders for contracts. The partnerships had to produce transfer of technology and training. The management of the projects had to be shared between foreign and Venezuelan executives. On the other hand, attractive contracting conditions were applied and stable work loads were offered. As a result, in 2001, 90 per cent of EPC contracts were executed by local EPC companies, up from 20 per cent in 1980. In the same year, there were more than 140 firms of various sizes and degrees of specialization.

## Annex E.   Financial services

Stability in the financial sector is essential for the achievement of the MDGs. Financial crises have plunged millions of people into poverty and set development efforts back decades. The burden of adjustment in such crises is inevitably borne by the poor. Nevertheless, developing countries are again confronted with requests to liberalize further their financial service regimes.

### Differing commitments to financial reform

Enhanced competition in the financial services sector was expected to result in lower fees; improved quality and choice of services; access to new products and technologies; and access to new sources of capital. Liberalization measures have included the withdrawal of government intervention by privatizing State-owned financial entities; freeing interest rates and leaving credit allocation to be determined by the market; the removal of regulations, either quantitative or qualitative that discriminate against foreign financial entities; and the removal of restrictions on intra-sectoral activities by financial entities. The approach of developing countries to financial reform has varied including (*a*) deregulation of domestic markets with restrictions on new entrants, either general or only to foreign providers, (*b*) reform has been accompanied by the liberalization of the capital account, while in other cases regulations restricting movement of capital were maintained, (*c*) withdrawal of all State ownership of financial entities was terminated, or the maintenance of State participation in development banks, (*d*) full liberalization of commercial presence combined with restrictions on cross-border trade and (*e*) different approaches to the speed of the reform and in the sequencing between financial sector liberalization and regulatory upgrading.

The liberalization of financial services has been given specific focus in the WTO, as a result of acute pressure by developed countries, to the extent that additional negotiations (concluding in 1998) were held in this sector, after the Uruguay Round, to obtain further liberalization. The GATS commitments reflect the policy tools that developing country governments have retained to manage the financial sector. These include limitations on the opening of new banks, restrictions on foreign ownership, nationality requirements for directors, no commitments regarding "new financial services", etc. Some have been aimed at reserving segments of the financial sector for disadvantaged segments of the population.[117] Despite the experience of financial crises over recent years, some FTAs have pushed financial liberalization even further.

---

117  The concluding meeting of the financial services negotiations was held up to the early hours of the morning as Malaysia successfully resisted attempts to dilute its pro-Bumiputera policy in the financial sector.

*Impact of liberalization*

Countries undertaking liberalization of the financial sector have experienced a fast increase in the participation of foreign financial entities in the market at the expense of domestic firms. Domestic financial entities have been bought by foreign firms or have left the market not being able to compete any longer. Concentration in the domestic market has taken place since, increasingly, a smaller number of financial entities control a larger share of the financial market. Financial liberalization has not always contributed to increasing lending to the private sector as a percentage of GDP. On the contrary, a sharp decline has been observed after the reform. SMEs and operators in the agriculture sector have been particularly affected by limited access to credit. Experience shows that countries should carefully assess the potential implications of reform on the basis of national realities,[118] designing appropriate financial services liberalization policies to suit country-specific conditions; determining the potential costs and benefits of reforms and also the appropriate pace and sequence of the process. In the absence of adequate prudential policy, liberalization may contribute to financial instability.

---

**Box 26.   The Thai experience**

The Thai experience and financial crisis in 1997 shows that "fast and furious" liberalization has not worked well. Liberalization should have been planned as a process and implemented in steps rather than being set out as an objective to be achieved through incoherent policy measures. The experience also demonstrates how challenging it is to adapt external fast developments to a country's needs and readiness. The rapidly growing banking system and the influx of short-term foreign capital proved, for instance, to be too much and too fast for the Thai authorities to catch up with on the regulatory front. While financial reform and the strengthening of the financial system are of paramount importance, they should be devised and implemented on a continuous basis and not only when an acute need or extraordinary circumstances force a country to undertake drastic reforms.[a]

a  WTO, Communication from Thailand—Assessment of Trade in Services, document TN/S/W/4, 22 July 2002.

---

## Annex F.   Distribution services

Liberalizing distribution services is seen as a means to increase productivity, lower prices, greater product choice and distribution formats, and technological innovation. However, small domestic competitors cannot compete with large retail chains thus eliminating employment opportunities for the poor. The concentration of owner-

---

118  International Monetary Fund, 2000, *International Capital Markets: Developments, Prospects, and Key Policy Issues*, Washington, D.C.: September 2000 (http://www.imf.org/external/pubs/ft/icm/2000/01/eng/index.htm).

ship at the world level can operate so as to marginalize small producers. Developing countries must devise policies in this sector that provide benefits for all, in the face of further requests for liberalization.

## Strategic role of distribution services

Distribution services are closely linked with other services such as transport, packaging, warehousing, financial services and commercial real estate development and have become a vehicle in international trade and competitiveness. The distribution chain has become shorter, and a direct relationship between producers and retailers has emerged, driven by enabling technologies and the desire to lower transaction costs. Rapid diffusion and incorporation of new business methods and technologies have brought about fundamental institutional and organizational changes related to procurement, inventory control, management methods and payment formula. The presence of large international retailers can become an avenue for increasing exports, incorporating domestic suppliers into the global procurement network, as well as being conducive to the improvement of local worker skills, especially in logistics, marketing and management.

## Concentration of ownership

Ownership in both retail and wholesale sectors has become highly concentrated. The top 200 retailers account for 30 per cent of worldwide retailing sales. The growing presence of foreign retailing conglomerates in many developing countries is transforming highly competitive markets, with tens of thousands of small firms competing in the different market segments, into a situation in which a small number of firms control most of the industry turnover. This has led to smaller local suppliers being forced out of the market.

The distribution sector accounts for a sizeable share of non-agricultural employment in developing countries—for example 6-7 per cent in India— and it is significantly higher than in developed countries.[119] Small shops play a crucial social role as employers of poor people who migrate from rural to urban areas; they perform therefore a crucial social role that big chains would be unable to perform. Moreover, shifting the social status of people from that of shop owners to that of shop employees has the effect of shrinking the middle class, with negative social and political implications.

The dominance of large firms in the distribution service sector is having a profound impact on the wholesale segment of the market, and on local suppliers of goods, in particular in the farm sector. Developing country suppliers of foodstuffs find themselves bearing the brunt of price competition among distribution chains while small farmers find themselves left out due to their inability to meet the quality and delivery standards imposed by the firms themselves.[120]

---

119 See UNCTAD, 2005, *Distribution Services*, TD/B/COM.1/EM.29/2, Geneva.
120 See chapter 4, *UNDP Human Development Report 2005*, op. cit.

## Conditions for liberalization

Developing countries are thus seeking trade-offs so as to obtain the benefits of the presence of large distribution chains while protecting and stimulating the role of small retail outlets as a source of employment for poor people, and ensuring access to distribution chains for small producers. This can be accomplished through techniques such as limitations on the number of branches of foreign chains, economic needs tests (which can be inscribed in GATS commitments), and the support to SMEs through training in management and distribution processes[121] and credit facilities.

Opening up the retail market without ensuring the necessary conditions for fair competition has often not yielded the expected welfare gains. Such action may need to be complemented by the setting up of vigorous and clear anti-trust legislation aimed at regulating cartels, predatory behaviour, abuses of market power and deceptive practices, and at promoting consumer welfare; policies aimed at supporting retail diversity and entrepreneurship; the extension of unfair contract law to business-to-business contracts; measures aimed at the proper implementation of trade marks and copyright law; the setting up of franchise law, including mandatory disclosure of information; and the development of soft law instruments, such as codes of good practices, which have proved very effective in regulating buyers' anti-competitive behaviour.

### Box 27.   Expansion of supermarket chains

In the food retail business, there has been an impressive expansion of supermarket chains both domestic and foreign, with Latin America leading the way among developing regions. Supermarkets' share rose from 20 per cent of total national food retailing in 1990 to 50-60 per cent of total turnover in 2002. The development of supermarket chains in Asia and Africa has followed a pattern similar to that of Latin America, but with a later take-off. The share of supermarket chains in grocery retail is currently around 33 per cent in Indonesia, Malaysia and Thailand and around 63 per cent in the Republic of Korea, Taiwan Province of China and the Philippines. On the other hand, supermarket penetration in India stands at only 5 per cent. The most recent venue for supermarket take-off is Africa, especially Eastern and Southern Africa; in South Africa, supermarket chains represents 55 per cent of total national groceries sales, while in Nigeria they still account for only 5 per cent.

---

121 In Colombia, for example, the modernization and liberalization of distribution services has had a negative impact on medium- and small-sized companies, which have been displaced from the market. The Government has, then, implemented a special programme—PYMECO—to support small retailers through training in management and distribution processes.

## Annex G.  Health services

The provision of health services to the poor is central to the achievement of MDGs
4, 5 and 6. The pressures for foreign participation in health sectors have arisen at a
moment when the impact of the WTO and other trade agreements on health is a
subject of major concern to the international community. Commitments on health
in GATS and other trade agreements can impact the provision of basic health services to the poor.[122] As already noted, the 2001 WTO Ministerial Declaration on
the Trade-Related Aspects of Intellectual Property Rights (TRIPS) Agreement and
Public Health was deemed necessary to protect developing countries against bilateral pressures from powerful trading partners who were undermining their rights to
generic access to medicines. International health experts have strongly and continually cautioned prudence to developing countries in committing themselves to allowing foreign providers of health services, including health insurance, companies from
entering their markets.

While the role of the private sector in providing health services varies from
country to country, most WTO members have declined to make commitments in
this sector. Many countries desire the latest medical technology and high-tech hospitals and training facilities. The existence of such facilities is also seen as an inducement to foreign investment. However, there is a concern that the foreign private sector
will drain human and financial resources from the national sectors, both public and
private, and lead to a two-tier health system, one for the rich and one for the poor. As
the greatest challenge facing developing countries in the health sector is to provide
affordable access to quality services for the rural poor, the presence of foreign private
suppliers could make little contribution to, and more likely frustrate, these efforts.

Foreign participation in the health services sector can also take place through
the provision of health insurance. International health experts consider that while,
in theory, greater access for health insurance companies could stimulate competition
and reduce costs, in actual practice, evidence shows that greater competition among
health insurers segments and destabilizes the market in addition to undermining
the ability to build larger, more equitable risk pools that spread costs between rich
and poor, healthy and sick. In particular, it is crucial to prevent wealthier population groups from opting out of national health insurance schemes. Foreign health
insurance should not operate in a manner that undermines universal compulsory
health insurance systems. The experience of some developing countries with Health
Maintenance Organizations (HMOs), which create a captive supply of medical staff,
has been particularly discouraging.[123] International health experts advise that the
entry of foreign suppliers makes it more urgent for countries to create an effective
regulatory framework for the health insurance sector, and that until such a system is

---

122 For links to the international debate on trade in health services see Choike, *Health and
Health Services, Goods for Sale* (www.choike.org/nuevo_eng/informes/1007.html).

123 See, for example, "Consensus paper on managed care organizations", developed by Association of Private Hospitals of Malaysia, 10 April 2001 (www.hospitals-malaysia.org).

in place it could be harmful for developing countries to make full commitments in the health insurance subsector under GATS financial service schedules.[124]

A number of developing countries are exporting health services. Patients come to developing countries for medical treatment not only because of lower costs, but also to obtain traditional medical treatment, and often to enjoy more labour-intensive and compassionate treatment from medical staff. However, health export policies can impact, both positively and negatively, domestic health care, in particular, access to health services by the poor. Such access on people living in poverty can depend on the number of medical staff and facilities in the exporting country and the regulatory structure that is established.[125]

Developing countries that expend resources on the treatment of foreign patients are likely to be diverting resources from domestic needs. In addition, by offering more attractive employment conditions, they exacerbate shortages of skilled staff in public facilities, on which the poor rely. The export of health services through Mode 2 ("health tourism") requires a comprehensive strategy based on an analysis of the potential gains and the impacts on the national health system and access for the poor. These impacts will differ among countries, as a function of specific characteristics of the health system of each potential exporting country, but, in many cases, could be negative.

## References

Abugattas, Luis, and Simonetta Zarrilli (2007). *Challenging Conventional Wisdom: Development Implications of Trade in Services*, UNCTAD Series on Trade, Poverty and Cross-cutting Development Issues. http://www.unctad.org

Adlung, Rolf (2005). *Public Services and the GATS,* WTO Working Paper ERSD-2005-03. Geneva. http://www.wto.org/English/res_e/reser_e/ersd200503_e.htm.

Adhikari, Ratnakar, and Yumiko Yamamoto (2005). *Flying Colours, Broken Threads: One Year of Evidence from Asia after the Phase-out of Textiles and Clothing Quotas, Tracking Report.* Colombo: UNDP Asia Pacific Trade and Investment Initiative. http://www.undprcc.lk.

_____ (2006). *Sewing Thoughts, How to Realize Human Development Gains in the post-Quota World, Tracking Report.* Colombo: UNDP Asia Pacific Trade and Investment Initiative. http://www.undprcc.lk/Publications/Publications/TC_Tracking_Report_April_2006.pdf.

Akyuz, Yilmaz (2005). "The WTO negotiations on industrial tariffs: what is at stake for developing countries". Geneva: Third World Network. http://www.twnside.org.sg/akyuz.htm.

Association of Private Hospitals of Malaysia (2001). "Consensus paper on managed care organizations", 10 April 2001. http://www.hospitals-malaysia.org.

---

124 See Debra Lipson, 2001, *GATS and Health Insurance Services,* Background Note for WHO Commission on Macroeconomics and Health, CMH Working Paper 4:7, June 2001 (http://www.cmhealth.org/docs/wg4_paper7.pdf).

125 See WHO/UNCTAD study *International Trade in Health Services: a Development Perspective* UNCTAD/ITCD/TSB/5, WHO/TFHE/98.1, Geneva: 1998.

Bacchetta, Marc, and Bijit Bora (2003). "Industrial tariffs and the Doha Development Agenda", WTO discussion paper. Geneva. http://www.wto.org/English/res_e/booksp_e/discussion_papers_e.pdf.

Baunsgaard, Thomas, and Michael Keen (2005). *Tax Revenue and (or?) Trade Liberalization.* IMF Working Paper WP/05/112.

Bellmann, Cristophe. "Latin American countries in bilateral and multilateral agricultural negotiations". Presentation to the Andean Development Corporation. http://www.caf.com/attach/11/default/Lat_am_Ag.pdf.

Bernal, Luisa (2005). "Methodology for the identification of special products and products for eligibility under Special Safeguard Mechanism by developing countries", ITCSD. Geneva. http://ww.ictsd.org/dlogue/2005-10-14/Luisa%20Bernal%20Methodlogy%20paper.pdf).

Bernier, Ivan (2004). "Recent FTAs of the United States as illustrations of their new strategy regarding the audio-visual sector". http://www.mcc.gouv.qc.ca/diversite-culturelle/eng/pdf/conf_seoul_ang_2004.pdf.

Blandford, David, and Tim Josling (2006). "Options for the WTO modalities for agriculture", International Food and Agricultural Trade Policy Council. http://www.agritrade.org/Publications/DiscussionPapers/WTO%20Modalities.pdf.

Chanda, Rupa (2006). "Intermodal linkages to services trade". OECD Trade Policy Working Paper No. 30.

Charlton, Andrew (2003). "Incentive bidding wars for mobile investment; economic consequences and potential reponses". OECD Development Centre Technical Paper 203, OECD. http://www.oecd.org/dataoecd/39/63/2492289.pdf.

Choike, "Health and health services, goods for sale, a portal on Southern civil societies". http://www.choike.org/nuevo_eng/informes/1007.html.

Commission on Intellectual Property Rights (2002). *Integrating Intellectual Property Rights and Development Policy.* London. http://www.iprcommission.org/graphic/documents/final_report.htm.

Correa, Carlos (2000). "Reviewing the TRIPs Agreement", in UNCTAD, *A Positive Agenda for Developing Countries: Issues for Future Trade Negotiations,* UNCTAD/ITCD/TSB/10. New York and Geneva: UNCTAD. http://www.unctad.org/en/docs/itcdtsb10_en.pdf.

_____ (2000). *Integrating Public Health Concerns into Patent Legislation in Developing Countries.* Geneva: South Centre. http://www.southcentre.org.

_____ (2000b). *Intellectual Property Rights, the WTO and Developing Countries: The TRIPS Agreement and Policy Options.* London and New York: Zed Books.

Das, B. L. (2005), *The Current Negotiations in the WTO, Options, Opportunities and Risks for Developing Countries.* London: Zed Books.

Deere, Carolyn (2000). *Net Gains: Linking Fisheries Management, International Trade and Sustainable Development.* IUCN, The World Conservation Union. http://www.users.ox.ac.uk.

FAO (2003). Support to the WTO Negotiations for the Cancun Ministerial Conference. Food and Agriculture Organization of the United Nations, Rome. http://www.fao.org/docrep/005/y4852e/y4852e00.htm.

Fernández de Córdoba, Santiago (2005). *Coping with Trade Reforms, Implications of the WTO Industrial Tariff Negotiations for Developing Countries.* Geneva: UNCTAD. http://www.unctad.org.

G33 proposals:

> Modalities for the designation and treatment of any agricultural product as a Special Product (SP) by any developing country member, JOB(05)304, 22 November 2005. http://www.agtradepolicy.org/output/resource/G33_proposal_SPs_22Nov05.pdf.

> SSM for developing countries, JOB(06)64, 23 March 2006 http://www.agtradepolicy.org/output/resource/G33_revised_proposal_SSM_23Mar06.pdf.

Gibbs, Murray (2004*a*). "Energy in the WTO: what is at stake?", in *Investment, Energy and Environmental Services: Promoting Human Development in WTO Negotiations,* Sieh Mei Ling, ed.

_____ (2004*b*). "Statement on investment policy and human development", in *Investment, Energy and Environmental Services: Promoting Human Development in WTO Negotiations,* Sieh Mei Ling, ed. Kuala Lumpur: University of Malaya, UNDP, and Malaysian Institute of Economic Research. http://www.um.edu.my.

Gibbs, Murray, Swarnim Wagle, and Pedro Ortega (2005). *The Great Maze: Regional and Bilateral Free Trade Agreements in Asia. Colombo:* UNDP Asia-Pacific Trade and Investment Initiative. http://www.undprcc.lk/Publications/Publications/Great_Maze_-_FTA_-_completed.pdf.

GRAIN, "One global patent system?" WIPO's Substantive Patent Law Treaty, GRAIN briefings 2003. http://www.grain.org/briefings/?id=159.

_____, Beyond UPOV—Examples of countries preparing non-UPOV sui generis plant variety protection systems for compliance with TRIPS, GRAIN briefings 1999. http://www.grain.org/briefings/?id=127.

Hathaway, Dale (2002). "A special agricultural safeguard: buttressing the market access reforms of developing countries", in *FAO Papers on Selected Issues Relating to the WTO Negotiations on Agriculture.* Food and Agriculture Organization of the United Nations, Rome. http://www.fao.org/docrep/005/Y3733E/y3733e05.htm.

Hausmann, Ricardo, and Dani Rodrik (2003). "Economic development as self-discovery". *Journal of Development Economics*, vol. 72, No. 2, pp. 603-633. http://www.nber.org/papers/W8952.

Hilary, John (2003). "GATS and water: the threat of services negotiations at the WTO". London: Save the Children UK. http://www.savethechildren.org.uk/scuk_cache/scuk/cache/cmsattach/21_GATS_and_water.pdf.

International Monetary Fund (2002). "International capital markets: developments, prospects, and key policy issues". International Monetary Fund, Washington, D.C. http://www.imf.org/external/pubs/ft/icm/2000/01/eng/index.htm.

Jales, Mario (2005). "Tariff reduction, special products and special safeguards: an analysis of the agricultural tariff structures of G33 countries". Geneva: International Centre for Trade and Sustainable Development. http://www.ictsd.org/dlogue/2005-06-16/Jales.pdf.

Jayanetti, Sanath (2003). *Movement of Natural Persons and Its Human Development Implications (Housemaids and Unskilled Migrant Workers).* UNDP Asia Trade Initiative on Trade and Human Development, Phase 1, technical support document. Hanoi. http://www.undprcc.lk/Publications/Publications.asp?C=4.

Kim, DoHoon (2006). "Trade promotion and economic development in Korea". Korea Institute for Industrial Economics and Trade, presentation in file with author, May 2006.

Khan, Zubair (2003). *The Impact of the post-ATC Environment on Pakistan's Textiles Trade*, UNDP Asia Trade Initiative on Trade and Human Development, Phase 1, technical support document. http://www.undprcc.lk/Publications/Publications.asp?C=4.

Lakhoua, Faycal (1998). "The Tunisian experience of 'Mise à Niveau': conceptual issues and policy orientations". Marrakech. http://www.worldbank.org/mdf/mdf2/papers/benefit/finance/lakhoua.pdf.

Lam Quoc Tuan (2003). *Trade in Fisheries and Human Development: Country Case Study-Viet Nam*, UNDP Asia Trade Initiative on Trade and Human Development, Phase 1, technical support document. Hanoi. http://www.undprcc.lk/Publications/Publications.asp?C=4.

Lipson, Debra (2001). "GATS and Health Insurance Services". Background Note for WHO Commission on Macroeconomics and Health, CMH Working Paper 4:7. http://www.cmhealth.org/docs/wg4_paper7.pdf.

Loftus, Alexander, and David McDonald (2001). "Of liquid dreams: a political ecology of water privatization in Buenos Aires". *Environment & Urbanization*, vol. 13, No. 2. http://www.queensu.ca/msp/pages/Project_Publications/Journals/Loftus.pdf.

Malhotra, Kamal (2006). "National trade and development strategies: suggested policy directions". Background paper for UNDP *Asia-Pacific Human Development Report, Trade on Human Terms: Transforming Trade for Human Development in Asia and the Pacific*. Colombo: UNDP.

Marconini, Mario (2003). *Acordos Regionais e o Comercio de Servicos: normativa internacional e interesse brasiliero*. Sao Paulo: Aduanieras.

Mathew, Sebastian (2003). *Trade in Fisheries and Human Development in India*. UNDP Asia Trade Initiative on Trade and Human Development, Phase 1, technical support document. http://www.undprcc.lk/Publications/Publications.asp?C=4.

OECD (2003). "Public-private partnerships in the urban water sector". Policy Brief. Organization for Economic Cooperation and Development. Paris. http://www.oecd.org/dataoecd/31/50/2510696.pdf.

OXFAM (2000). "Tax havens: releasing the hidden billions for poverty eradication". http://www.oxfam.org.uk/what_we_do/issues/debt_aid/tax_havens.htm.

Pal, Parthapratim (2006). "The ongoing negotiations on agriculture: some observations". Presentation at the workshop on *WTO-Related Issues for Government Officials in the SAARC Region*. New Delhi: The Energy and Resources Institute, 1-3 May 2006. http://www.teriin.org/events/docs/wtopresent/partha4.ppt.

Paz, Julio (2005). "Identificación de productos especiales y mecanismos de salvaguardia especial en el Perú". Geneva: ICTSD.

Peters, Ralf (2004). "Agriculture". At UNECA Ad Hoc Meeting on Agriculture. Tunis, November 2004. http://www.eca.org/trid/meetingss/Tunis.November2004.

Rahman, A. A. (2003). *Trade in Agriculture, Food Security and Human Development: Country Case Study for Malaysia*. UNDP Asia Trade Initiative on Trade and Human Development, Phase 1, technical support document. http://www.undprcc.lk/Publications/Publications.asp?C=4.

Rangnekar, Dwijien (2004). "The socio-economics of geographical indications: a review of empirical evidence from Europe". UNCTAD-ICTSD Project on IPRS and Sustainable Development. http://www.iprsonline.org/unctadictsd/docs/CS_Rangnekar2.pdf.

Rodríguez Cervantes, Silvia (2006). "FTAs: trading away traditional knowledge". GRAIN briefings 2006 http://www.grain.org/briefings_files/fta-tk-03-2006-en.pdf.

Rodrik, Dani (2004). "Industrial policy for the twenty-first century". CEPR Discussion Paper No. 4767. London: Centre for Economic Policy Research. http://www.cepr.org/pubs/dps/DP4767.asp.

_____ (2006). "What's so special about China's exports?" CEPR Discussion Paper No. 5484. London: Centre for Economic Policy Research. http://www.nber.org/papers/w11947.

Rudloff, B., and J. Simon (2004). "Comparing EU FTAs: sanitary and phytosanitary regulations". ECDPM in Brief. http://www.ecdpm.org.

Seih Mei Ling, ed. (2004). *Investment, Energy and Environmental Services: Promoting Human Development in WTO Negotiations*. Kuala Lumpur: UNDP, Malaysian Institute of Economic Research and University of Malaya. March 2004. http://www.um.edu.my.

Shin, Jang-Sup, and Ha-Joon Chang (2004). "Foreign investment policy and human development country study: Republic of Korea", in *Investment, Energy and Environmental Services: Promoting Human Development in WTO Negotiations*, Seih Mei Ling, ed. Kuala Lumpur: UNDP, Malaysian Institute of Economic Research and University of Malaya. http://www.um.edu.my.

Stiglitz, Joseph, and Andrew Charlton (2005). *Fair Trade for All*. Oxford: Oxford University Press, 2005.

Stiglitz, Joseph, and M. Shahe Emran (2004). "Price neutral tax reform with an informal economy". Econometric Society, 2004 North American Summer Meetings, p. 493.

Tokrishna, Ruangrai (2003). *The Fisheries Sector in Asian Countries, Sustainable Fisheries, Human Development and Trade Liberalization*. UNDP Asia Trade Initiative on Trade and Human Development, Phase 1, technical support document. http://www.undprcc.lk/Publications/Publications.asp?C=4.

Tsogtbaatar, Damedin. "Mongolia's WTO accession: expectations and realities of WTO membership". WTO Managing the Challenges of WTO Participation: Case Study 29, http://www.wto.org/English/res_e/booksp_e/casestudies_e/case29_e.htm.

Tullao, Teresa, and Michael Angelo Cortez (2003*a*). *MNP and Human Development in Asia*. UNDP Asia Trade Initiative on Trade and Human Development, Phase 1, technical support document. http://www.undprcc.lk/Publications/Publications.asp?C=4.

_____ (2003*b*). "Movement of natural persons between the Philippines and Japan: issues and prospects". Presentation at De La Salle University, Manila, September 2003. http://pascn.pids.gov.ph/jpepa/docs/tullao-revised_sept%209.PDF.

UNCTAD *World Investment Reports,* various years. http://www.unctad.org/Templates/Page.asp?intItemID=1485&lang=1.

_____ (1994). *Trade and Development Report 1994.* UNCTAD/TDR/14 and Supp.1, Geneva.

_____ (2000). *A Positive Agenda for Developing Countries: Issues for Future Trade Negotiations,* UNCTAD/ITCD/TSB/10, New York and Geneva. http://www.unctad.org/en/docs/itcdtsb10_en.pdf.

_____ (2001). *WTO Accessions and Development Policies.* UNCTAD/DITC/TNCD/11, New York and Geneva. http://www.unctad.org/en/docs/ditctncd11_en.pdf.

_____ (2003). *Managing "Request-Offer" Negotiations Under the GATS: The Case of Energy Services.* UNCTAD/DITC/TNCD/2003/5, Geneva.

_____ (2003). "Report of expert meeting on market access issues under Mode 4". Document TD/B/COM.1/64, Geneva, 27 November 2003.

_____(2004). *Trade and Gender: Opportunities, Challenges and the Policy Dimension.* UNCTAD/TD/392. http://www.unctad.org/en/docs/edm20042_en.pdf.

_____(2005). *Distribution Services*, TD/B/COM.1/EM.29/2.

_____(2005). *Energy and Environmental Services, Negotiating Objectives and Development Priorities*, Simonetta Zarrilli, ed., UNCTAD/DITC/TNCD/2005/3.

_____(2005a). "International trade in environmental and energy services and human development". Discussion paper. UNDP Asia Pacific Trade and Investment Initiative. http://ww.undprcc.lk/Publications/Publications/International_trade-completed.pdf.

_____(2005b). "International trade in textiles and clothing and development policy options", After the full implementation of the WTO Agreement on Textiles and Clothing (ATC) on 1 January 2005, policy paper. http://www.undprcc.lk/Publications/Publications/T&CPolicyPaper.pdf.

_____(2006). "UNCTAD Secretary-General, Statement to ECOSOC Round Table on Globalization and Labour Migration", 6 July 2006. New York: United Nations. http://www.unctad.org.

UNDP (2005). *Human Development Report 2005, International Cooperation at a Crossroads: Aid, Trade and Security in an Unequal World.* New York. hdr.undp.org/reports/global/2005/.

_____(2006). "Concept note on aid for trade", January 2006 http://www.undp.org/poverty/.

UNDP, et al. (2003). *Making Global Trade Work for People.* London and Sterling, Virginia: Earthscan.

VanGrasstek, Craig (2003). *U.S. Policy Towards Free Trade Agreements: Strategic Perspectives and Extrinsic Objectives.* UNDP Asia Trade Initiative on Trade and Human Development, Phase 1, technical support document. http://www.undprcc.lk/Publications/Publications.asp?C=4.

Vivas, David, and Christophe Spennemann (2006). "Diálogo regional sobre propiedad intelectual, innovación y desarrollo sostenible". UNCTAD/ICTSD Project on Intellectual Property and Sustainable Development, Costa Rica, May 2006. http://www.ictsd.org.

Vu Quoc Huy, et al. (2003). *Trade in Services, Movement of Natural Persons and Human Development: Country Case Study—Viet Nam.* UNDP Asia Trade Initiative on Trade and Human Development, Phase 1, technical support document. http://www.undprcc.lk/Publications/Publications.asp?C=4.

Wagle, Swarnim (2003). *The Development Dimensions of the Sri Lankan Geographical Indication of Camellia Sinensis (Ceylon Tea).* UNDP Asia Trade Initiative on Trade and Human Development, Phase 1, technical support document. http://www.undprcc.lk/Publications/Publications.asp?C=4.

_____(2003). *Geographical Indications: TRIPs and Promoting Human Development in Asia.* UNDP Asia Trade Initiative on Trade and Human Development, Phase 1, technical support document. http://www.undprcc.lk/Publications/Publications.asp?C=4.

WHO/UNCTAD (1998). "International trade in health services: a development perspective", UNCTAD/ITCD/TSB/5, WHO/TFHE/98.1, Geneva.

World Bank (2005). *Global Economic Prospects 2005: Trade, Regionalism and Development.* Washington D.C.

World Energy Council (2001). *Energy Markets in Transition: The Latin American and Caribbean Experience.* London: World Energy Council.

WTO (2001). "Matrix on trade measures pursuant to selected MEAs". Document WT/CTE/W/160/rev.1, 14 July 2001, Geneva. http://www.wto.org.

_____(2002). "Communication from Thailand: assessment of trade in services". Document TN/S/W/4, 22 July 2002, Geneva. http://www.wto.org.

_____(2003). WTO, Committee on Agriculture–Special Session. WTO Negotiations on Agriculture, poverty reduction: Sectoral initiative in favour of cotton. Joint proposal Benin, Burkina Faso, Chad and Mali. Document TN/AG/GEN/4, 16 May 2003. http://www.wto.org.

_____(2005). United States—Upland Cotton. Appellate Body Report, Dispute DS267, circulated 3 March 2005 http://www.wto.org/english/tratop_e/dispu_e/cases_e/ds267_e.htm.

_____(2006). "Recommendations of the Task Force on Aid For Trade", document WT/AFT/1, 27 July 2006 http://www.wto.org.

## Inter-governmental and civil society organizations and research institutions

BIMSTEC: www.bimstec.org

Bilaterals.org: Everything that is not happening at the WTO: www.bilaterals.org

Choike: www.choike.org

European Centre for Development Policy Management: www.ecdpm.org

European Commission External Trade Directorate: http://ec.europa.eu.comm/trade/

European Services Forum: www.esf.be

FTA Watch Malaysia: www.ftamalaysia.org

FTA Watch Thailand: www.ftawatch.org

Food and Agriculture Organization (webpage on trade): http://www.fao.org/trade/negoc_dda_en.asp

GRAIN: www.grain.org

India Ministry of Commerce: http://commerce.nic.in

Institute for Agriculture and Trade Policy: www.iatp.org, www.tradeobservatory.org

International Collective in Support of Fishworkers: www.icsf.net and www.icsf.org

International Textiles and Clothing Bureau: www.itcb.org.

Japan Ministry of Foreign Affairs: www.mofa.go.jp/policy

OECD: www.oecd.org

SUNS South North Development Monitor: www.sunsonline.org

Singapore Ministry of Trade and Industry Singapore FTAs: www.fta.gov.sg/fta

South Centre: www.southcentre.org

Third World Network: www.twn.org.sg, www.twnside.org

UNCTAD: www.unctad.org

UNDP Colombo Regional Centre (site of UNDP's Asia Pacific Trade and Investment Initiative): http://www.undprcc.lk/Our_Work/Trade_and_Investment.asp

UNDP: www.undp.org

United States Trade Representative Office: www.ustr.gov

World Bank Independent Evaluation group: www.worldbank.org/ieg/trade

World Trade Organization: www.wto.org

World Water Council: www.worldwatercouncil.org

Litho in United Nations
07-64609—June 2008—6,000
ISBN 978-92-1-104579-6

United Nations publication
Sales No. E.08.II.A.4